THE THIRD REICH FROM ORIGINAL SOURCES

THE NUREMBERG TRIALS

THE COMPLETE PROCEEDINGS

Vol 3 : The Policy to Exterminate the Jews

17th December 1945 - 4th January 1946

Edited and introduced by Bob Carruthers

This edition published in Great Britain in 2011 by
Coda Books Ltd, The Barn, Cutlers Farm Business Centre, Edstone,
Wootton Wawen, Henley in Arden, Warwickshire, B95 6DJ
www.codahistory.com

Copyright © 2011 Coda Books Ltd

All rights reserved. No part of this publication may be reproduced or transmitted in any form or by any means, electronic or mechanical, including photocopy, recording, or any information storage and retrieval system, without permission in writing from the publisher.

A CIP catalogue record for this book is available from the British Library

ISBN 978 1 908538 79 6

Originally published as
"The Trial of German Major War Criminals
Proceedings of the International Military Tribunal Sitting at Nuremberg,
Germany"
under the authority of
H.M. Attorney-General by His Majesty's Stationery Office
London : 1946

CONTENTS

Introduction 4

Twenty-First Day: Monday, 17th December, 1945 7

Twenty-Second Day: Tuesday, 18th December, 1945 54

Twenty-Third Day: Wednesday, 19th December, 1945 103

Twenty-Fourth Day: Thursday, 20th December, 1945 147

Twenty-Fifth Day: Wednesday, 2nd January, 1946 189

Twenty-Sixth Day: Thursday, 3rd January, 1946 228

Twenty-Seventh Day: Friday, 4th January, 1946 274

About Coda Books 320

Introduction

The trial of the German major war criminals is better known to posterity as the Nuremberg Trials. This was a revolutionary new form of justice which was without parallel in the history of warfare.

In the wake of six years of savagery, inhumanity and turmoil it was sensed that a series of summary executions would not bring closure to the years of violence which had seen unheralded scenes of brutality as civilian populations were targeted for bombardment on a scale never before witnessed.

In 1945, faced with the stark evidence of the appalling crimes against humanity committed by the Nazi regime, there was an understandable clamour, particularly from the Soviet camp, for a series of quick summary executions to draw the line under the past and allow the world to get back to civilised behaviour. Given the scale of the crimes and the gruesome evidence emerging from Dachau, Auschwitz and Bergen-Belsen, it was certainly difficult to argue against making a rapid example of men like Hermann Göring, the father of the Gestapo.

Fortunately clearer heads prevailed and it was felt necessary to create some form of judicial process which would mark the transition back from barbarism to the rule of law. However there was then no such thing as an international court and there was no precedent for the legal trial of defeated belligerents. The plan for the "Trial of European War Criminals" was therefore drafted by Secretary of War Henry L. Stimson and the War Department. Following Roosevelt's death in April 1945, the new president, Harry S. Truman, gave strong approval for a judicial process. After a series of negotiations between Britain, the US, the Soviet Union and France, details of the trial were finally agreed. The trials were to commence on 20th November 1945, in the Bavarian city of Nuremberg.

At the meetings in Potsdam (1945), the three major wartime powers, the United Kingdom, the United States, and the Union of Soviet Socialist Republics finally agreed on the principles of punishment for those responsible for war crimes during World War II. France was also awarded a place on the tribunal.

The legal basis for the trial was established by the London Charter, issued on August 8th, 1945, which restricted the trial to "punishment of the major war criminals of the European Axis countries". Some 200 German war crimes defendants were ultimately tried at Nuremberg, and 1,600 others were tried under the traditional channels of military justice. The legal basis for the jurisdiction of the court was that defined by the Instrument of Surrender of Germany. Political authority for Germany had been transferred to the Allied Control Council which, having sovereign power over Germany, could choose to punish violations of international law and the laws of war. Because the court was limited to violations of the laws of war, it did not have jurisdiction over crimes that took place before the outbreak of war on September 3rd, 1939.

Leipzig, Munich and Luxembourg were briefly considered as the location for the trial. The Soviet Union had wanted the trials to take place in Berlin, as the capital city of the 'fascist conspirators', but Nuremberg was chosen as the site for the trials for two specific reasons: firstly because the Palace of Justice was spacious and largely undamaged (one of the few civic buildings that had remained largely intact through extensive Allied bombing), and secondly that a large prison was also part of the complex.

Nuremberg was also considered the ceremonial birthplace of the Nazi Party, and hosted annual rallies. It was thus considered a fitting place to mark the Party's symbolic demise.

As a compromise with the Soviet Union, it was agreed that while the location of the trial would be Nuremberg, Berlin would be the official home of the Tribunal authorities. It was also agreed that France would become the permanent seat of the IMT and that the first trial (several were planned) would take place in Nuremberg.

Each of the four countries provided one judge and an alternate, as well as a prosecutor.

- Major General Iona Nikitchenko (Soviet main)
- Lieutenant Colonel Alexander Volchkov (Soviet alternate)
- Colonel Sir Geoffrey Lawrence (British main and president)
- Sir Norman Birkett (British alternate)
- Francis Biddle (American main)
- John J. Parker (American alternate)
- Professor Henri Donnedieu de Vabres (French main)
- Robert Falco (French alternate)
- The chief prosecutors were as follows
- Attorney General Sir Hartley Shawcross (United Kingdom)
- Supreme Court Justice Robert H. Jackson (United States)
- Lieutenant-General Roman Andreyevich Rudenko (Soviet Union)
- François de Menthon (France)

Assisting Jackson was the lawyer Telford Taylor, Thomas J. Dodd and a young US Army interpreter named Richard Sonnenfeldt. Assisting Shawcross were Major Sir David Maxwell-Fyfe and Sir John Wheeler-Bennett. Mervyn Griffith-Jones, later to become famous as the chief prosecutor in the Lady Chatterley's Lover obscenity trial, was also on Shawcross's team. Shawcross also recruited a young barrister, Anthony Marreco, who was the son of a friend of his, to help the British team with the heavy workload. Assisting de Menthon was Auguste Champetier de Ribes.

The International Military Tribunal was opened on October 18th, 1945, in the Palace of Justice in Nuremberg. The first session was presided over by the Soviet judge, Nikitchenko. The prosecution entered indictments against 24 major war criminals and six criminal organizations – the leadership of the Nazi party, the Schutzstaffel (SS) and Sicherheitsdienst (SD), the Gestapo, the Sturmabteilung (SA) and the "General Staff and High Command," comprising several categories of senior military officers.

The indictments were for:
- Participation in a common plan or conspiracy for the accomplishment of a crime against peace
- Planning, initiating and waging wars of aggression and other crimes against peace
- War crimes
- Crimes against humanity

Under the circumstances the Proceedings of the International Military Tribunal just about passes muster as an exercise in establishing a platform from which to dispense a reasonably balanced form of justice. There was, of course, the questionable involvement of Stalin's legal team and it was ironic that his crimes against peace and humanity matched, if not surpassed those of Adolf Hitler. Ribbentrop and Molotov between them had secretly carved up Poland and in so doing had certainly been guilty of crimes against peace, planning war. Stalin had also waged an aggressive was against Finland and had annexed the Baltic States. Had Stalin been on trial his own actions would have condemned him to a guilty verdict on all four counts, but history is always written by the victors, and Stalin's crimes were airbrushed out of history in order that his team could sit in judgement as if nothing untoward had ever happened.

It has been asked many times were the trials fair. In strict legal terms they certainly were not. Declaring the instruments of the Nazi state to be illegal was illogical and unreasonable, but this was certainly no Stalinist show trial with a guilty verdict and a hangman's noose already awaiting the defendants. Under the circumstances the court was incredibly well balanced as was evidenced by the fact that three of the Defendants were acquitted and others received comparatively light sentences. Of the twenty-four accused only twelve received death sentences.

Ultimately the process had its flaws but it did provide a civilised alternative to Stalin's suggestion that 50,000 to 100,000 German officers should be executed without trial, and it was to serve as a forerunner for the International Court now located at the Hague.

This is the third volume in the complete proceedings of the Nuremberg trial of the German major war criminals before the International Military Tribunal sitting at Nuremberg, Germany.

Taken from the original court transcript this volume covers the proceedings from 17th December 1945 to 4th January 1946 and represents an essential primary source for scholars and general readers alike. The transcripts are complete and contain the whole of the proceedings as taken from the original court documents.

This volume includes the testimony of Otto Ohlendorf, Dieter Wisliceny, Walter Schellenberg and Alois Hoellriegel regarding the official Nazi policy of the extermination of the Jews, as originally published under the authority of H.M. Attorney-General by His Majesty's Stationery Office London in 1946.

Ohlendorf was a German SS-Gruppenführer and head of the Inland-SD (responsible for intelligence and security within Germany), part of the SD. He was the commanding officer of Einsatzgruppe D, which conducted mass murder in Moldova, south Ukraine, the Crimea, and, during 1942, the north Caucasus. During the trial against Einsatzgruppen leaders, Ohlendorf was the chief defendant, and was also a key witness in the prosecution of many other indicted war criminals. Ohlendorf's frank, apparently reliable testimony was attributed to his distaste for the corruption that was rampant in Nazi Germany and a stubborn commitment to duty. He expressed no remorse for his actions, and was later convicted and executed for his war crimes in 1951.

Wisliceny was a member of the SS and rose to the rank of SS-Hauptsturmführer. He ghettoized and liquidated several Jewish communities in Greece, Hungary and Slovakia. His testimony during the Nuremberg Trials was also used in the trial of Adolf Eichmann in 1961. Wisliceny was extradited to Czechoslovakia, where he was tried and hanged for his crimes in 1948.

Walter Schellenberg was a German SS-Brigadeführer who rose through the ranks of the SS to become the head of foreign intelligence following the abolition of the Abwehr in 1944. After Germany's defeat he was sought after by the Allies as a valuable intelligence asset, and was in Denmark attempting to arrange his own surrender when the British took Schellenberg into custody in June 1945. During the Nuremberg Trials, Schellenberg testified against other Nazis, and in the 1949 Ministries Trial he was sentenced to six years' imprisonment.

Alois Hoellriegel was a member of the SS from 1939 and was Unterscharfuehrer at Mauthausen concentration camp. He was sentenced to death in 1947.

Bob Carruthers

Twenty-First Day: Monday, 17th December, 1945

THE PRESIDENT: (Lord Justice Sir Geoffrey Lawrence): I have four announcements to make on behalf of the Tribunal. I will read those announcements now and they will be posted upon the board in the Information Centre in German as soon as possible.

The first announcement is this: The attention of the Tribunal has been drawn to publications in the Press of what appear to have been interviews with some of the defendants in this case, given through the agency of their counsel. The Tribunal considers it necessary to state with the greatest emphasis that this is a procedure which cannot and will not be countenanced. Therefore, counsel are warned that they should observe the highest professional standards in such matters and should not use the opportunity afforded to them of conferring freely with their clients to act in any way as intermediaries between the defendants and the Press, and they must exercise the greatest professional discretion in making any statement on their own behalf.

The Tribunal recognises that in a trial of this kind, where the public interest is world-wide, it is in the highest degree important that all those who take part in the trial in any capacity whatever should be aware of their responsibility to see that nothing is done to detract from the proper conduct of the proceedings.

The Press of the world is rendering a very great service in giving publicity to the proceedings of the Tribunal, and the Tribunal feels that it may properly ask for the co-operation of all concerned to avoid anything which conflicts with the impartial administration of justice.

The second announcement that I have to make is this: The Tribunal understands that the counsel appointed under Article 9 of the Charter are in doubt whether they have been appointed to represent the groups and organisations charged in the Indictment as criminal, or to represent individual applicants who have applied to be heard under the said article.

The Tribunal directs that counsel represent the groups and organisations charged, and not the applicants. As the Tribunal has already directed, counsel will be entitled to call as witnesses representative applicants and may also call other persons whose attendance may be ordered by the Tribunal. Application to call any witness must be made in the ordinary way. The evidence of such witnesses and the arguments of counsel must be confined to the question of the criminal nature of the group or organisation. Counsel will not be entitled to call evidence or to discuss any question as to the individual responsibility of particular applicants, except in so far as this may bear upon the criminal character of the organisations. Counsel will be permitted, as far as possible, to communicate with applicants in order to decide what witnesses they wish to apply to call.

The third announcement is this:

The Chief Prosecutor for the United States has requested the Tribunal to make a change in its formal order which provided that only such portions of documents which are read in Court would be admitted as evidence. In order to meet the needs, so far as possible, of the members of the Tribunal, of the prosecution, and of counsel for the defendants, to have before them all the evidence in the case, the Tribunal, having carefully considered the request, makes the following order:

All documents may be filed in Court. The Tribunal shall only admit in evidence, however:

1. Documents or portions of documents which are read in Court;
2. Documents or portions of documents which are cited in Court, on the condition that they have been translated into the respective languages of the members of the Tribunal for their use; and that sufficient numbers in German are filed in the Information Centre for the use of defence counsel.

This does not apply to the documents of which the Court will take judicial notice, in accordance with Article 21 of the Charter, and the prosecution and the defendants will be at liberty to read those documents, or to refer to them without reading them.

Trial briefs and document books may be furnished to the Tribunal if sufficient copies thereof are, at the same time, filed for defence counsel in the Information Centre. As far as possible, these should be furnished in advance of their introduction in Court. In order to permit the Interpretation and Translation Division to make translations in time, it is suggested that all documents be submitted to the Division at least five days before they are to be offered in evidence.

This is the fourth announcement: The Tribunal has passed upon a number of applications for witnesses. Some of these have been granted, subject to their evidence being relevant. Some have been declined, and in some cases orders have been made that the witness be alerted; that is to say, that if he can be located, he be advised to hold himself in readiness to come here as a witness if the application is granted.

It is the desire of the Tribunal to secure for the defendants those witnesses who are material and relevant to their defence. To prevent the unnecessary prolonging of the trial, however, it is clear that the witnesses whose testimony is irrelevant or merely cumulative should not be summoned. At the conclusion of the prosecution's testimony, the Tribunal shall hear from defendants' counsel as to which of the witnesses granted or alerted they think necessary to bring here to testify. At that time, the Tribunal may hear from them further as to any witnesses that have been declined, if, in view of the case, it then appears to the Tribunal that the testimony of such witnesses is material and not cumulative.

Counsel appearing for any defendant may question any other defendant as to any relevant matter, and may interrogate him as a witness for that purpose. If the other defendant takes the stand in his own behalf, the right shall be exercised at the conclusion of his testimony.

Examination of witnesses called by other defendants: The same person has been requested as a witness by a number of defendants in some cases. It is only necessary that such witness be called to the stand once. He may then be interrogated by counsel for any defendant as to any material matter.

That is all.

I call on Counsel for the United States.

CAPTAIN HARRIS: May it please the Tribunal, we are resuming the presentation of evidence of the conspirators' plans for Germanisation and spoliation.

The next general subject upon which we propose to introduce evidence is the conspirators' plans for the spoliation and Germanisation of the Soviet Union.

As Mr. Alderman has shown, the invasion of the Soviet Union was the culmination of plans meticulously laid by the conspirators. We wish now to introduce evidence upon the conspirators' plans for the exploitation and Germanisation of the Soviet Union after their anticipated conquest. The Chief Prosecutor for the Soviet Union will demonstrate what the execution of these plans meant in terms of human suffering and misery. We submit that the few exhibits which we propose to offer at this time will show the following:-

1. The conspirators planned to remove to Germany all foodstuffs and raw materials from the South and southeast of the Soviet Union over and above the needs of the Nazi invading forces and the absolute minimum necessary to supply the bare needs of the people in these particular regions, who produced the materials which were to be removed to Germany. This region had previously supplied the northern area of the Soviet Union, which the conspirators called the forest zone. The latter zone embraced some of the leading industrial areas of the Soviet Union, including Moscow and Leningrad.

2. They deliberately and systematically planned to starve millions of Russians. Starvation was to be accomplished by the following means:

a. As indicated under point 1, products from the South and southeast of the Soviet Union, which ordinarily were sent to the industrial regions of the north, were to be forcibly diverted to Germany. Moreover, all livestock in the industrial regions was to be seized for use by the Wehrmacht and the German civilian population. The necessary consequence was that the population of the northern regions would be reduced to starvation.

b. They established the following order of priority in which food produced by the Russians would be allocated:

First, the combat troops.

Second, the remainder of troops in enemy territory.

Third, troops stationed in Germany.

Fourth, the German civilian population, and

Lastly, the population of the occupied countries.

Thus even Russians in the food surplus area of the Ukraine, who were not essential to the production of material for the German war machine, were to be systematically starved.

3. They planned the permanent destruction of all industry in the northern area of the Soviet Union in order that the remnants of the Russian population would be completely dependent upon Germany for their consumer goods.

4. They planned to incorporate a part of Galicia and all of the Baltic countries into Germany, and to convert the Crimea, an area North of the Crimea, the Volga territory, and the district around Baku into German colonies.

I now turn to the specific items of proof.

I first offer in evidence Document EC-472, Exhibit USA 315. This document is offered for the particular purpose of showing the status and functions of the Economic Staff East, Group LA. The exhibit which we shall next offer in evidence was prepared by this organisation. Document EC-472 is a directive issued by defendant Goering's office for "The Operation of the Economy in the Newly-occupied Eastern Territories." It is the second edition and it is dated Berlin, July, 1941. The first edition was obviously published some time before July, 1941. The document was found among the captured O.K.W. files at Fechenheim.

Under this directive, defendant Goering established the Economic Executive Staff East, which was directly responsible to him, and under it created the Economic Staff East. The Economic Staff East, in turn, was subdivided into four groups: The Chief of the Economic Staff, Group LA, Group W, and Group M. I now quote from Page

2, Lines 7-9 of the English text; in the German text it is at Page 7, Lines 7-9. I quote:-
> "Group LA. (Functions of nutrition and agriculture, the economy of all agricultural products, provision of supplies for the Army, in co-operation with the army groups concerned.)"

I next offer in evidence Document EC-126, which is Exhibit USA 316. This is a report dated 23rd May, 1941, which was before the invasion of the Soviet Union. It was found among the captured files of the O.K.W. It is entitled, "Economic Policy Directives for Economic Organisation East, Agricultural Group." It was prepared by the Economic Staff East, Group LA, the Agricultural Group, which, as shown by the exhibit introduced a moment ago, was an important part of the organisation which defendant Goering established to formulate plans for the economic administration of Russia.

The underscoring in the English text merely reflects the underscoring in the original.

The document begins with a recitation of facts pertaining to the production of agricultural products in the Soviet Union. It states that the grain surplus of Russia is determined by the level of domestic consumption and that this fact affords the basis upon which the planners must predicate their actions and economic policy. I now quote from the sixth and seventh paragraphs of Page 2 of the English text. The German text is the last three lines of Page 3, and the first five lines of Page 4. I quote:-

> "The surplus territories are situated in the black soil district (that is in the South and South-East) and in the Caucasus. The deficit areas are principally located in the Forest Zone of the North.
>
> Therefore, an isolation of the black soil areas will in any case place greater or lesser surpluses in these regions at our disposal. The consequences will be cessation of supplies to the entire forest zone, including the essential industrial centres of Moscow and Leningrad."

Next, I quote from the last 11 lines of Page 2 and all of Page 3 of the English text. The German text begins in the middle of line 6 of Page 5 and continues through to line 29 of Page 6. I quote:

> "This - the cessation of supplies - means:
>
> 1. All industry in the deficit area, particularly the manufacturing industries in the Moscow and Leningrad regions as absolute minimum necessary to supply the bare needs of the people in these particular regions, as well as the Ural industrial regions will be abandoned. It may be assumed that these regions today absorb an annual five to ten million tons from the food production zone.
>
> 2. The Trans-Caucasian oil district will have to be excepted, although it is a deficit area. This source of oil, cotton, manganese, copper, silk and tea must continue to be supplied with food in any case, for special political and economic reasons.
>
> 3. No further exception with a view to preserving one or the other industrial region or industrial enterprise must be permitted.
>
> 4. Industry can only be preserved insofar as it is located in the surplus region. This applies, apart from the above-mentioned oil field regions in the Caucasus, particularly to the heavy industries in the Donesz District (Ukraine). Only the future will show to what extent it will prove possible to maintain in full these industries, and in particular the Ukrainian manufacturing industries, after the withdrawal of the food surplus required by Germany.
>
> The following consequences result from this situation, which has received the

approval of the highest authorities, since it is in accord with the political tendencies (preservation of the Little Russians, preservation of the Caucasus, of the Baltic provinces, of White Russia, to the prejudice of the Great Russians):

"I. For the forest belt:

(a) Production in the forest belt (the food-deficit area) will become 'naturalised,' similar to the events during the World War and the Communist tendencies of the war, etc., viz: agriculture in that territory will begin to become a mere 'home production.' The result will be that the planting of products destined for the market, such as, in particular, flax and hemp, will be discontinued, and the area used therefor will be taken over for products for the producer (grain, potatoes, etc.). Moreover, discontinuance of fodder deliveries to that area will lead to the collapse of the dairy production and of pig-producing in that territory.

(b) Germany is not interested in the maintenance of the productive power of these territories, except for supplying the troops stationed there. The population, as in the old days, will utilise arable land for growing its own food. It is useless to expect grain or other surpluses to be produced. Only after many years can these extensive regions be intensified to an extent that they might produce genuine surpluses. The population of these areas, in particular the urban population, will have to face most serious distress from famine. It will be necessary to divert the population into the Siberian spaces. Since rail transport is out of the question, this too, will be an extremely difficult problem.

(c) In this situation, Germany will only draw substantial advantages by quick, non-recurrent seizure, i.e., it will be vitally necessary to make the entire flax harvest available for German needs, not only the fibers but also the oleaginous seeds.

It will also be necessary to utilise for German purposes the livestock which has no fodder base of its own, i.e., it will be necessary to seize livestock holdings immediately, and to make them available to the troops not only for the moment but in the long run, and also for exportation to Germany. Since fodder supplies will be cut off, pig and cattle holdings in these areas will of necessity drastically decline in the near future. If they are not seized by the Germans at an early date, they will be slaughtered by the population for their own use, without Germany getting anything out of it."

That is the end of that particular quotation. Our next quotation is from the first paragraph of Page 4 of the English text. The German text is at Page 7, the last two words of line 26 down to the beginning of line 31:-

"It has been demanded by the Fuehrer that the reduction of the meat ration should be ended by the autumn. This can only be achieved by the most drastic seizures of Russian livestock holdings, particularly in areas which are in a favourable transport situation in relation to Germany."

In the interests of expedition, your Honour, I am omitting some sections from this last exhibit, which I had originally intended to quote.

I skip now to Line 29 of Page 4 of the English text, beginning with the underscored words "in future", and quote to Line 48. In the German text it is at Page 8, third line from the bottom, continuing to Line 17 of Page 9.

"In future, southern Russia must turn its face towards Europe. Its food surpluses, however, will only be paid for if it purchases its industrial consumer goods from Germany or Europe. Russian competition from the forest zone must, therefore, be abolished.

It follows from all that has been said that the German administration in these territories may well attempt to mitigate the consequences of the famine which undoubtedly will take place, and to accelerate the return to primitive agricultural conditions. An attempt might be made to intensify cultivation in these areas by expanding the acreage under potatoes or other important food crops giving a high yield. However, these measures will not avert famine. Many tens of millions of people in this area will become redundant and will either die or have to emigrate to Siberia. Any attempt to save the population there from death by starvation by importing surpluses from the black soil zone would be at the expense of supplies to Europe. It would reduce Germany's staying power in the war and would undermine Germany's and Europe's power to resist the blockade. This must be clearly and absolutely understood."

I next quote from Page 5, Lines 18 to 30 of the English text. The German text is at Page 12, Lines 1 to 11.

"I. Supplies for the Army:

Germany's food situation in the third year of war demands imperatively that the Wehrmacht, in all its provisioning, shall not live off Greater German territory or that of incorporated or friendly areas from which this territory receives imports. This minimum aim, the provisioning of the Wehrmacht from enemy territory in the third year, and if necessary in later years, must be attained at any price. This means that one-third of the Wehrmacht must be fully provisioned by French deliveries to the army of occupation. The remaining two-thirds (and even slightly more in view of the present size of the Wehrmacht) must without exception be provisioned from the Eastern territory."

I now quote from Page 8 of the English text, the last nine lines. The German text is at Page 18, Lines 15 to 22:

"Thus it is not important under any circumstances to preserve the status quo, but what matters is a deliberate turning away from the existing situation and introducing Russian food resources into the European framework. This will inevitably result in an extinction of industry as well as a large part of the people in what so far have been the food-deficit areas."

It is impossible to state this alternative in sufficiently hard and severe terms."

My next quotation is from the first 10 lines of Page 9 of the English text. The German text is at Page 19, Lines 11 to 20:

"Our problem is not to replace intensive food production in Europe through the incorporation of new space in the East, but to replace imports from overseas by imports from the East. The task is two-fold:-

1. We must use the Eastern spaces for overcoming the food shortages during and after the war. This means that we must not be afraid of drawing upon the capital substance of the East. Such an intervention is much more acceptable from the European standpoint than drawing upon the capital substance of Europe's agriculture."

Finally, I quote from the remainder of Page 9 to the end of the penultimate paragraph of the English text. The German text appears at Lines 24 to 31 of Page 19.

"2. For the future New Order, the food-producing areas in the East must be turned into a permanent and substantial complementary source of food for Europe, through intensified cultivation and resulting higher yields.

The first-named task must be accomplished at any price, even through the most ruthless cutting down of Russian domestic consumption, which will require discrimination between the consuming and producing zones."

It is submitted, your Honour, that this document discloses, on its face, a studied plan to murder millions of innocent people through starvation. It reveals a programme of premeditated murder of millions of innocent people through starvation. It reveals a programme of premeditated murder on a scale so vast as to stagger the human imagination. Major Elwyn Jones, of the British delegation, will subsequently show that this plan was, in effect, the logical culmination of general objectives clearly announced by Adolf Hitler in Mein Kampf. Each defendant in the box was fully aware of these general objectives when he committed the acts with which he is charged.

I next introduce in evidence a document no less damaging than the one I have just quoted. This document is Number L- 221, which is Exhibit USA 317. This is a top secret memorandum, dated 16th July, 1941, of a conference at the Fuehrer's headquarters, concerning the war in the East. It seems to have been prepared by defendant Bormann because his initials appear at the top of Page 1. It was captured by the United States Counter-Intelligence branch.

The text of the memorandum indicates that the conference was attended by Hitler, Lammers and defendants Goering, Keitel, Rosenberg and Bormann.

The exhibit is particularly important for the light it throws upon the conspirators' plans to Germanise conquered areas of the Soviet Union. It is important also for its disclosure of the utterly fraudulent character of the whole Nazi propaganda programme. It shows how the conspirators sought to deceive the entire world; how they pretended to pursue one course of action when their aims and purposes were to follow precisely the opposite course.

I first quote from Page 1 of the English text, beginning at Line 14 of Page 1 and continuing through to Line 22 of Page 2. The German text is at Page 1, beginning with the last paragraph and continuing through to Line 19 of Page 2. I quote:-

"A. Now it was essential that we did not publicise our aims before the world; also there was no need for that, but the main thing was that we ourselves knew what we wanted. By no means should we render our task more difficult by making superfluous declarations. Such declarations were superfluous because we could do everything wherever we had the power, and what was beyond our power we would not be able to do anyway.

What we told the world about the motives for our measures ought to be conditioned, therefore, by tactical reasons. We ought to act here in exactly the same way as we did in the cases of Norway, Denmark, Holland, and Belgium. In these cases, too, we did not publish our aims, and it was only sensible to continue in the same way.

Therefore, we shall emphasize again that we were forced to occupy, administer, and secure a certain area; it was in the interest of the inhabitants that we provided order, food, traffic, etc., hence our measures. Nobody shall be able to recognise that it initiates a final settlement. This need not prevent our taking all necessary measures - shooting, desettling, etc. - and we shall take them.

But we do not want to make any people our enemies prematurely and unnecessarily. Therefore we shall act as though we wanted to exercise a

mandate only. At the same time we must know clearly that we shall never leave those countries. Our conduct therefore ought to be:-
 1. To do nothing which might obstruct the final settlement, but to prepare for it only in secret;
 2. To emphasize that we are liberators.
In particular:-

The Crimea has to be evacuated by all foreigners and to be settled by Germans only.

In the same way the former Austrian part of Galicia will become Reich Territory. Our present relations with Roumania are good, but nobody knows what they will be in the future. This we have to consider, and we have to draw our frontiers accordingly. One ought not to be dependent on the good will of other people. We have to plan our relations with Roumania in accordance with this principle.

We have now to face the task of cutting up the giant cake according to our needs, in order to be able:-
 first, to dominate it;
 second, to administer it;
 and third, to exploit it.

The Russians have now ordered partisan warfare behind our front. This partisan war again has some advantage for us; it enables us to eradicate everyone who opposes us.

Never again must it be possible to create a military power West of the Urals, even if we have to wage war for a hundred years in order to attain this goal. Every successor of the Fuehrer should know that security for the Reich exists only if there are no foreign military forces West of the Urals: it is Germany who undertakes the protection of this area against all possible dangers. Our iron principle is and has to remain:

We must never permit anybody but the Germans to carry arms."

I next quote from Page 3, Lines 19 to 31 of the English text. In the German text this is at the last 13 lines of Page 5:

"The Fuehrer emphasizes that the entire Baltic country will have to be incorporated into Germany.

At the same time, the Crimea, including a considerable hinterland (situated North of the Crimea), should become Reich territory; the hinterland should be as large as possible.

Rosenberg objects to this because of the Ukrainians living there. (Incidentally, it occurred to me several times that Rosenberg has a soft spot for the Ukrainians; thus he desires to aggrandise the former Ukraine to a considerable extent.)"

Departing from the text for just a moment, it may be noted parenthetically that this was the only aspect of the programme outlined by Hitler at this meeting to which Rosenberg objected in any way. Resuming the quotation:-

"The Fuehrer emphasizes furthermore that the Volga colony, too, will have to become Reich territory, also the district around Baku; the latter will have to become a German concession (military colony)."

Thus the programme, as outlined by the conspirators at this meeting of 16th July, 1941, called for the unlawful incorporation of a part of Galicia and all of the Baltic countries into Germany, and for the unlawful conversion of the Crimea and areas

North of it, the Volga territory, and the district around Baku, into German colonies.

In further support of this point, I invite the attention of your Honour to Document 1020-PS, already introduced in evidence by Mr. Alderman, as Exhibit USA 145. This document was not included in our document book, your Honour, but has been read into the record by Mr. Alderman, Pages 1202 and 1203. This document is entitled, "Instructions for a Reich Commissioner in the Baltic Countries and White Russia".

THE PRESIDENT: Where are you quoting from?

CAPTAIN HARRIS: Sir, it is not included in our document book, but it is in the record, at Pages 1202 and 1203. In the German text, the original of which we have here, it is at Pages 2 and 3.

> "The aim of a Reich Commissar for Estonia, Latvia, Lithuania, and White Ruthenia (last two words added in pencil) must be to strive to achieve the form of a German protectorate, and then transform the region into part of the Greater German Reich by Germanising racially possible elements, colonising Germanic races and banishing undesirable elements. The Baltic Sea must become a Germanic inland sea, under the guardianship of Greater Germany."

I now offer in evidence Document EC-3, which is Exhibit USA 318, which was likewise found among the captured O.K.W. files at Fechenheim. This document, your Honour, is offered as direct proof of the fact, to which we have previously referred, that even in the food surplus areas of the occupied regions of the Ukraine, the conspirators planned to allocate food on a basis which left virtually nothing for those persons who were not engaged in the compulsory production of commodities for the German war machine. This document, as well as Document EC-126, which was introduced a few moments ago, and others we offer, should, it is submitted, be read in the light of the explicit provision in Article 52 of the Hague Regulations of 1907, that requisitions in kind and services shall not be demanded from municipalities or inhabitants except for the needs of the army of occupation.

I first quote from our Page 3, Lines 21 to 23 of the English text of EC-3. In the German text it is Page 13, Lines 1 to 3. The particular document from which I am about to quote is a top secret memorandum, dated 16th September, 1941, concerning a meeting of German military officials presided over by defendant Goering. This is our Page 3, Sir, Lines 21 to 23 of EC-3. The memorandum was signed by General Nagel, liaison officer between defendant Goering's Four Year Plan Office and the O.K.W. I now quote:-

> "At this conference which was concerned with the better exploitation of the occupied territories for the German food economy, the Reich Marshal - Goering - called attention to the following..."

I next quote from the first two paragraphs of Page 4 of the English text. The German text is at Page 13, the third and fourth paragraphs:

> "It is clear that a graduated scale of food allocations is needed.
>
> First in line are the combat troops, then the remainder of troops in enemy territory, and then those troops stationed at home. The rates are adjusted accordingly. The supply of the German non-military population follows and only then comes the population of the occupied territories."

I now quote from another portion of this document, starting at Page 1 of the English text. This is a memorandum, dated 25th November, 1941, relating to the general principles of economic policy in the newly-occupied Eastern territories, as prescribed in a conference held in Berlin on 8th November, 1941. This memorandum was also written by General Nagel. It is on the stationery of the Liaison Staff of

Supreme Headquarters, Armament Procurement Office with the Reich Marshal Goering.

I quote from Lines 13 to the bottom of Page 1.

THE PRESIDENT: Is not this document, the part you are going to read now, merely cumulative of EC-126, which you have just read to us, that economic policy directive?

CAPTAIN HARRIS: It affords further proof, Sir, of the conspirators' plans to exploit the Eastern Occupied Areas. I can omit it, if you like, Sir.

THE PRESIDENT: It does not seem to add anything.

CAPTAIN HARRIS: Very well, Sir.

I shall pass on to the next point.

On 17th July, 1941, Hitler and the defendant Keitel issued a decree appointing defendant Rosenberg as the Reich Minister for the Occupied Eastern Territories. This was the day following the meeting at the Fuehrer's headquarters, which is reported in Document L-221 and from which we have already quoted at length.

The decree appointing Rosenberg as Reich Minister for the Occupied Eastern Territories is set forth in Document 1997-PS, which is Exhibit USA 319 and I offer it as evidence. I quote from Articles 2 and 4 on Page 1 of this decree. The German text is at Pages 27 and 28, Articles 2 and 4.

> "The civil administration in the newly-occupied Eastern territories, where these territories are not included in the administration of the territories bordering on the Reich or the Government General, is subject to the Reich Minister for the Occupied Eastern Territories.
>
> I appoint Reichsleiter Alfred Rosenberg as Reich Minister for the Occupied Eastern Territories. He will hold office in Berlin."

Defendant Rosenberg's views well fitted him for this task as one of the chief executors of the conspirators' plans in the Soviet Union. His views were plainly expressed in a speech delivered on 20th June, 1940, and are set forth in Document 1058-PS, now Exhibit USA 147. I refer your Honour to the first three sentences of the English text. The German text appears on Page 9, last five lines and continuing through to line 2 of Page 10. In the speech, defendant Rosenberg stated, and I quote:

> "The job of feeding the German people stands, this year, without a doubt, at the top of the list of Germany's claims on the East; and here the Southern territories and the Northern Caucasus will have to serve as a balance for the feeding of the German people. We see absolutely no reason for any obligation on our part to feed also the Russian people with the products of that surplus territory. We know that this is a harsh necessity, bare of any feelings."

I next offer in evidence Document EC-347, which is Exhibit USA 320. This document was likewise found among the captured files of the O.K.W. It contains a set of directives issued by defendant Rosenberg in his capacity as Reich Minister for the Occupied Eastern Territories.

I quote from the first two full paragraphs of Page 1 of this exhibit. The German text is at Page 39, Paragraphs 4 and 5. In these directives defendant Rosenberg stated, and I quote:- -

> "The principal task of the civilian administration in the occupied Eastern territories is to represent the interests of the Reich. This basic principle is to be given precedence in all measures and considerations. Therefore, the occupied territories, in the future, may be permitted to have a life of their own in a form yet to be determined. However, they remain parts of the Greater German

living space and are always to be governed according to this guiding principle. The regulations of the Hague Convention on Land Warfare, which concern the administration of a country occupied by a foreign belligerent power, are not applicable, since the U.S.S.R. is to be considered dissolved and, therefore, the Reich has the obligation of exercising all governmental and other sovereign functions in the interests of the country's inhabitants. Therefore, any measures are permitted which the German administration deems necessary and suitable for the execution of this comprehensive task."

THE PRESIDENT: Has not that been read before?

CAPTAIN HARRIS: Not to my knowledge, Sir.

THE PRESIDENT: Very well.

CAPTAIN HARRIS: Implicit in defendant Rosenberg's statement that the Hague Regulations are not applicable to the Soviet Union is the recognition by him that the conspirators' actions in the Soviet Union flagrantly violated the Hague Regulations. The statement indicates that the conspirators were utterly contemptuous of applicable principles of International Law.

Mr. Dodd has already introduced into evidence Document 294- PS, now Exhibit USA 185, in connection with the slave labor presentation. This document is a top-secret memorandum, dated 25th October, 1942, which was found in defendant Rosenberg's files. It was written by Braeutigam, who was a high official in defendant Rosenberg's Ministry for the Occupied Eastern Territories. I should like to quote two additional passages from this document. I quote from the English text Page 1, the first full paragraph, Lines 17 to 20. The German text is at Page 1, the first full paragraph, Lines 22 to 25.

> "In the East, Germany is carrying on a three-fold war: A war for the destruction of Bolshevism, a war for the destruction of the Greater Russian empire, and finally a war for the acquisition of colonial territory for colonising purposes and economic exploitation.
>
> With the inherent instinct of the Eastern peoples, the primitive man soon found out also that for Germany the slogan: 'Liberation from Bolshevism' was only a pretext to enslave the Eastern peoples according to her own methods."

This completes, your Honour, the list of the exhibits with respect to the Soviet Union which we propose to introduce at this time. As I mentioned at the outset of this presentation, these exhibits do not disclose all of the conspirators' plans with respect to the occupied countries, but they do, we submit, show a constant pattern, a pattern of ruthless Germanisation and destruction.

In conclusion we desire to offer in evidence two documents which disclose that German industrialists and financiers aided and abetted Himmler in his relentless programme of Germanisation, exploitation, oppression and destruction.

I first offer in evidence Document EC-454, which is Exhibit USA 321. This document was found in the vaults of the Stein Bank in Cologne among the files of the banker, Baron Kurt von Schroeder, by a joint British-American team, headed by Colonel Kellam on the British side and Captain Roth on the American side. It is a carbon copy of a letter from von Schroeder to Himmler, dated 27th August, 1943, and bears von Schroeder's initials. I quote it in its entirety:-

> "My very Honourable Reichsfuehrer:
>
> With great joy I learn of your appointment as Reichsminister of the Interior and take the liberty to extend my heartiest congratulations to you on assuming your new post.

A strong hand is now very necessary in the operation of this department and it is universally welcomed, but especially by your friends, that it was you who were chosen for this by the Fuehrer. Please be assured that we will always do everything in our power at all times to assist you in every possible way.

I am pleased to inform you at this opportunity that your circle of friends has again placed at your disposal this year a sum slightly in excess of RM 1,000,000 for special purposes.' An exact list showing the names of the contributors will be sent to you shortly.

Again all my very best wishes - as well as those of my family - I remain yours, in old loyalty and esteem.

Heil Hitler! Yours truly."

I next offer in evidence - and this is the final exhibit, your Honour - Document EC-453, which is Exhibit USA 322. This document was likewise found in the Stein Bank in Cologne by the above-mentioned joint British-American team. It is a carbon copy of a letter from von Schroeder to Himmler, dated 21st September, 1943, bearing von Schroeder's initials, with the enclosed list of contributors -

THE PRESIDENT: Captain Harris, on what principle do you suggest that either of these letters can possibly be evidence in this case?

CAPTAIN HARRIS: Your Honour, at the time the motion to postpone the trial as to Gustav Krupp was argued before this Tribunal, the British Chief Prosecutor specifically stated that if it should be the decision of the Tribunal that Krupp should be dismissed, the evidence as to the part which he, his firm, and other industrialists played in the preparation and conduct of the war would still be given to this Tribunal as forming part of the general conspiracy in which these defendants were involved, with divers other persons not now before the Court.

The evidence we are now offering, your Honour, is precisely of the type indicated by Sir Hartley Shawcross. It is evidence which goes to prove the length and breadth of the general conspiracy which is alleged in the Indictment. Evidence showing contributions to one of the leading conspirators, a conspirator who was in the forefront of the unlawful programme to plunder public and private property and to Germanise a large part of the world, is, it is submitted, relevant to this proceeding.

May I continue?

THE PRESIDENT: Yes.

CAPTAIN HARRIS: I quote the last letter, EC-453, in its entirety:-

"Dear Reichsfuehrer:

I thank you very much for your kind letter of the 14th of this month with which you made me very happy. At the same time I am enclosing a list with the total amount of funds made available to you by your circle of friends and totaling RM 1,000,000. We are very glad indeed to render some assistance to you in your special tasks and to be able to provide some small relief for you in your still further extended sphere of duties.

Wishing you, dear Reichsfuehrer, the best of luck, I remain in old loyalty and esteem.

Heil Hitler! Yours very truly."

I had intended, Your Honour, to quote the names of the contributors; but I shall not, if your Honour considers it unnecessary.

THE PRESIDENT: I don't think it would add to the expedition of the trial, do you?

CAPTAIN HARRIS: Very well, sir. I am exceedingly grateful to your Honour for your very kind attention.

THE PRESIDENT: Yes, Colonel Storey.

COLONEL STOREY: Does your Honour want to proceed now before the recess?

THE PRESIDENT: No, perhaps we had better adjourn now for 10 minutes.

(A recess was taken.)

COLONEL STOREY: If the Tribunal please, the remainder of the presentation during the week will be concerning the criminal organisations. The first to be presented now is the Leadership Corps, including some of the illustrative crimes against the churches, against the Jews, against the Trade Unions, and the operation of the "Einsatzstab Rosenberg" concerning the looting of art treasures.

On the threshold of presenting the proof establishing the criminality of the Leadership Corps of the Nazi Party it is pertinent to restate the prosecution's theory of this case. It is this. The Nazi Party was the central core of the Common Plan or Conspiracy alleged in Count 1 of the Indictment, a conspiracy which contemplated and embraced the commission of Crimes against the Peace, War Crimes and Crimes against Humanity as defined and denounced by the Charter.

The Leadership Corps, upon the evidence, was responsible for planning, directing and supervising the criminal measures carried into execution by the Nazi Party in furtherance of the conspiracy. More than this, as will be shown, the members of the Leadership Corps themselves actively participated in the commission of illegal measures in aid of the conspiracy. In the light of the evidence to be offered this Tribunal, the Leadership Corps may be fairly described as the brain, the backbone, and the directive arms of the Nazi Party. Its responsibilities are more massive and comprehensive than those of the army of followers it led and directed in the assault against the peace-loving peoples of the world. Accordingly, upon the record made in this case and now to be enlarged upon, the prosecution requests this Tribunal to declare that the Leadership Corps of the Nazi Party is a criminal group or organisation in accordance with Article 9 of the Charter.

At this time I should like to submit to the Tribunal the document book supporting the brief as Exhibit USA V.

If your Honour pleases - diverting from the manuscript - during the recess there was placed upon your bench the document book, which has each document marked by tab and each quoted portion embraced by red pencil marks for the assistance of your Honours. In addition, we have handed up two documents that have already been introduced in evidence: an enlarged copy of this chart, more detailed, which your Honours have before you, and another chart, in photostatic form, with reference to the Leadership Corps; and both of those will be identified later.

I now proceed to present the proof relating to the composition, the functions, and the responsibilities and powers of the Leadership Corps of the Nazi Party. First, what was the Leadership Corps -

DR. ROBERT SERVATIUS (Counsel for the Leadership Corps of the N.S.D.A.P.): After the last meeting I received a statement by Mr. Justice Jackson in which were proposals about the taking of evidence and the time for the discussion of certain questions which might arise. I cannot understand the scope of these proposals, and must therefore ask that I may at some time speak about these points again, if it is necessary.

THE PRESIDENT: Of course, counsel will have the opportunity of presenting a full argument in answer to the argument presented on behalf of the prosecution.

What I understood from Mr. Justice Jackson on Friday was that he proposed that the evidence on the question of criminal organisations should be presented first, and the argument presented afterwards.

Counsel for the organisations will, as I stated this morning, have the opportunity of calling evidence in answer to the evidence of the prosecution, and will also have the opportunity of presenting whatever argument they think right in answer to the evidence and argument presented on behalf of the prosecution.

COLONEL STOREY: First, what was the Leadership Corps of the Nazi Party? What persons made up its membership? What was its size and scope?

In considering the composition and organisational structure of the Leadership Corps it will be convenient for the Tribunal to refer to Document 2903-PS, which is this exhibit on the wall and which was introduced by Mr. Albrecht at the opening of the Trial. And, supplementing the chart on the wall, I now offer in evidence Document 2833-PS, Exhibit USA 22, which is a chart of the Leadership Corps of the Nazi Party, appearing at Page 9 of a magazine published by the Chief Education Office of the Nazi Party, entitled 'The Face of the Party.' It is this little photostatic copy that you have.' Later on we expect to put the big one on the wall.

These charts and the evidence to follow show that the Leadership Corps constituted the sum total of the officials of the Nazi Party. It included the "Fuehrer" at the top; the "Reichsleiter," on the horizontal line; the Reich office holders, immediately below; the five categories of leaders who were area commanders, called the "Hoheitstraeger" or "bearers of sovereignty." They are in the red-lettered or red-lined boxes at the bottom. They range all the way from the 40 odd Gauleiter in charge of large districts, down through the intermediate political leaders, the "Kreisleiter," the "Ortsgruppenleiter," the "Zellenleiter", and finally, to the "Blockleiter", who were charged with looking after 40 to 60 households, and, what may be best described as staff officers, attached to each of the five levels of the "Hoheitstraeger".

Organised upon a hierarchical basis, forming a pyramidal structure - as appears from the chart which your Honour holds in your hands - the principal political leaders on a scale of descending authority were:-

The Fuehrer, at the top.

The Reichsleiter, as I have mentioned, and the main office and officeholders.

The Gauleiter, who was the district leader, with his staff officers.

The Kreisleiter, who was the county leader, and his staff officers.

The Ortsgruppenleiter, the local chapter leader, and his staff officers.

The Zellenleiter, who was the cell leader, and his staff officers.

And then, finally, the Blockleiter with his staff officers.

I now offer in evidence Document 1893-PS. This is Exhibit USA 323. And this, if your Honour pleases, is the Organisation Book of the N.S.D.A.P., the National Socialist Party. It was edited by the defendant, Reich Organisation Leader of the N.S.D.A.P. - the late defendant - Dr. Robert Ley and it is the 1943 edition. A large part of the evidence to be offered relating to the composition of the Leadership Corps of the Nazi Party will be drawn from this primer of the Nazi organisations, and I shall later quote from it, and without so requesting the Tribunal each time to take judicial notice, I shall assume, in the absence of questions, that it is so understood. That is Document 1893, the English translation, that we will refer to.

I now proceed to offer evidence on the make-up and powers of the Reichsleitung or the Leadership Corps, which consisted of the Reichsleiter or Reich Leaders of the Nazi Party - and they are shown on that long horizontal list at the top of the chart - the "Hauptaemter" (main offices), and the "Aemter", or office holders.

The "Reichsleiter" of the Party were, next to Hitler, the highest office holders in the

Party hierarchy. All of the Reichsleiter in the main office and office holders within the Reichsleitung were appointed by Hitler and directly responsible to him.

I quote from the first paragraph of Page 4, Document 1893- PS:-

"The Fuehrer appoints the following political directors:
Reichsleiter and all political directors, to include the Directors of the Womens Leagues, within the Reich Directorate or Reichsleitung."

The significant fact to be grasped is that through the Reichsleitung perfect co-ordination of the Party and State machinery was guaranteed.

The Party manual puts it this way - and I quote from the fourth sentence of the third paragraph of Page 20 of that document. You will find the page number at the bottom, Page 20; It is a very short quotation. I quote:

"In the Reichsleitung the arteries of the organisation of the German people and of the German State merge."

If your Honour please, there is a little different translation in that portion in your book.

To prove -

THE PRESIDENT: Just a moment, please. It begins: "It is in the Reich Directorate where the strings of the organisation of the German people and of the German State merge." Is that it?

COLONEL STOREY: Yes, Sir, that is it. This translation says, "the arteries of the organisation of the German people and of the German State merge."

THE PRESIDENT: Yes

COLONEL STOREY: To prove that the Reichsleiter of the Leadership Corps included the most powerful coalition of political overlords in Nazi Germany, it is necessary only to put in evidence their names. The list of Reichsleiter now to be offered in evidence will include the following defendants now on trial before this Tribunal:-

Rosenberg, von Schirach, Frick, Bormann, Hans Frank, and the late defendant Robert Ley.

The evidence to be introduced will show that the defendant Rosenberg was the leader of an organisation named for him, the "Einsatzstab Rosenberg" - which is not shown on this chart, if Your Honour pleases - which carried out a vast programme of looting and plunder of art treasures throughout occupied Europe.

The evidence will further show that, as representative of the Fuehrer for the supervision of Nazi ideology and schooling, Rosenberg participated in an aggressive campaign to undermine the Christian churches and to supersede Christianity by a German National Church founded upon a combination of irrationality, pseudo-scientific theories, mysticism, and the discredited cult of the racial State. It will further be shown that the late defendant Ley, acting as the agent of Hitler and the Leadership Corps, directed the Nazi assault upon the independent labor unions of Germany, and that before destroying himself he first destroyed the bastion of republican society, a free and independent labor movement, replacing it by a Nazi organisation, the German Labor Front, or the D.A.F., and employed this organisation as a means of exploiting the German labor force in the interests of the conspiracy, and of instilling Nazi ideology among the ranks of the German workers.

It will be shown that the defendant Frick participated in the enactment of many laws which were designed to promote the conspiracy in its several phases.

The defendant Frick shares responsibility for the grave injury done by the officials of the Leadership Corps to the concept of the rule of law by virtue of his efforts to give the color of law and formal legality to a large volume of Nazi legislation which violated the rights of humanity, such as the Nazi discriminatory legislation designed to degrade, stigmatise, and eliminate the Jewish people of Germany and German occupied Europe.

Though the defendant Bormann is physically absent from the dock, the evidence as to his responsibility in directing and furthering the course of the Nazi conspiracy is here and expands with the record in this case. As Chief of the Party Chancellery, immediately under Hitler, the defendant Bormann was an extremely important force in directing the activities of the Leadership Corps. As will be shown, a decree of 16th January, 1942, provided that the participation of the Party in all important legislation, governmental appointments, and promotions had to be undertaken exclusively by Bormann. He took part in the preparation of all laws and decrees issued by the Reich authorities and gave his assent to those of the subordinate governments.

I now refer to Document 2473-PS, Exhibit USA 324. You will find that the English translation contains a list of the Reichsleiter of the N.S.D.A.P. set forth on Page 170 of this book. It was edited by the late defendant and Reichsleiter for Party Organisation, Robert Ley.

The names of the 15 Reichsleiter in office in 1943 will be found on Pages 1 and 2 of Document 2473-PS.

If the Tribunal please, I will not read all of them, but will call attention only to certain of them, as follows:

Martin Bormann, Chief of the Party Chancellery.

Then we pass over to Wilhelm Frick, Leader of the National Socialist fraction in the Reichstag, shown on the big chart over at the second box from the end on the right.

Joseph Goebbels, Reich Propaganda Leader of the N.S.D.A.P., shown also on the same level.

Heinrich Himmler, Reich Leader of the S.S., the Deputy of the N.S.D.A.P. for all questions of Germandom.

Robert Ley, Reich Organisation Leader of the N.S.D.A.P. and Leader of the German Labor Front.

Victor Lutze, Chief of Staff of the SA.

Alfred Rosenberg, representative of the Fuehrer for the supervision of all mental and ideological training and education of the N.S.D.A.P.

Baldur von Schirach, Reich Leader for the education of the youth of the National Socialist Party.

And then, finally, Franz Schwarz, Reich Treasurer of the National Socialist Party.

The principal functions of the Reichsleiter, which we might call directors, included the responsibility of carrying out the tasks and missions assigned to them by the Fuehrer or by the Chief of the Party Chancellery, the defendant Martin Bormann. The Reichsleiter were further charged with insuring that Party policies were being executed in all the subordinate areas of the Reich. They were also responsible for insuring a continual flow of new leadership into the Party. With respect to the function and the responsibilities of the Reichsleiter I now quote from Page 20 of Document 1893-PS:-

"The N.S.D.A.P. represents the political conception, the political conscience and the political will of the German nation. Political conception, political conscience and political will are embodied in the person of the Fuehrer. Based on his directive and in accordance with the programme of the N.S.D.A.P., the organs of the Reich Directorate directionally determine the political aims of the German people. It is in the Reich Directorate - or Reichsleitung - that the arteries of the organisation of the German people and State merge. It is the task of the separate organs of the Reich Directorate to maintain as close a contact as possible with the life of the nation through their sub- offices in the Gau...

The structure of the Reich Directorate is such that the channel from the lowest Party office upwards shows the most minute weaknesses and changes in the mood of the people....

Another essential task of the Reich Directorate is to assure a good selection of leaders. It is the duty of the Reich Directorate to see that there is leadership in all phases of life, a leadership which is firmly tied to National Socialist ideology and which promotes its dissemination with all of its energy....

It is the supreme task of the Reich Organisation Leader to preserve the Party as a well-sharpened sword for the Fuehrer."

The domination of the German Government by the top members of the Leadership Corps was facilitated by a circular decree of the Reich Minister of Justice, dated 17th February, 1934, which established equal rank for the offices within the Reichsleitung of the Leadership Corps and the Reich offices of the German Government. In this decree it was expressly provided that "The supreme offices of the Reich Party Directorate are equal in rank to the supreme Reich Government authorities". The Party Manual termed the control exercised over the machinery of the Government by the Leadership Corps "the permeation of the State apparatus with the political will of the Party".

At a later stage in this proceeding it will be shown that the Leadership Corps of the Nazi Party incontestably dominated the German State and Government. The control by the Leadership Corps of the German Government was facilitated by uniting in the same Nazi chieftains high offices within the Reichsleitung and the corresponding offices within the apparatus of the government. For example, as shown in Document 2903-PS, Goebbels was Reichsleiter in charge of Party propaganda, but he was also a cabinet minister in charge of propaganda and public enlightenment.

Himmler held office within the Reichsleitung as head of the Main Office for Folkdom, and also was Reichsfuehrer of the S.S. At the same time, Himmler held the governmental position of the Reich Commissioner for the Consolidation of Germandom, and was the governmental head of the German police system.

As will be shown, this personal union of high office in the Leadership Corps and high governmental position in the same Nazi Leaders greatly accommodated the plan of the Leadership Corps to dominate and control the German State and Government.

In addition to the Reichsleiter the Party Directorate included about 11 Hauptaemter, or main offices, and about four Aemter, or offices. As set forth in the exhibit, the Hauptaemter of the Party included such main organisations as those for personnel, training, technology (headed by the defendant Speer), folkdom (headed by Himmler), civil servants, communal policy, and the like. The Aemter or offices, of the Party within the Reichsleitung included the Office for Foreign Policy under the defendant Rosenberg which, the evidence will show, actively participated in plans for the launching of the war of aggression against Norway, the Office for Colonial Policy, the Office for Genealogy, and the Office of Racial Policy.

As will be shown by the chart of the Leadership Corps in the folder which your Honour has, certain of the main offices and offices within the Reichsleitung would appear again within the Gauleitung, or Gau Party Directorate, and the Kreisleitung, or Party County Directorate. It is thus shown that the Reichsleiter and the main office and office holders within the Reichsleitung exercised through functional channels, through the subordinate offices on lower regional levels, a total control over the various sectors of the national life of Germany.

I shall next take up the Gauleiter. As will be seen from this organisational chart of the Nazi Party now before the Tribunal as Exhibit USA 2, for Party purposes Germany was divided into major administrative regions, Gaue, which in turn were sub-divided into Kreise (counties), Ortsgruppen (local chapters), Zellen (cells), and in Blocks (blocks). A Gauleiter who was the political leader of the Gau or district was in charge of each Gau. Each Gauleiter was appointed by and was directly responsible to Hitler. I quote from Page 18 of this same Document 1893-PS, the Organisation Book of the N.S.D.A.P.:-

"The Gau represents the concentration of a number of Party counties or Kreise. The Gauleiter is directly subordinate to the Fuehrer.

The Gauleiter bears overall responsibility to the Fuehrer for the sector of sovereignty entrusted to him. The rights, duties, and jurisdiction of the Gauleiter result primarily from the mission assigned by the Fuehrer, and apart from that, from detailed directives."

The responsibility and function of the Gauleiter and his staff officers or office holders were essentially a political one, namely, to insure the authority of the Nazi Party within his area, to co-ordinate the activities of the Party and all its affiliated and supervised organisations, and to enlarge the influence of the Party over the people and life in his Gau generally. Following the outbreak of the war, when it became imperative to co-ordinate the various phases of the German war effort, the Gauleiter were given additional important responsibilities. The Ministerial Council for the Defence of the Reich, which was a sort of general staff for civilian defence, and the mobilisation of the German war economy, by a decree of 1st September, 1939 (1939 Reichsgesetzblatt, Part I, page 1565), appointed about 16 Gauleiter as Reich Defence Commissars, concerning which I ask the Tribunal to take judicial notice. Later, under the impact of mounting military reverses, and an increasingly strained war economy, more and more important administrative functions were put on a Gau basis. The Party Gaue became the basic defence areas of the Reich, and each Gauleiter became a Reich Defence Commissar by a decree of the Ministerial Council for the Defence of the Reich of 16th November, 1942 (1942 Reichsgesetzblatt, Part I, page 649), of which I ask the Tribunal to take judicial notice. In the course of the war additional functions were entrusted to the Gauleiter, so that at the end, with the exception of certain special matters, such as police affairs, almost all phases of the German war economy were co-ordinated and supervised by them. For instance, regional authority over price control was put under the Gauleiter as Reich Defence Commissars and housing administration was placed under the Gauleiter as Gau Housing Commissars. Toward the end of the war the Gauleiter were charged even with the military and quasi-military tasks. They were made commanders of the Volkssturm in their areas, and were entrusted with such important functions as the evacuation of civilian population in the path of the advancing Allied armies as well as measures for the destruction of vital installations.

The structure and organisation of the Party Gaue were substantially repeated in the lower levels of the Reich Party organisation such as the Kreise, Ortsgruppen, Zellen, and Blocks. Each of these was headed by a political leader who, subject to the Fuehrer principle, and the orders of superior political leaders, was a sovereign within his sphere. The Leadership Corps of the Nazi Party was in effect a "hierarchy of descending Caesars." Each of the subordinate Party levels, such as the Kreise, Ortsgruppen, and so on, was organised into offices, or Aemter, dealing with the various specialised functions of the Party. But the number of such departments and offices diminished as the Party unit dropped in the hierarchy, so that, while the Kreis office contained all, or almost all of the offices in the Gau (such as the deputy, the staff office leader, an organisation leader, school-leader, propaganda leader, Press office leader, treasurer, judge of the Party Court, inspector, and the like), the Ortsgruppe had less, and the Zellen and Blocks still less.

The Kreisleiter (or county leader):
The Kreisleiter was appointed and dismissed by Hitler upon the nomination of the Gauleiter and directly subordinate to the Gauleiter in the Party hierarchy. The Kreis usually consisted of a single county. The Kreisleiter within the Kreis, had in general the same position, powers, and prerogatives granted the Gauleiter in the Gau. In cities they constituted the very core of Party power and organisation. I quote again from Page 17 of Document 1893- PS, Page 17 the English translation:-

> "The Kreisleiter carries overall responsibility towards the Gauleiter within his zone of sovereignty for the political and ideological training and organisation of the Political Leaders, the Party members, as well as the population".

The Ortsgruppenleiter was the local chapter leader. The area of the Ortsgruppenleiter was comprised of one or more communes, or, in a town, a certain district. The Ortsgruppe was composed of a combination of blocks and cells according to local circumstances, and contained up to 1,500 households. The Ortsgruppenleiter also had a staff of office leaders to assist him in the various functional activities of the Party. All other political leaders in his area of responsibility were subordinate to and under the direction of the Ortsgruppenleiter. For example, the leaders of the various affiliated organisations of the Party, within his area, such as the German Labor Front and the Nazi organisations for lawyers, students, and civil servants, were all subordinate to the Ortsgruppenleiter. In accordance with the Fuehrerprinzip, the Ortsgruppenleiter, or Local Chapter Leaders, were appointed by the Gauleiter, and were directly under and subordinate to the Kreisleiter.

The Party manual provides as follows with reference to the Ortsgruppenleiter, and I quote from Pages 16 and 17 of Document 1893-PS:-

> "As Hoheitstraeger (Bearer of Sovereignty) he is responsible for all expressions of the Party will; he is responsible for the political and ideological leadership and organisation within his zone of sovereignty.
>
> The Ortsgruppenleiter carries the overall responsibility for the political results of all measures initiated by the offices, organisations, and affiliated association of the Party.
>
> The Ortsgruppenleiter has the right to protest to the Kreisleiter against any measures contrary to the interests of the Party with regard to a united political appearance in public."

The Zellenleiter:
The Zellenleiter was responsible for from four to eight blocks. He was the immediate superior of, and had control and supervision over, the Blockleiter. His mission and duties, according to the Party manual, corresponded to the missions of the Blockleiter. I quote from the last paragraph of Page 15, just one line of that same document: "The missions of the cell-leader correspond to the missions of the block-leader."

The Blockleiter:
The Blockleiter was the one Party official who was peculiarly in a position to have

continuous contact with the German people. The block was the lowest unit in the Party pyramidal organisation. The block of the Party comprised 40 to 60 households and was regarded by the Party as the focal point upon which to press the weight of its propaganda. I quote from Pages 13 and 14 of this same document:-

> "The household is the basic community upon which the block and cell system is built. The household is the organisational focal point of all Germans living in an apartment, and includes boarders, domestic help, etc. The Blockleiter has jurisdiction over all matters within his zone relating to the Movement, and is fully responsible to the Zellenleiter."

The Blockleiter, as in the case of other political leaders, was charged with planning, disseminating, and developing a receptivity to the policies of the Nazi Party among the population in his area of responsibility. It was also the expressed duty of the Blockleiter to spy on the population. I quote from Pages 14 and 15 of this same document:-

> "It is the duty of the Blockleiter to find people disseminating damaging rumours and to report them to the Ortsgruppe, so that they may be reported to the respective State authorities.
>
> The Blockleiter must not only be a preacher and defender of the National Socialist ideology towards the member of the Nation and Party entrusted to his political care, but he must also strive to achieve practical collaboration of the Party members within his block zone.
>
> The Blockleiter shall continuously remind the Party members of their particular duties towards the people and the state. The Blockleiter keeps a list (card file) about the households. In principle, the Blockleiter will settle his official business verbally, and he will receive messages verbally, and pass them on in the same way. Correspondence will only be used in cases of absolute necessity. The Blockleiter conducts National Socialist propaganda from mouth to mouth. He will eventually awaken the understanding of the eternally dissatisfied as regards the frequently misunderstood or wrongly interpreted measures and laws of the National Socialist Government. It is not necessary for him to fall in with complaints and gripes about possibly obvious shortcomings of any kind in order to demonstrate solidarity. A condition to gain the confidence of all people is to maintain absolute secrecy in all matters."

It will be shown that there were in Germany nearly half a million Blockleiter. Large though this figure may appear, there can be no doubt that these officials were in and of the Leadership Corps of the Nazi Party. Though they stood at the broad base of the Party Pyramid rather than at its summit, where rested the Reichsleiter, by virtue of this fact, they were stationed at close intervals throughout the German civil population.

THE PRESIDENT: I think, Colonel Storey, it would be an assistance to the Tribunal if you could tell us, that is, at some time convenient to yourself, approximately how many there were of each of these ranks in the corps.

COLONEL STOREY: If Your Honour please, that is the next subject.

THE PRESIDENT: Very well.

COLONEL STOREY: It may be doubted that the average German ever looked upon the face of Heinrich Himmler. But the man in the street in Nazi Germany could not have avoided an uneasy acquaintance with the Blockleiter in his own neighborhood. As it is the "cop on the beat" rather than the Chief Magistrate of the nation who symbolises law enforcement to the average man and woman, so it was the

Blockleiter who represented to the people of Germany the Police State of Hitler's Germany. In fact, as may be inferred from the evidence, the Blockleiter were "Little Fuehrers" with real and literal power over the civilians in their domains. As proof of the authority of the Blockleiter to exercise coercion and the threat of force upon the civil population, I quote from Document 2833-PS, which is an excerpt from Page 7 of the magazine entitled 'The Face of the Party,' Document 2833-PS. It is just a line of quotation:-

> "Advice and sometimes also the harsher form of education is employed if the faulty conduct of an individual harms this individual himself, and thus also the community."

Before I get to the numbers, I wanted to deal with the Hoheitstraeger.

THE PRESIDENT: Do not you think it is time to break off?

COLONEL STOREY: Yes.

THE PRESIDENT: Until 2 o'clock.

(A recess was taken until 1400 hours.)

COLONEL STOREY: Your Honour will notice that we have substituted an enlarged chart for the photostatic copy that was introduced in evidence this morning. Another thing I would like to call your Honour's attention to is the fact that the other chart, the big one, was dated 1945 and therefore did not show the defendant Hess, because of his flight to England in 1941, and it will be recalled that the defendant Hess occupied the position before Bormann directly under the Fuehrer in the Party organisation.

We now take up the Hoheitstraeger. The Hoheitstraeger, turning from the text, is shown on this chart very well, and all of those shown in the black block constitute the Hoheitstraeger, beginning with the Fuehrer and going down the vertical column clear down to the black line.

Within the Leadership Corps of the Nazi Party certain of the Political Leaders possessed a higher degree of responsibility than others, were vested with special prerogatives, and constituted a distinctive and elite group within the Party hierarchy. Those were the so-called "Hoheitstraeger" (Bearers of Sovereignty) who represented the Party within their areas of jurisdiction which are sections of Germany, the so-called Hoheitsgebiet. I now quote from Page 9 of the English translation of Document 1893-PS:-

> "Among the political leaders, the Hoheitstraeger assume a special position. Contrary to the other Political Leaders who have departmental missions, the Hoheitstraeger themselves are in charge of a geographical sector known as the Hoheitsgebiet (Sectors of Sovereignty).
> "Hoheitstraeger" are:
>   The "Fuehrer"
>   The "Gauleiter"
>   The "Kreisleiter"
>   The "Ortsgruppenleiter"
>   The "Zellenleiter"
>   The "Blockleiter"
> "Hoheitsgebiete" are:
>   The "Reich"
>   The "Gau"
>   The "Kreis"
>   The "Ortsgruppe"

The "Zelle"
The "Block"

Within their sector of sovereignty the Hoheitstraeger have sovereign political rights. They represent the Party within their sector. The Hoheitstraeger supervise all Party officers within their jurisdiction and are responsible for the maintenance of discipline. The directors of offices, etc., and of the affiliated organisations are responsible to their respective Hoheitstraeger as regards their special missions. The Hoheitstraeger are superior to all political leaders, managers, etc., within their sector.

The Hoheitstraeger of the Party are not to be administrative officials but are to move in a continuous vital contact with the Political Leaders of the population within their sector. The Hoheitstraeger are responsible for the proper and good supervision of all members of the nation within their sector.

The Party intends to achieve a state of affairs in which the individual German will find his way to the Party."

The distinctive character of the Politische Leiter constituting the Hoheitstraeger and their existence and operation as an identifiable group are indicated by the publication of a magazine entitled 'Der Hoheitstraeger' whose distribution was limited by regulation of the Reich Organisation Leader to the Hoheitstraeger and certain other designated Politische Leiter. I now refer to Document 2660- PS, which I offer in evidence as Exhibit USA 235, and I quote from the inside cover of this magazine which reads as follows:-

"'Der Hoheitstraeger, the contents of which is to be handled confidentially, serves only for the orientation of the competent leaders. It may not be loaned out to other persons."

Then follows a list of the Hoheitstraeger and other Political Leaders authorised to receive the magazine.

The magazine states, in addition, that the following are entitled to receive it - I would like to emphasise who these were,

"Commandants, Unit Commanders, and Candidates of Order Castles; The Reich Speakers, Shock Troop Speakers and Gau Speakers of the N.S.D.A.P.; the Lieutenant Generals and Major Generals of S.A., S.S., N.S.F.K. - which is the Flying Corps - and N.S.K.K. - the Motor Corps - Lieutenant Generals and Major Generals of the H.J. - that is the Hitler Jugend."

The fact that this magazine existed, that it derived its name from the commanding officers of the Leadership Corps, that it was distributed to the elite of the Leadership Corps, in other words, that a House Bulletin was circulated down the command channels of the Leadership Corps is probative of the fact that the Leadership Corps of the Nazi Party was a group or an organisation within the meaning of Article 9 of the Charter.

An examination of the contents of the magazine, 'Der Hoheitstraeger,' reveals a continuing concern by the Leadership Corps of the Nazi Party in measures and doctrines which were employed throughout the course of the conspiracy charged in the Indictment. I shall not trouble the Tribunal nor encumber the record by offering in evidence exhaustive enumeration of these matters; but it may serve to clarify the plans and policies of the inner elite of the Leadership Corps by indicating that a random sampling of articles published and policies advocated in the various issues of the magazine from February, 1937, to October, 1938, included the following: slanderous anti-Semitic articles, attacks on Catholicism and the Christian religion and clergy; the need for motorised armament; the urgent need for expanded Lebensraum and colonies; persistent attacks on the League of Nations; the use of the Block and Cell in achieving favourable Party votes; the intimate association between the Wehrmacht and the Political Leadership; the racial doctrines of Fascism, the cult of leadership; the role of the Gaue, Ortsgruppen, and Zellen in the expansion of Germany; and related matters all of which constituted elements and doctrinal techniques in the carrying out of the conspiracy charged in the Indictment.

The Political Leaders were organised according to the Leadership Principle. I quote from the fourth paragraph of Page 2 of Document 1893-PS, at the bottom of the page and top of Page 3:-

> "The basis of the Party organisation is the Fuehrer thought. The public is unable to rule itself either directly or indirectly. All Political Leaders stand as appointed by the Fuehrer and are responsible to him. They possess full authority toward the lower echelons. Only a man who has absorbed through the school of subordinate functions within the Party has a claim to the higher Fuehrer offices. We can only use Fuehrer who have risen from the ranks. Any Political Leader who does not conform to these principles is to be dismissed or to be sent back to the lower offices, as Blockleiter or Zellenleiter, for further training. The Political Leader is not an office worker but the Political Deputy of the Fuehrer. Within the Political Leadership of the State we are building the leadership of the Party. The type of the Political Leader is not characterised by the office which he represents. There is no such thing as a Political Leader of the N.S.B.O., etc., but there is only the Political Leader of the N.S.D.A.P."

Each Political Leader was sworn in yearly. According to the Party Manual the wording of the oath was as follows; and I quote from the second paragraph on Page 3, Document 1893-PS:- -

> "I pledge eternal allegiance to Adolf Hitler; I pledge unconditional obedience to him and the Fuehrers appointed by him."

The Organisation Book of the N.S.D.A.P. also provides, and I quote from Page 3, Paragraph 4, of the same document:-

> "The Political Leader is inseparably tied to the ideology and the organisation of the N.S.D.A.P. His oath only ends with his death or with his expulsion from the National Socialist Community."

Appointment of Political Leaders.

With respect to the appointment of the Political Leaders constituting the Leadership Corps of the Party, I quote from Page 4 of the Organisation Book, which is Document 1893-PS:-

> "The Fuehrer appoints the following Political Leaders:-
>
> (a) All Reichsleiter and all Political Leaders within the Reichsleitung (Reich Party Directorate) including women's leaders.
>
> (b) All Gauleiter, including the Political Leaders holding offices in the Gauleitung (Gau Party Directorate) including Gau women's leaders.
>
> (c) All Kreisleiter.
>
> The Gauleiter appoints:
>
> (a) The Political Leaders and women's leaders within the Gau Party Directorate.
>
> (b) The Political Leaders and the directors of women's leagues in the Kreis Party Directorate.
>
> (c) All Ortsgruppenleiter.

The Kreisleiter appoints the Political Leaders and the Directors of the Women's Leagues of the Ortsgruppen, including the Block and Cell Leaders...."

The power of Hoheitstraeger to call upon other Party formations.

The Hoheitstraeger among the Leadership Corps were entitled to call upon and utilise the various Party formations as necessary for the execution of the Nazi Party policies.

The Party Manual provides with respect to the power and authority of the Hoheitstraeger to requisition the services of the S.A.; and I quote from Page 11 of this same Document 1893-PS:-

"The Hoheitstraeger is responsible for the entire political appearance of the Movement within this zone. The S.A. leader of that zone is tied to the directives of the Hoheitstraeger in that respect. The Hoheitstraeger is the ranking representative of the Party to include all organisations within his zone. He may requisition the S.A. located within his zone from the respective S.A. leaders if they are needed for the execution of a political mission. The Hoheitstraeger will then assign the mission to the S.A.

Should the Hoheitstraeger need more S.A. for the execution of a political mission than is locally available, he then applies to the next higher office of sovereignty which, in turn, requests the S.A. from the S.A. office in his sector."

According to the Party manual, the Hoheitstraeger had the same authority to call upon the services of the S.S. and N.S.K.K. as they possessed with respect to the S.A.

With respect to the authority of the Hoheitstraeger to call upon the services of the Hitler Jugend, the Party Manual states - and I quote from Page 11, the last paragraph of that translation:-

"The Political Leader has the right to requisition the H.J. - that is the Hitler Jugend - in the same manner as the S.A. for the execution of a political action.

In appointing leaders of the H.J. and the D.J., the office of the H.J. must procure the approval of the Hoheitstraeger of his zone. This means that the Hoheitstraeger can prevent the appointment of leaders unsuited for the leadership of youth. If his approval has not been procured an appointment may be cancelled if he so requests."

An example of the use of the Party formations at the call of the Leadership Corps of the Party is provided by the action taken by the Reichsleiter for Party Organisation of the National Socialist Party, Dr. Robert Ley, leading to the deliberate dissolution of the Free Trade Unions on 2nd May, 1933. I quote from Document 392-PS, Exhibit USA 326, which is a copy of the directive issued by the defendant Ley on 21st April, 1933, reproduced on Pages 51-52 of the 'Social Life in New Germany' by Professor Mueller. In this directive the late defendant Ley directed the employment of the S.A. and the S.S. in the occupation of trade union properties and for taking trade union leaders into protective custody. I now quote from Paragraph 6 of Page 1 of Document 392-PS. It is the third or fourth paragraph from the bottom of the page:-

"S.A. as well as S.S. are to be employed for the occupation of trade union properties and for the taking of the parties concerned into protective custody.

The Gauleiter is to proceed with his measures on a basis of the closest understanding with the competent Regional Factory Cell Director."

I also quote from the second paragraph of Page 2 of that same document:-

"The following are to be taken into protective custody: All Trade Union Chairmen, the District Secretaries and the Branch Directors of the 'Bank for Workers, Employees and Officials, Inc.'"

I now offer in evidence Document 2474-PS, Exhibit USA 327, which is a copy of a decree issued by the defendant Hess as Deputy of the Fuehrer, dated 25th October, 1934, which under the authority of the Hoheitstraeger with respect to Party formations. I quote from the numbered Paragraphs 1, 5 and 6 of Page 1 of Document 2474-PS which reads as follows (Page 1 of the English translation):-

"The Political leadership within the Party and its political representation towards all offices, State or others, which are outside of the Party, lie solely and exclusively with the Hoheitstraeger (Bearers of Sovereignty) that is to say with me, the Gauleiter, Kreisleiter, and Ortsgruppenleiter. The departmental workers of the Party organisations, Reichsleiter, office directors, etc., as well as the leaders of the S.A., S.S., H.J., and the subordinate affiliations, may not enter into binding agreements of a political nature with State and other offices except when so authorised by their Hoheitstraeger.

In places where the territories of the units of the S.A., S.S., H.J. and the subordinate affiliations do not coincide with the zones of the Hoheitstraeger, the Hoheitstraeger will give his political directives to the ranking leader of each unit within his zone of sovereignty."

It was the official policy of the Leadership Corps to establish close and co-operative relations with the Gestapo. The Tribunal will recall that the head of the German Police and S.S., Himmler, was a Reichsleiter on the top level of the Leadership Corps. Without offering in evidence a decree issued by the defendant Bormann as Chief of Staff, Deputy of the Fuehrer, dated 26th June, 1935, I ask the Court to take judicial knowledge; and I quote:-

"In order to effect a closer contact between the offices of the Party and its organisations with the Directors of the Secret State Police (Gestapo), the Deputy of the Fuehrer requests that the Directors of the Gestapo be invited to attend all the larger official rallies of the Party and its organisations."

That is from the 1937 edition, Page 143, dated the 26th June, 1937, "The Decrees of the Deputy of the Fuehrer."

With reference to the meetings and conferences among the Hoheitstraeger of the Leadership Corps, it is the contention of the prosecution that the members of the Leadership Corps constituted a distinctive and identifiable group or organisation. It is strongly supported by the fact that the various Hoheitstraeger were under an absolute obligation to meet and confer periodically, not only with the staff officers on their own staffs, but with the political leaders and staff officers immediately subordinate to them. For example, the Gauleiter was bound to confer with his staff officers (such as his deputy and so forth, which included the school leader, propaganda leader, Press leader, his Gau Party Judge, etc.) every 8 to 14 days. Furthermore, the Gauleiter was obligated to meet with the various Gauleiter subordinate to him once every 3 months for a three-day convention, for the purpose of discussing and clarifying Nazi policies and directives, for hearing basic lectures on Party policy, and for the mutual exchange of information pertinent to the Party's current programme. The Gauleiter was also obliged to meet at least once a month with the leaders of the Party formations and affiliated organisations within his Gau area, such as the leaders of the S.A., and S.S., Hitler Jugend and others. In support of these statements, I quote from Page 8 of Document 1893-PS. I don't think it is necessary to read all of that.

"Leader conferences in the district:

A. District Leaders.", Page 8.

If your Honour pleases, with your permission I will omit the reading of that, because it was really summarised in my previous statement. I will quote

Subparagraph (d):-

"(d) The bearer of sovereignty will meet at least once a month with the leaders of the S.A., S.S., N.S.K.K., H.J., as well as the R.A.D. and the N.S.F.K. who are within the zone, for the purpose of mutual orientation."

The Organisation Book of the Party imposes a similar requirement of regular and periodical conferences and meetings upon all the other Hoheitstraeger, including the Kreisleiter, Ortsgruppenleiter, Zellenleiter and Blockleiter.

The clear consequence of such regular and compulsory conferences and meetings by all the Hoheitstraeger, both with their own staff officers and with the political leaders and staff officers subordinate to them, was that basic Nazi policies and directives issued by Hitler and the leader of the Party Chancellery, the defendant Bormann, directly through the chain of command of the Hoheitstraeger, and functional policies issued by the various Reichsleiter and Reich officeholders down functional and technical channels, were certain to be notified to, received and understood by, the bulk of the membership of the Leadership Corps.

If I may digress from my text and call attention to this chart, You will see the dotted lines connecting down from the Party level, Gau level, to similar offices in the lower level.

I next come to the statistics relating to the Leadership Corps of the Nazi Party and the evidence relating to the size of the Leadership Corps of the Nazi Party. As previously shown, the Leadership Corps comprised some of the officials of the Nazi Party including, in addition to Hitler and the members of the Reichsleitung, such as the Reichsleiter and the Reichs office holders, a hierarchy of Hoheitstraeger, which I have described, as well as the staff officers attached to the Hoheitstraeger. I now offer in evidence Document 2958-PS, Exhibit USA 325; and this is issue No. 8, 1939, of the official Leadership Corps organ 'Der Hoheitstraeger' similar to the one I exhibited a moment ago, and is for the year 1939. This shows that there were:-

40 Gaue and 1 Foreign Gau, each led by a Gauleiter;
that is 41;
808 Kreisleiter;
28,376 Ortsgruppenleiter;
89,378 Zellenleiter; and
463,048 Blockleiter.

However, as shown by the evidence previously introduced, the Leadership Corps of the Nazi Party was composed not only of the Hoheitstraeger, but also of the staff officers or officeholders attached to the Hoheitstraeger. The Gauleiter, for example, was assisted by a deputy Gauleiter, several Gau inspectors, and a staff which was divided into main offices (Hauptaemter) and offices (Aemter) including such departments as the Gau Staff Office, Treasury, Education Office, Propaganda Office, Press Office, University Teachers, Communal Policy, and so forth. As previously shown, the staff office structure of the Gau was substantially represented in the lower levels of the Leadership Corps organisation such as the Kreise, the Ortsgruppen, and so on. The Kreise and the smaller territorial areas of the Party were also organised into staff offices dealing with the various activities of the Leadership Corps. But, of course, the importance and the number of such staff offices diminished as the unit dropped in the hierarchy; so that, while the Kreisleiter staff contained all or most of the departments mentioned for the Gau, the Ortsgruppe had fewer departments and the lower ones fewer still. Firm figures have not been found as to the total number of staff officers, as distinguished from the Hoheitstraeger or political commanders themselves included within the Leadership Corps.

With respect to the scope and composition of the Leadership Corps of the Nazi Party, the prosecution adopts the view and respectfully submits to this Tribunal that, in defining the limits of the Leadership Corps, staff officers should only be included down to and including the Kreis. Upon this basis, the Leadership Corps of the Nazi Party constituted the Fuehrer, the members of the Reichsleitung, the five levels of the Hoheitstraeger, and the staff officers attached to the 40 odd Gauleiter and the 800 or 900 Kreisleiter. Adopting this definition of the Leadership Corps, it will be seen that the total figure for the membership of that organisation, based upon the statistics cited from the basic handbook for Germany, amounts to around 600,000. And by excepting the staff officers of the lower levels, as is provided in the Indictment and as just defined, and without prejudice to any later individual action against those excepted, we think the figure of around 600,000 is approximately correct.

It is true that this figure is based upon an admittedly limited view of the size of the membership of the Leadership Corps of the Nazi Party, for the evidence has shown that the Leadership Corps, in effect, embraced staff officers attached to the subordinate Hoheitstraeger and the inclusion of such staff officers in the estimation of the size of the Leadership Corps, if we had so recommended, would have been considerably enlarged so that he final figure, if we had included staff officers to the Blockleiter would have been 2,000,000 in round numbers.

THE TRIBUNAL (Mr. BIDDLE): What reason did you have for excluding them?

COLONEL STOREY: For this reason, your Honour. A person on the last level of Blockleiter might have called on an individual laborer who might have been on his staff, but he certainly would not have the discretion that a staff leader had, for example, or perhaps the Gauleiter, as a propaganda man who disseminated information down as well as helping to participate in plans and policies of the upper organisation.

The subordinate staff officers thus excluded were responsible functionally to the higher staff officers with respect to their particular specialty, such as propaganda, Party organisation, and so on, and to their respective Hoheitstraeger with respect to discipline and policy control and, as I mentioned, such higher staff officers also participated in planning and policy and passed those policies down through technical levels or technical channels as opposed to command channels.

"The Leadership Corps of the Nazi Party joined and participated in the Common Plan Or Conspiracy" is the next title.

The programme of the Nazi Party, proclaimed by Hitler on 24th February, 1920, contained the chief elements of the Nazi plan for domination and conquest. I now quote from Document 1708-PS, which is the Year Book for 1943, published by the Party, and edited by the late Robert Ley. This book contains the famous 25 points of the Party which I now offer in evidence as Exhibit USA 324. Departing from the text, I don't intend to quote these 25 Party objectives, but only refer to a few of them, and I quote from Page 1 of the English translation of Document 1708-PS.

> "We demand the unification of all Germans in Greater Germany on the basis of the right of self-determination of peoples."

Point 2 of that programme which I quote demanded unilateral abolition of the Peace Treaties of Versailles and St. Germain which I quote:-

> "We demand equality of rights for the German people in respect to the other nations; abrogation of the Peace Treaties of Versailles and St. Germain."

Point 3:-

> We demand land and territory (colonies) for the sustenance of our people and

colonisation by our surplus population."

Point 4:-

"Only a member of the race can be a citizen. A member of the race can only be one who is of German blood without consideration of confession. Consequently, no Jew can be a member of the race."

Point 6:-

"We demand that every public office, of any kind whatsoever, whether in the Reich, the county or municipality, be filled only by citizens. We fight the corrupting parliamentary regime, office-holding only according to party inclinations without consideration of character or abilities."

Point 22 (this is from Page 2 of the English translation of Document 1708-PS):-

"We demand the abolition of the mercenary troops and the formation of a National Army."

Back to Page 1 - another quotation:-

"The programme is the political foundation of the N.S.D.A.P. and accordingly the primary political law of the State.

All legal precepts are to be applied in the spirit of the Party Programme.

Since the taking over of control, the Fuehrer has succeeded in the realisation of the essential portions of the Party Programme from the fundamentals to the details.

The Party programme of the N.S.D.A.P. was proclaimed on the 24th February, 1920, by Adolf Hitler at the first large Party gathering in Munich and since that day has remained unaltered. The National Socialist philosophy is summarised in 25 points.

As previously mentioned, the Party programme was binding upon the Political Leaders and they were duty bound to support and carry out that Programme.

The Party Manual states, and I quote again from the middle of Page 1 of Document 1893-PS:-

"The Commandments of the National Socialists:-

The Fuehrer is always right.

The programme be your dogma; it demands your total devotion to the Movement. Right is what serves the Movement and thus Germany."

On Page 2 of the same document another brief quotation:

"The Leadership Corps is responsible for the complete penetration of the German nation with the National Socialist spirit."

The oath of the Political Leaders to Hitler has been previously mentioned. In this connection the Party Manual provides, and I quote from the second paragraph on Page 3 of the same document:-

"The Political Leader is inseparably tied to the ideology and the organisation of the N.S.D.A.P. His oath only ends with his death or with his expulsion from the National Socialist community."

While the "leadership principle" assured the binding nature of Hitler's statements, programme and policies upon the entire Party and the Leadership Corps thereof, the leadership principle also established the full responsibility of the individual Political Leader within the province and jurisdiction of his office or position.

The leadership principle applies not only to Hitler as the supreme leader but also to the Political Leaders under him, and thus permeated the entire Leadership Corps. I quote from the middle of Page 2 of Document 1893-PS:-

"The basis of the Party organisation is the Fuehrer idea. All Political Leaders stand as appointed by the Fuehrer and are responsible to him. They possess full authority toward the lower echelons."

The various Hoheitstraeger of the Leadership Corps were, in their respective areas, themselves Fuehrer. I quote from the third paragraph of Page 9 of this same document:-

"Within their sector of sovereignty, the Hoheitstraeger have sovereign political rights.

They are responsible for the entire political situation within their sector."

I again refer to and quote from Document 1814-PS, Exhibit USA 328, which is the Party Book. It is just a one sentence quotation, and it states:-

"The Party is an Order of 'Fuehrer'."

The subjugation of the entire membership of the Leadership Corps to the fiat of the leadership principle is clearly shown in the following passage from the Party Manual; it is this same document on Page 3:-

"A solid anchorage for all the organisations within the party structure is provided, and a firm connection with the sovereign leaders of the N.S.D.A.P. is created in accordance with the leadership principle."

Next is the subject:-

"The Nazi Party, directed by the Leadership Corps, dominated and controlled the German State and Government."

The Trial Brief dealing with the criminality of the Reich Cabinet sets forth the evidence as to the identity of various ministers comprising the Cabinet, and I shall not deal with that subject. The presence of the Reichsleiter and other prominent members of the Leadership Corps in the Cabinet facilitated the domination of the Cabinet by the Nazi Party and the Leadership Corps.

I omit the next paragraph down to the law of July, 1933.

A law of 14th July, 1933, outlawed and forbad the formation of any political parties other than the Nazi Party and made offenses against this a punishable crime, thereby establishing the one-party state and rendering the Leadership Corps immune from the opposition of organised political groups. I now quote from Document 1388-PS, that being the English translation of the Law against the Formation of New Political Parties stated in 1933 Reichsgesetzblatt, Part I, Page 479, and I quote the first two articles of this law, which read as follows:

"The National Socialist German Workers' Party constitutes the only political party in Germany. Whoever undertakes to maintain the organisational structure of another political party or to form a new political party will be punished with penal servitude up to three years or with imprisonment of from six months to three years, if the deed is not subject to a greater penalty according to other regulations."

I will omit the next paragraph.

I now quote from Document 1398-PS, which is the English translation of Law to Supplement the Law for the Restoration of the Professional Civil Service, dated 20th July, 1933, 1933 Reichsgesetzblatt, Part I, Page 518.

On 13th October, 1933: "A Law to Guarantee Public Peace" was enacted which provided, inter alia, that the death penalty or other severe punishment should be imposed upon any person who "undertakes to kill a member of the S.A. or the S.S., a trustee or agent of the N.S.D.A.P. out of political motives or on account of their official activity."

THE PRESIDENT: Which article are you reading?

COLONEL STOREY: Yes, Sir; 1398-PS. I am in error, Sir, it is 1394-PS just previous.

THE PRESIDENT: Which article are you reading?

COLONEL STOREY: I am afraid I have not the reference, but here is the quotation, I think it is on that one page. A Law to Guarantee Public Peace, and then it has to do . . . it is Article 2, I believe, Paragraph 2, Article 1.

I next refer to Document 1395-PS, which is the English translation of the Law on Security and the Unity of Party and State of 1st. December, 1933, and it was enacted "to secure the unity of Party and State." This law provided that the Nazi Party was the pillar of the German State and was linked to it indissolubly; it also made the Deputy of the Fuehrer (then Hess) and the Chief of Staff of the S.A. (then Roehm) members of the Reich Cabinet. I quote:-

> "After the victory of the National Socialist Revolution the National Socialistic German Workers' Party is the bearer of the concept of the German State and is inseparably the State. It will be a part of the public law. Its organisation will be determined by the Fuehrer.
>
> The Deputy of the Fuehrer and the Chief of Staff of the S.A. will become members of the Reich Government in order to insure close co-operation of the offices of the Party and S.A. with the public authorities."

This law was a basic measure in enthroning the Leadership Corps in a position of supreme political power in Germany, for it laid down that the Party, directed by the Leadership Corps, was the embodiment of the State and, in fact, was the State. Moreover this law made both the Fuehrer's Deputy and the Chief of Staff of the S.A., which was a Party formation subject to the call of the Hoheitstraeger, cabinet members, thus further solidifying the Leadership Corps' control of the cabinet. The dominant position of the Leadership Corps is further revealed by the provision that the Reichchancellor would issue the carrying out regulations of this law in his capacity as Fuehrer of the Nazi Party. The fact that Hitler, as Fuehrer of the Leadership Corps, could promulgate rules which would have statutory force and be published in the Reichsgesetzblatt, the proper compilation of State enactments, is but a further reflection of the reality of the Party's domination of the German State.

I now refer to Document 2775-PS, which is Exhibit USA 330, which is the English translation of certain extracts from Hitler's speeches to the 1934 and 1935 Party Congress at Nuremberg. I quote from the second extract in Document 2775-PS, which is a declaration by Hitler to the 1935 Party Congress and which reads - just one sentence:-

> "It is not the State which gives orders to us, it we who give orders to the State."

Upon the evidence, that categorical statement of the Fuehrer of the Leadership Corps, affirming the dominance of the Party over the State, cannot be refuted.

On the 30th June, 1934, Hitler, as head of the Nazi Party, directed the massacre of hundreds of S.A. men and other political opponents. Hitler sought to justify these mass murders by declaring to the Reichstag that "at that hour I was responsible for the fate of the German nation, and the supreme judge of the German people." The evidence relating to these events will be presented at a later stage in connection with the case against the S.A.

On the 3rd July, 1934, the Cabinet issued a decree describing the murders and the massacre of 30th June, 1934, in effect, as legitimate self-defence by the State. By this law the Reich Cabinet moved to make themselves accessories after the fact of these murders. The domination by the Party, however, makes the Cabinet's characterisation of these criminal acts by Hitler and his top Party leaders as State measures, consistent with political reality. I refer now to Document 2057-PS, which is the English translation of the Law Relating to the National Emergency Defence Measures of 3rd July, 1934, in the Reichsgesetzblatt of that year, Part I, Page 529, and I quote the single article of that law, which reads as follows: That is Document 2057. This still has reference to the blood purge:-

"The measures taken on 30th June and 1st and 2nd July, 1934, to counteract attempt at treason and high treason shall be considered as national emergency defence."

On 12th July, 1934, there was enacted a law defining the function of the Academy for German Law. I refer to Document 1391-PS, which is an English translation of the Statute of the Academy for German Law, 12th July, 1934, 1934 Reichsgesetzblatt, Part I, Pages 605 and 606.

"Closely connected with the agencies competent for legislation, it" - the Academy - "shall further the realisation of the National Socialist programme in the realm of the law."

On 30th January, 1933, Hitler, the Leader of the Nazi Party and Fuehrer of the Leadership Corps, was appointed Chancellor of the Reich. When President Von Hindenburg died in 1934, the Fuehrer amalgamated into his person the offices of Chancellor and Reich President. I refer to Document 2003- PS, which establishes that fact, and I do not quote. It is Reichsgesetzblatt 1934, Part I, Page 747.

By decree of the 20th December, 1934, Party uniforms and institutions were granted the same protection as those of the State. This law was entitled "Law Concerning Treacherous Acts Against the State and Party and for the Protection of Party Uniforms." This law imposed heavy penalties upon any person making false statements injuring the welfare or prestige of the Nazi Party or its agencies. It authorised the imprisonment of persons making or circulating malicious or baiting statements against leading personalities of the Nazi Party, and it provided punishment by forced labor for the unauthorised wearing of Party uniforms or symbols. I again refer to Document 1393, not quoting, which is the English translation and gives the authority.

Finally, by the law of 15th September, 1934, the swastika flag of the Party was made the official flag of the Reich. I refer to Document 2079, which is the English translation of the Reich Flag Law, found in Reichsgesetzblatt 1935, Part I, Page 1145. Just this one sentence - the quotation:-

"The Reich and National flag is the swastika flag."

The swastika was the flag and symbol of the Leadership Corps of the Nazi Party. By law it was made the flag of the State; a recognition that the Party and its corps of political leaders were the sovereign powers in Germany.

On 23rd April, 1936, a law was enacted granting amnesty for crimes which the offender had committed "in his eagerness to fight for the National Socialist ideals". I cite Document 1386, which is the English translation of the Law Concerning Amnesty, Reichsgesetzblatt 1936, Part I, Page 378.

In furtherance of the conspiracy to acquire totalitarian control over the German people, a law was enacted on 1st. December, 1936, which incorporated the entire German youth within the Hitler Youth, thereby achieving total mobilisation of the German youth. I cite Document 1392, containing that law, 1936, Reichsgesetzblatt, Part I, Page 993. The law further provided that the task of educating the German youth through the Hitler Youth was entrusted to the Reichsleiter of the German youth in the N.S.D.A.P. By this law a monopoly control over the entire German youth was placed in the hands of the top official, a Reichsleiter, of the Leadership Corps of the Nazi Party, the defendant Von Schirach.

On 4th February, 1938, the Fuehrer of the Leadership Corps of the Nazi Party, Hitler, issued a decree in which he took over direct command of the whole German Armed Forces. I cite Document 1915-PS, 1939 Reichsgesetzblatt, Part I, Page 111. Hitler says:-

"From now on, I take over directly the command of the whole Armed Forces."

By virtue of the earlier law of 1st August, 1934, Hitler combined the offices of the Reich President and the Chancellorship. In the final result, therefore, Hitler was Supreme Commander of the Armed Forces, the Head of the German State, and the Fuehrer of the Nazi Party.

With respect to this, the Party Manual states as follows, and I quote from Page 19 of Document 1893-PS:-

"The Fuehrer created the National Socialist German Workers' Party. He filled it with his spirit and his will, and with it he conquered the power of the State on 30th January, 1933. The Fuehrers will is supreme in the Party.

By authority of the law about the Chief of State of the German Reich, dated 1st August, 1934, the office of the Reich President has been combined with that of the Reich Chancellery. Consequently, the powers heretofore possessed by the Reich President were transferred to the Fuehrer, Adolf Hitler. Through this law, the conduct of the Party and State has been combined in one hand. By desire of the Fuehrer, a plebiscite was conducted on this law on 19th August, 1934. On this day, the German people chose Adolf Hitler to be their sole leader. He is responsible only to his conscience and to the German nation."

A decree of 16th January, 1942, provided that the Party should participate in legislation and official appointments and promotions. I cite as proof Document 2100-PS, which is the English translation of a directive concerning the application of the Fuehrer decree relating to the Chief of the Party Chancellery, 1942, Reichsgesetzblatt, Part I, Page 35. The decree further provided that such participation should be undertaken exclusively by the defendant Bormann, Chief of the Party Chancellery and Reichsleiter of the Leadership Corps. The decree provided that the Chief of the Party Chancellery was to take part in the preparation of all laws and decrees issued by Reich authorities, including those issued by the Ministerial Council for Defence of the Reich, and to give his assent to those of the Laender and of the Reich governments, the Laender being the German States. All communications between the State and Party authorities, unless within the Gau only, were to pass through Bormann's hands. This decree is of crucial importance in demonstrating the ultimate control and responsibility imputable to the Leadership Corps for governmental policy and actions taken in furtherance of the conspiracy.

On or about the 26th April, 1942, Hitler declared in a speech that, in his capacity as leader of the nation, Supreme Commander of the Armed Forces, Supreme Head of the Government, and as Fuehrer of the Party, his right must be recognised to compel with all means at his disposal, every German, whether soldier, judge, State official, or party official, to fulfill his desire. He demanded that the Reichstag officially recognise this asserted right, and on the 26th April, 1942, the Reichstag issued a decision in which full recognition was given to the rights of the Fuehrer which I have just asserted. I cite Document 1961-PS, which is the English translation of that decision, found in 1942 Reichsgesetzblatt, Part I, Page 247. I quote:-

"At the proposal of **THE PRESIDENT:** of the Reichstag, on its session of 26th April, 1942, the greater German Reichstag has unanimously approved of the rights which the Fuehrer has postulated in his speech, with the following

decision:-
> There can be no doubt that in the present war, in which the German people is faced with a struggle for its existence or annihilation, the Fuehrer must have all the rights postulated by him which serve to further or achieve victory. Therefore, without being bound by existing legal regulations, in his capacity as Leader of the Nation, Supreme Commander of the Armed Forces, Governmental Chief and Supreme Executive Chief, as Supreme Justice and as Leader of the Party, the Fuehrer must be in the position to force with all means at his disposal every German, if necessary, whether he be a common soldier or officer, low or high, official or judge, leading or subordinate official of the Party, worker or employer, to fulfill his duties. In case of violation of these duties, the Fuehrer is entitled, after conscientious examination, regardless of so- called well-deserved rights, to mete out due punishment and to remove the offender from his post, rank and position without introducing prescribed procedures.

At the order of the Fuehrer, this decision is hereby made public. Berlin, 26th April, 1942."

Hitler himself perhaps best summarised the political realities of his Germany which constituted the basis for the prosecution's submission that the Leadership Corps of the Nazi Party and its following effectively dominated the State. The core and crux of the matter was stated by Hitler in his speech to the Reichstag on 20th February, 1938, when he declared in effect that every institution in Germany was under the direction of the Leadership Corps of the Nazi Party.

I cite as the prosecution's final exhibit in support of the proposition that the Leadership Corps dominated the German State with resulting responsibility, Document 2715-PS, which is the book containing Hitler's speech to the Reichstag on the 20th February, 1938, as reported in 'Das Archiv', Volume 47, February 1938, Pages 1441 and 1442. I quote a brief excerpt from Document 2715-PS; and introduce it as Exhibit USA 331:-

> "National Socialism has given the German people that leadership which as Party not only mobilises the nation but also organizes it, so that on the basis of the natural principle of selection, the continuance of a stable political leadership is safeguarded for ever. National Socialism possesses Germany entirely and completely since the day when, five years ago, I left the house in Wilhelmsplatz as Reich Chancellor. There is no institution in this State which is not National Socialist. Above all, however, the National Socialist Party in these five years not only has made the nation National Socialist, but also has given itself that perfect organisational structure which guarantees its performance for all the future. The greatest guarantee of the National Socialist revolution lies in the complete domination of the Reich and all of its institutions and organisations, internally and externally, by the National Socialist Party. Its protection against the world abroad, however, lies in the new National Socialist Armed Forces. In this Reich, anybody who has a responsible position is a National Socialist. Every institution of this Reich is under the orders of the supreme political leadership. The Party leads the Reich politically, the Armed Forces defend it militarily. There is nobody in any responsible position in this state who doubts that I am the authorised leader of this Reich."

The supreme power which the Leadership Corps exercised over the German State and Government is pointed out by an article published in this same authoritative magazine 'Der Hoheitstraeger', in February, 1939. In this article, which was addressed to all Hoheitstraeger, the Leadership Corps is reminded that it has conquered the State, and it possesses absolute and total power in Germany. I cite Document 3230- PS, which is the English translation of an article entitled "Fight and Order", and I quote from this article, which trumpets forth in what we might term as accents of Caesarism, the battle call of the Leadership Corps in German life. I quote:-

> "Fight? Why do you always talk of fighting? You have conquered the State, and if something does not please you, then just make a law and regulate it differently. Why must you always talk of fighting? For you have every power. Over what grounds do you fight? Outer- political? You have the Wehrmacht - it will wage the fight if fight is required. Inner-political? You have the law and the police which can change everything with which you do not agree."

In view of the domination of the German State and Government by the -

THE PRESIDENT: Is this a good time to break off?

COLONEL STOREY: Yes, Sir.

(A recess was taken.)

COLONEL STOREY: In view of the domination of the German State and Government by the Nazi Party and the Leadership Corps thereof, as established by the foregoing and other evidence heretofore recited in the previous trial briefs, it is submitted that the Leadership Corps of the Nazi Party is responsible for the measures, including the legislative enactments, taken by the German State and Government in furtherance of the conspiracy formulated and carried out by the co-conspirators and the organisations charged with criminality in the present case.

I will now go to the overt acts and crimes of the Leadership Corps. The evidence now to be presented will establish that the membership of the Leadership Corps actively entered into a wide variety of acts and measures designed to advance the course of the conspiracy. The evidence will show that such participation by the Leadership Corps in the conspiracy embraces such measures as anti-Semitic activities; war crimes committed against members of the Allied Forces; participation in the forced-labor programme, measures to subvert and undermine the Christian religion and persecute the Christian clergy; the plundering and spoliation of cultural and other property in German occupied territories in Europe; participation in plans and measures leading to the initiation and prosecution of aggressive war; and, in general, the wide variety of measures embracing the Crimes against the Peace, War Crimes, and Crimes Against Humanity as defined and denounced by the Charter.

The first item of evidence we have to introduce is in connection with the participation of the Gauleiter and Kreisleiter, in what the Nazis describe as the "spontaneous uprising of the people" against the Jews throughout Germany on 9th and 10th November, 1938. We do not intend to introduce, by departing from the text, any evidence formerly introduced by Major Walsh on the persecution of the Jews, but only to show the connection of a few of the Party officials in connection with the assassination of an official of the German Embassy in Paris on the 7th of November.

The evidence relating to these pogroms has been thoroughly presented in connection with the prosecution's evidence in other phases of the case, particularly of the persecution of the Jews. I shall therefore limit myself to two documents and will request the Tribunal to recall that in the teletyped directive from S.S. Gruppenfuehrer Heydrich, issued on 10th November, 1938, to all police headquarters and S.D. districts, all chiefs of the State Police were ordered to contact the political leaders in the Gaue and the Kreise and to arrange with these high officials in the Leadership Corps the organisation of the so-called spontaneous demonstrations against the Jews.

The evidence previously presented shows that pursuant to this directive a large number of the Jewish shops and businesses were pillaged and wrecked, synagogues set on fire, individual Jews beaten up, and large numbers taken to concentration camps. This evidence forcibly illustrates the employment and participation of all the Kreisleiter and Gauleiter in illegal and inhuman measures designed to further the anti-Semitic programme which was an original and continuous objective of the Leadership Corps of the Nazi Party. I refer again to Document 3051-PS, Exhibit USA 240, and simply call your Honour's attention to the different political leaders who were named in that document, and I will not attempt to read nor refer to it again.

Departing again from the text, I want to offer at this time in evidence -

THE PRESIDENT: Colonel Storey, is it addressed to these various ranks in the Leadership Corps?

COLONEL STOREY: Your Honour, I notice on the first page it is addressed - I am not good in German - but to the State Police, to the S.D., and to some other S.D. officials.

THE PRESIDENT: What has that got to do with the Leadership Corps?

COLONEL STOREY: It has to do with directions to Party officials to take part in these demonstrations. In other words, through certain officials of the Leadership Corps this directive was dispatched and directed.

THE PRESIDENT: Are you sure the State Police and S.D. are any of the ranks in the Leadership Corps?

COLONEL STOREY: If your Honour will refer to this original chart, this big one, you will notice that the S.A., and S.S., and several of the organisations are listed on the left-hand part of that big chart. I think it is in the folder there on your Honour' desk. In other words, the close examination of that directive will show that they were to contact different political leaders in connection with the carrying into effect of this demonstration of the 9th and 10th November. That is the only purpose for which it is offered. It has been introduced in evidence, but the reason I mention it at this time-

THE PRESIDENT: I cannot see that it shows it. It seems to me to be a letter from the Chief of the Security Police to all headquarters and stations of the State Police.

COLONEL STOREY: I have not the English translation before me at this moment, your Honour.

THE PRESIDENT: Well, go on.

COLONEL STOREY: I now offer in evidence Document 3063-PS, Exhibit USA 332. This was a report from the Chief Party Judge Buch to the defendant Goering dated the 13th February, 1939, concerning actions taken by the Supreme Party Court for excesses in connection with the demonstrations of the 9th and 10th of November, 1938. I do not believe this, your Honour, is in the document book 3063.

THE PRESIDENT: Yes, it is.

COLONEL STOREY: I beg your pardon. I had forgotten whether it was in there or not. I quote a brief portion of it:-

> "When all the synagogues were burnt down in one night it must have been organised in some way and can only have been organised by the Party."

It is a long document, and that is the only portion I quote. I have not the reference to it.

THE TRIBUNAL (Mr. BIDDLE): What page?

COLONEL STOREY: I am sorry, Sir, I have not the reference book.

THE PRESIDENT: On Page 1. You have the document before you.

COLONEL STOREY:

"When all the synagogues burned down in one night it must have been organised in some way, and can only have been organised by the Party."

The first paragraph, Page 7.

Now I turn to illustrate the crimes against the Allied airmen. The members of the Leadership Corps of the Nazi Party participated in and shared the responsibility for the murder, beating, and ill-treatment of Allied airmen who landed in German or German- controlled territory. Many Allied airmen who bailed out of disabled planes over Germany were not treated as prisoners of war, but were beaten and murdered by German civilians with the active condonation, indeed at the instigation, of some of the Leadership Corps of the Nazi Party. Such a course of conduct by the Leadership Corps represented a flagrant and deliberate violation by the German Government of its obligations under the Geneva Convention to protect prisoners of war against acts of violence and ill-treatment.

As shown by Document 2473-PS - it is necessary to turn to that - which is a list of the Reichsleiter of the Nazi Party appearing in the National Socialist Yearbook of 1943, and by Document 2903, which is this large chart, Heinrich Himmler was the Reichsleiter of the Nazi Party and thus a top official in the Leadership Corps by virtue of his positions as Reichsfuehrer of the S.S. and Delegate for German Folkdom. I now offer in evidence an original order Signed by Himmler, Document R-110, as Exhibit USA 333.

It is dated 10th August, 1943, and I quote:

"It is not the task of the police to interfere in clashes between Germans and English and American terror fliers who have bailed out."

This order was transmitted in writing to all senior executive S.S. and police officers, and orally to their subordinate officers and to all Gauleiter. As shown in Document 2473-PS and by the chart, Joseph Goebbels -

THE PRESIDENT: I was only thinking that the police are not part of the Leadership Corps; are they?

COLONEL STOREY: But Himmler, if your Honour pleases, combined offices himself of the Reichsfuehrer of the S.S. and leader of the German police. He was an officer of the State; he was an officer of the Party; and he issued this to officials of the Leadership Corps.

THE TRIBUNAL (Mr. BIDDLE): And your point is, this order of Himmler's would be proof against the 600,000 members that you have spoken of?

COLONEL STOREY: Not against the members, but I said against the organisation as a criminal organisation, because from the top it disseminated orders of this type through the channels of the Leadership Corps.

THE PRESIDENT: But that is what I was putting to you, that it was not through the channels of the Leadership Corps, but through the channels of the police.

COLONEL STOREY: But the police, if your Honour pleases, were connected with the Leadership Corps, and Himmler stood at the top of both. It does not show on that chart but it shows on the other big chart, if your Honour pleases, with reference to Goebbels who was a very senior official in the Leadership Corps of the Nazi Party, by virtue of his position as propaganda leader of the Party.

In the issue of the 'Voelkischer Beobachter' of 29th May, 1944, there appeared an article written by Goebbels, the Reichsleiter for Party propaganda, in which he openly invited the German civilian population to punish Allied fliers shot down over Germany. I refer to Document 1676-PS, Exhibit USA 334, which is the issue of the 'Voelkischer Beobachter' containing this article inciting the people to the commission of war crimes. I now quote:-

> "It is possible only with the aid of arms to secure the lives of enemy pilots who were shot down during such attacks, for they would otherwise be killed by the sorely tried population. Who is right here? The murderers who, after their cowardly misdeeds, await a humane treatment on the part of their victims, or the victims who wish to defend themselves according to the principle: 'An eye for an eye, a tooth for a tooth'? This question is not hard to answer."

Reichsleiter Goebbels then proceeds to answer this question in the following language, and still quoting:-

> "It seems to us hardly possible and tolerable to use German police and soldiers against the German people when it treats murderers of children as they deserve."

On the 30th May, 1944, the defendant Bormann, Reichsleiter and Chief of the Party Chancellery, issued a circular letter on the subject which furnishes indisputable proof that British and American fliers, who were shot down, were lynched by the German population. I offer this circular letter of the defendant Bormann into evidence, Document 057- PS, it is up towards the top in the original book.

THE PRESIDENT: Have you got the original book?

COLONEL STOREY: Just a moment, your Honour.

After alleging that in recent weeks English and American fliers had repeatedly shot children, women, peasants, and vehicles on the highways, Bormann then states as follows in the second paragraph of the English translation. I quote:-

> "Several instances have occurred where members of the crews of such aircraft, who have bailed out or who have made forced landings, were lynched on the spot immediately after capture by the populace, which was incensed to the highest degree. No police measures or criminal proceedings were invoked against the German civilians who participated in these incidents."

The attention of the Tribunal is particularly invited to the fact that this letter of the defendant Bormann is distributed through the chain of command of the Nazi Party, expressly mentioning on the distribution list Reichsleiter, Gauleiter, Kreisleiter, and leaders of the incorporated and affiliated organisations of the Party. The defendant Bormann requested in the first paragraph of the second page, which is found in the English translation, that the local group leaders (Ortsgruppenleiter) be informed of the contents. of his circular letter orally - only by oral means.

The effect of Reichsleiter Bormann's circular letter may be seen in an order dated 25th February, 1945, which I now offer in evidence. It is Document L-154, Exhibit USA 335. It is an order from Albert Hoffmann, an important member of the Leadership Corps by virtue of his position as Gauleiter and National Defence Commissioner of the Gau Westfalen-South. It is addressed to all county councillors, mayors, police officials, and to county leaders and county chiefs of the Volkssturm.

> "Fighter bomber pilots who are shot down are in principle not to be protected against the fury of the people. I expect from all police officers that they will refuse to lend their protection to these gangster types. Authorities acting in contradiction to the popular sentiment will have to account to me. All police and gendarmerie officials are to be informed immediately of this, my

attitude."

The obligations-

THE PRESIDENT: Who is Hoffmann?

COLONEL STOREY: Albert Hoffmann was a member of the Leadership Corps by virtue of his position as Gauleiter and National Defence Commissar of the Gau Westfalen-South. In this connection, if your Honour pleases, I quote the provisions of the Geneva Convention, 27th July, 1929, Article 2, which provides - and I simply ask the Court to take judicial notice:-

> "Prisoners of war are in the power of the hostile power, but not of the individuals or corps who have captured them.
>
> They must at all times be humanely treated and protected, particularly against acts of violence, insults, and public curiosity.
>
> Measures of reprisal against them are prohibited."

THE PRESIDENT: Is that the 1907-

COLONEL STOREY: 1929, the Geneva Convention dated 27th July, 1929, and is Article 2, and it was also ratified by Germany and the United States. It is clear from the foregoing quoted provisions that the Geneva Prisoners of War convention imposes upon its signatories the strictest obligations to protect its prisoners of war from violence. The evidence just presented shows that the German State violated this provision. The evidence also proves that members of the Leadership Corps of the Nazi Party participated in the conspiracy to incite the German civilian population to take part in these atrocities.

Now I next turn to some illustrative crimes against foreign labor.

On 13th September, 1936, Reichsleiter of the Party Organisation, Dr. Robert Ley, addressed 20,000 people attending a session of the Party Congress. The official account of the Party rally states that the Fuehrer was received with "enthusiastic shouts of exaltation" when he strode through the hall with his deputy, his constant retinue, and several Reichsleiter and Gauleiter. I am referring to Document 2283-PS, and it is the 'Voelkischer Beobachter' of 14th September, 1936, Page 11, which we offer as Exhibit USA 337. In his speech Reichsleiter Robert Ley states that he had been mystified when the Fuehrer ordered him in "mid-April, 1933, to take over the trade unions, since I could not see any connection between my task as Organisational Leader of the Party and my new task." Ley continues by stating that very soon it became clear to him why his responsibilities as Reichsleiter of the Party Organisation and Leader of the German Labour Front made logical his selection by the Fuehrer as the man to direct the smashing and dissolution of the free trade unions; and I quote from that document:-

> "Very soon ... your decision, my Fuehrer, became clear to me and I recognised that the organisational measures of the Party could only come to full fruition when supplemented by the organisation of the people, that is to say by the mobilisation of the energies of the people and by their concentration and alignment. My tasks as Reichsleiter of the Party Organisation and as Leader of the German Labour Front were a completely homogeneous task; in other words, in everything I did, I acted as Reichsleiter of the Party Organisation. The German Labour Front was an institution of the Party and was led by it. The German Labour Front had to be organised regionally - according to the same principles as the Party. That is why trade union and employee associations had to be smashed unrelentingly, and the basis of construction was formed, as in the Party, by the cell and the local section."

On 17th October, 1944, Reichsleiter Rosenberg sent a letter to Reichsleiter Bormann which I introduce as Document 327- PS, Exhibit USA 338, in which he informed the latter that he had sent a telegram to the Gauleiter urging them not to interfere in the liquidation of certain listed companies and banks under his supervision. Rosenberg emphasizes to Bormann that any "delay of liquidation or independent confiscation of the property by the Gauleiter would impair or destroy an organised plan" for the liquidation of a vast amount of property.

On 7th November, 1943, the Chief of the General Staff of the Armed Forces delivered a lecture at Munich to the Reichsleiter and the Gauleiter. I now refer to Document L- 172, previously introduced in evidence as Exhibit USA 34. This is L-172. The Chief of Staff stated that his object was to give a review of the strategic position at the outset of the fifth year of war; and he stated that he realised that the Political Leaders in the Reich and Gau areas, in view of their burdensome tasks in supporting the German war effort, were in need of information he could give. He stated, in part, as follows:-

> "Reichsleiter Bormann has requested me to give you a review today of the strategic position in the beginning of the fifth year of war. No one - Fuehrer has ordered - know more or be told more than he needs for his immediate task, but I have no doubt at all in my mind, gentlemen, that you need a great deal in order to be able to cope with your tasks. It is in your Gau, after all . . . that all the enemy propaganda, and the malicious rumours concentrate that try to find themselves a place among our people... Against this wave of enemy propaganda and cowardice you need to know the true situation, and for this reason, I believe that I am justified in giving you a perfectly open and uncovered account of the state of affairs..."

Reichsleiter Bormann distributed to all Reichsleiter, Gauleiter, and leaders of Party affiliated organisations an undated letter of transmittal, which is Document 656-PS, Exhibit USA 339, on the National Socialist Party stationery, signed by Bormann, an order of the Supreme Command of the Wehrmacht, relating to self-defence by German guard personnel and German contractors and workers against prisoners of war. The order of the Wehrmacht referred to, states that the question of treatment of prisoners of war is continually being discussed by the Wehrmacht and Party bureaus. The order states that, should prisoners of war refuse to obey orders to work, the guard has "in the case of the most pressing need and danger, the right to force obedience with the weapon if he has no other means. He can use the weapon as much as is necessary to attain his goal..."

On 18th April, 1944 Reich Commissar Lohse, Reich Minister for the Occupied Eastern Territories, in a letter to Reich Youth Leader Axmann - I now offer in evidence Document 347- PS, Exhibit USA 340 - proposed that the Hitler Youth participate in and supervise the military education of the Estonian and Latvian Youth. Lohse states in the above letter that "in the military education camps, the young Latvians are trained under Latvian leaders in the Latvian language not because this is our ideal, but because absolute military necessity demands this." Lohse further stated in the above letter, and I quote:

> ". . . in contrast to the Germanic peoples of the West, military education is no longer to be carried out through voluntary enlistments but through legal conscription. The camps in Estonia and Latvia ... will have to be under German Leadership and, as military education camps of the Hitler Youth, they must be a symbol of our educational mission beyond Germany s borders... I consider the execution of the military education of the Estonian

and Latvian youth not only a military necessity but also a war mission of the Hitler Youth especially. I would be thankful to you, Party Member Axmann, if the Hitler Youth would put itself at our disposal with the same readiness with which they have so far supported our work in the Baltic area."

An order of the Reich Minister of the Interior, Frick, dated 22nd October, 1938, is Document 1438-PS, of which I ask the Court to take judicial notice, and I quote:

"The Reichsfuehrer S.S. and the Chief of the German Police ... can take the administrative measures necessary for the maintenance of security and order even beyond the legal limits otherwise set on such measures."

The above order related to the administration of the Sudeten German territory.

In a letter dated 23rd June, 1943, our Document 407-PS already in evidence as Exhibit USA 209, Gauleiter and Plenipotentiary for the Direction of Labour, Fritz Sauckel, wrote to Hitler advising him of the success of the forced labour programme as of that date and stating that, and I quote:

"You can be assured that the District (Gau) of Thueringen and I will serve you and our dear people with the employment of all strength."

I now offer in evidence Document 630-PS, Exhibit USA 342. If your Honour please, I call attention that this is on the personal stationery of Adolf Hitler, dated 1st September, 1939. It is addressed to Reichsleiter Bouhler and Doctor of Medicine Brandt, and it is signed personally by Adolf Hitler. I want to quote all of that document; it is short:

"Reichsleiter Bouhler and Dr. Brandt, M.D., are charged with the responsibility of enlarging the authority of certain physicians to be designated by name, in such a manner that persons who, according to human judgment, are incurable can, upon a most careful diagnosis of their condition of sickness, be accorded a mercy death.

(signed) A. Hitler."

A handwritten note on the face of the document states:

"Given to me by Bouhler on 27th August, 1940.

Signed, Dr. Guertner."

In a memorandum recording an agreement between himself and Himmler, the Minister of Justice Thierack stated that on the suggestion of Reichsleiter Bormann, an agreement had been reached between Himmler and himself with respect to "special treatment at the hands of the police in cases where judicial sentences were not severe enough."

I will offer Document 654-PS, Exhibit USA 218, which was previously introduced, and I want to quote one portion:

"The Reich Minister of Justice will decide whether and when special treatment at the hands of the police is to be applied. The Reich Fuehrer S.S. will send the reports, which he sent hitherto to Reichsleiter Bormann, to the Reich Minister of Justice.

"If the views of the Reich Fuehrer S.S. and the Reich Minister of Justice disagreed, the opinion of Reichsleiter Bormann will be brought to bear upon the case, and he will possibly inform the Fuehrer."

In the above note it is further stated:

"The delivery of anti-social elements from execution of their sentence to the Reichfuehrer of S.S. to be worked to death. Persons under preventative arrest, Jews, Gypsies, Russians and Ukrainians, Poles with more than three-year sentences, Czechs and Germans with more than eight-year sentences, according to the decision of the Reich Minister of Justice. First of all the worst anti- social elements amongst those just mentioned are to be handed over. I shall inform the Fuehrer of this through Reichsleiter Bormann."

With respect to the "administration of justice by the people," it continues:

"This is to be carried out step by step as soon as possible. I shall rouse the Party particularly to co- operate in this scheme by an article in the 'Hoheitstraeger.'"

And your Honours have already seen copies of that publication. I now skip Paragraphs 16 and 17.

A letter from R.S.H.A. (which is the Reich Security Main Office) to police chiefs, dated 5th November, 1942, which is Document L-316, Exhibit USA 346 - this was addressed to all police chiefs, dated 5th November, 1942 - recites an agreement between the Reichsfuehrer S.S. and the Reich Minister of Justice, approved by Hitler - I call the attention of your Honours to the red border around this original and its having the Party seal on it - providing that the ordinary criminal procedure was no longer to be applied to Poles and members of the Eastern populations. The agreement provided that such people, including Jews and Gypsies, should henceforth be turned over to the police. The principles applicable to a determination of the punishment of German offenders, including appraisal of the motives of the offender, were not to be applied to foreign offenders. I quote from Page 2 of the document:

"The offense committed by a person of foreign extraction is not to be regarded from the view of legal retribution by way of justice, but from the point of view of preventing dangers through police action.

From this it follows that the criminal procedure against persons of foreign extraction must be transferred from Justice to the Police.

The preceding statements serve for personal information. There are no objections if the Gauleiter are informed in the usual way should the need arise."

I now omit Paragraphs 19 and 20 of the text and refer to Document 1058-PS, previously introduced in evidence as Exhibit USA 147.

In a speech to a gathering of persons intimately concerned with the Eastern problem, on 20th June, 1941, Reichsleiter Rosenberg stated that the Southern Russian territories and the Northern Caucasus would have to provide food for the German people. I quote Rosenberg's words:

"We see absolutely no obligation on our part to feed also the Russian people with the products of that surplus territory. We know that this is a harsh necessity, bare of any feelings."

THE PRESIDENT: We have already had that read to us twice

COLONEL STOREY: I am sorry, Sir. I did not hear it. Strike it from the record.

I now refer to Document R-114. I believe it is the last one in the book, Exhibit USA 314.

Gauleiter Wagner, of the German-occupied areas of Alsace, prepared plans and took measures leading to the expulsion and deportation of certain groups within the Alsatian civilian population. His plans called for the forcible expulsion of certain categories of so-called undesirable persons as a means of punishment and compulsory Germanisation. The Gauleiter supervised deportation measures in Alsace from July to December, 1940, in the course of which 105,000 persons were either expelled or prevented from returning. A memorandum, dated 4th August, 1942, of a meeting of high S.S. and police officials convened to receive the reports and plans of the Gauleiter relating to the Alsatian evacuations, states that the persons deported were mainly "Jews, Gypsies, and other foreign racial elements, criminals, asocial and incurably insane persons, as well as Frenchmen and Francophiles." The memorandum further states the Gauleiter said that the Fuehrer had given him permission "to cleanse Alsace of all foreign, sick, or unreliable elements"; and that the Gauleiter emphasised the political necessity of further deportations. The memorandum further records that the S.S. and police officials present at the conference approve the Gauleiter's proposals for further evacuation.

I now skip over to the next paragraph 24.

A memorandum by Reichsleiter Bormann of a conference called by Hitler at his headquarters, 16th July, 1941, which is Document L-221, Exhibit USA 317.... I am sorry, I believe that one was quoted this morning. The only purpose in referring to it is in connection with the Reichsleiter. I believe Captain Harris quoted from that document this morning, and I will not read the quotation.

I call attention to the fact, however, that this conference was attended by Reichsleiter Rosenberg, Reich Minister Lammers, Field Marshal Keitel, the Reich Marshal, and Bormann, and lasted about 20 hours. The memorandum states that discussion occurred with respect to the annexation by Germany of various parts of conquered Europe. The memorandum also states that a long discussion took place with respect to the qualifications of Gauleiter Lohse, who was proposed by Rosenberg at this conference as Governor of the Baltic states.

Discussion also occurred, according to the memorandum, with respect a the qualifications of other Gauleiter and commissioners for the administration of various areas of occupied Russia. Goering stated, according to the memorandum, that he intended to appoint Gauleiter Terboven for "exploitation of the Kola Peninsula; the Fuehrer agrees".

I believe the next portion has been quoted, too. I now pass to the participation of the Leadership Corps in the suppression of the Christian Church and persecution of the clergy, and cite some illustrative crimes.

The evidence relating to the systematic effort of the defendants and co-conspirators to eliminate the Christian churches in Germany has been previously introduced in Exhibit USA Book "H" by Major Wallis with respect to the Nazi efforts to eliminate the Christian Church. The evidence now to be presented is limited to proving and pointing out the responsibility of the Leadership Corps of the Nazi Party and the members thereof, for illegal activities against the Christian Church and clergy.

The defendant Bormann issued a secret decree to all Gauleiter entitled, "Relationship of National Socialism and Christianity". And that is Document D-75, toward the top, I believe, your Honour. It is Exhibit USA 348. In this decree Reichsleiter Bormann flatly declares that National Socialism and Christianity are incompatible and that the influence of the churches in Germany must be eliminated. I quote from pertinent portions of this decree beginning with the first paragraph thereof, top of page 3, which reads as follows:

"National Socialist and Christian concepts are irreconcilable....

Our National Socialist ideology is far loftier than the concepts of Christianity which, in their essential points, have been taken over from Jewry. For this reason, also, we do not need Christianity.... If, therefore, in the future our youth learn nothing more of this Christianity whose doctrines are far below ours, Christianity will disappear by itself.... It follows from the irreconcilability of National Socialist and Christian concepts that a strengthening of existing confessions, and every assistance for originating Christian confessions, is to be rejected by us. A differentiation between the various Christian confessions is not to be made here. For this reason, also, the thought of an erection of an Evangelical National Church by merger of the various Evangelical churches has been definitely given up, because the Evangelical Church is just as inimical to us as the Catholic Church. Any strengthening of the Evangelical Church would merely react against us....

For the first time in German history, the Fuehrer consciously and completely has the leadership of the people in his own hand. With the Party, its components, and attached units the Fuehrer has created for himself, and thereby the German Reich Leadership, an instrument which makes him independent of the Church. All influences which might impair or damage the leadership of the people, exercised by the Fuehrer with the help of the N.S.D.A.P., must be eliminated. More and more the people must be separated from the churches and their organs, the pastors. Of course, the churches must and will, seen from their viewpoint, defend themselves against this loss of power. But never again must an influence on leadership Of the people be yielded to the churches. This influence must be broken completely and finally.

Only the Reich Government and, by its direction, the Party, its components and attached units have a right to leadership of the people. Just as the deleterious influences of astrologers, seers, and other fakirs are eliminated and suppressed by the State, so must the possibility of Church influence also be totally removed. Not until this has happened does the State leadership have influence on the individual citizens. Not until then are people and Reich secure in their existence for all the future...."

I next offer in evidence Document 070-PS, towards the beginning, Exhibit USA 349, which is a copy of a letter issued from Bormann's office, dated 25th April, 1941, to the defendant Rosenberg in his capacity as the Fuehrer's representative for the supervision of the entire mental and ideological training and education of the N.S.D.A.P. In this letter Bormann's office states that the measures have been taken leading to the progressive cancellation of morning prayers and other religious services, and their substitution by Nazi mottoes and slogans. I quote from the first paragraph of Document 070-PS:

"We are inducing schools more and more to reduce and abolish morning religious services. Similarly the confessional and general prayers in several parts of the Reich have already been replaced by National Socialist mottoes. I would be grateful to know your opinion on a future National Socialist morning service instead of the present confessional morning services which are usually conducted once per week...."

In a letter from Reichsleiter Bormann to Reichsleiter Rosenberg dated 22nd February, 1940, Document 098-PS, Exhibit USA 350, which I offer in evidence, Bormann declares to Rosenberg that the Christian religion and National Socialism are incompatible. Bormann cites, as examples of hostile...

THE PRESIDENT: Would you take care to give us the number the documents?

COLONEL STOREY: I beg your pardon, Sir.

THE PRESIDENT: This is 098-PS.

COLONEL STOREY: Document 098-PS.

THE PRESIDENT: The one before you referred to was 070-PS.

COLONEL STOREY: Yes - 070-PS.

THE PRESIDENT: Before that, D-75.

COLONEL STOREY: That's correct. With your Honour's permission, rather than quote the whole document I will summarise it: divergence between Nazism and the churches, the attitude of the latter on the racial question; celibacy of the priests; monasteries and nunneries, etc. Bormann further declares that the churches could not be subjugated through compromise but only through a new philosophy of life as prophesied in Rosenberg's writings. Bormann proposes the creation of a National Socialist Catechism in order to give that part of the German youth which declines to practice confessional religion a moral foundation and to lay a moral basis for National Socialist doctrines, which are gradually to supplant the Christian religions. Bormann suggests that some of the Ten Commandments could be merged with the National Socialist Catechism and states that a few new Commandments should be added, such as: "Thou shalt be courageous; Thou shalt not be cowardly; Thou shalt believe in God's presence in the living nature, animals, and plants; Thou shalt keep thy blood pure;" etc. He concludes that he considers the problem so important that it should be discussed with the members of the Reich Directorate as soon as possible.

And now a quotation from the fifth paragraph on the first page of that translation:

"Christianity and National Socialism are phenomena which originated from entirely different basic causes. Both differ fundamentally so strongly that it will not be possible to construct a Christian teaching which would be completely compatible with the point of view of the National Socialist ideology; just as the communities of Christian faith would never be able to stand by the ideology of National Socialism in its entirety..."

Then I quote from the last paragraph on Page 5 of that document:

"The Fuehrer's deputy finds it necessary that all these questions should be thoroughly discussed in the near future in the presence of the Reich Leaders (Reichsleiter) who are especially affected by them..."

I next offer in evidence Document 107-PS.

THE PRESIDENT: Do you suggest that these Blockleiter were actually present at that discussion?

COLONEL STOREY: Your Honour, in connection with the policy directives, the security of the sect goes from the top to the bottom, and if that policy is adopted they may by directive send for the Blockleiter. He is to discuss it in connection with the Reichsleiter, who are the Party Directors, and I assume that, if the Party Directors establish it as a policy, then they were to issue appropriate directives to the other subordinate members. Mr. Lambert has suggested also that it would not be possible to discuss this matter with all the Leadership Corps and therefore they discussed it with the Party Directors.

THE TRIBUNAL (Mr. BIDDLE): Does that show that he discussed it with the Directors?

COLONEL STOREY: No, Sir, that does not follow, but it shows that it was a subject of discussion for the Board of Directors of the Nazi Party.

THE PRESIDENT: Yes, but the question is, who are the Directors?

COL. STOREY: Five or six of them sit here, a total of 16.

THE PRESIDENT: Yes, but I thought that you were asking us to declare the whole of the organisation down to the Blockleiter as criminal.

COLONEL STOREY: That is true, your Honour, but this is one piece of evidence, one instance of the criminality of the organisation, and we cannot prove at each stage that all of them knew about it. We are trying to select different offenses and different crimes that were committed within the Party.

Document 107-PS, which is Exhibit USA 351, and which we now offer in evidence, is a circular letter, dated 17th June, 1938, addressed, by the defendant Bormann as Reichsleiter and Deputy of the Fuehrer, to all Reichsleiter and Gauleiter. Bormann's letter encloses a copy of rules, prepared by Reichsleiter Hierl, setting forth certain restrictive regulations with respect to participation of the Reich Labour Service in religious celebrations. I quote pertinent portions of the directions issued by Reichsleiter Hierl, beginning, with the first paragraph, the list of directions in Document 107-PS, on Page 1 of the English translation:

"The Reich Labour Service is a training school in which the German youth should be educated to national unity in the spirit of National Socialism....

What religious beliefs person has is not a decisive factor, but it is decisive that he first of all feels himself a German.

Every religious practice is forbidden in the Reich Labour Service because it disturbs the comradelike harmony of all working men and women.

On this basis, every participation of the Reich Labour Service in religious arrangements and celebration is not possible."

The Tribunal will appreciate that the position of the defendant Bormann as Deputy of the Fuehrer of the Leadership Corps of the Nazi Party and Chief of the Nazi Party Chancellery, and the position of the defendant Rosenberg as the Fuehrer's representative for the whole spiritual and philosophical education of the Nazi Party, give to the views of these defendants on religion and religious policy the highest official backing. The anti-Christian utterances and policies of these two defendants reveal a community of mind and intention amongst the most powerful leaders of the Party which was amply confirmed, as the evidence will show, by the actual treatment of the churches since 1933 and throughout the course of the conspiracy. I now offer in evidence Document 2349-PS, Exhibit USA 352, which is an excerpt from the book "The Myth of the 20th Century," written by the defendant Rosenberg. I quote from that document:

"The idea of honour - national honour - is for us the beginning and the end of our entire thinking and doing. It does not admit of any equal-valued centre of force alongside it, no matter of what kind, neither Christian love, nor the Free-Masonic humanity, nor the Roman philosophy."

I now offer in evidence Document 848-PS, Exhibit USA 353, which is a Gestapo telegram, dated 24th July, 1938, dispatched from Berlin to Nuremberg, dealing with demonstrations and acts of violence against Bishop Sproll in Rottenburg. The Gestapo office in Berlin wired its Nuremberg office a teletype account received from its Stuttgart office of disorderly conduct and vandalism carried out by Nazi Party members against Bishop Sproll. I quote from the fourth paragraph of Page 1 of the English translation of Document 848-PS, which reads as follows:

"The Party, on 23rd July, 1938, from 2100 hours on carried out the third demonstration against Bishop Sproll. Participants, about 2,500-3,000, were brought from outside by bus, etc. The Rottenburg populace again did not participate in the demonstration. This town took a rather hostile attitude toward the demonstrations. The action got completely out of hand of the Party member responsible for it. The demonstrators stormed the palace, beat in the gates and doors. About 150 to 200 people forced their way into the palace, searched through the rooms, threw files out of the windows and rummaged through the beds in the rooms of the palace. One bed was ignited. The Bishop was with Archbishop Groeber of Freiburg and the ladies and gentlemen of his menage in the chapel at prayer. About 25 to 30 people pressed into this chapel and molested those present. Archbishop Groeber was taken for Bishop Sproll. He was grabbed by the robe and dragged back and forth."

The Gestapo official in Stuttgart added that Bishop Groeber desires "to turn to the Fuehrer and to Reich Minister of the Interior Dr. Frick, anew," and the Gestapo official added that he had found a report of the demonstration after "suppressing counter mass meetings."

On 23rd July, 1938, the Reich Minister for Church Affairs, Kerrl, sent a letter to the Minister of State and Chief of the Praesidium Chancellery, Berlin, stating that Bishop Sproll had angered the population by abstaining from the plebiscite of 10th April. I now offer in evidence Document 849-PS, Exhibit USA 354. In this letter Kerrl stated that the Gauleiter and Governor of Wuerttemberg had decided that, in the interest of preserving the State's authority, and in the interest of quiet and order, Bishop Sproll could no longer remain in office. I quote from the third paragraph of the first page of the Document 849-PS:

"The Reich Governor had explained to the Ecclesiastical Board that he would no longer regard Bishop Sproll as head of the Diocese of Rottenburg, on account of his refraining from the election in the office and that he desired Bishop Sproll to leave the Gau area because he could assume no guarantee for his personal safety; that in the case of the return of the Bishop of Rottenburg, he would see to it that all personal and official intercourse with him on the part of State offices, as well as the Party offices and the Armed Forces, would be denied."

Kerrl further states in the above letter that his deputy had moved the Foreign Office through the German Embassy at the Vatican to urge the Holy See to persuade Bishop Sproll to resign his Bishopric. Kerrl concludes by stating that should the effort to procure the Bishop's resignation prove unsuccessful, "the Bishop would have to be exiled from the land or there would have to be a complete boycott of the Bishop by the authorities."

On 14th July, 1939, the defendant Bormann in his capacity as Deputy of the Fuehrer issued a Party regulation which provided that Party members entering the clergy or undertaking the study of theology would have to leave the Party. I now offer in evidence Document 840-PS, Exhibit USA 355, and this is a copy of a regulation by Bormann, relating to the admission of the clergy and students of theology into the Party. I quote from the last paragraph of the English translation, which reads - I quote from the second page near the end of the document:

"I decree that in the future Party members who enter the clergy or who turn to the study of theology have to leave the Party."

In this directive Bormann also refers to an earlier decree, dated 9th February, 1939, in which he had ruled that the admission of members of the clergy into the Party was to be avoided. In this decree, also, Bormann refers with approval to a regulation of the Reich Treasurer of the Party, dated 10th May, 1939, providing that "clergymen as well as other fellow Germans who are also closely connected with the Church cannot be admitted into the Party."

I now offer in evidence Document 3268-PS, Exhibit USA 356, which contains excerpts from the Allocution of His Holiness Pope Pius XII, to the Sacred College, 2nd June, 1945. In this address His Holiness, after declaring that he had acquired an appreciation of the great qualities of the German people in the course of 12 years of residence in their midst, expressed the hope that Germany could "rise to new dignity and a new life once it has laid the satanic specter raised by National Socialism, and the guilty have expiated the crimes they have committed." After referring to repeated violations by the German Government of the Concordat concluded in 1933, His Holiness declared as follows, and I quote from the last paragraph of Page 1 of the English translation of Document 3268-PS:

"The struggle against the Church did, in fact, become ever more bitter, there was the dissolution of Catholic organisations; the gradual suppression of the flourishing Catholic schools, both public and private; the enforced weaning of youth from family and Church; the pressure brought to bear on the conscience of citizens, and especially of civil servants; the systematic defamation, by means of a clever, closely organised propaganda, of the Church, the clergy, the faithful, the Church's institutions, teachings and history; the closing, dissolution, confiscation of religious houses and other ecclesiastical institutions; the complete suppression of the Catholic Press and publishing houses...

In the meantime the Holy See itself multiplied its representations and protests to governing authorities in Germany, reminding them, in clear and energetic language, of their duty to respect and fulfill the obligations of the natural law itself that were confirmed by the Concordat. In these critical years, joining the alert vigilance of a pastor to the long suffering patience of a father, our great predecessor, Pius XI, fulfilled his mission as Supreme Pontiff with intrepid courage.

But when, after he had tried all means of persuasion in vain, he saw himself clearly faced with deliberate violations of a solemn pact, with a religious persecution masked or open but always rigorously organised, he proclaimed to the world on Passion Sunday, 1937, in his Encyclical, 'Mit brennender Sorge' that National Socialism really was: the arrogant apostasy from Jesus Christ, the denial of His doctrine and of His work of redemption, the cult of violence, the idolatry of race and blood, the overthrow of human liberty and dignity...

From the prisons, concentration camps, and fortresses are now pouring out, together with the political prisoners, also the crowds of those, whether clergy or laymen, whose only crime was their fidelity to Christ and to the faith of their fathers or the dauntless fulfillment of their duties as priests...

In the forefront, for the number and harshness of the treatment meted out to them, are the Polish priests. From 1940 to 1945, 2,800 Polish ecclesiastics were imprisoned in that camp; among them was the Auxiliary Bishop of Wloclawek, who died there of typhus. In April last there were left only 816, all the others being dead except for two or three transferred to another camp. In the summer of 1942, 480 German-speaking ministers of religion were known to be gathered there; of these, 45 were Protestants, all the others Catholic priests. In spite of the continuous inflow of new internees, especially from dioceses of Bavaria, Rhenania and Westphalia, their number, as a result of the high rate of mortality, at the beginning of this year did not surpass 350. Nor should we pass over in silence those belonging to occupied territories, Holland, Belgium, France (among whom the Bishop of Clermont), Luxembourg, Slovenia, Italy. Many of those priests and laymen endured indescribable sufferings for their faith and for their vocation. In one case the hatred of the impious against Christ reached the point of parodying on the person of an interned priest, with barbed wire, the scourging and the crowning with thorns of our Redeemer."

THE PRESIDENT: I think perhaps it would be time now to adjourn.

(The Tribunal adjourned until 1000 hours on 18th December, 1945)

Twenty-Second Day:
Tuesday, 18th December, 1945

COLONEL STOREY: If the Tribunal please, before adjourning yesterday afternoon, your Honour properly asked a question or two about Documents 3051 and 3063, to which I think I have an answer that will help the Tribunal. Your Honour will recall, with reference to Document 3051-PS... I believe it might be of assistance to turn to that document.

THE PRESIDENT: Yes.

COLONEL STOREY: Your Honour asked yesterday afternoon, since this had to do with the S.D. and the S.S., how the Party was involved. And I should like to quote paragraph Number I on Page 2 of the English translation, which answers this question, and I am quoting:

"The Chiefs of the State Police, or their deputies, must get in contact by telephone with the Political Leaders (Gauleitung oder Kreisleitung) who have jurisdiction over their districts and have to arrange a joint meeting with the appropriate inspector or commander of the Order Police to discuss the organisation of the demonstration. At these discussions the Political Leaders are to be informed that the German Police have received from the Reichsfuehrer S.S. and Chief of the German Police the following instructions, in accordance with which the Political Leaders should adjust their own measures."

That had to do with the preparation for the general anti-Jewish uprisings.

Now, with reference to Document 3063, which follows just one or two documents below...

THE PRESIDENT: What was the document?

COLONEL STOREY: Number 3063 was the next, just below that one, if your Honour pleases.

THE PRESIDENT: Very well.

COLONEL STOREY: That, if you recall, your Honour, was a report from the Supreme Party Court Justice Buch to the defendant Goering, concerning punishment for the uprisings that followed the 9th and 10th of November demonstration. I should like to quote the portion signed by the defendant Goering. It is, I believe, the second page of the English translation.

It is dated: "Berlin, 2nd February, 1939."

"Dear Party Member Buch:

I thank you for forwarding the report of your special senate about the proceedings which were taken in regard to the excesses on the occasion of the anti-Jewish operations of the 9th and 10th of November, 1938, of which I have taken cognisance.

Heil Hitler!

yours,

Goering."

And then, passing, your Honour, to page number I, immediately following, of the English translation, I think the next two paragraphs will answer your Honour's question. I quote:

"On the evening of 9th November, 1938, the Reich Propaganda Director Party Member Dr. Goebbels told the Party Leaders assembled at a social evening in the old town hall in Munich that in the districts (Gauen) of Kurhessen and Magdeburg-Anhalt it had come to hostile Jewish demonstrations, during which Jewish shops were demolished and synagogues were set on fire. The Fuehrer, at Goebbels' suggestion, had decided that such demonstrations were not to be prepared or organised by the Party; but so far as they originated spontaneously, they were not to be discouraged either. In other respects, Party Member Dr. Goebbels carried out the purport of what was prescribed in the teletype of the Reich Propaganda Administration of 10th November, 1938.

It was probably understood by all the Party leaders present."

THE PRESIDENT: What does "12:30 to 1 o'clock" mean there?

COLONEL STOREY: That is the time of the teletype message, I assume, your Honour.

THE PRESIDENT: Yes.

COLONEL STOREY: "It was probably understood by all the Party leaders present, on the basis of the oral instructions of the Reich Propaganda Director, that the Party should not appear outwardly as the originator of the demonstrations but in reality should organise and execute them. Instructions to this end were telephoned immediately" - thus a considerable time before transmission of the first teletype - "to the bureaux of their districts (Gauen) by a large part of the Party members present."

Now, your Honour properly asked, yesterday afternoon, how the "Blockleiter" would be affected. Your Honour will recall that, in the instructions to the "Blockleiter" defining his offices, it was stated that his instructions would be received orally and they would be transmitted orally, and writing was never to be used except in extreme cases. Therefore I say that these quoted portions clearly indicate that the Party was in fact used in connection with these famous anti-Jewish demonstrations of 9th and 10th November, 1938.

Now, reverting to the text where I left off yesterday afternoon:

The Leadership Corps of the Nazi Party participated in the confiscation of church and religious property.

I offer in evidence Document 072-PS, which is Exhibit USA 357, which is a letter, dated 19th April, 1941, from Reichsleiter Bormann to Reichsleiter Rosenberg. This letter exposes the participation of the "Gauleiter" in measures relating to the confiscation of religious property.

I now quote from the last paragraph of Page 1 of the English translation of Document 072-PS, which reads:

"The libraries and art treasures of the monasteries confiscated in the Reich were to remain for the time being in their monasteries in so far as the 'Gauleiter' had not determined otherwise."

On 21st February, 1940, the Chief of the Security Police and S.D. Heydrich, wrote a letter to Reichsfuehrer S.S. Himmler, proposing that certain listed churches and monasteries be confiscated for the accommodation of so-called "racial Germans".

The Tribunal, of course, will recall Himmler's position.

After pointing out that, on political grounds, outright expropriation of religious property would not be feasible at the time, Heydrich suggested certain specious interim actions with respect to the church properties in question, to be followed progressively by outright confiscation.

I now offer in evidence R-101A - it is right towards the end of your Honour's Exhibits - as Exhibit USA 358.

If your Honour pleases, there are several of those documents under R-101, and at the bottom you will notice they are labeled "A", "B", and "C". The first one is R-101A, and I quote the first five paragraphs on Page 2 of the English translation:

> "Enclosed is a list of church possessions which might be available for the accommodation of racial Germans. The list, which I beg you to return, is supplemented by correspondence and illustrated material pertinent to the subject.
>
> For political reasons, expropriation without indemnity of the entire property of the churches and religious orders will hardly be possible at this time.
>
> Expropriation with indemnity or in return for assignment of other lands and grounds will be even less possible.
>
> It is therefore suggested that the respective authorities of the Orders be instructed that they make available the monasteries concerned, for the accommodation of racial Germans, and remove their own members to other less populous monasteries."

There is a marginal note opposite this paragraph that, translated means "very good."

> "The final expropriation of these properties thus placed at our disposal can then be carried out step by step in the course of time."

On 5th April, 1940, the Security Police and Security Service S.S. sent a letter to the Reich Commissar for the Consolidation of Germandom, enclosing a copy of the foregoing letter from Heydrich to Himmler of 21st February, 1940, proposing the confiscation of Church properties. The letter of 5th April, 1940, is included in the Document R- 101A, just introduced in evidence; and I quote from this second sentence of the first paragraph thereof, on Page 1 of the English translation of that document. It is the first paragraph of Page I:

> "The Reich Leader S.S. has agreed to the proposals made in the enclosed letter and has ordered the matter to be dealt with by collaboration between the Chief of the Security Police and Security Service and your office."

If your Honour pleases, I believe it is on Pare 1 of the document. It is from the second sentence of the first paragraph. It is on the same one as the tab, your Honour.

THE PRESIDENT: Yes, I have it.

COLONEL STOREY: I now offer in evidence Document R-101C, Exhibit USA 358. This is a letter dated 30th July, 1941, written by an S.S. Standartenfuehrer, whose signature is illegible, to the Reich Leader of the S.S. The letter supplies further evidence of the participation of the "Gauleiter" in the seizure of church property. I quote from the first three paragraphs of the English translation of Document R-101C:

> "In accordance with the report of 30th May, 1941, this office considers it its duty to call the Reich Leader's attention to the development which is taking place in the incorporated Eastern Countries with regard to seizure and confiscation of Church property.
>
> As soon as the Reich laws on expropriation had been introduced, the Reich Governor and 'Gauleiter' in the Wartheland adopts the practice of expropriating real estate belonging to churches for use as dwellings. He grants compensation to the extent of the assessed value, and pays the equivalent

amount into blocked accounts.

Moreover, the East German Estate Administration, Limited, reports that in the 'Warthegau' all real estate owned by the churches is being claimed by the local 'Gau' administration."

I next offer in evidence Document R-101D, which immediately follows Exhibit USA 358, already in evidence. This is a letter from the Chief Of Staff of the Main Office to Himmler, dated 30th March, 1942, dealing with the confiscation of church property. The letter evidences the active participation of the Party Chancellery in the confiscation of religious property.

In this letter the Chief of Staff, Main Office, reports to Himmler concerning the policy of the S.S. in suspending all payment of rent to monasteries and other church institutions whose property had expropriated. The letter discusses a proposal made by the Reich Minister of the Interior, in which the Party Chancellery prominently participated, to the effect that the church institutions should be paid amounts corresponding to current mortgage charges on the premises, without realising any profit. The writer further suggests that such payments should never be made directly to the ecclesiastical institutions but rather should be made to the creditors of the institutions:

I now quote from the fourth sentence on Page 3 of that document:

"Such an arrangement would be in line with the basic idea of the settlement originally worked out between the Party Chancellery and the Reich Minister of the Interior."

I understand the Reich Minister of Interior for 1933-1944 was the defendant Frick.

The Leadership Corps of the Nazi Party participated in the suppression of religious publications and interfered with free religious education.

In a letter dated 27th September, 1940, Reichsleiter and Deputy of the Fuehrer Bormann transmitted to the defendant Rosenberg a photostatic copy of a letter from Gauleiter Florian, dated 23rd September, 1940, which expresses the Gauleiter's intense disapproval, on Nazi ideological grounds, of a religious pamphlet entitled, "The Spirit and Soul of the Soldiers," written by a Major General von Rabenau.

I now offer in evidence Document 064-PS, Exhibit USA 359. It is an original letter signed by Rosenberg attaching the copy of that matter. It contains defendant Bormann's letter to Rosenberg, dated 27th September, 1940, transmitting the Gauleiter's letter of 23rd September, 1940, to the defendant Hess, in which the Gauleiter urges that the religious writings of General von Rabenau be suppressed. In his letter to the defendant Hess, Gauleiter Florian discusses a conversation he had with General von Rabenau at the close of a lecture delivered by the General to a group of younger Army officers at Aachen. This conversation illumines the hostile attitude of the Leadership Corps of the Nazi Party towards the Christian churches. I quote from the second sentence of the second paragraph of the second page of the Gauleiter's letter to the defendant Hess, which appears on Page 2 of the English translation - the second paragraph:

"After he had affirmed the necessity of the churches, Rabenau said, with emphasised self-assurance, something like the following:

'Dear Gauleiter, the Party is making mistake after mistake in the treatment of the churches. Obtain for me the necessary powers from the Fuehrer and I guarantee that I shall succeed in a few months in establishing peace with the churches for all time.'

After this catastrophic ignorance, I gave up the conversation.

Dear Party Member Hess, the reading of von Rabenau's pamphlet

'Spirit and Soul of the Soldiers' has reminded me again of this. In this brochure Rabenau affirms the necessity of the Church straightforwardly and clearly, even though he is prudently careful. He writes on Page 28: 'There could be more examples; they would suffice to show that a soldier in this world can scarcely get along without thoughts about the next one.'

Because von Rabenau has a false spiritual basis, I consider his activities as an educator in spiritual affairs to be dangerous, and I am of the opinion that his educational writings are to be dispensed with absolutely and that the publication section of the N.S.D.A.P. can and must renounce these writings. The churches with their Christianity constitute that danger against which the struggle must always be carried on."

That the Party Chancellery shared with the Gauleiter this hostility to the Christian Churches is further revealed by the defendant Bormann's instruction to the defendant Rosenberg, set forth in Bormann's letter of transmittal, that Rosenberg "take action" on the Gauleiter's recommendation that the General's writings be suppressed.

I now offer in evidence Document 089-PS, Exhibit USA 360, which is a letter from the defendant Bormann, as Deputy of the Fuehrer, to the defendant Rosenberg, dated 8th March, 1940, enclosing a copy of Bormann's letter of the same date to Reichsleiter Amann. Amann was a top member of the Leadership Corps by virtue of his position as Reichsleiter for the Press and Leader Of the Party Publishing Company. In this letter to Amann Bormann expresses his dismay and dissatisfaction that only 10 per cent of the 3,000 Protestant periodicals in Germany have ceased publication, for what are described as "paper saving" reasons. Bormann then advises Reichsleiter Amann that "the distribution of any paper whatsoever for such periodicals is barred."

I now refer to this Document 089-PS, and I quote the second paragraph of Bormann's letter to Amann, which appears on the first page - the second paragraph - of the English translation:

"I urge you to see to it, in any redistribution of paper to be considered later, that the confessional writing, which, according to experiences so far gathered, possesses very doubtful value for strengthening the power of resistance on the part of the people toward the external foe, receive still sharper restrictions in favour of literature politically and ideologically more valuable."

I next offer in evidence Document 101-PS, Exhibit USA 361, which is a letter from the defendant Bormann, again, to Reichsleiter Rosenberg, dated the 17th January, 1940, expressing the Party's opposition to the circulation of religious literature to the members of the German Armed Forces. Among the soldiers of the United Nations, the proposition that there are no atheists in the fox-holes received a wide and reverent acceptance. However, in this document there is a contrary meaning, and I quote from Page 1 of the English translation, which reads:

"Nearly all the districts" - (that is Gauen) - "report to me regularly that the churches of both confessions are administering spiritually to members of the Armed Forces. This administration finds its expression especially in the fact that soldiers are being sent religious publications by the spiritual leaders of their home congregations. These publications are, in part, very cleverly composed. I have repeated reports that these publications are being read by the troops and thereby exercise a certain influence on the morale.

I have, in the past, by sounding out at once the General Field Marshal, the High Command of the Armed Forces, and fellow Party Member Reich

Director Amann, sought to restrict considerably the production and shipment of publications of this type. The result of these efforts remained unsatisfactory. As Reichsleiter Amann has repeatedly informed me, the restriction of these pamphlets by means of the paper rationing cannot be achieved because the paper used for the pamphlets is being purchased on the open market.

If the influencing of the soldiers by the church is to be effectively combated, this will only be accomplished only by producing many good publications in the shortest possible time under the supervision of the Party.

At the last meeting of the Deputy Gauleiters, comments were made on this matter to the effect that no considerable quantity of such publications is available.

I maintain that it is necessary that in the near future we transmit to the Party Service Offices down to the Ortsgruppenleiter a list of additional publications of this sort which should be sent to our soldiers by the Ortsgruppen..."

The Leadership Corps also participated in measures leading to the closing and dissolution of theological schools and other religious institutions. I now offer in evidence Document 122-PS, Exhibit USA 362, which, again, is a letter from the defendant Bormann to the defendant Rosenberg in his capacity as the Fuehrer's Representative for the Supervision of Spiritual and Ideological Schooling and Education of the N.S.D.A.P. This letter is dated 17th April, 1939, and transmits to Rosenberg an enclosed photostatic copy of a plan suggested by the Reich Minister for Science, Education and Training for the combining and closing of certain specially listed theological faculties. In his letter of transmittal the defendant Bormann requested Reichsleiter Rosenberg, to take "cognizance and prompt action" with respect to proposed suppression of religious institutions. I now quote from the next to the last paragraph of Page 2 of the English translation, in which the plan to suppress the religious institutions is summarised, and which reads:

"To recapitulate, this plan would mean, in addition to the closing of the theological faculties at Innsbruck, Salzburg and Munich, which has already taken place, and the contemplated transfer of the faculty of Graz to Vienna - that is the disappearance of four Catholic theological faculties:

(a) The closing of three more Catholic theological faculties or higher schools and of four Evangelical theological faculties in the Winter Semester 1939/1940;

(b) the closing of one more Catholic and of three more Evangelical theological faculties in the near future."

From the foregoing evidence the inference is irresistible, that the Leadership Corps of the Nazi Party shares a responsibility for the measures taken to subvert the Christian Churches and persecute the Christian clergy, both in Germany and in German-occupied territories of Europe. The evidence just offered, together with that previously presented by the prosecution, demonstrates that there was a general participation by the Leadership Corps, ranging from the Reichsleiter to the Gauleiter, adhered to by the rank and file, in the deliberate programme undertaken to undermine Christian religion.

We stress the significance of the appointment of the defendant Rosenberg, whose anti- Christian views are open and notorious, as the Fuehrers "delegate" or "representative" for the whole spiritual and philosophical education of the Nazi Party. It was precisely this position which gave Rosenberg his seat in the Reichsleitung, the general staff of the Party, comprising all the Reichsleiter. But emphasis is placed not merely upon the fact that anti-Christs, such as the defendants Bormann and

Rosenberg, held directive positions in the Leadership Corps but also upon the fact that their directives and orders were passed down the chain of command of to the Leadership Corps and caused the participation of its membership in acts subversive to the Christian Church.

In Document D-75, which I believe has been previously introduced - and I am just going to quote one line from it - the defendant Bormann stated:

"Nazism and Christianity are irreconcilable concepts."

The defendant was never more right, but he erred grievously by his prophecy as to which of the two would first pass away.

I next turn to the responsibility of the Leadership Corps for the destruction of Free Trade Unions and the imposition of the conspiratorial control over the productive labour capacity of the German nation.

The evidence relating to the responsibility of the Nazi Conspirators for the destruction of the independent trade unions has been previously introduced in evidence in the USA Exhibit G, which was the document book containing the evidentiary materials relating to the destruction of the trade unions. The brief evidence, which I shall now present, is offered to prove the responsibility of the Leadership Corps of the Nazi Party for the smashing of the independent unions and the imposition of conspiratorial control over the productive labour capacity of the German nation.

Soon after the seizure of power prominent members of the Leadership Corps participated in the smashing and dissolution of the independent trade unions of Germany. The defendant Robert Ley, by direct virtue of his office as Reich Organisation Leader and Reichsleiter in the Leadership Corps, was directed by Hitler, in mid-April, 1939, to smash the independent unions.

I will pass on now to Document 392, Exhibit USA 326, and I quote, beginning at the top of Page 1 of the English translation:

"On Tuesday, 2nd May, 1933, the co-ordination action of the Free Trade Unions began.

The essential part of the action is to be directed against the General German Trade Union Federation and the General Independent Employees' Federation.

Anything beyond that which is dependent upon the Free Trade Unions is left to the discretion of the Gauleiter's judgment. The Gauleiter are responsible for the execution of the co-ordination action in the individual areas. Supporters of the action should be members of the National Socialist Factory Cell Organisations.

The Gauleiter is to proceed with his measures on the basis of the closest agreement with competent Gau or regional factory cell directors.

In the Reich, the following will be occupied:

The directing offices of the unions...."

Then it lists a number of offices, and I previously quoted who was to be taken into protective custody.

The next provision:

"Exceptions are granted only with the permission of the Gauleiter.

It is understood that this action is to proceed in a strongly disciplined fashion. The Gauleiter are responsible in this respect. They are to hold the direction of the action firmly in hand.

Heil Hitler!

(signed) Dr. Robert Ley."

The defendant Ley's order for the dissolution of the independent trade unions was carried out as planned and directed. Trade union premises all over Germany were occupied by the S.A. and the unions dissolved. On the 2nd May, 1933, the official N.S.D.A.P. Press Service reported that the National Socialist Factory Cell Organisation (N.S.B.O.) had "eliminated the old leadership of Free Trade Unions" and taken over their leadership.

I now offer in evidence Document 2224-PS, Exhibit USA 364, which are Pages 1 and 2 of the 2nd May, 1933, issues of the National Socialist Party Press Agency. I quote from Paragraph 5 of Page 1 of the English translation:

> "National Socialism, which today has assumed leadership of the German working class, can no longer bear the responsibility for leaving the men and women of the German working class, the members of the largest trade organisation in the world, the German Trade Union Movement, in the hands of people who do not know a fatherland that is called Germany. Because of that, the National Socialist Factory Cell Organisation (N.S.B.O.) has taken over the leadership of the trade unions. The N.S.B.O. has eliminated the former leadership of the trade unions of the General German Trade Unions Federation, and of the General Independent Employees' Federation...
>
> On 2nd May, 1933, the National Socialist Factory Cell Organisation (N.S.B.O.) took over the leadership of all trade unions; all trade union buildings were occupied and most stringent control has been exercised over financial and personnel matters of the organisations."

As shown by this evidence, the assault on the independent unions as directed by the defendant Ley, in his capacity as Reichsleiter in charge of Party Organisation, assisted by the Gauleiter and Party Formations, and included the seizure of trade union funds and property. In this connection I offer in evidence Document 1678-PS, exhibit Number USA 365. This document is a report of a speech by Reichsleiter Ley on the 11th September, 1937, to the fifth annual session of the German Labour Front. In this speech Ley shamelessly corroborates the confiscation of the trade union funds. I quote from Paragraph 4 of Page 1 of the English translation:

> "Once I said to the Fuehrer: 'My Fuehrer, actually I am standing with one foot in gaol, for today I am still the trustee of the comrades "Leipart" and "Imbusch," and should they some day ask me to return their money, then it will be found that I have spent it, either by building things, or otherwise. But they will never again find their property in the condition in which they handed it over to me. Therefore I would have to be convicted.'
>
> The Fuehrer laughed and remarked that apparently I felt extremely well in this condition.
>
> It was very difficult for us all. Today we laugh about it..."

The plan of the Nazi conspirators to eliminate the Free Trade Unions was advanced by the enactment, on 19th May, 1933, of a law which abolished collective bargaining between workers and employers and replaced it with a regulation of working conditions by Labour Trustees appointed by Hitler. I refer to Document 405-PS, which is the text of the law, 1933 Reichsgesetzblatt Vol. I, 285. After providing in Section 1 for the appointment by Hitler of trustees of labour, this law provides, and I quote from Section 2 of the English translation of Document 405-PS:

> "Until a new revision of the social constitution, the trustees are to regulate the conditions for the conclusion of labour contracts. This practice is to be legally binding for all persons, and replaces the system founded on combinations of workers, of individual employers or of combinations of employers..."

Having destroyed the independent unions and collective bargaining, the next step of the Nazi conspirators was to secure the Nazification in the field of industrial relations. I refer to Document 1861-PS, which is the text of the law of 20th January, 1931, 1934, Reichsgesetzblatt Vol. I, 45. This law was entitled the "Law Regulating National Labor," and it imposed the leadership principle upon industrial enterprisers and provided, in Section I, paragraph 1, that the enterpriser should be the leader of the plant and the workers would "constitute his followers." I now quote from Section I, paragraph 2, of the first page of Document 1861-PS:

> "The leader of the plant makes the decisions for the employees and labourers in all matters concerning the enterprise, as far as they are regulated by this law.
> He is responsible for the well-being of the employees and labourers. The employees owe him faithfulness according to the principles of factory community."

The Trade Unions having been dissolved and the leadership principle superimposed upon the relationship of management and labour, the members of the Leadership Corps joined in and directed measures designed to replace the independent unions by the German Labour Front, the D.A.F., an affiliated Party organisation. On the very day the Nazi conspirators seized and dissolved the free trade unions, the 2nd May, 1933, they publicly proclaimed that a "united front of German workers" would be formed, with Hitler as honourary patron, at a workers' congress on the 10th May, 1933. I quote from the next to the last paragraph of Page 2 of Document 2224-PS, which was a release of the Nazi Party Press Agency:

> "The National Socialist Party Press Agency is informed that a great Workers' Congress will take place on Wednesday, 10th May, in the Prussian House of Lords in Berlin. The United Front of German Workers will be formed there. Adolf Hitler will be asked to assume the position of Honourary Patron."

The Nazi conspirators employed the German Labour Front, the D.A.F., as an instrument for propagandising its millions of compulsory members with Nazi ideology. The control of the Leadership Corps over the German Labour Front was assured not only by the designation of Reichsleiter of the Party Organisation Ley as head of the D.A.F., but by the employment of a large number of 'Politische Leiter,' or Political Leaders, charged with disseminating and imposing Nazi ideology upon the large membership of the D.A.F. I now cite Document 2271-PS, Exhibit USA 328, which is the Party Organisation Book referred to yesterday, Pages 185-187; and I quote from the first page of the English translation, the first paragraph:

> "The National Socialist Factory Cell Organisation (N.S.B.O.) is a union of the Political Leaders of the N.S.D.A.P. in the German Labour Front.
> The N.S.B.O. is to undertake the organisation of the German Labour Front.
> The duties and responsibilities of the N.S.B.O. have passed over to the D.A.F.
> The Political Leaders who have been transferred from the N.S.B.O. to the German Labour Front guarantee the ideological education of the D.A.F. in the spirit of the National Socialistic idea."

Now, if your Honour pleases, in addition to the evidence heretofore presented, the prosecution submits that it is another evidence of crime that the Leadership Corps of the N.S.D.A.P. was responsible for the plundering of art treasures by the defendant Reichsleiter Rosenberg's "Einsatzstab Rosenberg". The definition of "Einsatzstab" is a "special staff," and I am told that the word "Einsatz" means "to give action to". In other words, it was a task force, a special staff.

This subject, digressing from the text, had been prepared in connection with the general subject of "Plundering of Art Treasures", and I shall now turn to the document books of the "Plundering of Art Treasures" because the citations now will be in this small book.

I now pass to your Honour Document Book "W", and, may I say, digressing from the text, that the trial address, which is very brief, has, as I have been told by the Translating Division, been translated into all four languages; and, as I understand, Colonel Dostert will distribute it to all parties in their respective languages.

Also, by way of explanation, at the beginning there is one reference here to the plundering of art treasures in the occupied portion of Poland, which does not bear directly upon this subject, but does on the general conspiracy: and I thought, in the interest of time, that we might follow the presentation, because it is very brief.

May it please the Tribunal, the sections of the Indictment which are to be proved at this point are those dealing with the plunder of public and private property under Count One, the Common Plan or Conspiracy. It is not my purpose to explore all phases of the ordinary plunder in which the Germans engaged. However, I would bring to the attention of the Tribunal and of the world the defendants' vast, organised, systematic programme for the cultural impoverishment of virtually every community of Europe and for the enrichment of Germany thereby.

Special emphasis will be placed on the activities of the Einsatzstab Reichsleiter Rosenberg; and the responsibility of the Leadership Corps in this regard is a responsibility that is shared by the defendants Rosenberg, Goering and Keitel, and by the defendant organisations: the General Staff, High Command, Gestapo, the Security Service, and the S.S.

Before I deal with the plunder of the cultural treasures by the Einsatzstab Rosenberg, I wish to reveal briefly the independent plundering operations conducted in the Government General of occupied Poland by authority of the defendant Goering and under the supervision of the defendant Frank, the Governor General.

In October, 1939, Goering issued a verbal order to a Dr. Muehlmann asking him to undertake the immediate securing of all Polish art treasures. Dr. Muehlmann himself gives evidence of this order in Document 3042, found in the document book last introduced as Exhibit USA 375.

THE PRESIDENT: Are the documents in Book W?

COLONEL STOREY: Book W; yes, Sir.

THE PRESIDENT: I was asking whether the documents in Book W are placed in order of number in PS?

COLONEL STOREY: They are; yes, Sir; and the first one is found on the first page. I beg your pardon; 3042 would be in numerical order toward the end, your Honour.

THE PRESIDENT: I have it. I was merely asking for general information.

COLONEL STOREY: These are consecutive. I would like to offer this affidavit and to read it in full. In short, it was obtained in Austria.

Kajetan Muehlmann states under oath:

"I have been a member of the N.S.D.A.P. since 1st April, 1938. I was Brigadier General (Oberfuehrer) in the S.S.

I was never an illegal Nazi.

I was the special deputy of the Governor General of Poland, Hans Frank, for the safeguarding of art treasures in the Government General, October, 1939 to September, 1943.

Goering, in his function as chairman of the Reich Defence Council, had commissioned me with this duty.

I confirm that it was the official policy of the Governor General Hans Frank, to take into custody all important art treasures which belonged to Polish public institutions, private collections and the Church. I confirm that the art treasures mentioned were actually confiscated; and it is clear to me that they would not have remained in Poland in case of a German victory, but they would have been used to complement German artistic property.

Signed and sworn to by Dr. Muehlmann."

On the 15th November, 1939, Frank issued a decree, which is published officially in The Law of the Government General, (Document 1773-PS, Exhibit USA 376). It is E.800, Article 1, Section 1. It is not in the document book. It is just a short quotation, of which we ask the Tribunal to take judicial notice. Quoting:

"All movable and stationary property of the former Polish State will be sequestered for the purpose of securing all manner of public valuables."

In a further decree of 16th December, 1939, appearing at Page E.810 of the same publication, Frank provided that all art objects in public possession in the Government General were to be seized for the fulfillment of public tasks of common interest, in so far as they had not already been seized under the decree of 13th November. The decree provided that, in addition to art collections and art treasures belonging to the Polish State, there will be considered as owned by the public those private collections which have not already been taken under protection by the Special Commissioner, as well as all ecclesiastical art property.

On the 24th September, 1940, Frank decreed that all property seized on the basis of the decree of 15th November, 1939, would be transferred to the ownership of the Government General, and this decree is also found at E.810 of the same publication.

It is impossible for me to furnish this Tribunal a complete Picture of the vastness of the programme for the cultural impoverishment of Poland carried out pursuant to the directives, as I cannot read into the record the 500-odd masterpieces catalogued in Document 1233-PS (Exhibit USA 377) or the many hundreds of additional items catalogued in Document 1709-PS, Exhibit USA 378. Now Document 1233-PS, which I hold in my hand, is a finely bound, beautifully printed catalogue, in which defendant Frank proudly lists and describes the major works of art which he had seized for the benefit of the Reich. This volume was captured by the Monuments, Fine Arts and Archives Division of the Third United States Army and was found in Frank's home near Munich. The introductory page describes the thoroughness with which the Government General stripped Poland of its cultural possessions. That is quoted in Document 1233-PS.

THE PRESIDENT: Will you hand that up?

COLONEL STOREY: I am quoting now from the introductory page, the English translation, the first paragraph. I might say by way of explanation, that this book lists the valuable art treasure by titles. I now quote from the introductory page:

"By reason of the decree of 16th December, 1939, by the Governor General of the Occupied Polish territories, the Special Commissioner for securing objects of art and culture was able to seize within six months almost all of the art objects of the country, with one exception: a series of Flemish Gobelins of the Castle of Crakow. According to the latest information these are now in France, so that subsequent seizure will be possible."

Going through this catalogue page by page we find that it included references to paintings by German, Italian, Dutch, French and Spanish masters, rare illustrated books, Indian and Persian miniatures, wood-cuts, the famous Veit-Stoss hand-carved altar (created here in Nuremberg and purchased for use in Poland), handicraft, articles of gold and silver, antique articles of crystal, glass and porcelain, tapestries, antique weapons, rare coins and medals. These articles were seized, as indicated in the catalogue, from public and private sources, including the National Museums in Crakow and Warsaw, the cathedrals of Warsaw and Lublin, a number of churches and monasteries, university libraries, and a great many private collections of the Polish nobility.

I wish now to offer in evidence the catalogue bearing our number 1233-PS. It is the one just introduced in evidence, and is Document 1709-PS. This latter report, in addition to listing the 521 major items described in the catalogue, lists many other items, which though generally no less important from an artistic standpoint, were considered by the Germans to be of secondary importance from the point of view of the Reich.

It is interesting to note with what pains the defendant Frank opted to conceal his real purpose in seizing these works of art. The cover of the catalogue itself states that the objects listed were secured and safeguarded. Strangely enough, it was found necessary to safeguard some of the objects by transporting them to Berlin and depositing them in the depot of the Special Deputy or in the safe of the Deutsche Reichsbank, as is indicated on Page 80 of Document 1709-PS, Exhibit USA 378. The items referred to as having been transported to Berlin are listed in the catalogue of treasures safeguarded and their numbers are 4, 17, 27, 35, and so on. Thirty-one extremely valuable and world-renowned sketches of Albrecht Duerer, taken from the collection of Lubomirski in Lemberg, were likewise safeguarded. At Page 68 of this report, Dr. Muehlmann states that he personally handed these sketches to Goering, who took them to the Fuehrer at his headquarters.

Numerous objects of art, paintings, tapestries, plates, dishes, as well as other dinnerware, were also safeguarded by Frank, who had the Special Deputy to deliver these objects to an architect for the purpose of furnishing the castle at Crakow and the Schloss Kressendorf, which were his residences. It was apparently Frank's belief that these items would be safer in his possession, used to grace his table and dazzle his guests, than they would be in the possession of the rightful owners.

There is no doubt whatever that virtually all the art treasures of Poland were seized for the use of Germany and would never have been returned in the event of German victory. Dr. Muehlmann, a noted German art authority, who directed the seizure programme for the period of four years and was endowed by Frank with sufficient authority to promulgate decrees generally applicable throughout the territory, has stated the objectives of the programme in no uncertain terms in the affidavit to which I have just referred.

So much for Poland.

I now direct the attention of the Tribunal to the activities of the Einsatzstab Rosenberg, an organisation which planned and directed the looting of the cultural treasures of nearly all Europe. To obtain a full conception of the vastness of this looting programme, it will be necessary to envision Europe as a treasure-house in which is stored the major portion of the artistic and literary product of two thousand years of Western Civilisation. It will further be necessary to envision the forcing of this treasure-house by a horde of vandals, bent on systematically removing to the Reich these treasures, which are, in a sense, the heritage of all of us, to keep them there for the enjoyment and enlightenment of Germans alone. Unique in history, this art seizure programme staggers one's imagination and challenges one's credulity. The documents which I am about to offer in evidence will present undeniable proof of the execution of the policy to strip the occupied countries of the accumulated product of centuries of devotion to art and the pursuit of learning.

May I digress here a moment and state that we are not going to offer all the documents and all the details, because our Soviet and French colleagues will offer a great many of the detailed documents in support of their case on War Crimes.

I now offer in evidence Document 136-PS as Exhibit USA 367. That is an order of Hitler dated the 29th January, 1940, which set into motion the art seizure programme that was to envelop the continent. I now offer the original. I call your Honour's attention to this original, being signed by Adolf Hitler, and I believe it is in the famous Jumbo type. I quote the order in its entirety. It is very short:

> "The 'Hohe Schule' is to become the Centre for National Socialistic ideological and educational research. It will be established after the conclusion of the war. I order that the preparations already initiated be continued by Reichsleiter Alfred Rosenberg, especially in the way of research and setting up of the library.
>
> All sections of the Party and State are required to co- operate with him in this task."

Although the above order makes no specific mention of the seizure of art treasures, the programme had extended by the 5th November, 1940, beyond its original scope to include the seizure of Jewish art collections.

I now offer in evidence Document 141-PS, Exhibit USA 368, which is a certified copy of an order signed by Goering, dated 5th November, 1940, in which he states:

> "In conveying the measures taken until now for the securing of Jewish art treasures by the Chief of the Military Administration, Paris, and the Einsatzstab Rosenberg, the art objects brought to the Louvre will be disposed of in the following way:
>
> 1. Those about which the Fuehrer has reserved for himself the decision as to their use.
> 2. Those which serve to complete the Reichsmarshal's collection.
> 3. Those library books, the use of which seem useful to the establishment of the higher institutes of learning, and which come within the jurisdiction of Reichsleiter Rosenberg.
> 4. Those which are suitable for sending to the German museums."

Thus, early in 1940, eleven months after the initiation of the programme for establishment of the library for ideological research, the original purpose had been expanded so as to include the seizure of works of art, not only for the benefit of research, but for the delectation of the Fuehrer and Goering and the enhancement of the collections of German museums.

Impelled as they were by the perfidious dream of subjugating a continent, the Nazi conspirators could not content themselves merely with the exploitation of the cultural riches of France, but rapidly extended their activities to the other occupied countries. I now offer in evidence Document 137-PS as Exhibit USA 379. That is a copy of an order signed by the defendant Keitel, dated 5th July, 1940, and I should like to read that brief order in full:

> "To: The Chief of Army High Command, Chief of the Armed Forces in the Netherlands.
>
> Reichsleiter Rosenberg has suggested to the Fuehrer that:
>
> 1. The State libraries and archives be searched for documents valuable to Germany.
> 2. The Chancelleries of the high church authorities and lodges be searched for political maneuvers directed against us and that the material in question be seized.

The Fuehrer has ordered that this suggestion be followed and that the Gestapo, supported by the archivists of Reichsleiter Rosenberg, be put in charge of the researches. The Chief of Security Police, SS Gruppenfuehrer Heydrich, has been informed. He will communicate with the competent military commanders in order to execute this order.

These measures will be executed in all regions of the Netherlands, Belgium, Luxembourg, and France occupied by us.

It is requested that subordinate services be informed.

Chief of Army High Command:

Signed Keitel."

From the Netherlands, Belgium, Luxembourg, and France the Einsatzstab's activities ultimately were expanded still further to Norway and Denmark. I now offer in evidence Document 159-PS, Exhibit USA 380, which is the copy of an order signed by Utikal, Chief of the Einsatzstab, dated the 6th June, 1944, from which it is seen that a special mission of the Einsatzstab was sent to Norway and Denmark.

As the German Army penetrated to the East, the fingers of the Einsatzstab reached out to seize the cultural riches thus made available to them, and their activities were extended to the Occupied Eastern Territories, including the Baltic States and the Ukraine, as well as to Hungary and Greece. I now offer in evidence Document 153-PS, Exhibit USA 381, being a certified copy of a letter from Rosenberg to the Reich Commissioner for the East and Reich Commissioner for the Ukraine, dated 27th April, 1942. The subject of the letter is stated to be as follows:

"Formation of a Central Unit for the Seizure and Securing of Objects of Cultural Value in the Occupied Eastern Territories." In the last paragraph of that document, I quote:

"With the Commissioners of the Reich a special department within Department II (political) will be set up for a limited time for the seizure and securing of objects of cultural value. This department is under the control of the head of the main group of Einsatzstab of Reichsleiter Rosenberg for the occupied territories."

THE PRESIDENT: Perhaps this would be a good time to break off for ten minutes.

(A recess was taken.)

COLONEL STOREY: Activities were initiated in Hungary as indicated by Document 158-PS, Exhibit USA 382, which I now offer in evidence. This was a copy of a message initialed by Utikal, Rosenberg's Chief of Staff. The first paragraph of this document states:

"The Einsatzstab of Reichsleiter Rosenberg for the occupied territories has dispatched a Sonderkommando under the direction of Stabseinsatzsfuehrer Dr. Zeiss, who is identified by means of his Service Book Number 187, for the accomplishment of the missions of the Einsatzstab in Hungary outlined in the Fuehrer's Decree of 1st March, 1942."

I now offer into evidence Document 171-PS, Exhibit USA 383, which is an undated report on the "Library for Exploration of the Jewish Question." The fifth paragraph states:

"The most significant book-collections today belonging to the stock of the Library for Exploration of the Jewish Question are the following..."

The ninth item of the list which follows refers to "Book- collections from Jewish Communities in Greece (about 10,000 volumes)."

It was only natural that an operation conducted on so vast a scale, extending as it did to France, Belgium, the Netherlands. Luxembourg, Norway, Denmark, the Occupied Eastern Territories. the Baltic States, the Ukraine, Hungary and Greece, should call upon a multitude of other agencies for assistance. Among the other agencies co-operating in the plunder programme were several of those which stand indicted here as Criminal Organisations. The co-operation of the Wehrmacht High Command was demanded by the Hitler order of 1st March, 1942, which I now offer in evidence as our Document 149-PS, Exhibit USA 369, which is signed personally by Adolf Hitler and is also in the Jumbo type. The order decrees the ideological fight against the enemies of National Socialism to be a military necessity, and reaffirms the authority of the Einsatzstab Rosenberg to conduct searches and seizures of suitable material for the Hohe Schule. The fifth paragraph states:

> "The measures of execution concerning co-operation with the Wehrmacht are assured by the Chief of the O.K.W. with the consent of Reichsleiter Rosenberg."

While I am on that document, which is referred to later, I should like to read the other portions. I call attention of your Honour to the distribution. It is distributed to all duty stations of the Armed Forces, the Party, and the State. It says:

> "Jews, Freemasons, and related ideological enemies of National Socialism are responsible for the war which is now being waged against the Reich. The co-ordinated, ideological fight against those powers is a military necessity. I have therefore charge Reichsleiter Rosenberg to carry out this task in co-operation with the chief of the O.K.W. His 'staff for special purposes' in the occupied territories is authorised to search libraries, record-offices, lodges and other ideological and cultural institutions of all kinds for suitable material, and to confiscate the said material for the ideological task of the N.S.D.A.P. and the later scientific research work of the 'Hohe Schule.' The same regulation applies to cultural material which is in possession of Jews; and of unobjectionable origin."

The final passage is:

> "The necessary measures within the territories of the East under the German Administration are determined by Reichsleiter Rosenberg in his capacity as Reichsminister for the Occupied Eastern Territories."
>
> Signed: Adolf Hitler."

THE PRESIDENT: Colonel Storey, I think the Tribunal would find it convenient, and it would save time, if the documents, when they are referred to, were read in full in so far as you want to read them, rather than returning to read one passage and then returning to a document later on.

COLONEL STOREY: Yes, Sir. May I explain why that was, Sir? I was trying to fit in this presentation with the Leadership Corps. It was quoted in two places and I didn't notice it until I started.

THE PRESIDENT: What I am saying is that I think it is much easier to follow the documents if all the parts of the document which you wish to read are read at one time, rather than to read one sentence, then come back to another sentence, and then possibly come back to a document for a third sentence. I don't know whether that will be possible for you to do.

COLONEL STOREY: We will try to work it out that way, Sir.

THE PRESIDENT: Thank you.

COLONEL STOREY: Co-operation of the S.S. and the S.D. is indicated in a letter from Rosenberg to Bormann dated 23rd April, 1941, Document 071-PS, Exhibit USA 371, which I now offer in evidence. This letter states in the fifth sentence of the first numbered paragraph:

"It is understood that the confiscations are not executed by the regional authorities, but that this is conducted by the Security Service (S.D.) as well as by the police."

Farther down in the same paragraph it is stated:

It has been communicated to me in writing by a Gauleiter that the chief office of the Reich Security (R.S.H.A.) of the S.S. has claimed the following from the library of a monastery: The Catholic Handbook, Albertus Magnus; Edition of the Church Fathers, History of the Papacy, by L. V. Pastor; and other works."

The second and last paragraph stated that:

I should like to remark in this connection that this affair has already been executed on our side with Security Service (S.D.) in the most loyal fashion."

The defendant Goering showed special diligence in furthering the purposes of the Einsatzstab Rosenberg, a diligence which will be readily understood in view of the fact that he himself directed that second in priority only to the demands of the Fuehrer were to be "those art objects which served the completion of the Reichsmarshal's - that is Goering's - - collection."

On 1st May, 1941, Goering issued an order to all Party, State and Wehrmacht services, which I am now offering into evidence as Document 1117-PS, Exhibit USA 384. It is an original bearing Goering's signature. This order requested all Party, State and Wehrmacht services, and I now quote:

"... to give all possible support and assistance to the Chief of Staff of Reichsleiter Rosenberg's staff.... The above-mentioned persons are requested to report to me on their work, particularly on any difficulties which might arise."

On 30th May, 1942, Goering claimed credit for a large degree of the success of the Einsatzstab. I offer in evidence a captured photostatic copy of a letter from Goering to Rosenberg, showing Goering's signature, which bears our No. 1015-I-PS, and which I offer in evidence as Exhibit USA 385. The last paragraph of this letter states as follows:

"...On the other hand I also support personally the work of the Einsatzstab wherever I can do so, and a great part of the seized cultural goods can be accounted for because I was able to assist the Einsatzstab with my organisations."

If I have tried the patience of the Tribunal with numerous details as to the origin, the growth and the operation of the art looting organisation, it is because I feel that it will be impossible for me to convey to you a full conception as to the magnitude of the plunder without conveying first to you information as to the vast organisational work that was necessary in order to enable the defendants to collect in Germany cultural treasures of staggering proportions.

Nothing of value was safe from the grasp of the Einsatzstab. In view of the great experience of the Einsatzstab in the complex business of the organised plunder of a continent, its facilities were well suited to the looting of material other than cultural objects. Thus, when Rosenberg required equipment for the furnishing of the offices of the administration in the East, his Einsatzstab was pressed into action to confiscate Jewish homes in the West. Document L- 188, which is Exhibit USA 386, and which I now offer in evidence, is a copy of a report submitted by the director of Rosenberg's office, West, operating under the Ministry for the Occupied Eastern Territories. I wish to quote at some length from this document and I call the Tribunal's attention to the third paragraph on Page 3 of the translation:

"The Einsatzstab Reichsleiter Rosenberg was charged with the carrying out of this task" - that is, the seizure of art possessions - "in addition to this seizure of property, at the suggestion of the Director West of the Special Section of the Einsatzstab, it was proposed to the Reichsleiter that the furniture and other contents of the unguarded Jewish homes should also be secured and dispatched to the Minister for the Occupied Eastern Territories for use in the Eastern Territories."

The last paragraph on the same page states:

"At first all the confiscated furniture and goods were dispatched to the administrations of the Occupied Eastern Territories. Owing to the terror attacks on German cities which then began, and in the knowledge that the bombed-out people in Germany ought to have preference over the Eastern people, Reichsminister and Reichsleiter Rosenberg obtained a new order from the Fuehrer according to which the furniture, etc., obtained through the N Action was to be put at the disposal of bombed-out people within Germany."

The report continues with a description of the efficient methods employed in looting the Jewish homes in the West (top of Page 4 of translation).

"The confiscation of Jewish homes was carried out as follows: So-called confiscation officials went from house to house when no records were available of the addresses of Jews who had departed or fled, as was the case, for instance, in Paris, in order to collect information as to abandoned Jewish homes... They drew up inventories of those homes and subsequently sealed them... In Paris alone about twenty confiscation officials confiscated more than 38,000 homes. The transportation of the contents of these homes was completed with all the available vehicles of the Union of Parisian Removal Contractors, who had to provide up to 150 trucks, and 1,200 to 1,500 French laborers."

If your Honour pleases, I am omitting the rest of the details of that report because our French colleagues will present them later.

Looting on such a scale seems fantastic. But I feel I must refer to another statement, for, though the seizure of the contents of over 71,000 homes and their shipment to the Reich in upwards of 26,000 railroad cars is by no means a petty operation, the quantities of plundered art treasures and books and their incalculable value, as revealed in the document I am about to offer, will make these figures dwindle by comparison.

I next refer to the stacks of leather-bound volumes in front of me, to which the Justice referred in his opening statement.

These thirty-nine volumes which are before me contain photographs of works of art secured by the Einsatzstab and are volumes which were prepared by members of the Rosenberg staff. All of these volumes bear our Number 2522-PS, and I offer them in evidence as Exhibit USA 388.

I am passing to your Honours eight of these volumes, so that each one of you - they are all different - might see a sample of the inventory. I call your Honours' attention to the inside cover page. Most of them have an inventory, in German, of the contents of the book, and then follows a true photograph of each one of these priceless art treasures separated by fine tissue paper.

There are thirty-nine of these volumes that were captured by our forces when they overran a part of Southern occupied German areas.

THE PRESIDENT: Is there anything known about the articles photographed here?

COLONEL STOREY: Yes, Sir: I will describe them later. I believe each one of them is identified in addition to the inventory.

THE PRESIDENT: I meant whether the articles, the furniture or pictures themselves, have been found.

COLONEL STOREY: Yes, Sir, most of them were found in an underground cavern, I believe in the Southern part of Bavaria; and these books were found by our staff in co- operation with the group of U.S. Army people who have assembled these art treasures and are now in the process of returning them to the rightful owners. That is where we got these books.

I should like to refer, while your Honour are looking at these, just to the aggregate totals of the different paintings. Here are the totals as shown by Document 1015-B-PS, which is in the document book. As they are totalled, I don't think your Honours need follow the document; you can continue looking at the books if you like.

"Up to 15th July, 1944, the following had been scientifically inventoried:

21,903 Art Works.

5,281 paintings, pastels, water-colours, drawings.

684 miniatures, glass and enamel paintings, books and manuscripts.

583 plastics, terra-cottas, medallions and plaques.

2,477 articles of furniture of value to art history.

583 textiles (Gobelins, rugs, embroideries, Coptic materials, majolica, ceramics, jewellery, coins, art treasures made with precious stones).

5,825 objects of decorative art (porcelains, bronzes, faience, majolica ceramics, jewelry, coins, art objects with precious stones).

1,286 East Asiatic art works (bronzes, plastics, porcelains, paintings, folding screens, weapons).

259 art works of antiquity (sculptures, bronzes, vases, jewellry bowls, cut stones, terracottas)."

The mere statement that 21,903 art works have been seized does not furnish an adequate conception of their value. I refer again to the statement in the document: "The extraordinary artistic and material value of the seized art works cannot be expressed in figures" and to the fact that they are objects of such a unique character that their evaluation is entirely impossible. These thirty-nine volumes are by no means a complete catalogue. They present, at the most, pictures of about 2,500 of the art treasures seized, and I ask you to imagine that this catalogue had been completed and that, in the place of thirty-nine volumes, we had 350 to 400 volumes. In other words, if they were prepared in inventory form as these thirty-nine volumes, to cover all of them, it would take 350 to 400 volumes.

We had arranged, your Honours, to project just a few of these on the screen, but before we do that, which is the end of this part of the presentation, I should like to call your Honours' attention to Document 015-PS. It is dated 16th April, 1943. It is a copy of a letter from Rosenberg to Hitler. The occasion for the writing of this letter was the birthday of the Fuehrer, to commemorate which Rosenberg presented some folders of photographs of pictures seized by the Einsatzstab. And I imagine, although we have no authentic evidence, that probably some of these were prepared for that occasion. In the closing paragraph of the letter, Document 015-PS, Exhibit USA 387, he says:

"I beg of you, my Fuehrer, to give me a chance during my next audience to report to you orally on the whole extent and state of this art seizure action. I beg you to accept a short written intermediate report of the progress and extent of the art seizure action, which will be used as a basis for this later oral report, and also to accept three volumes of the temporary picture catalogues which, too, show only a part of the collection you own. I shall deliver further catalogues, which are now being compiled, when they are finished."

Rosenberg then closes with this touching tribute to the aesthetic tastes of the Fuehrer, tastes which were satisfied at the expense of a continent, and I quote:

"I shall take the liberty during the requested audience to give you, my Fuehrer, another twenty folders of pictures, with the hope that this short occupation with the beautiful things of art which are so near to your heart, will send a ray of beauty and joy into your revered life."

THE PRESIDENT: Will you read all the passage that you began; five lines above that beginning with the words, "These photos represent -"

COLONEL STOREY:

"These photos represent an addition to the collection of fifty-three of the most valuable objects of art delivered some time ago to your collection. This folder also shows only a small percentage of the exceptional work and extent of these objects of art seized by my service command (Dienststelle) in France and put into a safe place in the Reich."

If your Honours please, at this time we would like to project on the screen a few of these photographs. The photographs of paintings which we are now about to project on the screen are taken from a single volume of the catalogue and are mere representative of the many volumes of pictures of similar works. The other items, photos of which are to be projected, were picked from various volumes on special subjects. For example, the Gobelin tapestry which you are about to see is merely one picture from an entire volume of tapestry illustrations. Each picture that you will see is representative of a number of volumes of similar pictures, and each volume from which these single pictures were taken represents approximately a tenth of the total number of volumes which would be necessary to illustrate all the items actually plundered by the Einsatzstab. We will now have the slides, just a few of them.

(Photographs were projected on the screen in the court room.)

This first picture is a portrait of a woman, painted by the Italian painter Palma Vecchio.

The next picture is a portrait of a woman by the Spanish painter Velasquez.

This picture is a portrait of Lady Spencer by the English painter Sir Joshua Reynolds.

This picture is a painting by the French painter Watteau.

This is a painting of "The Three Graces" by Rubens.

This is a portrait of an old woman by the famous painter Rembrandt.

This painting of a young woman is by the Dutch painter Van Dyck.

Now this picture is a sample of sixteenth century jewelry in gold and enamel, decorated with pearls.

This is a seventeenth century Gobelin tapestry.

This picture is of a Japanese painting from the catalogue volume on East Asiatic art.

This is an example of famous china.

This is a picture of a silver-inlaid Louis XIV cabinet.

The last picture is of a silver altar piece of the fifteenth or sixteenth century, of Spanish origin.

That is the last picture.

I call to your attention again that each of the pictures you have just seen is merely representative of a large number of similar items illustrated in the thirty-nine volume catalogue which is, in itself, only partially complete. There is little wonder that the Fuehrer's occupation with these beautiful things of art, which were nearest to his heart, should have sent a ray of beauty and joy into his revered life. I doubt that any museum in the world, whether the Metropolitan in New York, the British Museum in London, the Louvre in Paris or the Tretiakov Gallery in Moscow, could present such a catalogue as this; in fact, should they pool their treasures the result would certainly fall short of the art collection that Germany amassed for herself, at the expense of the other nations of Europe. Never in history has a collection so great been amassed with so little scruple.

It is refreshing, however, to know that the victorious Allied armies have recovered most of such treasures, principally hidden away in salt mines, tunnels, and secluded castles; and the proper governmental agencies are now in the process of restoring these priceless works of art to their rightful owners.

I shall next refer to Document 154-PS, which is a letter dated the 5th July, 1942, from Doctor Lammers, Reich Minister and Chief of the Chancellery, to the highest Reich authorities and services directly subordinate to the Fuehrer. This letter states and implements the Hitler order that was introduced in evidence, and explains that the Fuehrer delegated authority to Rosenberg's staff to search for and seize cultural property by virtue of Reichsleiter Rosenberg's position as representative of the Fuehrer for the supervision of the whole ideological and political education of the N.S.D.A.P.

The Tribunal will recall, however, that it is by virtue of holding this office that defendant Rosenberg occupied a place within the Reichsleitung or Party Directorate of the Leadership Corps. That is Exhibit USA 370, and it is offered merely for the purpose of showing the address to the highest Reich authorities and services directly subordinate to the Fuehrer.

In a letter to the defendant Bormann, dated the 23rd April, 1941, the defendant Rosenberg protested against the arbitrary removals by the S.D. and other public services from libraries, monasteries, and other institutions - and he proposed that in the claims by the S.D. and his representative the final regulation as to the confiscation should be made by the Gauleiter. This letter has been offered previously as 071-PS, and I quote, beginning with the next to the last sentence at the bottom of page one of the English translation - I am sorry, your Honour, that is in the other book -

THE PRESIDENT: You cited 071-PS this morning.

COLONEL STOREY: Yes, Sir, and I will forego that at the moment, your Honour, because it refers to the other book. Finally, in connection with the presentation of this subject, I submit that the summary of evidence establishes that the defendants and their conspirators, Rosenberg and Bormann, acting in their capacity as political leaders of the Leadership Corps of the Nazi Party and as members thereof, participated in the Conspiracy or Common Plan alleged in Count I of the Indictment and committed acts constituting the crimes alleged. Accordingly we submit: (I) The Leadership Corps of the Nazi Party is a group or organisation in the sense in which those terms are used in Article 9 of the Charter; (2) The defendants and conspirators, Rosenberg and Bormann, committed the crimes defined in Article 6 of the Charter, and in that capacity as members of the Political Leaders of the Leadership Corps of the Nazi Party.

It was at all times the primary and central design and purpose of the Leadership Corps of the Nazi Party to direct, engage, and participate in the execution of the

Conspiracy which contemplated and involved the commission of the Crimes as defined in Article 6 of the Charter.

And I should like now to call attention again to a chart which was identified in the beginning - I believe by Major Wallis; it was taken from the publication which is entitled 'The Face of the Party.' This chart emphasises, more clearly than I can state the total and thorough control over the life of the German, beginning at the age of ten, at the bottom of the chart, and continuing through the various categories.

Notice the age of ten to fourteen, the Jungvolk. Then it goes to the Adolf Hitler School on the right, twelve to eighteen. The Hitler Jugend, fifteen to eighteen; the S.A., the N.S.K.K., N.S.F.K., nineteen to twenty. And then the labour service over at the left; and then again to the S.A., S.S., N.S.K.K., N.S.F.K.; and then into the Wehrmacht, and up through to the top box on the left of the top row of men, the Political Leaders of the N.S.D.A.P. Next, all of those buildings up there, as I understand, are the academies of the N.S.D.A.P., and then finally, at the top, to the Political Leaders of the German Volk, thus showing the complete evolution. This is the final exhibit, and with that I close the presentation of the Leadership Corps. The next presentation is the Reich Cabinet, the "Reichsregierung." We will take just a few moments.

If your Honour please, there is one thing Colonel Seay called my attention to. I refer to it merely for the record. In one of the previous documents, 090-PS, Exhibit USA 372, which is in the other document book, there was a statement that clearly established that the expenses of the Einsatzstab Rosenberg, that is, the staff's operational expenses, were financed by the Nazi Party.

If the Tribunal please, I now offer Document Book "X," which I believe has been passed to your Honours; and also Colonel Dostert's staff has prepared a chart of the "Reichsregierung" in different languages, and I believe your Honours have copies. There is one copy, here in German that I shall be glad to pass to counsel who are especially concerned with this case. They have one copy in German. I don't know who it is-

THE PRESIDENT: You mean counsel for the Reich Cabinet?

COLONEL STOREY: Yes, Sir. May I say also, by preliminary reference, that we examined the records in the collection office this morning, and only one letter of intervention has been filed on behalf of the Reich Cabinet, and that was by the defendant Keitel.

We will now consider the "Reichsregierung." Some preliminary remarks about this group have already been placed before the Tribunal by Mr. Albrecht in his comments upon the Government chart. It will be necessary, however, for sake of coherence, to repeat briefly some of the statements made by him, and therefore we beg the indulgence of the Tribunal.

The "Reichsregierung," meaning Reich Cabinet, unlike most of the other groups named in the Indictment, was not especially created by the Nazi Party to carry out or implement its nefarious schemes and purposes. The "Reichsregierung" - commonly referred to as the Cabinet - had, before the Nazis came to power, a place in the constitutional and political history of the country. As with other cabinets of duly constituted governments, the executive power of the realm was concentrated in that body. The Nazi conspirators realised this only too well. Their aim for totalitarian control over the State could not be secured - they realised - except by acquiring, holding and utilising the top level machinery of the State. And this they did.

Under the Nazi regime the "Reichsregierung" gradually became a primary agent of the Nazi Party with functions and policies formulated in accordance with the objectives and methods of the Party itself. The institution of the "Reichsregierung" became - at first gradually and then with more rapidity - polluted by the infusion of the Nazi conspirators into the Cabinet. Many of them - sixteen to be exact - sit before you today in the dock. There was no plan, scheme or purpose - however vile or inhuman or illegal in any sense of the word - that was not clothed with the semblance of legality by the Nazi "Reichsregierung." It is for that reason that we will ask this Tribunal - after the proof has been offered - - to declare that body, as defined in the Indictment, to be a Criminal Organisation. The proof will be divided into two main categories, the first of which will tend to establish the composition and nature of the "Reichsregierung" under the Nazis, as well as delineating briefly its functions and powers, while the second will tend to establish - and conclusively we believe - the reasons why the brand of criminality should be affixed to that group.

The term "Reichsregierung" literally translated reads "Reich Government." Actually, as we said, it was commonly taken to refer to the ordinary Reich Cabinet. In the Indictment the term "Reichsregierung" is defined to include not only those persons who were members of the ordinary Reich Cabinet, but also those persons who were members of the Council of Ministers for the Defence of the Reich, and the Secret Cabinet Council. However, the really important subdivision of the three is - as the proof will show - the ordinary Cabinet. Between it and the other two there was in reality only an artificial distinction. There existed, in fact, a unity of personnel, actions, functions, and purposes that obliterated any academic separation. As used in the Indictment, the term "ordinary Cabinet" means Reich Ministers, that is, heads of departments of the Central Government, Reich Ministers without portfolio, State Ministers acting as Reich Ministers, and other officials entitled to take part in meetings

I might state here that there were, altogether, forty-eight persons who held positions in the ordinary Cabinet. Seventeen of them are defendants before the Tribunal. Bormann is absent. Of the remaining thirty-one, eight are believed to be dead.

Into the ordinary Cabinet were placed the leading Nazi collaborators, the trusted henchmen, and then, when new governmental agencies or bodies were created, either by Hitler or the Cabinet itself, the constituents of these new bodies were taken from the roles of the ordinary Cabinet.

In 1933 when the first Hitler Cabinet was formed on 30th January, there were ten ministries that could be classified as departments of the Central Government. I have here a typed copy of the minutes of the first meeting of that Cabinet. These were found in the files of the Reich Chancellery and bear the typed signature of one Weinstein, the counsellor of the ministry, who was described in the minutes as responsible for the protocol, that document already appears in Document B; but I again refer the Tribunal to Page 4 of the translation, which is Document 351, as shown in your document book, and contains a list of those present.

THE PRESIDENT: 351-PS?

COLONEL STOREY: Yes, Sir, 351-PS, Exhibit USA 389.

The ten ministers referred to therein are set forth. They are - and I read:

"Reich Minister for Foreign Affairs, the defendant von Neurath; Reich Minister of the Interior, the defendant Frick; Reich Minister of Finance, von Krosigk; Reich Minister of Economy" -and then I skip to the bottom of the page - "Reich Minister of Food and Agriculture, Dr. Hugenberg; Reich Minister Of Labour, Seldte; Reich Minister of Justice" - no name is given, the post was filled two days later by Guertner - Reich Defence Minister von Blomberg; and the Reich Postmaster-General and Reich Minister for

Transportation, von Eltz Ruebenach."

In addition you will note that the defendant Goering was there as Reich Minister - he had no portfolio then - and as Reich Commissar for Aviation. Dr. Peregke was there as Reich Commissar for Procurement of Labour. Two State Secretaries were present: Dr. Lammers of the Reich Chancellery and Dr. Meissner of the Reich Presidential Chancellery.

THE PRESIDENT: In the copy I have, the defendant Goering appears as the Reich Minister for Aviation.

COL. STOREY: Yes, Sir. I mentioned that he appears as Reich Minister and as Reich Commissar for Aviation.

THE PRESIDENT: Oh, I see. I was reading from the first two pages of the document. You were reading from Page 4?

COLONEL STOREY: Yes.

THE PRESIDENT: Very well.

COLONEL STOREY: I am informed that the Ministry was created later, but he is named Reich Commissar for Aviation.

In addition the defendant Funk was present as Reich Press Chief, and the defendant von Papen was present as Deputy of the Reich Chancellor and Reich Commissar for the State of Prussia.

Not long after that date new ministries or departments were created, into which leading Nazi figures were placed. On 13th March, 1933, the Ministry of Popular Enlightenment and Propaganda was created. The decree setting it up appears in the 1933 Reichsgesetzblatt, Part I, Page 104, our document 2029-PS.

I assume that the Court will take judicial notice of the laws and decrees, as we have mentioned in the previous proceeding.

The late Goebbels was named as Reich Minister of Popular Enlightenment and Propaganda. On 5th May, 1933, the Ministry of Air (1933 Reichsgesetzblatt, Part I, Page 241, our Document 2089-PS). On 1st May, 1934, the Ministry of Education. I refer to 1934 Reichsgesetzblatt, Part I, Page 365, our Document 2078-PS. On 16th July, 1935, the Minister for Church Affairs (1935 Reichsgesetzblatt, Part I, Page 1029, our Document 2090-PS). The defendant Goering was made Air Minister; Bernhard Rust, Gauleiter of South Hanover, was named Education Minister and Hans Kerrl named Minister for Church Affairs.

Two ministries were added after the war started. On 17th March, 1940, the Ministry of Armaments and Munitions was established (1940 Reichsgesetzblatt, Part I, Page 513, our Document 2091-PS) The late Dr. Todt, a high Party official, was appointed to this post. The defendant Speer succeeded him. The name of this department was changed to "Armaments and War Production" in 1943 (1943 Reichsgesetzblatt, Part I, Page 529, our Document 2092-PS). On 17th July, 1941, when the seizure of the Eastern territories was in progress, the Ministry for the Occupied Eastern Territories as created. The decree appointing the defendant Rosenberg to the post of Minister of this department has already been received in evidence as Exhibit USA 319.

During the years 1933 to 1945 one ministry was dropped - that of Defence - which was later called "War." This took place in 1938 when on 4th February Hitler took over command of the whole Armed Forces. At the same time he created the "Chief of the Supreme Command of the Armed Forces," or, in other words, the Chief of the O.K.W. This was the defendant Keitel. The decree accomplishing this change is published in the 1938 Reichsgesetzblatt, Part I, at Page 111. It appears in our Document Book as 1915-PS, and I would like to quote a brief portion of that decree.

It begins at the bottom of the second paragraph:

"He - referring to the Chief of the Supreme Command of the Armed Forces - is an equal in rank to a Reich Minister."

"At the same time, the Supreme Command takes the responsibility for the affairs of the Reich Ministry of War; and, by my order, the Chief of the Supreme Command of the Armed Forces exercises the authority formerly belonging to the Reich Minister."

Another change in the composition of the Cabinet during the years in question should be noted. The post of Vice-Chancellor was never refilled after the defendant von Papen left on 30th July, 1934.

In addition to the heads of departments that I have outlined, the ordinary Cabinet also contained Reich Ministers without portfolio. Among these were the defendants Hans Frank; Seyss-Inquart, Schacht, after he left the Economics Ministry, and von Neurath, after he was replaced as Minister of the Interior. There were other positions that were also an integral part of the Cabinet. These were the Deputy of the Fuehrer, the defendant Hess, and later his successor, the Leader of the Party Chancellery, the defendant Bormann; the Chief of Staff of the S.A., Ernst Roehm, for 7 months prior to his assassination; the Chief of the Reich Chancellery, Lammers; and, as we have already mentioned, the Chief of the O.K.W., the defendant Keitel. These men had either the title of or the rank of Reich Minister. I have already read portions of the law creating the Chief of the O.K.W., where his importance in Cabinet affairs is delineated. The importance of the defendants Hess and Bormann will soon be expounded, while that of the Chief of the Reich Chancellery, Lammers, will also soon become self-evident.

But there were others, such as State Ministers acting as Reich Ministers. Only two persons fell within this category: the Chief of the Presidential Chancellery, Otto Meissner, and the State Minister of the Protectorate of Bohemia and Moravia, Karl Hans Frank. In addition, the Indictment names - as belonging to the ordinary Cabinet - "others entitled to take part in Cabinet meetings." Many governmental agencies were created by the Nazis between the years 1933 and 1945, but the peculiarity of such creations was that in most instances such new posts were given the right to participate in Cabinet meetings. Here the list is long but significant. Thus those entitled to take part in Cabinet meetings were the Commanders-in-chief of the Army and the Navy, the Reich Forest Master, the Inspector-General for Water and Power, the Inspector-General of German Roads, the Reich Labour Leader, the Reich Youth Leader, the Chief of the Foreign Organisation in the Foreign Office, the Reichsfuehrer S.S. and Chief of the German Police in the Reich Ministry of the Interior, the Prussian Finance Minister and the Cabinet Press Chief.

These, then, were the posts and some of the personnel in the ordinary Cabinet. They were all positions of such common knowledge and notoriety that the Tribunal can take judicial notice. Further, they all appear on the chart entitled "Organisation of the Reich Government," which was authenticated by the defendant Frick and is in evidence as Exhibit USA 3, which Mr. Albrecht introduced on the second day of the Trial. They are also capable of proof by laws and decrees published in the Reichsgesetzblatt and by notices in the semi-official monthly publication entitled 'Das Archiv,' which was edited by an official of the Ministry of Popular Enlightenment and Propaganda - all of which I submit are within the judicial purview of the Tribunal. The persons who held these posts in the ordinary Cabinet varied between the years 1933 and 1945.

Does your Honour wish to adjourn at 12:45?

THE PRESIDENT: Yes, perhaps we had better.

(A recess was taken until 1400 hours.)

COLONEL STOREY: If the Tribunal please, the persons who held these posts in the ordinary Cabinet varied between the years 1933 and 1945. Although it is not encumbent upon us to prove who they were, since the group and not the individuals are under consideration, nevertheless their names are already before this Tribunal in the original governmental chart, Exhibit USA 3. Since it will be of interest to the Tribunal to see what persons - and 17 of them are defendants here - held any particular positions in the Cabinet, a table has been prepared which lists all the departments and posts I have mentioned, and the encumbents thereof, during the years 1933 to 1945. The German equivalents of the titles are also shown and, with the permission of the Tribunal, I will now distribute this table to its members. Copies have likewise been filed in the defendants' Information Centre. The table also is annotated with citations to sources verifying the facts shown - all of which, however, were of common knowledge during the period in question.

Diverting from the text: This is simply prepared for the convenience of the Tribunal in connection with the studying of the briefs and the documents. As I said at the outset, the proof will show that there was only an artificial distinction between the ordinary Cabinet, the Secret Cabinet Council, and the Council of Ministers for the Defence of the Reich. This is evident in the first instance by the unity of personnel between the three subdivisions. Thus on 4th February, 1938, Hitler created the Secret Cabinet Council. If your Honours will refer to this big chart, you will notice under 1938 there is a red line pointing down to the Secret Cabinet Council created during that year. This decree appears in the 1938 Reichgesetzblatt, Part I, at Page 112. It is in our document book as Document 2031-PS, and I should like to quote from it.

THE PRESIDENT: It is not in Book X, is it?

COLONEL STOREY: Yes, Sir; 2031-PS.

THE PRESIDENT: 2031?

COLONEL STOREY: Yes, Sir; I beg your pardon, it is under the Laws and Decrees Section.

> "To advise me in conducting the foreign policy I am setting up a Secret Cabinet Council.
>
> As President of the Secret Cabinet Council I nominate: Reich Minister Baron von Neurath.
>
> As members of the Secret Cabinet Council I nominate: Reich Minister for Foreign Affairs Joachim von Ribbentrop; Prussian Prime Minister, Reich Minister of the Air, Supreme Commander of the Air Force, General Field Marshal Hermann Goering; the Fuehrer's Deputy, Reich Minister Rudolph Hess; Reich Minister for the Enlightenment of the People and Propaganda, Dr. Joseph Goebbels; Reich Minister and Chief of the Reich Chancellery, Dr. Lammers; Supreme Commander of the Army, General Walther von Brauchitsch; Supreme Commander of the Navy, Grand Admiral Dr. (honorary) Raeder; Chief of the Supreme Command of the Armed Forces, Lt.-Gen. Wilhelm Keitel."

It will be noted that every member was either a Reich Minister or, as in the case of the Army, Navy, and O.K.W. heads, had the rank and authority of a Reich Minister.

On 30th August, 1939, Hitler established the Council of Ministers for the Defence of the Reich, better known as the Ministerial Council. This was the so-called Cabinet. The decree appears in the 1933 Reichsgesetzblatt, Part I, at Page 1539. I now refer to Document 2018-PS of the Laws and Decrees, and I quote paragraph 1:

"1. From members of the Reich Defence Council shall be set up a standing Committee to be known as the Ministerial Council for the Defence of the Reich.

2. The standing members of the Ministerial Council for Defence of the Reich shall be:

General Field Marshal Goering as chairman;
The Fuehrer's Deputy - the defendant Hess;
Commissioner General for Reich Administration - the defendant Frick;
Commissioner General for Economy - the defendant Funk;
Reich Minister and Chief of the Reich Chancellery - Dr. Lammers;
Chief of the High Command of the Armed Forces - the defendant Keitel.

3. The chairman may draw on any other members of the Reich Defence Council including further personnel for advice."

Again it will be seen that all were also members of the ordinary Cabinet. But this use of the Cabinet as a manpower reservoir, from whom the trusted collaborators were selected, becomes particularly poignant when we consider the actions of the Nazi conspirators which were not published in the Reichsgesetzblatt, which were concealed from the world and which were part and parcel of their conspiracy to wage aggressive war. It will have been noted that the decree setting up the Ministerial Council, one to which I have just referred ,contained this sentence:

"Out of the Reich Defence Council a standing committee shall be set up as a
A Ministerial Council for Defence of the Reich."

There is evidence already before this Tribunal establishing the creation - by the Cabinet - on 4th April, 1933, of this really secret war-planning body. I refer the Tribunal to Exhibit USA 24, which appears in our document book as Document 2261-PS. That document contains the unpublished Reich Defence Law of 21st May, 1935. As to the membership of that Council when first created, I have here a copy of the second session of the working committee of those delegated for the Reich Defence, dated 22nd May, 1933, and signed by the defendant Keitel. It appears in our document book as EC- 177, Exhibit USA 390. The composition of the Reich Defence Council appears on Page 3 of the original and also on Page 3 of the translation:

THE PRESIDENT: I thought you were going to refer to 2261-PS.

COLONEL STOREY: If your Honour pleases, I just referred to it as being an exhibit already in evidence, and said that it was one of the unpublished Reich Defence Laws. That was the only purpose in referring to it.

THE PRESIDENT: You were referring to EC-177. Where is it?

COLONEL STOREY: In the document book, your Honour, just this side of the Laws and Decrees.

The quotation is from the top of Page 3 of the translation:

"Composition of the Reich Defence Council:
President: Reich Chancellor
Deputy: Reichswehr Minister
Permanent Members:
Minister of the Reichswehr
Minister for Foreign Affairs
Minister of the Interior
Minister of Finance
Minister of Economic Affairs

Minister for Public Enlightenment and Propaganda
Minister of Air Chief of the Army Command Staff
Chief of the Navy Command Staff

Depending on the case: the remaining members, further personnel, e.g. leading industrialists," etc.

All but the Chiefs of the Army and Navy Command Staff were, then, component parts of the ordinary Cabinet. The composition of his Defence Council was changed in 1938. I refer the Tribunal to Exhibit USA 36, which appears in our Document Book as No. 2194-PS. This contains the unpublished Reich Defence Law of 4th, paragraph 10, 4th September, 1938.

I now quote from paragraph 10, entitled "The Reich Defence Council," which is found at Page 4 of the copy of the law in the original, and I now quote from Page 6 of the English translation, the top of the page:

"2. The Fuehrer and Reich Chancellor is chairman in the R.V.R. His permanent deputy is General Field Marshal Goering. He has the right to call conferences of the R.V.R. Permanent members of the R.V.R. are:

Reich Minister of Air and Supreme Commander of the Air Force.
Supreme Commander of the Army,
Supreme Commander of the Navy,
Chief of the O.K.W.,
Deputy of the Fuehrer,
Reich Minister and Chief of the Reich Chancellery,
President of the Secret Cabinet Council,
General Plenipotentiary for the Reich Administration,
General Plenipotentiary for Economics,
Reich Minister for Foreign Affairs,
Reich Minister of the Interior,
Reich Finance Minister,
Reich Minister for Public Enlightenment and Propaganda,
President of the Reich Bank Directory,

The other Reich Ministers and the Reich Offices directly subordinate to the Fuehrer and the Reich Chancellor will be consulted, if necessary. From time to time additional personages may be summoned as the case demands."

THE PRESIDENT: Colonel Storey, it would help me, if you explained to me what conclusions you are asking us to draw from these documents.

COLONEL STOREY: If your Honour pleases, we were trying to show the progressive domination of the Reich Cabinet by the defendants and the members of this group, so that, as your Honour will see as we proceed, they could pass laws and decrees secretly by circulatory process or, in effect, at their will. I realise it is a little detailed, but we are trying to show the composition and how it was set up, and the conclusions will be drawn later.

By that time the Supreme Commanders of the Army and Navy had been given ministerial rank and authorised to participate in Cabinet meetings. I cite 1938 Reichsgesetzblatt, Part I, Page 215.

May we at this time call the attention of the Tribunal to two members of the Defence Council who also appear in the Ministerial Council under the same title: the Plenipotentiary for Administration and the Plenipotentiary for Economy? The former post was held by the defendant Frick, while the latter was first held by the defendant Schacht and then by the defendant Funk, who signed the decree in that capacity.

These facts are verified by the defendant Frick in Exhibit USA 3, which is the Nazi Governmental organisation chart previously referred to.

As we will show later, these two posts had many of the other ministries subordinated to them for war-planning aims and purposes. They, together with the Chief of the O.K.W., formed a powerful triumvirate that is known as the "3-Man College" shown in the three boxes down from 1935-1938, which figured prominently, as the proof will disclose, in the plans and preparations to wage aggressive war. The holders of these positions vere Cabinet members: the defendants Frick, Funk and Keitel.

This utilisation of the ordinary Cabinet as a supply centre fo other governmental agencies, and the cohesion between all of the groups, is perhaps quickly seen on the chart which is shown.

The points I have been making are illustrated on the chart. We are not offering this chart in evidence, although all facts thereon already have been proved or will be proved. The chart is also designed to depict (to the left of the line running down the right centre) the chronological development of the offshoots of the ordinary Cabinet. Thus in the main box entitled "Reich Cabinet" (which appears directly under Hitler) certain dates appear.

I think I will omit the part that describes those lines because it is self-evident.

The Ministerial Council for the Defence of the Reich was created in 1944; the Delegate for Total War Effort was Goebbels. These agencies were, next to Hitler, the important Nazi functionary bodies. In every case, as the chart shows, they were occupied by persons taken from the ordinary Cabinet. The arrow running from the Reich Defence Council to the Ministerial Council for the Defence of the Reich, is intended to reflect the fact shown previously, that the latter was formed out of the former. We will, for other points of this presentation, refer again to the chart, especially to that portion to the right which relates to ministries.

The unity, cohesion and inter-relationship of the subdivisions of the "Reichsregierung" was not the result of a co-mixture of personnel alone. It was also realised by the method in which it operated. The ordinary Cabinet consulted together both by meetings and through the so-called circulation procedure. Under this procedure, which was predominantly used when meetings were not held, drafts of laws prepared in the individual ministries were distributed to the other Cabinet members for approval or disapproval.

The man primarily responsible for the circulation of drafts of laws under this procedure was Dr. Lammers, the Leader and Chief of the Reich Chancellery. I have here an affidavit executed by him concerning that technical device, which we offer in evidence as Exhibit USA 391, Document 2999-PS. It is short and I should like to quote all of it:

"I, Hans Heinrich Lammers, being first duly sworn, depose and say:

I was Leader of the Reich Chancellery from 30th January, 1933, until the end of the war. In this capacity I circulated drafts of proposed laws and decrees, submitted to me by the Minister who had drafted the law or decree, to all members of the Reich Cabinet. A period of time was allowed for objections, after the expiration of which the law was considered as having been duly accepted by the various members of the Cabinet. This procedure continued throughout the entire war. It was followed also in the Council of Ministers for the Defence of the Reich.

Signed: 'Dr. Lammers' - and sworn to before Colonel Hinkel."

As an illustration of how the circulation procedure worked I have here a memorandum dated 9th August, 1943, which bears the facsimile signature of the defendant Frick and is addressed to the Reich Minister and Chief of the Reich Chancellery. Attached to the memorandum is a draft of the law in question and a carbon copy of a letter dated 22nd December, 1943, from the defendant Rosenberg to the Reich Minister of the Interior, containing his comments on the draft. I now offer Document 1701-PS as Exhibit USA 392, and I call your Honour's attention to the big red border around the enclosure. The quoted portion is from Page 1 of the translation and Page 1 of the original. Quoting:

"To the Reich Minister and Chief of the Reich Chancellery.

For the information of the other Reich Ministers. Subject: Law on the Treatment of Asocial Elements of the Community.

In addition to my letter of 19th March, 1942.

After the draft of the Law on the Treatment of Asocial Elements of the Community has been completely re-written, I am sending the enclosed new draft with the consent of the Reich Minister of Justice, Dr. Thierack, and ask that the law be approved in the circulatory manner. The necessary number of prints is attached."

The same procedure was followed in the Council of Ministers when that body was created. And the decrees of the Council of Ministers were also circulated to the members of the ordinary Cabinet.

I have here a carbon copy of a memorandum found in the files of the Reich Chancellery by the Allied Armies, and addressed to the members of the Council of Ministers, dated 17th September, 1939, and bearing the typed signature of Dr. Lammers. It is Document 1141-PS, Exhibit USA 393, from the English translation, the last paragraph just above Dr. Lammers' signature, I quote:

"Matters submitted to the Council of Ministers for the Reich Defence have heretofore been distributed only to the members of the Council. I have been requested by some of the Reich Ministers who are not permanent members of the Council to inform them of the drafts of the decrees which are being submitted to the Council, so as to enable them to check those drafts from the point of view of their respective offices. I shall follow this request so that all of the Reich Ministers will in future be informed of the drafts of decrees which are to be acted upon by the Council for the Reich Defence. I therefore request peermission to add forty-five additional copies of the drafts, as well as of the letters which usually contain the arguments for the drafts, to the folders submitted to the Council."

Von Stutterheim, who was an official of the Reich Chancellery, comments on this procedure, at Page 34 of a pamphlet entitled "The Reich Chancellery," which I now offer in evidence, Document 2231-PS ...

THE PRESIDENT: Colonel Storey, I do not understand what the importance of the last document is.

COLONEL STOREY: The last document, if your Honour pleases, is in further evidence of the approval of the laws, and of the passing of laws by a circulatory process.

THE PRESIDENT: We already have Dr. Lammers' affidavit.

COLONEL STOREY: It might be considered strictly cumulative, if that is what your Honour has in mind.

THE PRESIDENT: Well, if it is cumulative, we do not really want to hear it.

COLONEL STOREY: Yes, Sir; I will ask then that it be stricken from the record.

I really overlooked the fact that it was cumulative. Miss Boyd and Commander Kaplan tell me that the Document 2231-PS is probably also corroborative of the same process, and I will, therefore, not offer it.

I have already stated that for a time the Cabinet consulted together through actual meetings. The Council of Ministers did likewise, but those members of the Cabinet who were not already members of the Council also attended the meetings of the Ministerial Council. And when they did not attend in person they were usually represented by State Secretaries of the Ministries. We have here minutes of six meetings of the Council of Ministers as of 1st, 4th, 8th and 19th September, 1939, also of 16th October and 15th November, 1939. These original documents were found in the files of the Reich Chancellery. I offer them in evidence as Document 2852-PS, Exhibit USA 395. It will only be necessary to point out for our purposes at this time a few of the minutes. I call the attention of the Tribunal to the meeting held on 1st September, 1939, which is probably the first meeting since the Council was created on the 30th August, 1939; and I read from that document which shows who was present, beginning at the top of the English translation:

> "Present were the permanent members of the Council of Ministers for Defence of the Reich: The Chairman, General Field Marshal Goering; the Deputy of the Fuehrer, Hess;" - for some unknown reason a line appears through the name Hess - "the Plenipotentiary for Reich Administration, Dr. Frick; the Plenipotentiary for Economy, Funk; the Reich Minister and Chief of the Reich Chancellery, Dr. Lammers; and the Chief of the High Command of the Armed Forces, Keitel, represented by Major-General Thomas."

These were the regular members of the Council. Also present were the Reich Minister for Food and Agriculture, Darre; and seven State Secretaries: Koerner, Neumann, Stuckart, Posse, Landfried, Backe, Syrup. These State Secretaries were from the several ministries or other top Reich authorities, as, for example, to name a few: Koerner was the deputy of the defendant Goering in the Four Year Plan; Stuckart was in the Ministry of the Interior; Landfried was in the Ministry of Economics; Syrup was in the Ministry of Labour. These later positions appear on the government chart which is already in evidence. Now the meeting of the Council, I will omit that one.

And then there came the names of nine State Secretaries...

THE TRIBUNAL (Mr. BIDDLE): Colonel Storey, the last document shows only that certain members of the Cabinet were at the Cabinet meeting.

COLONEL STOREY: Yes, it shows no more than that. I am going on a little farther, to show that the S.S. Gruppenfuehrer was present also, and other people were present.

THE TRIBUNAL (Mr. BIDDLE): What does that show?

COLONEL STOREY: In other words, that they called in these subordinate people, as in the meeting of the ministers.

THE TRIBUNAL (Mr. BIDDLE): What would that show?

COLONEL STOREY: Well, it just shows the permeation of the Party and the subordinate agencies, showing they could use the Reich Cabinet for whatever purpose they wanted and to devise laws any way they wanted. They called in these people, in subordinate positions, to sit with them when they were passing Cabinet measures. I can also call your Honour's attention to the Ministerial Council for Defence. The Cabinet was supposed to be a Ministerial-rank Cabinet meeting, and as I just started to show, they called in the S.S. Gruppenfuehrer Heydrich to this meeting.

THE PRESIDENT: There could be no doubt, could there, that there was a Reich

Cabinet?

COLONEL STOREY: No, Sir.

THE PRESIDENT: And that the Reich Cabinet made decrees by this circulatory method? There is no doubt about that.

COLONEL STOREY: That is right, Sir.

THE PRESIDENT: What does this document have to do with that?

COLONEL STOREY: It shows who participated, and how they were there in their Party rank; and I will omit the rest, with reference to these other individuals.

THE PRESIDENT: But we have had ample evidence before, haven't we, as to who formed the Reich Cabinet?

COLONEL STOREY: Yes. Well, I will omit the rest with reference to other people who participated, and just skip over to Page 23 for the record. Before leaving these minutes, and as indicative of the activities of the Reichsregierung, I would like to call the attention of the Tribunal to some of the decrees passed and minutes discussed at these meetings. At the first meeting of 1st September, 1939, fourteen decrees were ratified by the Council. Of this group I call the attention of the Tribunal to Decree No. 6, appearing on Page 2 of the translation, and I quote:

THE PRESIDENT: I do not think you gave us the number.

COLONEL STOREY: I beg your pardon, Sir. It is the Reichsgesetzblatt No. 1, Page 1681, of which we ask the Tribunal to take judicial notice. That decree was about the organisation of the administration and about the German Security Police in the Protectorate of Bohemia and Moravia. That appears in the translation of 2852-PS. Another one that was passed is dated 19th September, 1938, on Page 6 of the translation, and I quote from the bottom of Page 6:

"The Chairman of the Council, General Field Marshal Goering, made comments regarding the structure of civil administration in the occupied Polish territory. He expressed his intentions regarding the economic evacuation measures in this territory. Then the questions of decreasing wages, and the question of working hours and the support of members of families of drafted workers were discussed."

There are a number of miscellaneous points of discussion appearing, and in paragraph 2 of the minutes I quote the following, as it appears on Page 7:

"The chairman directed that all members of the Council should regularly receive the situation reports of the Reichsfuehrer S.S. Then the question of the population of the future Polish Protectorate was discussed and the housing of Jews living in Germany."

Finally, I call the attention of the Tribunal to the minutes of the meeting of 15th November, 1939, Page 10 of the translation, where, among other things, the treatment of Polish prisoners of war was also discussed.

We submit that this document not only establishes the close working union between agencies of the State and Party, especially with the notorious S.S., but also tends to establish, as charged in the Indictment, that the Reichsregierung was responsible for the policies adopted and put into effect by the government, including those which comprehended and involved the commission of crimes referred to in the Indictment. But a mere working alliance would be meaningless unless there were power. And the Reichsregierung had the power. Short of Hitler himself, it had practically all the power a government can exercise. The prosecution has already offered evidence on how Hitler's Cabinet and the other Nazi conspirators secured the passage by the Reichstag of the "Law for the Protection of the People and the Reich" of 24th

March, 1933, which has been previously referred to in our Document 2001-PS, and which vested the Cabinet with legislative powers even to the extent of deviating from previously existing constitutional law; how such powers were retained even after the members of the Cabinet were changed; and how the several States, provinces, and municipalities, which had formerly exercised semi-autonomous powers, were transformed into the administrative organs of the Central Government. The ordinary Cabinet emerged all-powerful from this rapid succession of events. The words of the defendant Frick are eloquent upon that achievement. I have an article of his which he wrote for the 1935 National Socialist Year Book, Document 2380-PS, which I offer in evidence as Exhibit USA 396, and I quote from Page 213 of the original, and it is on Page 1 of the English translation, the second paragraph:

"The relationship between the Reich and the States has been put on an entirely new basis never known in the history of the German people. It gives to the Reich Cabinet (Reichsregierung) unlimited power, it even makes it its duty to build a completely unified leadership and administration of the Reich. From now on there is only one national authority: that of the Reich. From now on, there is only one national authority: that of the Reich. Thus, the German Reich has become a unified State, and the entire administration in the States is carried out only by order of, or in the name of, the Reich. The State borders are now only administrative-technical boundaries, but no longer boundaries of sovereignty.

In calm determination, the Reich Cabinet (Reichsregierung) realises step by step, supported by the confidence of the entire German people, the great longing of the Nation: the creation of the unified National Socialist German State."

THE PRESIDENT: Colonel Storey.

COLONEL STOREY: Yes, Sir?

THE PRESIDENT: That document seems to me to be merely cumulative. You have established, and other counsel on behalf of the United States have established, that the Reich Ministers had power to make laws, and the question is whether you have given any evidence as to the criminal nature of the Reich Cabinet.

COLONEL STOREY: If your Honour pleases, again it was included for the purpose of connecting one of the defendants here-

THE PRESIDENT: What I was pointing out was that it was merely cumulative.

COLONEL STOREY: Yes, all right, Sir. It may be strictly cumulative. I will omit the next reference, which will probably also be cumulative and turn over to -

THE PRESIDENT: The same document, you mean?

COLONEL STOREY: No, Sir. There is another document that I was going to offer, No. 2849. There is a quotation from another book; it probably bears on the same point. I will omit it also. The next is a reference to the Ministerial Council's being given legislative power. I do not believe this has been introduced before, that the Council itself was given legislative powers. That is in Article 2 of the decree of 30th August, 1939, Document 2018-PS; the ordinary Cabinet continued to legislate throughout the war.

Obviously, because of the fusion of personnel between the Ministerial Council and the ordinary Cabinet, questions were bound to arise as to what form should lend its name to a particular law. Thus Dr. Lammers, the Chief of the Reich Chancellery and a member of both agencies, wrote a letter on 14th June, 1942, to the Plenipotentiary for Reich Administration about this question.

This next document, if the Court please, it may not be necessary to read. It generally shows that both agencies continued to legislate side by side, and it would really be cumulative evidence. There were others that possessed legislative powers, besides the ones I have mentioned. Hitler, of course, had legislative power. Goering, as Deputy of the Four Year Plan, could and did issue decrees that had the effect of law, and the Cabinet delegated power to issue laws which could deviate from the existing ones, to the Plenipotentiaries of Economy and Administration and the Chief of the O.K.W., and to the so-called "3-Man College," the "3-Man College" having authority to legislate. This was done in the war-planning law, the Secret Defence Law of 1938, Document 2194-PS, Exhibit USA 36. These three officials, Frick, Funk and Keitel, however, were, as we have proved, also members of the Council of Ministers, as well as being part of the ordinary Cabinet.

It can, therefore, be readily said, in the language of the Indictment, that the Reichsregierung possessed legislative powers of a very high order in the system of German government; and that they exercised such powers has in part already been demonstrated. I refer to that merely to show that it was a Secret Cabinet law - without quoting - that the executive and administrative powers of the Reich were concentrated in the Central Government primarily as the result of two basic Nazi laws that reduced the separate States (called Laender) to mere geographical divisions. If your Honour pleases, these laws are cited, and I believe it would be cumulative evidence if I undertook to chronicle them. I pass to the part at the bottom of Page 29.

> There were other steps taken towards centralisations. Let us see what powers the ordinary Cabinet would wield as a result. We have here a publication of 1934, which was edited by Dr. Wilhelm Stuckart, State Secretary in the Reich Ministry of the Interior, and Dr. Harry V. Rosen v. Hoewel, another official with the title of "Oberregierungsrat," in the Reich Ministry of the Interior. It is entitled "Administrative Law," Document 2959-PS, and I offer it as Exhibit USA 399. It details the powers and functions of all the ministers of the ordinary Cabinet, from which I will select but a few to illustrate the extent of control vested in the Reichsregierung. The quotation is from Page 2 of the translation and Page 66 of the original. "The Reich Ministers. There are at present twenty-seven Reich Ministers, namely...."

May I say that the only purpose in offering this is to show over what each Minister had jurisdiction and to what his authority extended; for example, the Reich Minister for Foreign Affairs - it details what he handles. The Reich Minister of the Interior follows in detail on the matters entrusted to his jurisdiction, and so on.

THE PRESIDENT: Colonel Storey, may I ask you what has that to do with the criminality of the Reich Cabinet?

COLONEL STOREY: The point, as I see it, again though it may be cumulative, your Honour, is to show how these defendants, and the others with them, formed a Cabinet, formed the Ministries, formed these councils, so that they could give semblance of legality to any action they determined to take, whether they were in session or not, and according to the dictates of the respective Ministers, in other words, showing a complete domination.

THE PRESIDENT: I should have thought that was amply shown already.

COLONEL STOREY:

> "In view of the anticipated lifting of the ban for Party membership, the Fuehrer, as the first step in this regard, personally carried out the enlistment into the Party of the members of the Cabinet who so far had not belonged to it; and he handed them simultaneously the Gold Party Badge, the supreme

badge of honour of the Party.

In addition, the Fuehrer awarded the Gold Party Badge to Generaloberst Freiherr von Fritsch; Generaladmiral D. h. c. Raeder; the Prussian Minister of Finance, Professor Popitz; and the Secretary of State and Chief of the Presidential Chancellery, Dr. Meissner.

The Fuehrer also honoured with the Gold Party Badge the Party Members State Secretary Dr. Lammers, State Secretary Funk, State Secretary Koerner, and State Secretary General of the Air Force Milch."

It was thus possible to refuse the Party membership thus conferred. Only one man did this, however, von Eltz- Ruebenach, who was the Minister of Postal Services and Transportation at the time. I have here an original letter, dated 30th January, 1937, from von Eltz-Ruebenach to Hitler, and it is in his own personal handwriting. It is Document 1534-PS which I desire to offer as Exhibit USA 402, and I quote it in toto:

"Berlin (W8), 30th January, 1937.
Wilhelm Street, 79.

My Fuehrer:

I thank you for the confidence you have placed in me during the four years of your leadership and for the honour you do me in offering to admit me into the Party.

My conscience forbids me, however, to accept this offer. I believe in the principles of positive Christianity and must remain faithful to my Lord and to myself. Party membership would mean that I should have to face, without contradiction, the steadily increasing attacks by Party officers on the Christian confessions and on those who want to remain faithful to their religious convictions.

This decision has been infinitely difficult for me, for never in my life have I performed my duty with greater joy and satisfaction than under your wise State leadership.

I ask to be permitted to resign.

With German greetings,

Yours very obediently,

(Signed) BARON VON ELTZ."

But the Nazis did not wait until all members of the Cabinet...

THE PRESIDENT: Was Baron von Eltz permitted to resign?

COLONEL STOREY: As I understand, your Honour, every one of them was a member except this one, and he declined and offered his resignation which was accepted. The Nazis did not wait until all members of the Cabinet were Party members. Shortly after it came to power, it quickly assured themselves of active participation in the work of the Cabinet. On 1st. December, 1933, the Cabinet passed a law securing the unity of Party and State. That has been introduced previously and I will not refer to it any more. It is referred to here as our Document 1395.

THE PRESIDENT: Why is Baron von Eltz shown as a member of the Cabinet in 1938?

COLONEL STOREY: Your Honour, please, the "1938" simply refers to the time the Secret Cabinet Council was created. It does not have to do with when any of these people came to the Cabinet.

THE PRESIDENT: I see.

COLONEL STOREY: In other words, all these arrows show that these different agencies were created during those years.

THE PRESIDENT: Yes, I follow it.

COLONEL STOREY: I say, for your Honour' information, that in this list of all of the Cabinet members and the members of the Reichsregierung from 1933 his name is shown in the list that we handed to your Honour.

THE PRESIDENT: Up to 1937?

COLONEL STOREY: No, Sir from 1933 right up to 1945 his name is listed. If your Honour will recall, we handed in a separate list and it does contain the Baron's name, with the authority of his appointment, etc..

THE PRESIDENT: You mean, that is a mistake?

COLONEL STOREY: No, Sir; it is not a mistake.

THE PRESIDENT: He did not resign?

COLONEL STOREY: He did resign, but your Honour asked if his name was shown up here and I said that in the separate list showing the list of all members of the Reichsregierung, from 1933 to 1945, the Baron's name was included and the proper reference is made in this separate list for your Honour's guidance.

I have here a copy of an unpublished decree signed by Hitler, dated 27th July, 1934. It is Document D-138, Exhibit USA 403, and it is in the section headed "Laws and Decrees," if your Honour pleases, and I offer it in evidence. This is a decree of Adolf Hitler:

> "I decree that the Deputy of the Fuehrer, Reich Minister Hess, will have the capacity of a participating Reich Minister in connection with the preparation of drafts for laws in all Reich administrative spheres. All legislative work is to be sent to him when it is received by the other Reich Minister concerned. This also applies in cases where no one else participates except the Reich Minister making the draft. Reich Minister Hess will be given the opportunity to comment on drafts suggested by experts.
>
> This order will apply in the same sense to legislative ordinances. The Deputy of the Fuehrer in his capacity of Reich Minister can send as representative an expert on his staff. These experts are entitled to make statements to the Reich Ministers on his behalf."
>
> (Signed) Adolf Hitler."

The defendant Hess himself has some pertinent comment to make regarding his right of participation on behalf of the Party. And I now offer in evidence Document D-139, Exhibit USA 404. This is an original letter signed by Rudolf Hess and is dated the 9th October, 1934, on the stationery of the N.S.D.A.P., and it is addressed to the Reich Minister of Public Enlightenment and Propaganda.

I now quote the entire document:

> "By a decree of the Fuehrer dated 27th July, 1934, I have been granted the right to participate in the legislation of the Reich as regards both formal laws and legal ordinances. This right must not be rendered illusory by the fact that I am sent the drafts of laws and decrees so late, and am then given a limited time, so that it becomes impossible for me to deal with the material concerned during the given time. I must point out that my participation means taking into account the opinion of the N.S.D.A.P. as such, and that in the case of the majority of drafts of laws and decrees, I consult with the appropriate departments of the Party before making my comment. Only by proceeding in this manner can I do justice to the wish of the Fuehrer as expressed in the decree of the Fuehrer of 27th July, 1934. I must therefore ask the Reich

Ministers to arrange that drafts of laws and decrees reach me in sufficient time. Failing this, I would be obliged in future to refuse my agreement to such drafts from the beginning and without giving the matter detailed attention - in all cases where I am not given a sufficiently long period for dealing with them.

Heil. (Signed) R. Hess."

A handwritten note appears attached to the letter. I quote from Page 2 of the translation:

"Berlin, 17th October, 1935.

1. The identical letter seems to have been addressed to all Reich Ministers. In our special field the decree of 27th July, 1934, has hardly become applicable so far. A reply does not seem called for.

2. File in File 7B.

(Signed) 'R.'"

The participating powers of Hess were later broadened. I now refer to Document D-140, Exhibit USA 405; and it is a letter dated the 12th April, 1938, from Dr. Lammers to the Reich Ministers. I offer it in evidence and quote from the English translation, Paragraph 3:

"The Deputy of the Fuehrer will also have participation where the Reich Ministers give their agreement to the State Laws and legislative ordinances of States, under paragraph 3 of the first decree concerning reconstruction of the Reich of 2nd February, 1934 (Reich Law Gazette I, 81). Where the Reich Ministers have already, at an earlier date been engaged in the preparation of such laws or legislative ordinances, or have participated in such preparation, the Deputy of the Fuehrer likewise becomes participating Reich Minister. Laws and legislative decrees of the Austrian State are equally affected hereby."

(Signed) Dr. Lammers."

THE PRESIDENT: Colonel Storey, may I ask you what those three documents are supposed to prove?

COLONEL STOREY: In the first place, your Honour, the one I have just referred to shows that they passed laws over conquered territory; that one related to Austria. The one signed by Hess, just before, gives him almost unlimited power as regards both formal and legal ordinances and over administrative districts; and in addition, I think, your Honour, the most important point is that Hess says: "You must send them to me long enough in advance so that I may consult with the Party and the appropriate Party members and get their reaction."

THE PRESIDENT: Is that relied upon as evidence of criminality, that he took the trouble to find out what other Ministers thought?

COLONEL STOREY: I think it is a part of the general conspiracy showing the domination of Party and State by the Nazi Party and particularly the Leadership Corps.

THE PRESIDENT: I thought I had already said that it appeared to us - and I think I speak on behalf of all the Tribunal - - that that matter had been amply proved and that we wished you to turn to the question of criminality of the Reich Cabinet.

COLONEL STOREY: May I assume, your Honour, that we need to offer no further proof that the Party itself had to do with the making of these laws as suggested by the defendant Hess? I thought it was incumbent upon us to prove that the Party dominated this Cabinet, and particularly the Leadership Corps.

THE PRESIDENT: You are dealing now with the Reich Cabinet and I think the Tribunal is satisfied that the Reich Cabinet had full powers to make laws.

COLONEL STOREY: I think that we go a little step further and undertake to show, if we have not already shown, that the way and manner in which they did it by consulting the Party was criminal. Now, I have some other laws to cite here in corroboration of that, but, if the Tribunal is satisfied, I do not see any use in citing them.

THE PRESIDENT: I do not think the Tribunal would imagine that they made laws without consulting somebody. Perhaps it would be a convenient time to break off for ten minutes.

(A recess was taken.)

COLONEL STOREY: If your Honour pleases, when we adjourned we were speaking of these laws that had been passed, and certainly I do not want to offer any redundant evidence or any that is not necessary. I therefore am briefly referring to the laws which we propose to offer now.

The Party, as your Honour will recall, had 25 fundamental points which they had set out to achieve, as introduced in evidence yesterday. Those points, your Honour will recall, related to everything from the abrogation of the Treaties of Versailles and St. Germain to the obtaining of greater living space, and so forth.

Now, we propose to cite various decrees and laws passed by this Cabinet carrying into effect what we contend were the criminal purposes of the Party, and to show that the Reich Cabinet was asked by the Party to give semblance of legality to their alleged criminal purposes. That is the only reason we expect to chronicle or to mention the laws that were passed in pursuance thereof. And I shall proceed, as your Honour suggests, merely to list a group of the laws that seek to establish the co-called 25 points of the Nazi Party. Perhaps, with your Honour's permission, I will just refer to a few of them as being indicative of the type of laws that were passed to further their 25 points.

For example, in implementation of this point, the Nazi Cabinet enacted, among others, the following laws:

The law of 3rd February, 1938, concerning the obligation of German citizens in foreign countries to register. That is cited in the Reichsgesetzblatt.

The law of the 13th March, 1938, relating to the reunion of Austria with Germany-

THE PRESIDENT: Were these were all passed by the Reich Cabinet?

COLONEL STOREY: Yes.

THE PRESIDENT: Well, are you not going to cite the laws?

COLONEL STOREY: Yes, but I was going to show them as illustrative; that is the 1938 Reichsgesetzblatt, Part I, Page 237.

The law of 21st November, 1938, for the re-integration of the German Sudetenland with Germany, 1938, Reichsgesetzblatt, Part I, Page 1641.

The incorporation of Memelland into Germany, 23rd March, 1939, Part I, Page 559, of the 1939 Reichsgesetzblatt.

With reference to Point 2...

THE PRESIDENT: Would you give me the place where the 25 points are set out? Have you got a reference to that?

COLONEL STOREY: Yes, Sir; it appears in Document 1708-PS, in document book A.

THE PRESIDENT: Thank you.

COLONEL STOREY: I believe we referred to it yesterday.

THE PRESIDENT: That is sufficient.

COLONEL STOREY: Yes, Sir.

Now, as an illustration, Point 2 of that Party platform - which, as your Honour will recall, demanded the cancellation of the Treaties of Versailles and St. Germain - the following acts of the Cabinet in support of this part of the programme may be mentioned:

Proclamation of 14th October, 1933, to the German people concerning Germany's withdrawal from the League of Nations and the Disarmament Conference, 1933 Reichsgesetzblatt, Part I, Page 730.

Law of 16th March, 1935, for the establishment of the Wehrmacht and compulsory military service, 1935 Reichsgesetzblatt, Part I, Pages 369 to 375.

Now, with reference to Point 4 of the Party platform, which said:

"Only those who are members of the 'Volk' can be citizens. Only those who are of German blood, without regard to religion, can be members of the 'Volk.' No Jew, therefore, can be a member of the 'Volk.'"

That is Point 4.

Among other Cabinet laws, this point was implemented by the law of 15th July, 1933, for the recall of naturalisation and deprivation of citizenship of these people, 1933 Reichsgesetzblatt, Part I, Page 480.

The law of 7th April, 1933, which said that persons of non- Aryan descent could not practise law, 1933 Reichsgesetzblatt, Part I, Page 188.

The law of 25th April, 1933, restricting the number of non- Aryans in schools and higher institutions of learning, 1933 Reichsgesetzblatt, Part I, Page 225.

The law of 29th September, 1933, excluding persons of Jewish blood from the peasantry, 1933 Reichsgesetzblatt, Part I, Page 685.

Another one, 19th March, 1937, excluded Jews from the Reich Labour Service , 1937 Reichsgesetzblatt, Part I, Page 325.

There is another one of 6th July, 1938, prohibiting Jews from participating in six different types of businesses, 1938 Reichsgesetzblatt, Part I, Page 823.

Point 23 of that Party platform proclaimed,:

"We demand legislative action against conscious political lies and their broadcasting through the Press."

To carry out this point I give a few of the Cabinet laws that were passed. One of 22nd September, 1933, which established the Reich Culture Chamber, 1933 Reichsgesetzblatt, Part I, Page 661.

One concerning editors, of 4th October, 1933, 1933 Reichsgesetzblatt, Part I, Page 713.

Another one with reference to restrictions as to the use of the theater, on 15th May, 1934.

THE PRESIDENT: The use of what?

COLONEL STOREY: Theatre shows. 1934 Reichsgesetzblatt, Part I, Page 411.

THE PRESIDENT: What is the date of that?

COLONEL STOREY: 15th May, 1934.

Now, passing from those illustrative laws, the ordinary Cabinet did, in fact, enact most of the legislation which set the stage for and put into execution the Nazi Conspiracy described under Count One of the Indictment. Many of these laws have been referred to previously by the prosecution. All the laws to which I shall refer or have referred to were enacted specifically in the name of the Cabinet. A typical introductory paragraph reads, and I quote:

"The Reich Cabinet has enacted the following law which is hereby promulgated." In other words, that shows it is a Cabinet law.

THE PRESIDENT: That applies to all the ones you have just given us?

COLONEL STOREY: Yes, Sir. That is a typical heading.

In connection with the acquiring of control of Germany under Count One of the Indictment, I refer to some of the following laws.

Here is a law of the 14th July, 1933, against the establishment of new parties. I believe I referred to that yesterday. That is 1933 Reichsgesetzblatt, Part I, Page 479.

Another of 14th July, 1933, providing for the confiscation of property of Social Democrats and others, 1933 Reichsgesetzblatt, Part I, Page 479.

I have already referred to that law of 1st December, 1933, which consolidated the Party and State, which is found in 1933 Reichsgesetzblatt, Part I, Page 1,016. In the course of consolidating the control of Germany these laws were enacted, and I give a few illustrations:

21st March, 1933, creating special courts. That is in 1933 Reichsgesetzblatt, Part I, Page 136. Law of 31st March, 1933, for the integration of all the States into the Reich, 1933 Reichsgesetzblatt, Part I, Page 153.

THE PRESIDENT: Will you repeat that, integration of what?

COLONEL STOREY: Integration of the States - that is the separate States into the Greater Reich.

Here is one of 30th June, 1933, eliminating non-Aryan civil servants or civil servants married to non-Aryans, 1933 Reichsgesetzblatt, Part I, Page 433.

The law of the 24th April, 1934, creating the People's Court, 1934 Reichsgesetzblatt, Part I, Page 341. And that was the same Court your Honour saw functioning in one of the films exhibited last week.

The law of 1st August, 1934, uniting the office of President and Chancellor, 1934 Reichsgesetzblatt, Part I, Page 747.

I am not introducing all of them or referring to all of them.

Here is a law of the 18th March, 1938, that provides for the submission of one list of candidates to the electorate of the entire Reich, 1938 Reichsgesetzblatt, Part I, Page 258.

Nazi extermination of political internal resistance in Germany through the purge of their political opponents and through acts of terror, which are set forth in Paragraph III(d) 3(b) of Count One, was facilitated or legalised by the following Cabinet laws, translations being found in Document Book F, which has previously been submitted. I will just refer to a few of these as they are translated in that book.

Here is one of 14th July, 1933, that prohibits the establishment of new parties and contains a penal clause. That is found in 1933 Reichsgesetzblatt, Part I, Page 479. Here is one of 20th December.

THE PRESIDENT: You have already given that one.

COLONEL STOREY: I believe so, yes, Sir.

Here is a law of the 3rd July, 1934, concerning measures for emergency defence of the State, and which legalised their own purge. That is in 1934 Reichsgesetzblatt, Part I, Page 529.

Law of 20th December, 1934, on treacherous acts against the State and Party and for protection of the Party uniforms, 1934 Reichsgesetzblatt, Part I, Page 1269.

Here is one of 24th April, 1934, that makes the creation of a new or continuance of existing political Parties an act of treason, 1934 Reichsgesetzblatt, Part I, Page 341.

Here is one of the 28th June, 1935, that changes the Penal Code, 1935 Reichsgesetzblatt, Part I, Page 839.

Here is the last one I will mention: 16th September, 1939, permitting second prosecution of an acquitted person before a Special Court, the members of which were named by Hitler, 1939 Reichsgesetzblatt, Part I, Page 1841.

Now, next are some laws that related to the extermination of the trade unions, which I have already cited, and they are in Document Book G. I will not refer to them. Then the laws abolishing collective bargaining. I have referred to those; I will pass them.

In fact, even the infamous Nuremberg Laws of 15th September, 1935, although technically passed by the Reichstag, were nevertheless worked out by the Ministry of the Interior. This is verified by a work of Dr. Franz A. Medicus, entitled "Ministerialdirigent", published in 1940. It is Document 2960-PS, Exhibit USA 406. I would like to refer to the paragraphs at Page 62 of the original publication, and translated in our Document 2960-PS, beginning the first paragraph:

> "The work of the Reich Ministry of Interior forms the basis for the three 'Nuremberg Laws' passed by a resolution of the Reichstag on the occasion of the Reich Party Meeting of Freedom. The 'Reich Citizenship Law' as well as the 'Law for the Protection of German Blood and German Honour' opened extensive tasks for the Ministry of the Interior not only in the field of administration. The same applies to the 'Reich Flag Law' that gives the foundation for the complete reorganisation of the use of the flag."

A few decrees of the Council of Ministers which similarly supplied the legal basis for the criminal acts and conduct of the conspirators, about which the Tribunal has already heard and will hear more, relate to those of 5th August, 1940, which imposed a discriminatory tax on Polish workers in Germany; and that is in 1940 Reichsgesetzblatt, Part I, Page 1077.

Also the law of 4th December, 1941, which imposed penal measures against the Jews and the Poles in the Eastern Occupied Countries; 1941 Reichsgesetzblatt, Part I, Page 759.

The last one was concerning the employment of Eastern Workers, which I referred to this morning.

Almost immediately upon Hitler's coming into power, the Cabinet commenced to implement the Nazi conspiracy to wage aggressive war. Three of the documents that establish this point have already been introduced in evidence. They are EC-177, 2261-PS, and 2194-PS, respectively. Document EC-177, which is Exhibit USA 390, is a long copy of the minutes, and I beg the indulgence of the Tribunal for referring to it again, EC-177...

THE PRESIDENT: Is it in this book?

COLONEL STOREY: Yes, Sir, EC-177. Your Honour, I did not intend to quote from that. I am simply referring to it as being the minutes of the second session of the working committee of the delegates for Reich Defence and being signed by the defendant Keitel.

Document 2261 consists of a letter dated the 24th June, 1935, 2261-PS. That transmits a copy of a secret, unpublished Defence Law of 21st May, 1935, and also a copy of a decision of the Reich Cabinet of the same date in the Council for Defence of the Reich. These have been previously introduced, but they are illustrative laws passed by this Cabinet.

Document 2194 also transmits a copy of the secret, unpublished Reich Defence Law, 4th September, 1938.

I will skip down to the laws passed by the Reich Defence Council, on Page 50, for the record.

The Reich Defence Council was a creation of the Cabinet. On 4th April, 1933, it was decided to form that agency. The decision of the Cabinet, attached to Document

2261-PS, which is Exhibit USA 24, Page 4 of the translation, Paragraph 1, proves that fact. The two secret laws contained in Document 2261, as well as in document 2194, were passed by the Cabinet; nor was this a case of one group setting up an entirely distinct group to do its dirty work. The Cabinet put itself into the picture. This might have been a difficult task to accomplish before the Nazis assumed power - but with the Nazis in control, things could move swiftly, and I now refer again to Document EC-177, but I will not undertake to quote from that (although the quotation is set out here).

There is only one point in that connection which would not be cumulative. It is Page 5 of the translation and Page 8 of that original of EC-177, on the question of security and secrecy, that I think would be pertinent to the criminal nature. I quote:-

"Question has been brought up by the Reich Ministries. The secrecy of all Reich Defence work has to be maintained very carefully. Communications with the outside by messenger service only has been settled already with the Post Office, Finance Ministry, Prussian Ministry of the Interior and the Reichswehr Ministry. Main principle of security: no document must be lost, since otherwise enemy propaganda would make use of it. Matters communicated orally cannot be proved; they can be denied by us in Geneva. Therefore the Reichswehr Ministry has worked out security directives for the Reich Ministries and the Prussian Ministry of the Interior."

I will omit the next reference. I believe I will pass over to the affidavit of defendant Frick, on Page 60.

THE PRESIDENT: What is that?

COLONEL STOREY: It is, if your Honour pleases, Document 2986- PS. Exhibit USA 409, the original affidavit, signed by the defendant Frick. I believe defendant Frick sums up pretty well how the work was carried on.

"I, Wilhelm Frick, being first duly sworn, depose and say: I was Plenipotentiary for Reich Administration from the time when this office was created until 20th August, 1943. Heinrich Himmler was my deputy in this capacity. Before the outbreak of the war my task as Plenipotentiary for Reich Administration was the preparation of organisation in the event of war, such as, for instance, the appointment of liaison men in the different Ministries who would keep in touch with me. As Plenipotentiary General for Reich Administration I, together with the Plenipotentiary for Economy and the O.K.W., formed what was called a '3-Man College.' We were also members of the Reich Defence Council, which was to plan preparations and decrees in case of war, which later were published by the Ministerial Council for the Defence of the Reich. Since, as soon as the war started, everything had to be done speedily and there would have been no time for planning, such measures and decrees were prepared in advance, in case of war. All one then had to do was to pull out of the drawer the war orders that had been prepared. Later on, after the outbreak of the war, these decrees were enacted by the Ministerial Council for Defence of the Reich."

Signed and sworn to by Dr. Wilhelm Frick, on the 19th November, 1945."

To sum up this particular phase of the proof, the Cabinet by its own decision and its own laws created a large war- planning body - the Reich Defence Council - the members of which were taken from the Cabinet. Within the Council they set up a small working committee, again composed of Cabinet members and certain defence officials, a majority of whom were appointed from the Cabinet members, and to streamline the action, they placed all of its Ministries - except Air, Propaganda, and

Foreign Affairs - into the Groups headed respectively by the Plenipotentiaries for Economy and Administration and the O.K.W., and everything was organised in and for the greatest of secrecy.

That is this "3-Man College."

Now, in conclusion, if your Honour pleases, I would like at this time to summarise briefly the proof concerning the Reichsregierung.

From 1933 to the end of the war, the Reichsregierung comprised the dominant body of influence and leadership below Hitler in the Nazi Government. The three sub-divisions were included in the term Reichsregierung in the Indictment: the ordinary Cabinet, the Secret Cabinet Council, and the Council of Ministers for Defence of the Reich. Yet, in reality, there existed only an artificial, illusory boundary between the three.

The predominant sub-division was, of course, the ordinary Cabinet, which was commonly referred to as the Reichsregierung.

In it were the leading political and military figures in the Nazi Government; 17 of the 22 defendants before this Tribunal were integral parts of the ordinary Cabinet.

I should like now to name these defendants and to indicate the positions they held in the Reichsregierung:-

MARTIN BORMANN, Leader of the Party Chancellery.

KARL DOENITZ, Commander-in-Chief of the Navy.

HANS FRANK, Reich Minister without Portfolio.

WILHELM FRICK, Minister of the Interior, Plenipotentiary for Reich Administration, Reich Minister without Portfolio.

WALTER FUNK, Minster of Economics, Plenipotentiary for Economy.

HERMANN GOERING, Minister for Air, Reich Forest Master.

RUDOLF HESS, Deputy of the Fuehrer.

WILHELM KEITEL, Chief of the O.K.W.

CONSTANTIN H. K. VON NEURATH, Minister for Foreign Affairs, President of the Secret Cabinet Council.

FRANZ VON PAPEN, Vice-Chancellor.

ERICH RAEDER, Commander-in-Chief of the Navy.

JOACHIM VON RIBBENTROP, Minister for Foreign Affairs.

ALFRED ROSENBERG, Minister of the Occupied Eastern Territories.

HJALMAR SCHACHT, Acting Minister of Economics, Reich Minister without Portfolio, President of the Reichsbank, Plenipotentiary for War Economy.

BALDUR VON SCHIRACH, Reich Youth Leader.

ARTHUR SEYSS-INQUART, Reich Minister without Portfolio.

ALBERT SPEER, Minister for Armaments and War Production.

From the ordinary Cabinet there came not only the members of the Secret Cabinet Council and the Council of Ministers for Defence of the Reich, but also the members of the War Planning Group, the Nazi Secret Reich Defence Council. When it was deemed essential for the purposes of the conspiracy to wage aggressive war, that power was concentrated in a few individuals. Again these individuals were drawn from the ordinary Cabinet. Thus the Plenipotentiaries for Economy and Administration were also Ministers of the ordinary Cabinet and members of the Reich Defence Council and Ministerial Council.

Under them were grouped practically all the Ministers of the ordinary Cabinet.

Where political considerations of foreign policy required that another select group be chosen to act as advisors, the Secret Cabinet was created and populated with members of the ordinary Cabinet.

The Reichsregierung was dominated by the Nazi Party through the control exercised over its legislation by the Deputy of the Fuehrer, Hess, and later by the Leader of the Party Chancellery, Bormann. Party control was also effected through the individual membership of all members, and the union of various key Cabinet and Party positions in one man. As a result of this fusion of the Party and State, an enormous concentration of political power was gathered into the Cabinet.

The laws enacted by the Cabinet established the framework within which the Nazi conspirators established their control of Germany, set forth in Count I of the Indictment, by virtue of which they were enabled to commit the crimes alleged in Counts I, 2, 3 and 4 of the Indictment. The Cabinet enacted harsh penal laws, discriminatory laws, confiscatory laws, in violation of the principles of justice and humanity. Decrees enacted by the Ministerial Council during the war clothed the criminal acts of the Nazi conspirators with a semblance of legality. As an instrument of the Party the Cabinet effectively implemented the notorious-points of the Party programme. Finally, the Cabinet, almost immediately upon the coming into power of Hitler, became a war-planning group through its establishment in 1933 of a Reich Defence Council and its active participation in the schemes and plans for waging aggressive war.

It is, therefore, most respectfully submitted that, by virtue of all of the foregoing, the Reichsregierung, as defined in Appendix D, Page 35, of the Indictment, should be declared a criminal group within the meaning of Article 9 of Section II of the Charter.

That concludes, if your Honour pleases, this presentation, and the next subject is the S.A.

It will take a minute or two to get ready for that.

May it please the Tribunal, I passed up Document Book "Y," which contains the English translations of the documents relied upon in this presentation.

The organisation which I shall now present for your consideration is the Sturmabteilung, the organisation which the world remembers as the "Brown Shirts" or "Storm Troops," the gangsters of the early days of Nazi terrorism. It came to be known in later years as the S.A., and I shall refer to it in that manner in the course of my presentation.

The S.A. was the first of the organisations conceived and created by the Nazis as the instrument and weapon to effectuate their evil objectives, and it occupied a place of peculiar and significant importance in the scheme of the conspirators. Unlike some of the other organisations, the functions of the S.A. were not fixed or static. On the contrary, it was an agency adapted to many designs and purposes; and its role in the conspiracy changed from time to time - always corresponding with the progression of the conspiracy through its various phases towards the final objective: abrogation of the Versailles Treaty and acquisition of the territory of other peoples and nations. If we might consider this conspiracy as a pattern, with its various parts fitting together like the pieces of a jigsaw puzzle, we would find that the piece representing the S.A. constituted a link in the pattern vitally necessary to the presentation and development of the entire picture.

The S.A. participated in the conspiracy as a distinct and separate unit, having a legal character of its own. This is shown by Document 1725-PS, which is tabbed in the document book, of which the Court will take judicial notice. It is an Ordinance passed in March, 1935, Reichsgesetzblatt, Part I, Page 502. It declares that the S.A. and certain other agencies were thereafter to be considered "Components" of the

Nazi Party. This Ordinance further provided in Article 5 - and it is on the second page of the English translation, right after the word "Article 5" - I quote:-

> "The affiliated organisations can possess their own legal character."

Similarly the organisation book of the Nazi Party characterised the S.A. as an "entity." Document 3220-PS, which I now offer, is an excerpt from the 1943 edition of the Organisation Book, Page 358 of the original, and I quote from the English translation. It is there declared:-

> "The Fuehrer prescribes the law of conduct and commands its use. The Chief of Staff represents the S.A. as a complete entity on the mandate of the Fuehrer."

I am sure the evidence will demonstrate and characterize the S.A. as an entity and organisation having a legal character of its own. This evidence will show that while the S.A. was composed of many individual members, these members acted collectively and cohesively as a unit. They were closely bound and associated together by many common factors, including: uniform membership standards and disciplinary regulations; a common and distinctive uniform; common aims and objectives; common activities, duties and responsibilities; and - probably the most important factor of all - a fanatical adherence to the philosophies and ideologies conceived by the Nazi conspirators.

This is partially demonstrated by Document 2354-PS, which again is simply an excerpt from the Organisation Book of the Nazi Party. It is found on Page 7 of the English translation. It provides that membership in the S.A. was voluntary, but that the S.A. man should withdraw if

> "he can no longer agree with S.A. views or if he is not in a position to fulfill completely the duties imposed upon him as a member of the S.A."

The S.A. man was well schooled in the philosophies, attitudes and activities which he was expected and required to adopt and reflect in his daily life. Cohesion of thought and uniformity of action with respect to such matters was in part obtained by the publication and distribution of a weekly periodical entitled Der S.A.-Mann (The S.A. Man). This publication was principally devoted to the creation and fostering of the various aspects of Nazi ideology which constituted the doctrinal motives of many of the conspirators.

May I digress from my text and say to the Tribunal that we have here on the table all of these publications, beginning with the year 1934, up through and including the year 1939; the official weekly newspaper entitled Der S.A.-Mann, meaning the S.A. man, published in Munich, had wide distribution and was on sale at news stands and distributed throughout Germany and occupied countries.

In addition, Der S.A.-Mann served to report upon and document the activities of the S.A. as an organisation and those of its constituent groups. I shall have occasion at a later point to refer to certain portions of this publication for the consideration of the Tribunal.

The general organisational arrangement or plan of the S.A. will be demonstrated to the Tribunal by the documents which will subsequently appear. At this point I may say simply that this proof will show that the S.A. developed from scattered bands of street ruffians to a well-knit cohesive unit organised on a military basis, with military training and military functions, and, above all, with an aggressive, militaristic and warlike spirit and philosophy. It extended throughout the entire Reich territory and was formed vertically into local groups and divisions. Horizontally, there were special units including military cavalry, communications, engineer and medical units. Your Honours will observe the chart that I will introduce officially a little later in the Court.

Co-ordination of these various groups and branches was strictly maintained by the S.A. Headquarters and operational offices, and those offices were located in Munich.

The relationship between the S.A. and the N.S.D.A.P. is the next subject.

The case against the S.A. is a strong one and its basis or foundation consists of its significant and peculiar relationship and affiliation with the Nazi Party and the principal conspirators.

It is submitted that a relationship or association among the alleged conspirators constitutes important and convincing evidence of their joint participation in an established conspiracy; and this principle is particularly applicable because the affiliation between the S.A. and the Nazi leaders was closely maintained and adhered to and was adapted to the purpose of enabling the conspirators to employ the S.A. for any use or activity which might be necessary in the course of effectuating the objectives of the conspiracy.

Thus we find that the S.A. was, in fact, conceived and created by Hitler himself in the year 1921 at the very inception of the conspiracy.

> Hitler retained direction of the S.A. throughout the period of the conspiracy, delegating the responsibility for its leadership to a Chief of Staff. Hitler, in fact, was often known throughout Germany as O.S.A.F., or "Oberster S.A. Fuehrer," or, translated, "the highest S.A. Fuehrer."

The defendant Goering was an early member of the S.A. and he maintained a close affiliation with it throughout the course of the conspiracy.

The defendant Hess participated in many of the early battles of the S.A. and was leader of an S.A. group in Munich.

The defendants Frank, Streicher, von Schirach, and Sauckel each held a position of Obergruppenfuehrer in the S.A., a position corresponding to the rank of Lieutenant-General; and the defendant Bormann was a member of the Staff of the S.A. High Command.

The close relationship between the S.A. and the leaders of the Nazi Party is demonstrated by the fact that the Hoheitstraeger of the Nazi Leadership Corps were authorised to call upon the S.A. for assistance in carrying out particular phases of the Party programme. This was established yesterday by Document 1893-PS, from which, your Honours will recall, I quoted from a number of times in connection with the presentation of the Leadership Corps. It was declared in that excerpt, Page 11 of the English translation, as your Honour will recall, that the Hoheitstraeger were empowered to call upon the S.A. for the execution of political missions connected with the movement. This responsibility of the S.A. to the Party is also shown by Document 2383-PS, which is an ordinance for the execution of the Hitler decree, which I now offer in evidence as Exhibit USA 410. I quote from Page 3 of the English translation. If your Honour will turn to Page 3 of the English translation, it is the fourth paragraph on that page:-

> "The formations of the N.S.D.A.P., with exception of the S.S., for whom special provisions apply, are subordinated to the bearer of sovereignty (Hoheitstraeger) politically and in respect to commitments. Responsibility for the leadership of the units rests in the hands of the unit leader."

It was in accordance with such authority, as proved yesterday in the Leadership Corps presentation, that the S.A. was used in the seizure of trade union properties.

In addition the S.A. demonstrated its close affiliation to the Nazi Party by participating in various ways in election proceedings. This is shown in Document 2168-PS, which is a pamphlet entitled "The S.A.", which is Exhibit USA 411; and this pamphlet depicts the history and general activities of the S.A., written by an S.A.

Sturmfuehrer named Bayer, upon orders from S.A. headquarters. In that pamphlet, and I quote on Page 4 of the English translation, down towards the bottom of the page, the last paragraph, beginning on line 3:

"At the foremost front the labour and the struggle of the S.A. was not in vain. They stood at the foremost front of election fights."

THE PRESIDENT: I am sorry, will you tell me which page?

COLONEL STOREY: It is Page 4 of the English translation, down at the last paragraph, if your Honour pleases, beginning at the third line:

"...the labour and the struggle of the S.A. was not in vain. They stood at the foremost front of election fights."

Adolf Hitler, himself, on the 2nd September, 1930, took over the leadership of the S.A. as the Supreme S.A. Fuehrer. He himself guided his S.A. in the fateful election fight of the year 1930.

Further evidence of the interest and participation of Nazi leaders in the activities of the S.A. is to be found in these five bound volumes, which consist of the issues of the S.A. newspaper, Der S.A.-Mann, from the year 1934 to 1939 inclusive; and I should like, at this time, to ask that each of these bound volumes be marked for identification, because each of them will be referred to from time to time during this presentation. They will begin with Exhibit USA 414, 415, 416, 417 and 418 and they are referred to by appropriate document numbers, which I will refer to when the quoted portions come in the English translation.

Throughout these volumes there appear photographs portraying the participation of Nazi leaders in S.A. activities. I should like at this time to describe a few of the photographs, and I will indicate the page numbers upon which they appear.

If your Honour pleases, we set out a number of these photographs, but I should like, at this time, to exhibit to the Tribunal and pass into evidence one of the photographs appearing in the January, 1937, issue. It is a photograph of Goering at the ceremonies held upon the occasion of his being made Obergruppenfuehrer of the Feldherrnhalle Regiment of the S.A. on the 23rd January, 1937, and we offer in evidence the photograph and the page of the newspaper. We will pass it up to your Honours if you would like to see it. We offer it in evidence.

Here is another photograph of Goering, leading the Feldherrnhalle Regiment of the S.A. in parade on the 18th September, 1937, is shown at Page 3. The other photograph was at Page 3 of the January, 1937, edition of the S.A.- Mann.

I call the attention of your Honour to a few of the other photographs that appear. Here is a photograph of Hitler greeting Huehnlein, bearing the caption: "The Fuehrer Greets Corps Fuehrer Huehnlein at the Opening of the International Automobile Fair - 1935." That is dated the 23rd March, 1935, at Page 6.

Here is another photograph of Himmler and Huehnlein, who was the Fuehrer of the N.S.K.K., and Lutze, who was Chief of Staff of the S.A., bearing the caption: "They lead the soldiers of National Socialism," on 15th June, 1935, Page 1.

Another photograph shows Hitler at an S.A. ceremony, carrying the S.A. battle flag, and the picture bears the caption: "As in the fighting years the Fuehrer, on the Party Day of Freedom, dedicates the new regiments with the Blood Banner," 21st September, 1935, Page 4.

I pass on. Here is a photograph of Goering in the S.A. uniform, reviewing S.A. marching troops, under the caption, "Honour Day of the S.A.," 21st September, 1935, Page 3.

THE PRESIDENT: Colonel Storey, is there any doubt that Hitler and Goering were members of the S.A.?

COL. STOREY: No, Sir, but the purpose in showing those photographs, if your Honour pleases, was to show the militaristic character of the S.A. If there is no question about that and it is cumulative, then I will pass on.

The work of the S.A. did not end with the seizure by the Nazis of the German Government, but affiliation between the S.A. and the Nazi leaders was continued after the acquisition by the Nazis of the control of the German State. The importance of the S.A. in connection with the Nazi Government and control of Germany is shown by the law of 1st. December, 1933. I have already referred to that, that is the union of Party and State. However, there is one paragraph that has not been quoted before, if your Honour pleases, and I would like to call your attention to it. It is our Document 1395-PS, and it appears in the English translation on Page 1, and I quote Article 2:

"The Deputy of the Fuehrer and the Chief of Staff of the S.A. become members of the Reich Government in order to insure close co-operation of the offices of the Party and S.A. with the public authorities."

Similarly, in Document 2383, which I referred to a moment ago - I will merely refer to it again - that is 2383-PS, Page 11, the last paragraph:

"The Party and State offices must support the S.A. in this training effort and evaluate the certificate of possession of the S.A. defence insignia accordingly."

That the Nazis at all times possessed complete control of the S.A. is shown by the so-called "Roehm Purge" of June, 1934. Evidence concerning this matter is to be found in the "Voelkischer Beobachter" of 1st July, 1934, at Page 1. I will not quote from that.

Roehm had been Chief of Staff of the S.A. for several years and was responsible for the development of the S.A. into a powerful organisation with definite programmes and objectives.

Members of the S.A. were required to take a personal oath of fidelity to him. But when his policies conflicted with those of the Nazi leaders, he was removed and murdered and replaced by Victor Lutze. This drastic action was accomplished without revolt or dissension in the ranks of the S.A. and with no change in the objectives or programme of the organisation. The S.A. remained - I quote - "a reliable and strong part of the National Socialist Movement" - this is Document 2407-PS, Exhibit USA 412, the English translation of the "Voelkischer Beobachter." It is the last paragraph in the English translation, just above the name "Adolf Hitler."

"... It is my wish that the S.A. be built up as a reliable and strong part of the National Socialist movement, full of obedience and blind discipline. They must help to create and form the new German citizens."

The importance of the S.A. in the Nazi plan for the utilisation of the people of Germany is shown in Hitler's pronouncement: "The Course for the German Person," which appears in the issue of Der S.A.-Mann, of 5th September, 1936, at Page 22. It is our Document 3050-PS, Exhibits USA 414-418; and it is at Page 29 of the English translation; Page 29, of Document 3050-PS, the paragraph in the middle of the page; and I quote:

"The boy, will enter the 'Jungvolk,' and the lad, he will enter the Hitler Youth; the young man will go into the S.A., into the S.S., and into other units, and the S.A. and S.S. men will one day enter into the labour service and from there go to the Army, and the soldier of the 'Volk' will return again into the organisation of the movement, the Party, in the S.A. and S.S., and never again will our 'Volk' decay as it once decayed."

And so we see that at all times during the conspiracy the relationship between the S.A. and the Nazi Party was such that the S.A. was constantly available to the conspirators as an instrument to further their aims. The S.A. was created by the conspirators at the inception of the Nazi movement. It was at all times subject to the direction of Adolf Hitler. Seven of the defendants held positions of leadership and responsibility in the organisation, and at all times the S.A. was subject to the call of the "Hoheitstraeger." The S.A. stood at the forefront of the election fights, and co-operation between the offices of the Party, of the S.A., and of the State was assured by law.

So it was declared by Victor Lutze, the former Chief of Staff of the S.A., in a pamphlet entitled "The Nature and Tasks of the S.A." - and it is our Document 2471-PS. We offer the original in evidence as Exhibit USA 413; and I quote from the top of Page 1 of the English translation. I believe I will read that whole paragraph, the first paragraph at the top of the page:

"Before touching the real subject matter, I must tell you first, in order to clear up any uncertainty about my own position, that I never speak primarily as a member of the S.A., but as a National Socialist, since the S.A. cannot be independent of the National Socialist movement but can only exist as a part of it."

I should next like to present to the Tribunal evidence which will demonstrate the principal functions and activities performed by the S.A. pursuant to the relationship which I have described above and in furtherance of the objectives of the conspiracy. These activities may be logically classified or divided into four distinct phases or aspects, each of which, I might add, corresponds with a particular phase in the progress of the conspiracy toward the objectives alleged in the Indictment.

The first phase consists of the use of the S.A. and its members as the instrument for the dissemination of the ideology and fanaticism of the Nazis throughout Germany. The employment of the S.A. for this purpose continued throughout the entire period of the conspiracy, as will, I am sure, be apparent from the evidence.

The second phase relates to the period prior to the Nazi seizure of power. During this period the S.A. was a militant and aggressive group of fighters or gangsters whose function was to combat, physically and violently, all opponents of the Party.

The third phase relates to the period of several years following the Nazi seizure of power. During this period the S.A. participated in various measures designed to consolidate the control of the Nazis, including such Nazi- inspired programmes as the dissolution of the trade unions, the persecution of the Church, and the Jewish persecutions, to which I have already alluded. During this period they continued to serve as a force of political soldiers whose purpose was physically to combat members of political parties which were considered hostile or opposed to the Nazi Party.

The fourth aspect of the S.A. activities consisted of its employment as an agency for the building up of an armed force in Germany in violation of the Treaty of Versailles, and for the preparation of the youth of Germany - mentally and physically - for the waging of an aggressive war.

I should now like to discuss what I consider the highlights of the evidence relating to these four phases.

The first phase is in connection with the dissemination of ideology.

The first function of the S.A. consisted of its responsibility for disseminating the doctrines and ideologies, acceptance of which was necessary for the fulfilment of the Nazi objectives. From the very start the Nazi leaders emphasised the importance of this mission. During the course of the conspiracy the S.A. undertook many duties and responsibilities, but one responsibility which remained constant throughout was that of being propagandist of the National Socialist ideology.

I now refer, your Honour, to the English translation of Document 2760-PS, Exhibit USA 256, which is an excerpt from Mein Kampf, and it is shown at Page 5 of the translation of the document. This is the third paragraph on Page 5 of the document, and I quote:-

> "As the directing idea for the inner training of the Sturmabteilung, the dominant intention always was, aside from all physical education, to teach it to be the unshakeable convinced defender of the National Socialist idea."

I might add that Hitler's pronouncement as to the function of the S.A. in this respect became, in effect, the guiding principle of S.A. members, for Mein Kampf was taken to express the basic philosophy of the S.A.

In Document 2354-PS, which is an excerpt from the Organisation Book of the Party, at Page 1 of the English translation - it is quoted in the text - I quote Paragraph 1:

> "Education and training, according to the doctrine and aims of the Fuehrer as they are set down in Mein Kampf and in the Party programme, for all phases of our living and of our National Socialist ideology."

This same document - the Organisation Book of the Party - refers to the SA's function as the propagandist of the Party.

I believe the next one, if your Honour pleases, would merely be cumulative of what we have already referred to.

THE PRESIDENT: Perhaps this would be a convenient time to break off.

COLONEL STOREY: All right, Sir.

The Tribunal adjourned until 19th December, 1945, at 1000 hours.

Twenty-Third Day: Wednesday, 19th December, 1945

DOCTOR SAUTER (Counsel for the defendant von Schirach): Mr. President, yesterday a table was shown on the screen, in which the construction of the Reich Cabinet was exposed, which is under accusation as an organisation. And on this chart, under the heading "Other Participants in the Meetings of the Cabinet," the defendant von Schirach was also mentioned. The defendant von Schirach has explained to me and asked me to inform the Court that he never took part in any meeting of the Reich Cabinet; that he was never named a member of the Reich Cabinet; that he never took part in any resolution passed by the Reich Cabinet.

THE PRESIDENT: The point that the defendant is taking seems to me to be premature. This is not the stage for you to argue the question whether your client is a member of the Reich Cabinet or not. The argument upon the whole question will take place after the evidence and after the prosecution have had the opportunity of putting forward their arguments as to the criminal nature of the Reich Cabinet. You or other counsel on behalf of those concerned will be able to put forward your arguments. We do not desire to hear arguments now about the criminal nature, but to hear the evidence. Is that clear?

DOCTOR SAUTER: Yes. I shall then return to this point while the witnesses are being heard, and shall then bring witnesses to prove that the defendant von Schirach was never a member of the Reich Cabinet.

COLONEL STOREY: If the Tribunal please, yesterday afternoon we had just started on the participation of the S.A. in the first point - the dissemination of ideology or propaganda. In an article which appeared in Der S.A.-Mann, at Page 1 of the issue of January, 1934, which is Document 3050-PS, and I refer to Page 25 of the English translation - Document 3050-PS, Page 25, if your Honour pleases - the portion shown in red brackets. It is dated the 6th January, 1934:

> "The new Germany would not have come into existence without Der S.A.-Mann, and the new Germany would continue to exist if Der S.A.-Mann would now, with the feeling of having fulfilled his duty, quietly and unselfishly and modestly step aside, or if the new State would send him home, much like the Moor who has done his duty. On the contrary, Der S.A.-Mann, following the will of the Fuehrer, stands as a guarantor of the National Socialist revolution before the gates of power, and will remain standing there at all times. For there are still gigantic missions awaiting fulfillment which would not be thinkable without the presence and the active co-operation of the S.A. What has been accomplished up till now, the taking over of the power in the State, and the ejection of those elements which are responsible for the pernicious developments of the postwar years, as bearers of Marxism, Liberalism, and Capitalism, are only the preliminaries, the spring-board, for the real aims of National Socialism. Being conscious of the fact that the real National Socialist construction work would be building in an empty space, without the taking over of power by Adolf Hitler, the Movement and Der S.A.-Mann as the aggressive bearer of its will, primarily have directed all of their efforts to achieve the goal by continued striving, and to obtain the foundation or the realisation of their desires in the State by force. Out of this

comes the further mission of the S.A. for the completion of the German revolution: first, to be the guarantor of the power of the National Socialist State against all attacks from without as well as from within: second, to be the high institute of education of the people for the living National Socialism."

The function of S.A. as the propagandist of the Party was more than a responsibility which S.A. took unto itself. It was the responsibility recognised by the law of Germany. Document 1395-PS, is a copy of the law entitled, "Law on Securing the Unity of Party and State," which I have referred to before - and it was promulgated by the Reich Cabinet in 1933 - I desire to read Article 3, on Page 1 of the English translation:

"The members of the National Socialist German Party and the S.A., including their subordinate organisations, as the leading and driving force of the National Socialist State, will bear greater responsibility toward the Fuehrer, People, and State. In case they violate these duties they will be subject to special jurisdiction by Party and State. The Fuehrer may extend these regulations in order to include members of other organisations."

Thus were the S.A. members the ideology bearers of the Nazi Party - the soldiers of an idea - to use the expression employed by the Nazi writers. And permit me to emphasize that the S.A. was the propagandist agency, the principal agency employed by the conspirators to disseminate their fanaticism among the people of Germany.

If your Honour pleases, I had ended the quotation. I am sorry if I did not refer to it.

I need hardly point out the importance of this function to the successful carrying out of the conspiracy, for it is self-evident that the Nazis could not have carried their conspiracy to the stages which they did, had not the minds of the people of Germany been cruelly and viciously influenced and infected with their evil ideologies.

I now proceed to the other functions of the S.A. which I mentioned previously. The next is its use in the early stages of the conspiracy, as the "strong-arm" of the N.S.D.A.P. In the early stages of the Nazi movement, the employment of the S.A. as the propagandist instrument of the Party, involved, and was combined, with the exercise of physical violence and brutality.

As said by Hitler in Mein Kampf - and this excerpt appears at Page 4 of Document 2760-PS, Page 4 of the English translation, Exhibit USA 256 - I quote:

"The young Movement from the first day, espoused the standpoint that its idea must be put forward spiritually, but that the defence of this spiritual platform must, if necessary, be secured by strong-arm means."

I will read the rest of that paragraph:

"Faithful to its belief in the enormous significance of the new doctrine, it seems obvious to the movement that, for the attainment of its goal, no sacrifice can be too great."

So, in the early days of the Nazi movement, in order that the Nazis might better spread their fanatical philosophies, the S.A. was employed as a terroristic group, so as to gain for the Nazis possession and control of the streets. That is another way of saying that it was a function of the S.A. to beat up and terrorize all political opponents. The importance of this function is indicated in Document 2168-PS, Exhibit USA 411, which was written by S.A. Sturmfuehrer Bayer on orders from S.A. headquarters. I refer to Page 3 of the English translation of that document, the third paragraph from the bottom:

"Possession of the streets is the key to power in the State - for this reason the S.A. marched and fought. The public would never have received knowledge of the agitative speeches of the little Reichstag faction and its propaganda, or of the desires and aims of the Party, if the martial tread and battle song of the S.A. Companies had not beat the measures for the truth of a relentless criticism of the state of affairs in the governmental system. They wanted the Young Movement to keep silent. Nothing was to be read in the Press about the labour of the National Socialists, not to mention the basic aims of its platform. They simply did not want to awaken any interest in it. However, the martial tread of the S.A. took care that even the drowsiest citizens had to see at least the existence of a fighting troop."

The importance of the work of the S.A. in the early days of the movement was indicated by Goebbels in a speech which appeared in Das Archiv, October, 1935. This is our Document 3211-PS, Exhibit USA 419. It is on the first page of the English translation, No. 3211, quoting:-

"The inner-political opponents did not disappear due to mysterious unknown reasons, but because the Movement possessed a strong arm within its organisation, and the strongest arm of the Movement is the S.A. The Jewish question will not be solved separately, but by laws which we enact, for we are the anti-Jewish Government."

Specific evidence of the activities of the S.A. during the early period of the Nazi movement, from 1922 to 1931, is found in a series of articles appearing in Der S.A.-Mann, entitled "S.A. Battle Experiences Which We Will Never Forget." Each of these articles an account of a street or a meeting-hall battle waged by the S.A. against a group of political opponents in the early days of the Nazi struggle for power. These articles demonstrate that during this period it was the function of the SA to employ physical violence in order to destroy and subvert all forms of thought and expression which might be considered hostile to the Nazi aims or philosophy.

A number of such articles have been translated, and the titles are sufficiently descriptive to constitute evidence of the activities the S.A. in the early stages of the Nazi movement. I should like to quote from a few of these titles by giving the page reference of this big newspaper volume.

Here is one of 24th February, 1934, Page 4. The title: "We Subdue the Red Terror."

The 8th September, 1934, Page 12. The article is entitled: "Nightly Street Battles on the Czech Border."

The 6th October, 1934, Page 5: "Street Battle in Chemnitz."

Another one of the 20th October, 1934, Page 7. The title: "Victorious S.A."

I will skip several of them. Here is one of 26th January, 1935, Page 7. The title: The S.A. Conquers Rastenburg."

Another on 23rd February, 1935, Page 5: "Company 88 Receives Its Baptism of Fire."

One of 20th October, 1934, Page 7. The article is: "S.A. Against Sub-Humanity."

Finally, I mention the one of 10th August, 1935, Page 10. The title is, "The Blood Sunday of Berlin."

And then there is a portrait in the article of 11th September, 1937, Page 1, which symbolises the S.A.-Mann as the "Master of the Streets."

For an example of the nature of these articles, one appeared the Franken edition of the S.A.-Mann for 30th October, 1937, Page 3. It is entitled, "9th November, 1923, in Nuernberg," and I should like to quote from Pages 14 and 15 of Document 3050-PS, which is an English translation of this article:-

"We stayed overnight in the Colosseum (that means Nuernberg). Then in the morning we found out what had happened in Munich. 'Now a revolution will also be made in Nuernberg', we said. All of a sudden the Police came from the Master Guard and told us that we should go home, that the 'putsch' in Munich had failed. We did not believe that and we did not go home. Then came the State Police with fixed bayonets and drove us out of the hall. One of us then shouted: 'Let's go to the Cafe Habsburg!' By the time we arrived, however, the Police again had everything surrounded. Some shouted then, 'The Jewish place will be stormed.... Out with the Jews!' Then the police started to beat us up. Then we divided into small groups and roamed through the town, and wherever we caught a Red or a Jew we knew, a fist fight ensued.

Then in the evening we marched, although the Police had forbidden it, to a meeting in Fuerth. On our way the police again attempted to stop us. It was all the same to us. In the next moment in our anger we attacked the police so that they were forced to flee. We marched on to Geissmann Hall. There again they tried to stop us. But the Landsturm, which was also there, attacked the protection forces like persons possessed and drove them from the streets. After the meeting we dissolved and went to the edge of town. From there we marched in close column back to Nuernberg. In Will Street near Plaerrer the police came again. We simply shoved them aside. They did not dare to attack, for this would have meant a blood bath. We decided beforehand not to take anything from anyone. In Fuerth they had already noticed that we were up to no good. A mass of people accompanied us on the march. We marched with unrolled flags and sang so that the streets resounded: 'Comrade give me your hand; we want to stand together firmly; even if they misunderstand the S.A., the spirit must not die; Swastika on the steel helmet, black-white-red armband; we are known as Storm Troop (S.A.) Hitler!"

I now skip to the use of the S.A. to consolidate the power of the Party.

The third function of the S.A. was to carry out various programmes designed to consolidate Nazi control of the German State, including particularly the dissolution of the trade unions and the Jewish persecutions.

The S.A. groups were employed to destroy political opposition by force and brutality wherever necessary. An example of this is shown in Document 3221-PS, Exhibit USA 422, and that is an original affidavit made in the State of Pennsylvania, in the United States of America, by William F. Sollman, which we now quote in its entirety:-

"William F. Sollman, Pendle Hill School, Wallingford, Pennsylvania, being duly sworn according to law, deposes and says: From 1919 until 1933 I was a Social- Democrat and a member of the German Reichstag. Prior to 11th March, 1933, I was Editor-in-Chief of a chain of daily newspapers with my office in Cologne, Germany, which led the fight against the Nazi Party. On 9th March, 1933, members of the S.S. and S.A. came to my home in Cologne and destroyed the furniture and my personal records. At that time I was taken to the Brown House in Cologne, where I was tortured, being beaten and kicked for several hours. I was then taken to the regular Government prison in Cologne, where I was treated by two medical doctors and released the next day. On 11th March, 1933, I left Germany.

Signed and sworn to."

Prior to the organisation of the Gestapo on a national scale, local S.A. meeting places were designated as arrest points, and the S.A. members were employed in the taking into custody of Communists and other persons who were actually or supposedly hostile to the Nazi Party. This activity is described in Document 1759-PS, Exhibit USA 420, which is an original affidavit made by Raymond H. Geist. Mr. Geist was formerly United States Consul in Berlin. He is now in Mexico City. I should like to quote from a portion of his affidavit, the first being on Page 5 of the English translation, about the middle of the page, starting:-

> "At the beginning of the Hitler regime, the only organisation which had meeting-places throughout the country was the S.A. (Storm Troopers). Until the Gestapo could be organised on a national scale, the thousands of local S.A. meeting-places became the arrest points. There were at least 50 of these in Berlin. Communists, Jews, and other known enemies of the Nazi Party were taken to these points, and if they were enemies of sufficient importance they were immediately transferred to the Gestapo Headquarters. During 1933 and 1934, when the Gestapo became universally organised, the S.A. were gradually eliminated as arresting agents, and the S.S. were incorporated as administrative and executive officials into the Gestapo. By the end of 1934, the S.A. had been fairly well eliminated and the S.S., the members of which wore elegant black suits and were therefore called Elite Guards, became almost identical as functionaries with the Gestapo."

I now pass to Page 7 of this same Document, Page 7 of the English translation. It begins:-

THE PRESIDENT: Colonel Storey, does that mean that the S.A. were eliminated for the purpose of arrest or for other purposes too?

COLONEL STOREY: No, Sir. As I understand, Sir, the S.A. reached its height of popularity in 1934, and immediately after the Roehm purge began to decline. In the meantime, the S.S., which originated out of the S.A., was growing and became really the strong part, and grew and prospered after that. So I think the evidence will show that after 1934 the S.A. started a rapid decline in its importance.

Now, on Page 7 of the English translation I should like to quote a part of the Consul's report, beginning in the middle of the page. Another American, Herman I. Roseman, made an affidavit which stated:-

> "'Yesterday, 10th March, 1933, in the afternoon about 4:30, I came out of K.D.W. with my fiancee, Fraulein Else Schwarzlose, residing in Wilmersdorf (giving the address). A man in S.A. uniform stepped on my toe purposely, obviously offended me and said 'Pardon.' I said 'Bitte,' and walked ahead. He then followed me and kicked me saying, "Na und?" A police man saw this and walked ahead, paying no attention to attacks made on me. Then I took my passport out of my pocket, showed it to the second policeman, and said that I was an American citizen, but he walked ahead, obviously not able to afford me protection, or at least being unwilling to do so. The S.A. man continued to attack me, struck me in the face, wounded me over the eye, and continued to do me bodily harm. During this attack, all the time my walking along, we reached another policeman, and I applied to him, showing my passport and said: 'I am an American and am entitled to protection.' He shrugged his shoulders and said 'What can I do?' By this time the S.A. man had obviously attacked me enough and walked away.
>
> Upon my appeal, the policeman brought my fiancee and me to the station house at 13 Bayreuther Strasse. My fiancee and I reported to the officer in charge. He heard the story and said that he was sorry, but that there was nothing to do. My face was bleeding. The policeman said that he had orders not to interfere in any affair in which an S.A. man took part. I then asked him

what I could do to protect myself. He said that there was nothing to do but to wait until the situation was better. He added that the police were absolutely powerless, and were under the direction of the S.A., and that there were S.A. Sturm Abteilungen in the police itself. Thereupon I departed...."

Now on the next page, on Page 8, is another American, Mrs. Jean Klauber, and I quote from her affidavit.

"On the night of Friday, 10th March, 1933, she and her husband had retired for the night when they were awakened by a prolonged ringing of their apartment bell. They heard pounding upon the street door and a demand for immediate entry, and at the same time a threat to break the door down. The street door was opened by the janitor's wife, and a party of four or five men entered and went at once to the apartment of the deponent, where they again rang and pounded on the door. Mr. Klauber asked who was there and was answered - 'The police.' He opened the door and a party of four or five men in brown uniforms, one wearing a dark overcoat and carrying a rifle, pushed in, jostling Mr. and Mrs. Klauber aside. One asked Mrs. Klauber where the telephone was and she indicated the room where it was to be found, and started to go there. Thereupon, she was knocked down by one of them. They went on to the bedroom where Mr. and Mrs. Klauber followed them, and there they demanded their passports.

Mr. Klauber went to the wardrobe to get his, and was stopped, being asked by the intruders whether he was carrying any weapons. Being clothed only in pajamas, his denial was accompanied by a gesture indicating his garb. He then turned to the wardrobe, opened it, and reached for one of his four suits hanging therein where he thought the passport was, and was immediately attacked from behind by all but one of the intruders, who beat him severely with police clubs, the one with the overcoat and rifle standing by. Remarks were shouted such as, 'Look! Four suits, while for fourteen years we have been starving.' Mrs. Klauber tried to inquire the reason for their actions, and was answered- 'Jews. We hate you. For fourteen years we have been waiting for this, and tonight we will hang many of you.'

When the intruders stopped beating Mr. Klauber he was unconscious, and they again demanded the passports of Mrs. Klauber. Mrs. Klauber found her American passport and her German passport (required by local authorities as the wife of a German citizen and issued by the police at Munich after her arrival here), and the intruders took both in spite of Mrs. Klaubers protests that she was American. She then searched for her husbands passport, laid hold of his pocket-book, and in her excitement offered it to them. Though full of money they refused it, and again demanded the passport. Mrs. Klauber then found it and handed it over.

Then the intruders returned to the unconscious Mr. Klauber saying: 'He hasn't had enough yet,' and beat him further. Then they left, saying, 'We are not yet finished,' and just as they departed, one of them said to Mrs. Klauber, 'Why did you marry a Jew? I hate them' and struck her on the jaw with his police club...."

That is the end of the affidavit. Now continuing, the next paragraph is the statement of the Consul:

"I personally can verify that the police had been instructed not to interfere; and that is, that there was official sanction for these activities. Affidavits taken from numerous victims attest this fact. I had become acquainted with the two police officers stationed at the corner of Bellevuestrasse and Tiergartenstrasse near where the Consulate General was located; these officers told me that they and all the other police officers had received definite instructions not to interfere with the S.A., the S.S., or the Hitler Youth."

In addition, S.A. members served as guards at concentration camps during this consolidating period, and participated in the persecution and mistreatment of persons imprisoned therein. I now refer to Document 2824-PS, which is a book entitled, Concentration Camp at Oranienburg. It is Exhibit USA 423. This was by an S.A.-Sturmbannfuehrer named Schaefer, who was the commander of the concentration camp at Oranienburg. I quote the excerpt on the first page of the English translation, reading:-

"The most trusted, boldest S.A. men were selected in order to give them homes in the camp, since they were the permanent camp guards, and in such a manner we created a cadre of experienced guardsmen who were constantly prepared to be employed."

Further evidence concerning the operation of the concentration camps by the S.A. is found in Document 787-PS, Exhibit USA 421. This is a report to Hitler from the public prosecutor of Dresden concerning the nolle-prosequi of one Vogel, who was accused of mistreatment of persons imprisoned in the concentration camp. I quote from that report:

"The prosecuting authority in Dresden has indicted Oberregierungsrat Erich Vogel in Dresden on account of bodily injury while in office. The following subject matter is the basis of the process:

Vogel has belonged to the Gestapo office of the State of Saxon since its foundation and is chief of Main section II, which formerly bore the title ZUB. In the process of combating efforts inimical to the State, Vogel carried out several so-called 'borderland actions' in the year 1933, in which a large number of politically unreliable persons and persons who had become political prisoners in the border territories, were taken into 'protective custody and brought to the Hohnstain protective custody camp.

In the camp serious mistreatment of the prisoners has been going on at least since the summer of 1933. The prisoners were not only, as in the protective custody camp Bredow near Stettin, beaten into a state of unconsciousness for no reason, with whips and other tools, but were also tortured in other ways, as for instance with a drip- apparatus especially constructed for the purpose, under which the prisoners had to stand so long that they came away with serious purulent wounds on the scalp. The guilty S.A.-leaders and S.A.-men were sentenced to punishments of six years to nine months of imprisonment by the main criminal Court of the provincial court in Dresden on 15th May, 1935. Vogel, whose duties frequently brought him to the camp, took part in this mistreatment, in so far as it happened in the reception room of the camp during completion of the reception formalities, and in the supply room, during issuing of the blankets. In this respect it should be pointed out that Vogel was generally known to the personnel of the camp - because of his function as head of the ZUB - and his conduct became at least partly a standard for the above-named conduct of the S.A. leaders and men."

I want to read the remainder of that quotation. I am sorry, I have not got it here. There is a little portion there that should be read immediately following my statement - I will skip to the quotation just below:

"Vogel stayed in the reception room a long time and watched these proceedings without doing anything about them. In his presence for instance, the S.A.-man Mutze dealt such blows to one man, without provocation, that he turned on him. As already stated, Vogel not only took no steps against this treatment of the prisoners, but he even made jokes about it and stated that it amused him the way 'things were popping' here.

In the supply room, Vogel himself took a hand in the beating amid the general severe mistreatment. The S.A. men there employed whips and other articles and beat the prisoners in such a manner that serious injuries were produced, the prisoners partly became unconscious and had to lie in the dispensary a long time. Vogel was often present in the supply room during the illtreatment. At least in the following cases he personally laid violent hands upon prisoners."

And then skipping down:

- "the prisoner was laid across the counter in the usual manner, held fast by the head and arms, and then beaten for a considerable time by the S.A. men with whips and other articles. Along with this Vogel himself took part in the beating for a time, and after this mistreatment slapped him again, so that the prisoner appeared green and blue in the face. The prisoner is the tinsmith Hans Kuehitz, who bore the nickname 'Johnny.' Upon his departure, Vogel gave the head of the supply room, Truppfuehrer Meier from five to six reichsmarks with the stated reason that the S.A. men 'had sweated so.' The money was then distributed by Meier to those S.A. comrades who had taken part in the ill treatment."

Another activity of the S.A. during the days just following the Nazi seizure of power was to act as auxiliary police. This is shown in Document 3252-PS, Exhibit USA 424. This publication is a book written about Hermann Goering.

THE PRESIDENT: Colonel Storey, is that a document which shows on its face that the man was punished for this conduct?

COLONEL STOREY: I think it does; yes, Sir. I think it does.

THE PRESIDENT: I think that fact ought to be stated.

COLONEL STOREY: I believe it is stated, Sir. You see in the beginning it says that the prosecuting authority in Dresden had indicted Vogel on account of bodily injury, and I thought it stated that he had been punished.

THE PRESIDENT: The document does appear to state it, but I think you ought to state it in Court. The document ends up with - paragraph three -

COLONEL STOREY: It does state that he was punished. The purpose of introducing it was to show what actually took place.

I now turn to Document 3252-PS. As I have just mentioned, the book is entitled, "Hermann Goering, the Man and His Work," by Erich Gritzbach, in which it is declared that the ranks of the Security Police were strengthened by the S.A. and which was characterised as the most reliable instrument of the movement. I should like to quote on the first page of Document 3252-PS, the English translation - it is the fourth paragraph:

"The present reorganisation of the Security Police is hardly noticed by the public. Their ranks are strengthened by the S.A., the most reliable instrument of the movement. The Auxiliary Police have given effective aid by their fighting spirit, in the struggle against the Communists and other enemies of the State, not only to Goering, but have, driven by their National Socialist desire for a new spirit within the executive police, assisted in their rigid organisation."

I now skip to the S.A. participation in the Jewish pogrom of 10th - 11th November, 1938, shown by Document 1721-PS, Exhibit USA 425. This is a confidential report of the S.A.- Brigadefuehrer to his Group Commander, dated 29th November, 1938, in the English translation, starting at the beginning. Without reading the addresses, it is to S.A. Group Electoral Palatinate (Kurpfalz) Mannheim.

"The following order reached me at 3 o'clock on 10th November, 1938.

On the order of the Gruppenfuehrer, all Jewish synagogues within the 50th Brigade are to be blown up or set on fire immediately.

Neighboring houses occupied by Aryans are not to be damaged. The action is to be carried out in civilian clothes. Rioting and plundering are to be prevented. Report of execution of orders to reach the brigade Fuehrer or office by 8.30.

I immediately alerted the Standartenfuehrer and gave them the most exact instructions; the execution of the order began at once.

I hereby report that the following were destroyed in the area of:" -

Then there follows a list of 35 synagogues that were destroyed.

I just refer to a few of them:-

"No. 1. The Synagogue at Darmstadt, Bleichstrasse, destroyed by fire.

No. 4. The Synagogue at Graefenhausen, interior and furnishings wrecked."

And then under "Standarte 145":-

"The synagogue at Bensheim, destroyed by fire."

And then the next four items are synagogues destroyed by fire. In Standarte 168, eight synagogues are shown to have been destroyed by fire.

In Standarte 168, the synagogue in Beerfelden was blown up, and then follow several others where the furnishings were wrecked. In Standarte 221, the synagogue and chapel in Gross- Gerau was destroyed by fire, and the next one torn down and the furnishings destroyed. And then it is signed by the Fuehrer of Brigade 50, by the signature which is illegible, "Brigadefuehrer."

In connection with the persecution of the Jews, we again find the S.A. performing its function of propaganda agency for the Nazis. In this connection it was the function of the S.A. to create and foster among the people an anti-Jewish spirit and sentiment, without which the terrifying Crimes against Humanity perpetrated against the Jewish race certainly would not have been tolerated by any civilised peoples. Substantial and convincing evidence of this function is to be found in these bound volumes of Der S.A.- Mann. Throughout the period covered by these volumes there appeared in this publication article after article consisting of the most cruel and vicious sort of anti- religious propaganda, designed to engender and foster hatred and hostility toward the Jewish race.

I will refer to only a few of the titles appearing. On 27th July, 1935, at Page 4, the title is "Finish up with the Jew." That is shown, if your Honour pleases, in Document 3030, Pages 16 to 18 there listed. In the issue of 2nd February, 1935, Page 5, "The Jewish World Danger"; on 20th July, 1935, Page 4, "Jewish Worries"; on 1st June, 1935, Page 1, "Jews Are Not Wanted Here." And then follows a statement: "Then, also, outside of the last German village the sign will stand, 'Jews Are Not Wanted Here'; and then, finally, "no German citizen will again cross the threshold of a Jewish store. To achieve this goal is the mission of the S.A. man as the political soldier of the Fuehrer. Next to his word and his explanations stands his example."

Then further on 17th August, 1935, Page 1, "God Save the Jew." Then another under 5th October, 1935, Page 6, the title "The Face of the Jew" (with a portrait of a Jew holding the hammer and sickle).

I will just refer to one or two more of them. Here is one on 23rd November, 1935, Page 2. The title, "The Camouflaged Benjamin - Jewish Cultural Bolshevism in German Music."

Here is one of 2nd January, 1937, Page 6, a hideous-looking picture, the title being "Roumania to the Jews?"

I give the final quotation, the last one, 3rd February, 1939, Page 14, the title being "Friends of World Jewry - Roosevelt and Ickes."

The impressive thing about all these articles is the fact that it was not intended that the philosophies expressed in them should be confined to members of the S.A.; on the contrary, the plan was to educate the members of the S.A. with this iniquitous philosophy, and for the S.A., in turn, to be employed for its dissemination into the minds of the German people. This fact is demonstrated in the introduction to a series of anti-Jewish articles in the paper of 5th December, 1936, at Page 6. I will just read the title. It is found on Page 28 of the same document and the title is as follows: "Grave-Diggers of World Culture." Also on that same page, 28, I quote this statement:-

"We suggest that the comrades especially take notice of this series of articles and see that they are further circulated."

In addition, intensive campaigns were conducted to persuade the public to purchase and read Der S.A.-Mann and the various issues were posted in public places so that the general public might read them. Der S.A.-Mann itself contained several photographs which show particular issues posted upon street bulletin boards; and there are several photographs showing advertising displays, one of which, for example, reads as follows - this is in the issue of 31st October, 1936:-

"Der S.A.-Mann belongs in every house, every hotel, every inn, every waiting room, and every store."

Also in the issue of 24th August, 1935, at Page 3, there was a group picture of S.A. men on trucks and in front of the trucks were large signs, one of which read:-

"Read the 'Stuermer' and you will know the Jew."

On the same page of the publication I mentioned there is a photograph of what appears be a public rally, at which there is displayed a large poster reading: "He who knows the Jew, knows the Devil!"

THE PRESIDENT: Colonel Storey, the Tribunal expressed its view yesterday that they did not desire to hear cumulative evidence. Is this not rather cumulative?

COLONEL STOREY: I agree with your Honour that possibly it is. I am trying to draw the line on it. I will omit the rest of them.

Now we will pass to the final phase of the function of the S.A. in the conspiracy.

THE PRESIDENT: Perhaps we had better adjourn now for 10 minutes.

(A recess was taken.)

COLONEL STOREY: If your Honour pleases, I have just started on the function of the S.A. in the conspiracy, that is its participation the programme for preparation for warfare.

In this connection, your Honour asked this morning a question about the arresting and police activities of the S.A., and I mentioned that they had declined after 1934. For fear there was some misapprehension, I would like to state that as a police organisation and as an arresting agency they declined steadily after 1934.

We go now into the phase where they went into military preparations, the next phase, and that is the phase with which I deal now. If your Honour pleases, I have here an official government publication issued by the British Government in 1943, the title being, "The Nazi Party and Organisations," and I should like to quote as to the organisation and membership of the S.A. from that publication. It is the most authoritative that I have been able to find, and I would like to quote briefly from it:-

"The S.A. was founded in 1921 as a para-military organisation to protect Nazi meetings and leaders, to throw out interrupters and hecklers, to fight political enemies, and to provide pre-military training at a time when the legal 'Reichswehr' vas limited to 100,000 men. Their highest leader is Hitler himself; his deputy is called the Stabschef (Chief of Staff of the S.A.; from 1930 to June, 1934, it was Roehm; from then onwards till his death in May, 1943, Victor Lutze; since August, 1943, Wilhelm Schepmann.) In January, 1933, the S.A. had only 300,000 members. After the seizure of power, its strength increased quickly; at present it has a membership of 1,500,000 to 2,000,000" Now, the date of this is 1943.

We again find the S.A. employed to inculcate a particular Nazi ideology into the minds of the people of Germany. At this point it was the function of the S.A. to prepare Germany - mentally - for the waging of a vicious and aggressive war.

At all times, and especially during the period from 1933 to 1939, S.A. leaders emphasised to S.A. members the duty and responsibility of creating and fostering a militaristic spirit throughout Germany. In 1933 Hitler established the so- called S.A. sports programme, and at that time, according to Sturmfuehrer Bayer, in his pamphlet "The S.A.," which I have previously introduced in evidence as Document 2168-PS, the S.A. at that time was "commissioned to obtain and increase the preservation of a warlike power and a warlike spirit as the expression of an aggressive attitude."

In 1937 Hitler renewed the so-called sports programme and, as recited in Document 3050-PS, which is the English translation of these newspaper articles, on Page 12, he made a statement: "for the fostering of a military spirit."

The Organisation Book of the Party is to the same effect, in Document 3220-PS, which is Exhibit USA 323. I quote from a portion of that document - paragraphs 1 to 3 on Page 1 of the English translation, beginning at the first paragraph:-

"While the political organisation of the N.S.D.A.P. has carried out the political leadership, the S.A. is the training and education instrument of the Party for the realisation of the world philosophical soldier-like attitude.

In conformity with the directives of the Fuehrer given at the time of the Reich Party Meeting of Freedom, the S.A. is, as the voluntary political soldiery, the guarantor of the National Socialist Movement, of the National Socialist Revolution, and of the resurgence of the German people.

Consequently, the young German in the S.A. is being inculcated in the first instance from the standpoint of world philosophy and character, and trained as the bearer of the National Socialist armed will.

Equally important is a suitable education and training of the yearly age groups which the S.A. has to accomplish after they have served their time in the Army. It is the task to keep them for their lifetime in all their spiritual, mental and physical powers on the alert to work for the Movement, the People and the State. They should find their best home in the S.A. All that which could divide them economically, culturally, professionally, or socially is being overcome in the S.A. by the spirit of comradeship and manly dignity.

In that manner the S.A. is forming a decisive factor on the path to a popular community. Its spirit should radiate with soldierly tradition and the possibility of application on all existing units outside the movement. To guard them is thus an important mission of the S.A."

A number of the articles which were obviously designed to serve as war propaganda material have been translated; in other cases it has been deemed sufficient to translate merely the titles of articles, the titles in themselves being so descriptive that they disclose the nature and substance of the articles. I should like to refer to a few of these titles on this subject. They are shown on the English translation - Document 3050-PS, and they are listed on Page 1.

On the question of the Nazi "Lebensraum" philosophy: there is, first, in the issue Of 5th January, 1935, Page 13, the article "The German Living Space." The issue of 10th October, 1936, Page 15, "Our Right, Our Colonies." Another, of 14th October, 1938, Page 3, the title "Space and Folk"; "Colonies for Germany," 2nd January, 1937, Page 4. I should like to quote briefly from that article. I believe that it is on Page 1 of the English translation, Document 3050-PS:-

"The German Ambassador in London, Herr von Ribbentrop, recently, on occasion of a reception in the 'Anglo- German Fellowship' has renewed, in a speech which aroused great interest, the indubitable claim of Germany for the restitution of its colonies which had been snatched away.

Shortly thereafter the Reichsbank president and Reich Minister of Economics, Dr. Schacht, published in the English magazine, 'Foreign Affairs' a detailed article on the German colonial problem."

That is on Page 2, I believe, of the English translation.

"For the rest, Dr. Schacht laid out the categorical demand that Germany must, in order to solve the problem of its raw materials, get colonies, which must be administered by Germany, and in which the German standard currency must be in circulation."

Now, the next group are articles dealing with the Versailles Treaty, and I will only quote from a few of them on Page 3 of that same translation. Here is one of 7th April, 1934, Page 14, "What is the Situation regarding our battle for Equal Rights?" Another is entitled "The Dictate of Versailles," 30th June, 1934, Page 15. Here is a part of it:- -

"The Dictate of Versailles established the political, economical, and financial destruction of Germany in 440 artfully - one could also say devilishly - devised paragraphs; this work of ignominy is a sample of endless and partly contradictory repetitions in constantly new forms. Not too many have occupied themselves with this thick book to any great extent, for one could only do it with abomination."

Another title is 7th July, 1934, Page 15, "The Unbearable Limitations on our Fleet." Another one: 19th January, 1935, Page 13, "Versailles after 15 Years." I read a part of it:-

"This terrible word 'Versailles', since a blind nation ratified it, has become a curse for all those who have comprehended the gist of this monstrous product of hatred. The Versailles dictate is Germany's fate in the fullest sense of the word. Every German has been affected by this fate during the past 15 years. Therefore, every German down to the last man must also grasp the contents of this dictate so that one single desire, that for its absolute destruction, fills the whole German 'Volk'."

I shall omit the other quotation. The last one I shall refer to is "Versailles Will be Liquidated," 13th February, 1937. If your Honour pleases this is the last paragraph on Page 4 of the English translation. I quote:-

"The National Socialist Movement has again achieved a victory, for since the beginning of the fight there was written on their flags: The liquidation of the Versailles Treaty. For this fight the S.A. marched year after year."

A third group consists of articles describing preparations for war, purportedly being carried on by other nations, found on Page 5 of the same document and I shall refer to just a few of them:

The issue of 26th January, 1935, Page 14, "Military Training of English Youth," showing pictures of Eton students wearing the traditional Eton dress - tall hats and frock coats - marching with rifles.

Another one is "The Army of the Soviet Union," dated 16th March, 1935, Page 14.

Another one, 4th April, 1936, Page 15, "The Red Danger in the East."

Another one, 29th August, 1936, Page 10, "Russia Prepares for World War."

Another one, 19th June, 1937, Page 7, "Red Terrorism Nailed Down."

I shall omit the rest of them.

Now, the next is the S.A. participation in the aggressive war phase of the conspiracy - the preparation by S.A. of the youth of Germany for participation in aggressive warfare. I hardly think I need emphasize that one of the most important steps in carrying out the conspiracy was the training of the youth of Germany in the technique of war, and their preparation physically and spiritually for the waging of aggressive war. To the S.A. was delegated this most important responsibility. I have here Document 3215-PS, Exhibit USA 426, which I offer in evidence, and it is an excerpt from Das Archiv which contains Hitler's characterisation of the task of the S.A. in this respect. It is on Page 1 of the English translation of 3215-PS. I start the reading where it says, "Already in 1920-":

"Already in 1920 by the founding of the National Socialist Sports Troop (S.A.) the Fuehrer established the extensive mission of this S.A. at that time in which he declared in the protocol of its charter:

The Sports Troop (S.A.) shall be the bearer of the military thought of a free people."

In the same sense the Fuehrer said in his book, Mein Kampf:

"Give the German Nation six million bodies perfectly trained in sport, all fanatically inspired by the love of the Fatherland and trained to the highest offensive spirit, and a National Socialist State will, if necessary, have created an army out of them in less than two years."

The military character of the S.A. is demonstrated by its organisational composition. I refer to the chart on the wall, which is our Document 2168-PS, and it is taken from this book, being the pamphlet of the S.A.-Sturmfuehrer, and the chart is taken from the official book. I refer merely to the chart and call to the attention your Honour that it was organised into units closely corresponding to those of the German Army. As the Tribunal will see, the organisational scheme consisted of divisions. Going from the top in that pyramidal structure, we see at the top the division; next the brigade, then the regiment, the battalion, the company, the platoon and at the bottom, the squad.

In addition, there were special units and branches, including cavalry, signal corps, engineer corps, and medical corps. There were also, as Bayer pointed out in his pamphlet, three officer training schools. Similarly, S.A. members wore distinctive uniforms adapted to military functions, bore arms, and engaged in training, forced marches, and other military exercises.

S.A. members, moreover, were governed by general service regulations, which closely resembled service regulations of an armed force. They are contained in Document 2820-PS, Exhibit USA 427, which I offer in evidence. If your Honour pleases, they are found at Page 3 of the translation of Document 2820. I will merely refer to a few of them. They provide for punishment, designating them as penal regulations, for disobedience of orders and infractions. The punishments which are provided demonstrate the militaristic character of the S.A. and include the following:

Reprimand in private; reprimand in presence of superiors and announcement thereof at formations; prohibition of the right to wear service uniform; house arrest, arrest and confinement in gaol; demotion in rank, prohibition of right to carry weapons.

Preparation for war through the S.A. training programme was begun in Germany as early as 1933, but the scope of this programme was not made public because of the fact that it actually constituted a violation of the Treaty of Versailles. The strict secrecy with which the programme was surrounded is shown in Document D-44, Exhibit USA 428, which I offer in evidence.

On Page 1 of the English translation - this is from the Supreme Command of the S.A., Chief of Staff, and it has to do with publications on the S.A., is the following:

"Further to my instruction Z II 1351Z33 dated 11th July 33, I find cause to ask all S.A. authorities to exercise the greatest caution with regard to any publicity given to the S.A. service, not only in the Press, but also in the information and news sheets of the individual S.A. units.

Only during the last few days, the Reich Ministry of the Interior, at the request of the Foreign Office, has given strict instructions to all Reich authorities according to which the most severe control is to be exercised on all publications which might give other countries an occasion to allege German infringements of the terms of the Versailles Treaty.

As is known from the Geneva negotiations, our opponents have piled up material collected in Germany and submitted to them, which they use against us on every occasion during the conferences.

From this point of view, the information sheets circulating among the subordinate S.A. units cause the liveliest concern. I hold all higher S.A. leaders responsible that any such internal information sheets, appearing in the district of their command, are submitted to the most stringent control before they go into print, and I feel compelled to draw attention to the liability to prosecution for treason as pronounced in official instructions issued in the last few days in cases where such reports, printed no doubt in good faith, are published and therefore exposed to the danger of falling into the wrong hands.

On principle, pictures of the special technical units of the S.A. and S.S., in particular of the motorised signals, and possibly also of the air squads which now exist outside these formations, are forbidden, such pictures enabling other countries to prove the alleged formation of technical troop units."

Similarly, secrecy was provided for in the order assigning a Wehrmacht officer to the S.A. in January, 1934, to assist in the S.A. training programme. This Document, 2823-PS, Exhibit USA 429, which is a copy of a memorandum of S.A. Headquarters dated 20th January, 1934, designates an officer of the Wehrmacht to assist the military training of S.A. members. and it goes on to provide, and I quote from paragraph 7 of the English translation of Document 2823-PS:-

"For the purpose of camouflage, Lt. Col. Auleb will wear S.A. uniform with the insignia of rank according to more detailed regulations of the Supreme

S.A. Leaders."

The military training programme of the S.A. was for many years conducted under the guise of a sports programme. This plan was created by Hitler as early as 1920 by the founding of what he called the Sports Programme. The fact that the so-called Sports Programme was in reality closely associated with, and, in fact, a means of providing military training for the German youth is shown by the following characterisation it by Lutze, the Chief of Staff of the S.A., in an article written in 1939. I now refer to Document 3215-PS, Exhibit USA 426, and I quote excerpts of the English translation on Page 2:

"This goal was also served by the decrees of the Fuehrer to the S.A. in 1935 regarding the renewing of, in 1936 regarding the charter of, and in 1937 regarding the yearly repetitive exercises required for the S.A. sport badge. Parallel to this decree of the Fuehrer for the betterment and military indoctrination, organisational and training measures were taken within the S.A. Based on the conception that the preservation and intensification of the military power of our people must especially be promoted by military and physical exercises, a systematic training was carried out especially in these schools.

In twenty-five 'group schools' and in three 'Reichsfuehrer' schools of the S.A., 22,000 to 25,000 officers and non-coms have been trained yearly since 1934 in special educational courses until they earned the education and examination certificates. In clearly outlined directives the training goal which had to be achieved yearly was stepped up, and at the same time annual Reich competitive contacts of the S.A. were established. Hand in hand with the training of the Fuehrer Corps and the organisations belonging to it went the training for the front on the broadest basis."

In connection with the military training of the sports programme, I refer to Document 2354, Exhibit USA 430, which demonstrates the tests and standards required for obtaining the sports award, on Page 2 of the English translation. I am not going read all of it, if your Honour pleases, but just refer to a few of them:

"Group II: Military sports; 25-kilometer march with pack; firing of small-caliber arms; aimed throwing of hand grenades, 200 meter cross-country race over four obstacles with gas masks; swimming or bicycling; basic knowledge of first aid in case of accidents-"

I will pass the others.

In 1939 the S.A. Sports Programme was formally recognised in a decree issued by Hitler as a military training programme and the S.A. was openly declared to be an agency for pre-and post-military training, that is, for military training prior to and following service in the Wehrmacht. I have Document 2383-PS-

THE PRESIDENT: Colonel Storey, you have just drawn our attention to a Document 3215-PS, which shows that from 1934 onwards, 25,000 officers and non-commissioned officers were trained by the S.A.

COLONEL STOREY: Yes, Sir.

THE PRESIDENT: Isn't that sufficient to show the military nature of the organisation?

COLONEL STOREY: I think so. This was just the decree of Hitler. May I just refer to it by reference for the record? I will not read the decree.

THE PRESIDENT: Go on; what are you referring to?

COLONEL STOREY: Document 2383-PS, Page 11 of the English translation contains a copy of the decree legalising the training programme for pre-and post-military training.

It would have been one thing for the S.A. to conduct a military training programme for its members, but the S.A. programme was not confined to its members. The entire youth of Germany was enlisted into a feverish programme of military training.

I refer to a quotation in Document 2354-PS, from the same organisation book, which is at Page 2 of the English translation, in which the Chief of Staff Lutze said, and I quote briefly:

> "In order to give expression to the fostering of a valiant spirit in all classes of the German people, I further decree that this S.A. Sports Insignia can also be earned by persons who are not members of the movement, provided they comply racially and ideologically with the National Socialist requirements."

Document 2168-PS shows that responsibility for conducting the nation-wide programme was lodged in the operational main office of the SA. Page 8 of the English translation says, and I quote:

> "Prepare the physical military training of all Germans capable of bearing arms, and as a preparation therefor organise physical exercises and sports, so that the widest strata of the population are reached and will be kept in a militarily active condition both physically and spiritually, as well as in respect to character and ideology up until the last years of their lives."

I pass from that phase now.

Document 3215-PS is an excerpt from Das Archiv, and I refer to Pages 2 to 3 of the English translation beginning at the bottom of Page 2, and I quote:

> "Next to the companies of the S.A. were the S.A. Sport Badge Associations, in which all the militaristic nationals entered who were prepared to answer the call of the S.A. for the preservation of military proficiency. Up until now about 800,000 nationals outside the S.A. could successfully undergo the physical training as well as the political-military training of the S.A. on the basis of the S.A. sport badge."

The military programme of the S.A. was not that of a mere marching and drill society. It embraced every phase of the technique of modern warfare. This is particularly demonstrated by consideration of the articles on military training which appeared publicly throughout the issues of the S.A.-Mann. I should like to refer to only a few of the titles, and they are set out on Pages 8 and 10 of Document 3050. It is a very long list, and I will only refer to five or six.

> There is one of them, 17th February, 1934, Page 7, "Pistol Shooting"; 21st April, 1934, Page 13, "What every S.A. man must now about Aviation"; 19th May, 1934, Page 13, "Chemical Warfare"; 2nd June, 1934, Page 14, "Modern Battle Methods in the View of the S.A. Man"; 4th August, 1934, Page 13, "The Significance of Tanks and Motors in the Modern War."

I will omit references to the remainder.

Similarly, the issues of the S.A.-Mann contain many photographs and articles demonstrating and portraying S.A. participation in military exercises, including forced marching, battle maneuvers, obstacle runs, small-caliber firing, and so on. I merely refer these to your Honour, and they are shown on Pages 11 to 13 of Document 3050. Just one or two titles: 24th August, 1935, Page 2, "The S.A. Is and remains the Shock Troop of the Third Reich." Here is one showing the connection with the Wehrmacht: 2nd September, 1938, Page 1, "The S.A. and the Wehrmacht," with pictures of S.A. men on field maneuvers throwing hand grenades.

I will omit the rest of those.

Convincing evidence demonstrating the participation of the S.A. in the conspiracy is found in the fact that care was taken at all times to co-ordinate the military training of the S.A. with the requirements of the Wehrmacht. This is shown by Document 2821-PS, Exhibit USA 431, Page 1 of the English translation, quoting:
> "Permanent liaison between the Reich Defence Ministry and the Supreme Commander of the S.A... has been assured."

Another document, 3215-PS, which is an excerpt from Das Archiv, sets forth the co-operation and collaboration with the Wehrmacht, and specialised military training, and it was stated in a speech of the Chief of Staff of the S.A., Document 3215-PS, Page 2 of the English translation, Exhibit USA 426:
> "In the course of this development also special missions for military betterment were set for the S.A. The Fuehrer charged the S.A. with the cavalry and motor training and appointed S.A. Obergruppenfuehrer Litzmann as Reich Inspector with the mission of securing, through the S.A., cavalry recruits for the requirements of the German Wehrmacht. In close co-operation with parts of the Wehrmacht, special certificates were created for the signal, engineer and medical units which, like the cavalry certificate of the S.A., are valued as a statement of preference for employment in these units."

Your Honour, we have two or three more quotations about co-operation with the Wehrmacht, but I believe they would be cumulative, and I will omit them. I will refer only to Document 2383-PS, Exhibit USA 410. I will read a portion of the decree:
> "The Fuehrer: In amplification of my decrees of 15th February, 1935, and of 18th March, 1937 regarding the award of the S.A. Sports Insignia and the yearly repetitive exercises, I raise the S.A. Sports Insignia to the S.A. Military Insignia and make it a basis for pre- and post-military training. I designate the S.A. as the Standard Bearer of this training."

I pass now to Page 48 for the record.

The specialised training given S.A. members, in accordance with the requirements of the technical branches of the Wehrmacht, is described in Document 2168 by S.A. Sturmfuehrer Bayer, Exhibit USA 411, and it is Page 13 of the English translation:
> "On the one hand, the young S.A. man who from his branch in the S.A. enters the Armed Forces (Wehrmacht) already has many abilities which facilitate and speed up technical training; while on the other hand those very soldiers, who, having served their time in the Armed Forces return to the S.A., keep themselves, by constant training, physically and mentally fit, and impart their knowledge to their fellows.
>
> Thus they contribute a considerable portion to the increase of the armed strength and armed spirit of the German people."

And then passing down: "The S.A. each year is able to furnish many thousands of trained young men to our Wehrmacht." I will omit the rest of that.

I simply call attention now to Page 3 of an issue of Der S.A.-Mann dated 3rd February, 1939, which contains a photograph of Chief of Staff Lutze addressing a group of his men. This photograph bears the caption, "We will be the Bridge between the Party and the Wehrmacht."

The second reference shows a photograph of General Brauchitsch and Chief of Staff Lutze reviewing an S.A. unit.

Now, I pass to Document 3214-PS, which is Exhibit USA 432. There is only one page of it. Quoting:
> "It was announced that S.A. men and Hitler Youths liable to military service

can fulfil their military duty in the S.A. Regiment 'Feldherrnhalle,' the Commander of which is General Field Marshal, S.A. Obergruppenfuehrer Goering. The regiment for the first time was employed in the occupation of the Sudetenland as Regiment of the Luftwaffe, with special tasks under its Fuehrer and Regimental Commander, S.A. Gruppenfuehrer Reimann."

THE PRESIDENT: Up to now you have brought evidence to our notice showing that the S.A. was voluntary. This shows it was conscripted. When did it become conscripted?

COLONEL STOREY: As I understand it, your Honour, if you joined the S.A. you got out of conscription, but once you were in it they could use you as desired. In other words, the S.A. was a voluntary organisation.

THE PRESIDENT: That is the evidence you have given up to date.

COLONEL STOREY: Yes, Sir.

THE PRESIDENT: Well, when did it become liable to conscription or used as a substitute for conscription?

COLONEL STOREY: May I ask Mr. Burdell, who has been working on it, to answer that question?

MR. BURDELL: If your Honour pleases, there never was conscription in the S.A. As this document shows, document 3214, service in the Feldherrnhalle Regiment of the S.A. took the place of conscription. This first sentence in Document 3214, which reads, "It was announced that S.A. men and Hitler Youths liable to military service can fulfill their military conscription in the S.A. Regiment 'Feldherrnhalle,'" means, as I understand it, that S.A. men who are conscripted, that is S.A. men who are drafted after they have joined the S.A., may serve their conscription by remaining in the S.A. or by transferring to the Feldherrnhalle Regiment of the S.A.

The next paragraph of Document 3214 designates the requirements that must be fulfilled before the S.A. man can join this Feldherrnhalle Regiment, but if he fulfills those requirements he may join that regiment, and having done so, that serves the purpose or serves the function of conscription in the Wehrmacht.

I hope that answers your Honour's question.

COLONEL STOREY: In view of the above we would accept the S.A. to have been used as a striking force in the first steps of the aggressive war launched by Germany and as a basis for so-called Commando Groups, and such was the case. S.A. units were among the first Nazi military machine to invade Austria in the spring of 1938, as was proudly announced in an article appearing in Der S.A.-Mann, 19th March, 1938, Page 10, the article entitled, "We Were There First."

The S.A. participation in the occupation of the Sudetenland is also shown by Document 3036, Exhibit USA 102, and that is an affidavit by Gottlieb Berger, a former office holder in the S.S., who was assigned to the Sudeten-German Free Corps. I quote paragraphs 1 and 2 of the affidavit.

"1. In the fall of 1938 I held the rank and title of Oberfuehrer in the S.S. In mid-September I was assigned as S.S. Liaison Officer with Konrad Henlein's Sudeten German Free Corps at their headquarters in the castle at Dorndorf outside Bayreuth. In this position I was responsible for all liaison between the Reichsfuehrer S.S. Himmler and Henlein" - your Honour will recall Henlein was the leader in the Sudetenland - "and in particular, I was delegated to select from the Sudeten Germans those who appeared to be eligible for membership in the S.S. or V.T. (Verfuegungstruppe). In addition to myself, Liaison Officers stationed with Henlein included an Obergruppenfuehrer from the N.S.K.K., whose name I have forgotten, and S.A. Obergruppenfuehrer Max Juettmer, from the S.A. In addition, Admiral Canaris, who was head of the O.K.W. Abwehr, appeared at Dorndorf nearly every two days and conferred with Henlein."

Your Honours will recall that the "Abwehr" was the Intelligence Organisation.

2. In the course of my official duties at Henlein's Headquarters I became familiar with the composition and activities of the Free Corps. Three groups were being formed under Henlein's direction: One in the Eisenstein area, Bavaria; one in the Bayreuth area; one in the Dresden area; and possibly a fourth in Silesia. These groups were supposedly composed of refugees from the Sudetenland who had crossed the border into Germany, but they contain Germans with previous service in the S.A. and the N.S.K.K. (Nazi Motor Corps) as well. These Germans formed the backbone of the Free Corps.

On paper the Free Corps had a strength of 40,000 men. Part of the equipment furnished to Henlein, mostly haversacks, cooking utensils and blankets, was supplied by the S.A."

The adaptability of the S.A. to whatever purpose was required of it is demonstrated by its activities subsequent to the outbreak of the war. During the war the S.A. continued to carry out its military training programme, but it also engaged in other functions. Its wartime activities are set out in Document 3219-PS, which is Exhibit USA 433, and Document 3216-PS, Exhibit USA 434, which excerpts from Das Archiv.

I quote first, briefly, from Document 3219, the whole text, exclusive of the heading:

"The Chief of Staff of the S.A., Wilhelm Schepmann, gave further orders to increase the employment of the S.A. in the homeland war areas, because of the requirements of total war employment. This was done in numerous conferences with leaders of the S.A. divisions.

As a result of these conferences, as well as of measures already carried out earlier for the totalisation of the war employment, the S.A. has placed 86 per cent. of its main professional Fuehrer Corps at the disposal of the Front, even though the war missions of the S.A. have increased in the fields of pre-military training, the S.A. penetration into new parts of the Reich, the air war employment, the State and national guard, etc., during wartime.

The S.A. as a whole has given at present 70 per cent. of its some million members to the Wehrmacht."

I call the attention of your Honours to the statement of the membership of 26th August, 1944. I quote briefly from Document 3216, the English translation, just one sentence:

"By order of the Chief of Staff of the S.A., the S.A. unit Government-General was established, the command of which was taken over by Governor General S.A. Obergruppenfuehrer Dr. Frank."

I next offer in evidence an affidavit, being Document 3232-PS, Exhibit USA 435, by Walter Schellenberg:

"From the beginning of 1944 the S.A. also participated in many of the functions which had previously been entrusted only to the S.S., the Sipo and Army; for instance, the guarding of concentration camps and of prisoner-of-war camps, the supervision of forced laborers in Germany and occupied territories. This co-operation of the S.A. was planned and arranged for by high officials in Berlin as early as the middle of 1943."

This concludes my presentation of the principal points of evidence concerning the participation of the S.A. in the conspiracy, but before I leave the subject, I should like to present to the Tribunal a few facts which establish the participation in the conspiracy by defendant Goering, in his capacity as an S.A. member or leader.

In 1923, Goering became commander of the entire S.A. This is shown in the pamphlet, "The S.A.," which is already in evidence, and the notation concerning Goering's command appears at Page 2 of the translation, which I do not intend to quote but will merely refer to.

Goering's intention to employ the S.A. as a terroristic force to destroy political opponents is shown by a speech made by him on 3rd March, 1933, at a Nazi demonstration in Frankfurt. It is Document 1856-PS, Exhibit USA 437. It is an excerpt from a book entitled, "Hermann Goering, Speeches and Essays." I quote: Goering said-

> "Certainly I shall use the power of the State and the police to the utmost, my dear Communists, so draw no false conclusions. It will be a fight to the death, in which my fist will knuckle your neck; I shall lead with those down there the Brown Shirts."

The importance of the S.A. under Goering in the early stages of the Nazi movement is shown by Document 3259-PS, Exhibit USA 424, and it is an English translation from the same book, 3259-PS. This is a letter written to Goering by Hitler and I quote it:

> "My dear Goering,
>
> "When in November, 1923, the Party tried for the first time to conquer the power of the State, you, as Commander of the S.A., created, within an extraordinarily short time, that instrument with which I could dare struggle. Highest necessity had forced us to act, but by a wise providence at that time we were denied success. After receiving a grave wound, you again entered the ranks, as soon as circumstances permitted, as my most loyal comrade in the battle for power. You contributed essentially to creating the basis for the 30th January. Therefore, at the end of the year of the National Socialist Revolution, I desire to thank you wholeheartedly, my dear Party Comrade Goering, for the great services you have rendered to the National Socialist Revolution and consequently to the German people.
>
> "In cordial friendship and grateful appreciation,
>
> Yours,
>
> Adolf Hitler."

Although Goering did not retain command of the S.A., he at all times maintained close affiliation with the Organisation. This is shown by the the photographs of him participating in the activities which I have already introduced in evidence. Similarly, in 1937, he became the Commander of the Feldherrnhalle Regiment of the S.A. The Tribunal will recall, also my reference to the participation of that regiment in the occupation of the Sudetenland.

Now, finally, the evidence considered in the foregoing section of this brief, demonstrates the participation of the S.A. as an Organisation in the conspiracy alleged in Count One. Thus, the S.A. was first employed by the conspirators to destroy, by force and brutality, all opponents of National Socialism and to gain possession of the streets. Thereafter, upon the seizure of control by the N.S.D.A.P., the S.A. was used to consolidate and to strengthen Nazi power, and to persecute cruelly and destroy all so-called "enemies" of the State, including Jewry and the Church. During the period 1934 to 1939, the S.A. was employed for the actual preparation and training of the German people for war, and participated in aggressive warfare.

The S.A. was at all times employed by the conspirators to promote and disseminate the ideology of the Nazi Movement throughout Germany, and particularly, to perform the function of disseminating anti-Jewish propaganda and creating and fostering a militaristic and warlike spirit among the people of Germany

Conspiracy through its various phases; and the conclusion, we think, is irresistible, that the S.A. was an Organisation devoted exclusively to the task of assisting the defendants and their co-conspirators in carrying out the objectives of the Conspiracy.

Thus, in this sense, the S.A., as well as its members, were in fact co-conspirators and participants in a conspiracy which contemplated and involved Crimes Against Peace and Crimes Against Humanity and War Crimes.

That concludes the presentation of the S.A., your Honour, and the next is the S.S., by Major Farr.

Do your Honours want to go ahead with that now?

THE PRESIDENT: Perhaps we had better adjourn then, until 2 o'clock.

(A recess was taken until 1400 hours.)

MAJOR FARR: May it please the Tribunal, the next organisation to be dealt with is the S.S. The document books in this case are lettered " Z." For convenience in handling the books, because of the bulk of documents, we have divided them into two volumes. I shall in referring to a document number, refer to the volume in which that document appears.

About a week or ten days ago there appeared in a newspaper, circulated in Nuremberg, an account of a visit by that paper's correspondent to a camp in which S.S. prisoners-of-war were confined. The thing which particularly struck the correspondent was the one question asked by the S.S. prisoners. Why are we charged as war criminals? What have we done except our normal duty?

The evidence now to be presented to the Tribunal will, we expect, answer that question. It will show that just as the Nazi Party was the very heart - the core - of the conspiracy, so the S.S. was the very essence of Nazism. For the S.S. was the elite group of the Party, composed of the most thoroughgoing adherents of the Nazi cause, pledged to blind devotion to Nazi principles, and prepared to carry them out without any question and at any cost-a group in which every ordinary value has been so subverted that its members can ask " What is there unlawful about the things we have done?"

During the past weeks the Tribunal has heard evidence of the conspirators' criminal programme for aggressive war, for concentration camps, for the extermination of the Jews, for enslavement of foreign labour and illegal use of prisoners-of-war, for deportation and Germanisation of inhabitants of conquered territories. Through all this evidence the name of the S.S. ran like a thread. Again and again that organisation and its components were referred to. It is my purpose to show why it performed a responsible role in every one of these criminal activities, why it was - and, indeed, had to be - a criminal organisation.

The creation and development of such an organisation was, indeed, essential for the execution of the conspirators' plans. Their sweeping programme and the measures they were prepared to use and did use, could be fully accomplished neither through the machinery of the Government nor of the Party. Things had to be done for which no agency of government and no political party-even the Nazi Party-would openly take full responsibility. A specialised type of apparatus was needed, an apparatus which was to some extent connected with the Government and given official support but which, at the same time, could maintain a quasi-independent status, so that it acts could be attributed neither to the Government nor to the Party as a whole. The S.S. was that apparatus.

Like the S.A., it was one of the seven components or formations of the Nazi Party, referred to in the Decree on the Enforcement of the Law for Securing the Unity of Party and State, Of 29th March, 1935, published in the Reichsgesetzblatt for that year, Part I, Page 503. That decree will be found in our Document 1725-PS. I shall not read it. I assume that the Court will take judicial notice of it. The status of the S.S., however, was above that of the other formations. As the plans of the conspirators progressed, it acquired new functions, new responsibilities, and an increasingly more important place in the regime. It developed during the course of the conspiracy into a highly complex machine, the most powerful in the Nazi State, spreading its tentacles into every field of Nazi activity.

The evidence which I shall present will be directed, first, towards showing very briefly the origin and early development of the S.S. ; second, how it was organised- that is, its structure and its component parts ; third, the basic principles governing the selection of its members and the obligations they undertook; and finally, its aims and the means used to accomplish them, the manner in which it carried out the purposes of the conspirators, and thus was a responsible participant in the crimes alleged in the Indictment.

The history, Organisation and publicly announced functions of the S.S. are not controversial matters. They are not matters to be learned only from secret files and captured documents. They were recounted in many publications, circulated widely throughout Germany and the worldofficial books of the Nazi Party itself and books, pamphlets and speeches by S.S. and State officials published with S.S. and Party approval. Throughout the presentation of the case I shall frequently refer to five or six such publications, translations of which-in whole or in part-appear in the document books. Although I shall quote portions of them, I shall not attempt to read them all in full, since I assume that the contents of such authoritative publications may be judicially noticed by the Tribunal.

Now to take up the origin of the S.S. The first aim of the conspirators - as the evidence already presented to the Court has shown - was to gain a foothold in politically hostile territory, to acquire mastery of the streets and to combat any and all opponents with force. For that purpose they needed their own private, personal police Organisation. Evidence has just been introduced in the case against the S.A.-showing how that Organisation was created to fill such a role. But the S.A. was outlawed in 1923. When Nazi Party activity was again resumed in 1925, the S.A. remained outlawed. To fill its place and to play the part of Hitler's own personal police, small mobile groups known as protective squadrons (Schutzstaffel) were created. This was the origin of the S.S. in 1925. With the reinstatement of the S.A. in 1926, the S.S. for the next few years ceased to play a major role. But it continued to exist as an Organisation within the S.A. - under its own leader, however - the Reichsfuehrer S.S. This early history of the S.S. is related in two of the authoritative publications to which I have referred: the first is a book by S.S. Standartenfuehrer Gunter d'Alquen, entitled 'Die S.S.' This book - a pamphlet of some 30 pages - is an authoritative account of the history, mission and Organisation of the S.S., published in 1939. As indicated on its frontispiece, it was written at the direction of the Reichsfuehrer S.S., Heinrich Himmler. Its author, S.S. Standartenfuehrer Gunter d'Alquen, was the editor of the official S.S. publication 'Das Schwarze Korps.' This book is our Document 2284-PS, I offer it in evidence Exhibit USA 438. The passage to which I refer will be found on Pages and 7 of the original, and on Page i of the translation.

I shall not now read that passage.

The second publication is an article by Himmler, entitled " Organisation and Obligations of the S.S. and the Police." It was published in 1937 in booklet containing a series of speeches or essays by important officials of Party and the State - known as "National Political Course for the Arm Forces from 15th to 23rd January, 1937." The article by Himmler, which I refer, appears on Pages 137-161 of that pamphlet. Large extra from it make up our Document 1992-A-PS. I offer the essay by Himml as Exhibit USA 439. The passage to which I referred appears on Page 137 of the original and Page 1 of the translation, our Document. 1992-A-PS. I shall have occasion to quote from both these publications, but with respect to this matter of history, I assume that these references to the pertinent passages in them are enough.

As early as 1929 the conspirators recognised that their plans required organisation in which the main principles of the Nazi system, specifically the racial principles, would not only be jealously guarded but would carried to such extremes as to inspire or intimidate the rest of the population - an organisation in which, also, there would be assured complete freedom on the part of the leaders and blind obedience on the part of the members. The S.S. was built up to meet this need. I quote from d'Alquen's book 'Die S.S.', at Page 7 - this passage appears in our Document 2284-PS, at Page 4 of the translation, paragraph 4:

"On 16th January, 1929, Adolf Hitler appointed his tested comrade of long standing, Heinrich Himmler, as Reichsfuehrer S.S. Heinrich Himmler assumed charge therewith of the entire Schutzstaffel, totalling at the time 280 men, with the express and particular commission of the Fuehrer to form this organisation into an elite troop of the Party, a troop dependable in every circumstance. With this day the real history of the S.S. begins as it stands before us today in all its deeper essential features, firmly anchored in the National Socialist movement. For the S.S. and its Reichsfuehrer, Heinrich Himmler, its first S.S. men, have become inseparable in the course of these battle-filled years."

Carrying out Hitler's directive, Himmler proceeded to build up out of this small force of men an elite organisation - to use d'Alquen's words: " composed of the best physically, the most dependable, and the most faithful men in the Nazi movement." I read another passage from d'Alquen, at Page 12 of the original, Page 6 of the translation, paragraph 5:

"When the day of seizure of power had finally come, there were 52,000 S.S. men, who in this spirit bore the revolution in the van, marched into the new State which they began to help to form everywhere, in their stations and positions, in profession and in science, and in all their essential tasks."

The conspirators now had the machinery of government in their hands. The initial function of the S.S. - that of acting as private army and personal police force - was thus completed. But its mission had in fact really just begun. That mission is described in the Organisation Book of the N.S.D.A.P. for 1943. The pages from that book dealing with the S.S. - Pages 417 to 428 - are translated in out Document 2040-PS. The organisation's book has already been offered in evidence as Exhibit USA 303. The passage to which I refer appears on Page 417 of the original, and on Page 1, paragraph 2, of the translation, our Document 2640-PS:

"Missions

The most original and most eminent duty of the S.S. is to serve as the protectors of the Fuehrer.

By decree of the Fuehrer, the sphere of duties has been enlarged to include the internal security of the Reich."

This new mission - protecting the internal security of the regime - was somewhat more colourfully defined by Himmler in his pamphlet "The S.S. as an Anti-Bolshevist Fighting Organisation," published in 1936. It is our Document 1851-PS. I offer this document in evidence as Exhibit USA 440. The definition to which I refer appears at the bottom of Page 29 of the original, on the third page of the translation, middle of the paragraph:

"We shall unremittingly fulfil our task, the guaranty of the, security of Germany from the interior, just as the Wehrmacht guarantees the safety of the honour, the greatness, and the peace of the Reich from the exterior. We shall take care that never again in Germany, the heart of Europe, will the Jewish-Bolshevistic revolution of subhumans be able to be kindled either from within or through emissaries from without. Without pity we shall be a merciless sword of justice for all those forces whose existence and activity we know, on the day of the slightest attempt, may it be today, may it be in decades or may it be in centuries."

This conception necessarily required an extension of the duties of the S.S. into many fields. It involved, of course, the performance of police functions. But it involved more. It required participation in the suppression and extermination of all internal opponents of the regime. It meant participation in extending the regime beyond the borders of Germany, and, therefore, came to mean eventually participation in every type of activity designed to secure a hold over those territories and populations which, through military conquest, had come under German domination.

The expansion of S.S. duties and activities resulted in the creation of several branches and numerous departments and the eventual development of a highly complex machinery. Those various branches and departments cannot be adequately described out of the context of their history. That description I hope will emerge fully as evidence of the activities of the S.S. is presented. But it may be appropriate to anticipate, and at this point to say a word about the structure of the S.S.

For this purpose, a glance at a chart depicting the organisation of the S.S. as it appeared in 1945 may be helpful. There are being handed to the Tribunal small copies of this chart, two in English, one in French and one in Russian. In addition, there are handed eight larger copies of the chart in the original German, which bears on it the photostat of the affidavit of Gottlieb Berger, formerly Chief of the S.S. Main Office, who examined the chart, and stated that it correctly represented the organisation of the S.S.

I now offer in evidence the chart of the Supreme and Regional Command of the S.S. as Exhibit USA 445.

At the very top of the chart is Himmler, the Reichsfuehrer S.S., who commanded the entire organisation. Immediately below - running across the chart and down the right-hand side, embraced within the heavy line - are the twelve main departments constituting the Supreme Command of the S.S. Some of these departments have been broken down into the several offices of which they were composed, as indicated by the boxes beneath them. Other departments have not been so broken down. It is not intended to indicate that there were not subdivisions of these latter departments as well. The breakdown is shown only in those cases where the constituent offices of some department may have a particular significance in this case.

These departments and their functions are described in two official Nazi publications: the first is the Organisation Book of the N.S.D.A.P. for 1943 (our

Document 2640-PS) already introduced in evidence as Exhibit USA 323. The description, which I shall not now read, appears on Pages 419-420 of the original and Pages 2 to 4 of the translation. The second is an S.S. manual, which bears the title: "The Soldier Friend - Pocket Diary for the German Armed Forces - Edition D: Waffen S.S." It was prepared at the direction of the Reichsfuehrer S.S. and issued by the S . S. Main Office for the year ending 1942. It is our Document 2825-PS. I offer it in evidence as Exhibit USA 441. The description to which I refer appears on Pages 20 to 22 of the original, and Pages 1 and 2 of the translation. I will later have occasion to read the description of the functions of some of the departments in full. But I assume that the Court will take judicial notice of the entire passages to which I have referred. In addition, the departments are listed in a directory of the S.S., published by one of the main departments of the S.S. This document was found in the files of the Personal Staff of the Reichsfuehrer S.S., the first department on the left of the chart. It is entitled "Directory for the Schutzstaffel of the N.S.D.A.P., 1st November, 1944." It is marked "Restricted " and bears the notation "Published by S.S. Fuehrungshauptamt, Kommandant of the General S.S.," which is the fifth box from the left. It is our Document 2769-PS. I offer it in evidence as Exhibit USA 442. It is simply a list of the names of the departments and offices with their addresses and telephone numbers, and corroborates the statements in the two earlier publications to which I referred.

Returning now to the chart - following down the central spine from the Reichsfuehrer S.S. to the regional level, we come to the Higher S.S. and Police Leader, commonly known as H.S.S.P.F., the Supreme S.S. Commander in each region. I shall refer to his functions at a later point. Immediately below him is the breakdown of the organisation of the Allgemeine or General S.S. To the left are indicated two other branches of the S.S. - the Death Head Units (Totenkopf Verbaende) and the Waffen S.S. To the right, under the H.S.S.P.F., is the S.D. All of these components, together with the S.S. Police Regiments, are specifically named in the Indictment - Appendix B, Page 36 - as being included in the S.S.

Now a word as to these components. Up to 1933, there were no such specially designated branches. The S.S. was a single group - a group of 44 "volunteer political soldiers." It was out of this original nucleus that the new units developed.

The "Allgemeine " - that is, General S.S. - was the common basis, the main stem out of which the various branches grew. It was composed of all members of the S.S. who did not belong to any of the special branches.

It was the backbone of the entire organisation. The personnel and officers of the main departments of the S.S. Supreme Command were members of this branch. Except for high-ranking officers and those in staff capacities in the main offices of the S.S. Supreme Command, its members were part-time volunteers. As the evidence will show, its members were utilised in about every phase of S.S. activity. They were called upon in the anti-Jewish pogroms of 1938 ; they took over the task of guarding concentration camps during the war; they participated in the colonisation and resettlement programme. In short, the term "S.S." normally meant the General S.S.

It was organised on military lines, as will be seen from the chart, ranging from district (Oberabschnitt) and sub-district (Abschnitt) down through the regiment, battalion, company, to the platoon. Until after the beginning of the war it constituted numerically the largest branch of the S.S. In 1939 d'Alquen, the official S.S. spokesman, said, and I quote from his book, our Document 2284-PS, Page 9, paragraph 3, of the English translation, and Page 18 of the original document:

"The strength of the General S.S., 240,000 men, is sub-divided today into 14 corps, 38 divisions, 140 infantry regiments, 19 mounted regiments, 14 communication battalions and 19 engineer battalions as well as motorised and medical units. This General S.S. stands fully and wholly on call as in the fighting years . . ."

Similar reference to the military organisation of the General S.S. will be found in Himmler's speech "Organisation and Obligations of the S.S, and the Police," our Document 1992-A-PS, at Page 4 of the translation. and in the Organisation Book of the N.S.D.A.P. for 1943, our Document 2460-PS, at Pages 4 and 5 of the translation.

Members of this branch, however, with the exception of certain staff personnel - were subject to compulsory military service. As the result of the draft of members of the General S.S. of military age into the Army, the numerical strength of active members considerably declined during the war. Older S.S. men and those working in or holding high positions in the main departments of the Supreme Command of the S.S. remained. Its entire strength during the war was probably not in excess of 40,000 men.

The second component to be mentioned is the Security Service of the Reichsfuehrer S.S., almost always referred to as the S.D. Himmler described it in his speech, "Organisation and Obligations of the S.S. and the Police " - our Document 1992-A-PS. I quote a passage from Page 8, last paragraph of the translation, Page 151 of the original, paragraph 3:

"I now come to the Security Service (S.D.) ; it is the great ideological Intelligence Service of the Party, and, in the long run, also that of the State, During the time of struggle for power it was only the Intelligence Service of the S. S. At that time we had, for quite natural reasons, an Intelligence Service with the regiments, battalions and companies." - He refers there to the regiments, battalions and companies of the General S. S. - " We had to know what was going on on the opponents' side, whether the Communists intended to hold a meeting today or not, whether our people were to be suddenly attacked or not, and similar things. I had already separated this service in 1931 from the troops " (I note that it appears in the mimeographed translation as 1941, but, as will appear from a passage on the next pages of the translation, it was 1931 to which he was referring) "from the units of the General S.S., because I considered it to be wrong not to do so. For one thing, secrecy is endangered, then the individual men, or even the companies, are too likely to discuss everyday problems."

Although, as Himmler put it, the S.D. was only the Intelligence Service of the S.S. during the years preceding the accession of the Nazis to power, it became a much more important organisation shortly thereafter. It had been developed into such a powerful scientific espionage system under its chief, Reinhard Heydrich, that on 9th June, 1934, just a few weeks before the blood purge of the S.A., it was made, by decree of the defendant Hess, the sole Intelligence and Counter-intelligence agency of the entire Nazi Party. I refer in support of that statement to d'Alquen's book, Die S.S., our Document 2284-PS, at Page 11 of the translation. I shall not pause to quote that passage. The Organisation and numbers of the S.D., as they stood in 1937, were thus described by Himmler -I quote again from his article "Organisation and Obligations of the S.S. and the Police," our Document 1992-A-PS, at Page 9 of the translation, second paragraph, Page 151 of the original, paragraph 4:

"The Security Service had already been separated from the troop in 1931 and separately organised. Its higher headquarters coincide today with the Oberabschnitte and Abschnitte " (I refer to the "Abschnitte" and

"Oberabschnitte" indicated on the chart) "and it has also field offices, its own organisation of officials, and a great many command posts, and is approximately three to four thousand men strong, or at least it will be when it is built up."

Up to 1939, its headquarters was the S.S. Main Security Office (Sicherheitshauptamt), which, as I shall shortly show, became amalgamated in 1939 in the Reich Main Security Office (R.S.H.A.) one of the S.S. main departments shown on the chart before you - the sixth box from the left. The closer and closer collaboration of the S.D. with the Gestapo and Criminal Police - which eventually resulted in the creation of this R.S.H.A. - and the activities in which the S.D. engaged in partnership with the Gestapo, will be taken up in the presentation of the case against the Gestapo. The S.D. was, of course, at all times an integral and important component of the S.S. But it is more practicable to deal with it in connection with the activities of the whole repressive police system with which it functioned.

The third component to be mentioned is the "Waffen S.S." - the combat arm of the S.S. - created, trained and finally utilised for purposes of aggressive war. The reason underlying the creation of this combat branch was described in our Document 2640-PS, the Organisation Book of the Nazi Party for 1943. It appears on Page 427A of the original Page 5, paragraph 7 of the translation:

"The Armed S.S. originated out of the thought: to create for the Fuehrer a selected long-service troop for the fulfilment of special missions. It should make it possible for members of the General S.S., as well as for volunteers who fulfil the special requirements of the S.S., to fight in the battle for the evolution of the National Socialist idea, with weapon in hand, in unified groups, partly within the framework of the Army."

The term "Waffen S.S." did not come into use until after the beginning of the war. Up to that time there were two branches of the S.S. composed of full-time, professional, well-trained soldiers - the so-called "S.S. Verfuegungstruppe " - translatable perhaps as S.S. Emergency Troops - and the " S.S. Totenkopf Verbaende " -The, Death Head Units. After the beginning of the war, the units of the S.S. Verfuegungstruppe were brought up to division strength, and new divisions were added to them. Parts of the S.S. Death Head Units were formed into a division - the " S.S. Totenkopf Division." All these divisions then came to be known collectively as the Waffen S.S."

Let me now trace that development. I quote again from the Organisation Book of the Nazi Party for 1943, our Document 2640-PS, Page 427B of the original, Page 5, last paragraph of the translation:

"The origin of the Waffen S.S. goes back to the decree Of 17th March, 1933, establishing the ' Stabswache' with the original strength Of 120 men. Out of this small group developed the later-named ' S.S. Verfuegungstruppe' (S.S. Emergency Force), and the 'Leibstandarte S.S. Adolf Hitler.' In the course of the war these groups grew into divisions."

THE PRESIDENT: Major Farr, is it necessary to go into this degree of detail about the Organisation of the S.S.?

MAJOR FARR: Sir, it seemed to me that it is highly important to know exactly what is the organisation with which we are dealing. There has been, I understand, a suggestion made to the Court that certain portions of this organisation are not criminal. It is contended by some that the part they played was a perfectly innocuous one, and it seems to me that before we can determine whether the organisation as a whole is criminal, whether any portion of it is severable, then we must know what the organisation is.

THE PRESIDENT: Would it not be possible to leave that question to evidence in rebuttal, if the defendants are setting up that any particular branch of the S.S. is not criminal?

MAJOR FARR: If we adequately lay the basis for our case now, it may not be necessary for us to make any rebuttal. We may satisfy the defendants that there is nothing in the contention that any portion of the S.S. is a lawful portion. The point I am particularly trying to make now is: there has been a good deal of contention that the " Waffen S.S. " is severable ; that whatever may be said, for example, about the S.D. or the Death Head Units, the " Waffen S.S." is something different-the " Waffen S.S. " is part of the Army. I think it is important to establish at the outset that the "Waffen S.S." is as much a part of the S.S., as integral a part of the whole Organisation, as any of the other branches. I propose, therefore, to show the development of the " Waffen S.S.," growing out of the S.S. Emergency Troop, and to call to the attention of the Tribunal evidence showing how the " Waffen S.S." is an integral part of the S.S. as a whole.

THE PRESIDENT: Well, you must take your own course.

MAJOR FARR: The "S.S. Verfuegungstruppe" were described in a top secret Hitler order, dated the 17th August, 1938. It is our Document No. 647-PS. I offer it in evidence as Exhibit USA 443. That document will be found in Volume I of the document book. I quote from Section II of that order, which appears on Page 2 of the translation, at the top of the page, and also on Page 2 of the original.

"II. The Armed Units of the S.S.

A. (The S.S. Verfuegungstruppe)

i. The S.S. Verfuegungstruppe is neither a part.of the Wehr macht nor a part of the Police. It is a standing armed unit exclusively at my disposal. As such and as a unit of the N.S.D.A.P. its members are to be selected by the Reichsfuehrer S.S. according to the philosophical and political standards which I have ordered for the N.S.D.A.P. and for the Schutzstaffe. Its members are to be trained and its ranks filled with volunteers from those who are liable to serve in the army having finished their duties in the compulsory labour service. The service period for volunteers is 4 years. It may be prolonged for S.S. Unterfuehrer. Such regulations are in force for S.S. leaders. The regular compulsory military service (para. 8 of the law relating to military service) is fulfilled by service of the same amount of time in the S.S. Verfuegungstruppe."

I want to quote a further short passage from that decree which will be found on Page 3 of the translation, in the middle of the page, and on Page 4 of the original order:

III. Orders in Case of Mobilisation A. The employment of the S.S. Verfuegungstruppe in case of mobilisation is a double one.

I. By the Supreme Commander of the Army within the wartime army. In that case it comes completely under military laws and regulations, but remains a unit of the N.S.D.A.P. politically.

2. In case of necessity, in the interior according to my orders, in that case it is under the Reichsfuehrer S.S. and Chief of the German Police.

In case of mobilisation, I myself will make the decision about the time, strength and manner of the incorporation of the S.S. Verfuegungstruppe into the war-time army; these things will depend on the inner-political situation at that time."

Immediately after the issuance of this decree, and the Court will recall it was issued in August of 1938, this militarised force was employed with the Army for aggressive purposes-the taking over of the Sudetenland. Following this action, feverish preparation to motorise the force and to organise new units such as anti-tank, machine gun and reconnaissance battalions were undertaken pursuant to further directives of the Fuehrer. By September, 1939, the force was fully motorised, its units had been increased to division strength and it was prepared for combat. These steps are described in the Nationalist Socialist Yearbook for the years 1940 and 1941. I offer in evidence Pages 365 to 371 of the 1940 Yearbook. It is our Document 2164-PS. It will be Exhibit USA 255. I offer Pages 191 to 193 of the 1941 Yearbook - which is our Document 2163-PS - as Exhibit USA 444. Since the Yearbook is an official publication of the Nazi Party, edited by Reichsleiter Robert Ley and published by the Nazi Party publishing company, I assume that the Court will take judicial notice of the contents of these exhibits.

After the launching of the Polish invasion and as the war progressed, still further divisions were added. The Organisation Book of the Nazi Party for 1943 - our Document 2640-PS - lists some eight divisions and two infantry brigades as existing at the end of 1942. I refer to Page 427b of the original, Page 5, last paragraph of the translation. This was no longer an emergency force. it was an S.S. army and hence came to be designated as the Waffen S.S. Himmler referred to this spectacular development of this S.S. combat branch in his speech at Posen on 4th October, 1943, to S.S. Gruppenfuehrers. That speech has already been introduced in evidence at an earlier stage in the case, as Exhibit USA 170 - It is our Document 1919-PS.

I shall quote from that speech, Page 51 of the original, Page 2 of the translation, second paragraph, headed "The S.S. in War-Time."

"Now I come to our own development, to that of the S.S. in the past months. Looking back on the whole war, this development was fantastic. It took place at an absolutely terrific speed. Let us look back a little to 1939. At that time we were a few regiments, guard units, 8,000 to 9,000 strong - that is, not even a division, all in all 25,000 to 28,000 men at the outside. True, we were armed, but we really only got our artillery regiment as our heavy arm two months before the war began."

I continue, quoting from the same speech a passage found on Page 8 of the English translation and on Page 103 of the original. The passage in the translation appears at about the middle of the page.

"In the hard battles of this year, the Waffen S.S. has been welded together in the bitterest hours from the most varied divisions and sections, and from these it formed: body-guard units (Leibstandarte), military S.S. (Verfuegungstruppe), Death Head Units, and then the Germanic S.S."

Although tactically under the command of the Wehrmacht while in the field, it remained as much a part of the S.S. as any other branch of the organisation. Throughout the war it was recruited, trained, administered and supplied by the main offices of the S.S. Supreme Command. Ideologically and racially, its members were selected in conformity with S.S. standards.

I shall read a passage relating to the recruiting standards of the Waffen S.S. published in the S.S. Manual, "The Soldier Friend," our Document 2825-PS, which appears on Page 7 of the English translation, first paragraph on Page 36, paragraph 2, of the the original. I quote:

> "Today at last is the longed for day of the entrance examinations where the examiners and physicians decide whether or not the candidate is ideologically and physically qualified to do service in the Waffen S.S.
>
> Everyone has acquainted himself with the comprehensive Manual for the Waffen S.S., of which the principal points are as follows:
>
>> I. Service in the Waffen S.S. counts as military service. Only volunteers are accepted."

THE TRIBUNAL (MR. BIDDLE): What is the purpose of reading all this evidence ? What has what you just read got to do with what you are presenting ?

MAJOR FARR: Sir, I want to prove, as I said a moment ago, one thing first; that the Waffen S.S. is an integral, component part of the S.S. I want to establish that it is completely administered and controlled by the Supreme Command of the S.S. That is one thing.

The second thing I want to prove is this; that service in the Waffen S.S. is voluntary service, just as membership in the Allgemeine S.S. or Death Head Units is voluntary service. It is true that there were some instances towards the close of the war when a few men were conscripted into the Waffen S.S., but that was the exception and not the rule. In quoting from the Recruiting Standards of the Waffen S.S., appearing in this booklet which was published in 1942, and which indicates that at that time service in the Waffen S.S. was open only to volunteers, I think I am serving the purpose of proving one of the two points which I think ought to be estab lished.

I want to read, if I may, one further paragraph from that translation. I shall read the paragraph indicating that service is voluntary. Now I want to read the third requirement, which shows that service was open only to persons who could meet the ideological and other standards of the S.S. as a whole.

If the Tribunal is satisfied on the point that service in the Waffen S.S. is essentially voluntary and that the Waffen S.S. is an integral part of the S.S., I do not want to impose further by reading further evidence.

THE PRESIDENT: I think the Tribunal is satisfied on both those points, up to the present time, that it is voluntary and is an integral part of the S.S.

MAJOR FARR: If the Court is satisfied on both those points, I shall not pursue, any further, the introduction of this particular evidence.

THE PRESIDENT: It may, as you say, be possible to show that there were some members conscripted into it at a later date, but we have not had that evidence yet.

MAJOR FARR: No, your Honour, you have not.

All I want to show is that it is, normally, voluntary, and that the Waffen S.S. is an integral part of the whole organisation. If the Court is completely satisfied on that point I shall proceed no further with the description of the Waffen S.S.

I shall pass on now, therefore, to a description of the "S.S. Totenkopf Verbaende", the Death Head Units, which is the fourth component to be mentioned.

The origin and purpose of the Totenkopf Verbaende were succinctly described by d'Alquen in his book, "The S.S.", our Document 2284-PS, and I shall read from Page 10 of the English translation, paragraph 5, a passage that appears on Page 20 of the original, paragraph 3.

> "The S.S. Death Head Units form one part of the barracked S.S They arose from volunteers of the General S.S. who were recruite for the guarding of concentration camps in 1933.
>
> Their mission, apart from the indoctrination of the armed political soldier, is to guard enemies of the States who are held in concentration camps.

The S.S. Death Head Units enforce on their members 12 years' service. They are composed mainly of men who have already fulfilled their duty to serve in the Wehrmacht. This time of service is counted in full."

Since the Death Head Units - like the "S.S. Verfuegungstruppe" - were composed of well-trained professional soldiers, they were also a valuable nucleus for the Waffen S.S. The secret Hitler order of 17th August, 1938, Document 647-PS, which has already been introduced in evidence, provided for the tasks of the "S.S. Totenkopf Verbaende" in the event of mobilisation. The Toterikopf Verbaende were to be relieved from the duty of guarding concentration camps and transferred as a skeleton corps to the "S.S. Verfuegungstruppe". I quote from that order, a passage found on Page 5 of the translation, paragraph 4, Page 9 of the original:

"5. Regulations in case of Mobilisation:-
The S.S. Totenkopf Verbaende form the skeleton corps for the reinforcement of the S.S. Verfuegungstruppe (police reinforcement) and will be replaced in the guarding of the concentration camps by members of the General S.S. who are over 45 years of age and have had military training."

If I may point out to the Court, the purpose in offering that bit of evidence is to show that the foundation was laid for the "Allgemeine S.S.", the General S.S., to take over the duties of guarding concentration camps after the war had started. The Totenkopf Verbaende were originally created for that purpose. When the war came they went into the Waffen S.S. and their duties were taken over by members of the General S.S.

The final component, which was specifically referred to in the Indictment, is the S.S. Police Regiments. I shall very shortly turn to the steps by which the S.S. assumed control over the entire Reich Police. Out of the police, special militarised forces were formed, originally known as S.S. Police Battalions and later expanded to S.S. Police Regiments.

I quote from Himmler's Posen speech, our Document 1919-PS, Page 3 of the translation, next to the last paragraph, Page 58 of the original.

"Now to deal briefly with the tasks of the regular uniformed police and the Sipo - they still cover the same field. I can see that great things have been achieved. We have formed roughly 30 police regiments from police reservists and former members of the police - police officials, as they used to be called. The average age in our police battalions is not lower than that of the security battalions of the Armed Forces. Their achievements are beyond all praise. In addition, we have formed Police Rifle Regiments by merging the police battalions of the 'savage peoples'. Thus, we did not leave these police battalions untouched but blended them in the ratio of about 1 to 3."

The results of this blend of militarised S.S. police and "savage peoples" will be seen in the evidence which I shall later introduce, relating to extermination actions, conducted by them in the Eastern territories - exterminations which were so eminently successful and so ruthlessly conducted that even Himmler could find no words adequate for their eulogy.

THE PRESIDENT: We will adjourn now for 10 minutes.

(A recess was taken.)

MAJOR FARR: Each of the various components which I have described played its part in carrying out one or more functions of the S.S. The personnel composing each differed. Some were part-time volunteers; others, professionals, enlisted for different periods of time. But every branch, every department, every member, was an integral part of the whole organisation. Each performed his assigned role in the manifold tasks for which the organisation had been created. No better witness to this fact could be called upon than the Reichsfuehrer S.S., whose every effort was to insure the complete unity of the organisation. I quote his words, taken from his Posen speech, our Document igig-PS, Exhibit USA 170- 1 read from Page 104 of the original, fourth line from the top of the page, from the English translation, Page 8.

> "It would be an evil day if the main offices, in performing. their tasks with the best, but mistaken intentions, made themselves independent by each having a downward chain of command. I really think that the day of my overthrow would be the end of the S.S. It must be, that this S.S. organisation with all its branches-the General S.S. which is the common basis of all of them, the Waffen S.S., the regular uniformed police, the Sipo, with the whole economic administration, schooling, ideological training, the whole question of kindred, is, even under the tenth Reichsfuehrer S.S., one block, one body, one Organisation."

And continuing, about the middle of Page 8 of the translation, and at the bottom of Page 104 of the original speech:

> "The regular uniformed police and Sipo, General S.S. and Waffen S.S. must now gradually be amalgamated too, just as this is and must be the case within the Waffen S.S. This applies to matters concerning filling of posts, recruiting, schooling, economic organisation, and medical services. I am always doing something towards this end, a bond is constantly being drawn around these actions of the whole to cause them to grow together. Alas, if these bonds should ever be loosened-then everything-you may be sure of this-would sink back into its old insignificance within one generation, and in a short space of time."

I now turn to the underlying philosophy of the S.S., the principles by which its members were selected and the obligations imposed upon them. To understand this organisation, the theories upon which it was based must be kept clearly in mind. They furnish the key to all its activities. It is necessary, therefore, to consider them in some detail.

The fundamental principle of selection was what Himmler called that of Blood and Elite. The S.S. was to be the living embodiment of the Nazi doctrine of the superiority of Nordic blood-the carrying into effect of the Nazi conception of a master race. To put it in Himmler's own words, the S.S. was to be a " National Socialist Soldier Order of Nordic Men ". In describing to the Wehrmacht the reasons behind his emphasis on'racial standards of selection and the manner in which they were carried out he said-and I quote from our Document 1992-A-PS, Page I of the translation, last paragraph, Page 138, paragraph I of the original:

> "Accordingly, only good blood, blood which history has proved to be leading and creative and the foundation of every State and of all military activities, only Nordic blood, can be considered. I said to myself that, should I succeed in selecting from the German people for this organisation as many people as possible a majority of whom possess this desired blood, in teaching them military discipline and, in time, the understanding of the value of blood and the entire ideology which results from it, then it will be possible actually to create such an elite organisation as would successfully hold its own in all cases of emergency."

Further on, on Page 5 of the translation-I beg your pardon, on Page 4 of the translation, first line, Page 140 of the original, bottom paragraph, he says, referring to the method by which applicants were selected:

"They are very thoroughly examined and checked. Of ioo men we can use on the average 10 or 15, no more. We ask for the political record of his parents, brothers and sisters, the record of his ancestry as far back as 1750, and naturally the physical examination and his record from the Hitler Youth. Further, we ask for a eugenic record showing that no hereditary disease exists in his parents or in his family."

THE PRESIDENT: (interposing) I do not seem to get the point of this. We have already been told that the S.S. was a Corps d'Elite, and all this is showing the details of the choice.

MAJOR FARR: That is correct; it is showing the details of the choice.

THE PRESIDENT: But that has nothing to do with its being a criminal organisation, has it?

MAJOR FARR: I think it has, your Honour. I want to make again, if I may, two points. The very essence of this organisation was that of race. Its racial standards of selection had two purposes: One, to make it an organisation which would be an aristocracy not only for Germany, but which would be in a position to dominate all of Europe. For that purpose, not only were strict racial standards imposed for selection, but a great drive was made to perpetuate the S.S. stock, to build up a group of men who would be in a position to take over Europe when it was conquered.

There was nothing questionable about that aim. Himmler explicitly said time and time again: " What we are after is to make ourselves the super-class which will be able to dominate Europe for centuries." That was one of the fundamental purposes of the S.S., and it was a purpose which was not kept by Himmler to himself, but a purpose which was explained and publicly announced again and again.

THE PRESIDENT: You have npt yet shown us where it was announced, have you?

MAJOR FARR: I have not, Sir, and I am coming to that very shortly, but I wanted first to show your Honour what the racial basis of selection was. That is one aspect of the racial selective process.

The second was this: The negative side of the racialism. Not only did Himmler intend to build up an elite which would be able to take over Europe, but he indoctrinated that elite with hatred for all " inferior "-to use his words-races.

Now, I think unless it is clearly understood that that is the basis of the S.S., we cannot understand the organisation. I am quite prepared, if the Tribunal desires, not to go further into a discussionof the detail of the process of selection. I do think it important that I quote to the Tribunal the publicly announced basis for selection.

With the Tribunal's permission then, I would like to quote one passage from the Organisation Book for the Nazi Party, which explains the racial basis on which the S.S. was founded. That is our Document 2640-PS, which has already been introduced in evidence as Exhibit USA 323- 1 quote from Page V7 of the German text and from Page i of the translation, fourth paragraph, entitled "Selection of Members." And I quote this because this is not a hidden pronouncement. This is what the official Nazi Party publication said the S. S. was:

"Selection of Members.

For the fulfilment of these missions a homogeneous, firmly welded fighting force has been created bound by ideological oaths, whose fighters are selected out of the best Aryan humanity.

The conception of the value of the blood and soil serves as directive for the selection for the S.S. Every S.S. man must be deeply imbued with the sense and essence of the National Socialist Movement. He will be ideologically and physically trained so that he can be employed individually or in groups in the decisive battle for the National Socialist ideology.

Only the best and thoroughbred Germans are suited for commitment in this battle. Therefore it is necessary that an uninterrupted selection is maintained within the ranks of the S.S., first superficially, then more and more thoroughly."

Now, I would like to proceed to quote a paragrapb on the same page, three paragraphs down, with respect to obedience. It appears on Page 418 of the original, second paragraph. It runs:

"Obedience is unconditionally demanded. It arises from the conviction that the National Socialist ideology must reign. He who possesses it and passionately supports it, submits himself voluntarily to the compulsion of obedience. Therefore, the S.S. man is prepared to carry out blindly every order which comes from the Fuehrer or is given by one of his superiors, even if it demands the greatest sacrifice of himself."

There are stated the two fundamental principles of the S.S. (i) Racial selection; (2) Blind obedience.

Now, let me state what Himmler conceived that this organisation was to be used for. I quote from his address to the officers of the S.S. Leib standarte "Adolf Hitler" on the " Day of Metz," our Document 19i8-PS, Exhibit USA 304. I quote from Page 12 of the original document, the middle of the page; from the translation Page 3, last paragraph. I will begin the translation with the third sentence of that paragraph:

"The ultimate aim for these 11 years during which I have been the Reichsfuehrer S.S. has been invariably the same. To create an order of good blood which is able to serve Germany, which unfailingly and without sparing itself can be made use of because the greatest losses can do no harm to the vitality of this order, the vitality of these men, because they will always be replaced. To create an order which will spread the idea of Nordic blood so far that we will attract all Nordic blood in the world, take away the blood from our adversaries, absorb it so that never again, looking at it from the viewpoint of the grand policy, Nordic blood in great quantities and to an extent worth mentioning will fight against us. We must get it and the others cannot have it. We never gave up the ideas and the aim, conceived so many years ago. Everything we have done has taken us some distance further on the way. Everything we are going to do will lead us further on the way."

Now, one further quotation from the same document, which shows very explicitly why there was the building up of this order of Nordic blood, appears on Page 3 of the translation, the same document from which I have just quoted, about the middle of the first paragraph. It appears on Page 11 of the original speech, about the middle of the page. That is the speech to the officers of the S.S. Leibstandarte "Adolf Hitler."

"Please understand we would not be able to hold the great Germanic Reich which is about to take shape. I am convinced that we can hold it, but we have to prepare for that. If once we have not enough sons, those who come after us will have to become cowards. A nation which has an average of four sons per family can venture a war; if two of them die, two transmit the name. The leadership of a nation having one or two sons per family will have to be fainthearted in any decision, on account of their own experience because they will have to tell themselves: We cannot afford it. Look at France, which is the best example. France had to accept from us a dictate."

Domination of Europe through a Nazi elite required more, however, than a positive side of racialism.

THE TRIBUNAL (Mr. BIDDLE): Is that one of the crimes you allege, domination of Europe through an elite ?

MAJOR FARR: One of the crimes alleged is a 'conspiracy to dominate Europe, preparation for aggressive war, leading to the ultimate colonisation of Europe for the benefit of the conspirators. One of the instruments, we submit, used for carrying out that policy, was the S.S. The conspirators began, at the very beginning, the creation of the S.S., to build it up so that it would be the elite through which Germany would be able to dominate and rule the conquered territories.

We think that this conception of the S.S. has played a vital part in the conspiracy. It has bearing on the whole programme of the conspirators. Now, this certainly, in itself-

THE PRESIDENT: Yes, but, Major Farr, what you have to show is not the criminality of the people who used the weapon; the criminality of the people who composed the weapon.

MAJOR FARR: I think I have to show two things, certainly the criminality of the persons who composed the weapons, but it seems to me I must also show that that weapon played a part in the conspiracy because the Indictment alleges-

THE PRESIDENT: I should have thought you had shown that over and over again, that the S.S. were a part of the weapon. If there was a criminal conspiracy, then the S.S. were one of the weapons which were used by the conspirators. But what you have got to show in this part of the case is that the persons who formed that weapon were criminal and knew of the criminal objects of the S.S.

MAJOR FARR: I quite agree I have to show that. I suppose I have to show, before showing that the persons involved knew of the criminal aims of the Organisation, what those criminal aims were. I was simply attempting to show the Tribunal that one of those aims which I submit as criminal was a plan to dominate Europe, and that the S.S. was one of the means by which that was to be done.

Now, this is just one aspect of the S.S. criminality. I am quite ready not to proceed any further with the point if the Court already has the point, and thinks that the evidence of that aspect of its criminality is sufficient. I certainly do not want to labour the point too hard.

I will now proceed further with the point as to the building up of the S.S. as a racial elite to take over ; but I do think one other thing is important, and that is the negative side of that racialism: the hatred of other races. Himmler made some very striking points along that line as to what the S.S. was to be in relation to it. I quote from his Posen speech, that is, our document 1919-PS. The passage in question appears on Page 23 of the original speech, middle of the page, and will be found on Page I of the English translation, third paragraph.

I quote:

"One basic principle must be the absolute rule for the S.S. man. We must be honest, decent, loyal, and comradely to members of our own blood and to nobody else. What happens to a Russian, to a Czech, does not interest me in the slightest."

The next few sentences from that same paragraph have already been read into evidence, and I shall not repeat them. But I do want to quote, in the same paragraph, the conclusion that Himmler draws from what he just said. This sentence is about seven lines from the bottom of the paragraph, beginning:-

"That is what I want to instil into this S.S. and what I believe I have instilled in them as- one of the most sacred laws of the future."

Now these principles-that is, the conception of being an elite which was to take over Europe, and the conception of hatred toward inferior races, which was instilled in the S.S.-these were principles which were publicly reiterated over and over again so that the newest recruit was thoroughly steeped in them.

I quote from Himmler's Kharkov speech, which appears in the same document 1919-PS.

THE TRIBUNAL (Mr. BIDDLE): Can you not just give us the meaning of the speech without quoting from it; can you just refer to it ? I

MAJOR FARR: I will be very glad to do that, if the Court will take judicial notice of it. I will refer you to the passage I have in mind. The passage in question appears on Page 14 of the translation, about fifteen lines from the bottom of the page; it appears on Page 17 of the original, at about the middle of the page.

In that passage, after having talked at great length about the racial struggle, Himmler tells his commanding officers-and be is'making this speech to the commanding officers of three divisions of the Waffen S.S.-he tells his officers that the thing which he wants so thoroughly instilled into every recruit in the Organisation, so that he becomes saturated with it, is the necessity of the S.S. standing firm and carrying on the racial struggle without mercy.

On the same point one further quotation-if the Tribunal will bear with me-and I think this is important because this, again, is a public quotation, found in the Organisation Book of the Party. That is our document 2640-PS. It is a very short passage, appearing on Page V8 of the original, and Page i of the English translation, the third paragraph from the end of the page in the translation:

"He openly and unrelentingly fights the most dangerous enemies of the State: Jews, Freemasons, Jesuits, and political clergymen."

Now these were the fundamental principles of the S.S.: racial superiority and blind obedience. A necessary corollary of these two principles was ruthlessness. The evidence that we will introduce on these activities will show how successfully the S.S. learned the lesson it was taught.

The S.S. had to, and did, develop a reputation for terror which was Farefully cultivated. Himmler himself publicly attested it as early as 1936 in his pamphlet, " The S.S. as an Anti-Bolshevist Fighting Organisation " our document 185I-PS, which has already been introduced into evidence as exhibit USA 44o. I quote two sentences which appear at page 29 Of the original pamphlet, and on page 4 of the translation, the first two sentences:

"I know that there are some people in Germany who become sick when they see these black coats. We understand the reason for this and do not expect that we shall be loved by too many."

The role which the S.S. was required to play demanded that it remain constantly the essence of Nazism and that its elite quality should never be diluted.

As evidence that even in 1943 the S.S. standards were still being main tained, I offer in evidence a letter written to the defendant Kaltenbrunner by Himmler. This letter is our Document 2768-PS. It is a letter from the Reiclisfuehrer S.S., written at his field command post and bearing the date 24th April, 1943, 1 offer it as Exhibit USA 447. 1 quote from the first paragraph of that letter:

"Referring again to the matter which we discussed some time agothat is, the admission of Sipo officials into the S.S.-I wish to clarify again: I want an admission only if the following conditions are fulfilled:

I. If the man applies freely and voluntarily.

2. If, by applying strict and peace-time standards, the applicant fits

racially and ideologically into the S.S., guarantees according to the number of his children a really healthy S.S. stock, and is neither in, degenerate, nor worthless."

Then, continuing with the third paragraph:

"I beg not only that you will act accordingly in the future, but especially also that numerous admissions into the ranks of the S.S. in the past be re-examined and revised according to these instructions."

Now I have appended this, to indicate to the Tribunal the normal manner in which a man became a member of the S.S. This is discussed by Himmler in our Document 1992-A-PS, at Page 142 of the original, and Page 5 Of the translation. If the Court thinks that it can take judicial notice of that passage, I shall not trouble to read it. What it does is to describe how a young man comes into the S.S. normally, at the age of 18, serves an appren ticeship and receives his instructions in S.S. ideology, takes the S.S. oath, receives the S.S dagger, and how long he remains in the General S.S. I will not trouble to read that paragraph, since I assume that the Court will take judicial notice of it.

I do think it may be worth quoting the very brief oath which the S.S. man takes. That oath is quoted in the Waffen S.S. recruiting pamphlet, entitled, "The S.S. Calls You," our Document 3429-PS, which I offer in evidence as Exhibit USA 446. The oath appears on Page 18 of that pamphlet, and on Page 2 of the translation, in the middle of the page. I quote the oath

The Oath of the S.S. Man:

"I swear to you, Adolf Hitler, as Fuehrer and Reichschancellor, loyalty and bravery, I vow to you, and to those you have named to command me, obedience unto death, so help me God."

I turn now to a consideration of the activities of the S.S., the manner in which it carried out the purposes of the conspirators and performed its function of guarding the internal security of the Nazi regime. The proof of the elite Nazi quality and thorough reliability of the S.S.-the test by which it won its spurs-occurred on the 30th of June, 1934, when it participated in the purge of the S.A. and other opponents or potential opponents of the Nazi regime. That was the first real occasion for the use of this specialised Organisation, which could operate with the blessing of the Nazi State, but outside the law.

I offer in evidence an affidavit by the defendant Wilhelm Frick, signed and sworn to herein Nuremberg on the i 9th of November, 1945 - It is our Document 2950-PS- I offer it as Exhibit USA 448. 1 shall quote a portion of that affidavit, beginning about the middle of the first paragraph of the affidavit, the tenth line in the original.

"Many people were killed - I do not know how many - who actually did not have anything to do with the 'putsch.' People who just were not liked very well, as for instance, Schleicher, the former Reich Chancellor, were killed. Schleicher's wife was also killed, as was Gregor Strasser, who had been the Reich Organisation Leader and second man in the Party after Hitler. Strasser, at the time he was murdered, was not active in political affairs any more. However, he had separated himself from the Fuehrer in November or December of 1932. The S.S. was used by Himmler for the execution of these orders to suppress the 'putsch'."

It was in recognition of its services in this respect that the S.S. was raised to the status of a component of the Party equal in rank to the S.A., and other similar ranking. I ask the Court to take judicial notice of a passage which appears on Page i of the V614scher Beobachter of z6th July, 1934- It is our Document 1857-PS,

Exhibit USA 412. 1 shall read the translation of that passage, which is very brief:

"The Reich Press Office announces the following Order of the Fuehrer. In consideration of the greatly meritorious service of the S.S., especially in connection with the events Of 3oth June, 1934, 1 raise it to the standing of an independent Organisation within the N.S.D.A.P. The Reiclisfuehrer S.S., like the Chief of Staff, is, therefore, directly subordinate to the highest S.A. leader."

By its action on 30th June, the S.S. proved itself. It was, therefore, the type of Organisation which the conspirators wanted for the first necessary step in their programme, the acquisition of control over the police, because one of the first steps essential to the security of any regime is control of the police. The aim of the conspirators was to fuse the S.S. and the police, to merge them into a single, unified repressive force.

I turn now to the consideration of the development whereby the S.S. and the police became intermingled. Shortly after the seizure of power the conspirators began to develop, as a part of the State machinery, secret political police forces, originating in Prussia in the Gestapo established by decree of the defendant Goering in 1933, and this development will be dealt with in the case against the 'Gestapo. By 1934, the Reichsfuehrer S.S. had become the chief of these secret political police forces in all the States of Germany except Prussia, and deputy chief of the Prussian Gestapo. In that capacity he infiltrated these forces with members of the S.S. until a virtual identity of membership of the S.S. and the Gestapo was achieved.

On 17th June, 1936, by the Decree on the Establishment of a Chief of the German Police, published in the Reichsgesetzblatt for 1936, Part 1, Pages 487 and 488, our Document 2073-PS, of which I assume the Court will take judicial notice, the new post of Chief of the German Police was created in the Ministry of the Interior. Under the terms of the decree Himmler was appointed to this post with the title of "Reiclisfuehrer S. S., and Chief of the German Police in the Ministry of the Interior."

The combination of these two positions, that of leader of the S.S., and head of all the police forces in the Reich, was no accident, but was intended to establish a permanent relation between the two bodies, and not a mere 44 transitory fusion of personnel." The significance of this combination of these two positions was referred to by Hitler in his secret order of 17th August, 1938, on the organisation and mobilisation of the S.S., our Document 647-PS, which I introduce in evidence as Exhibit USA 443, from which I will now quote just the preamble, which will be found on the first page of our Document 647-PS, and at the beginning of the original order. I quote:

"By means of the nomination of the Reichsfuehrer S.S. and Chief of the German Police in the Ministry of the Interior on June 17th, 1936, (Reichsgesetzblatt I, Page 487), 1 have created the basis for the unification and reorganisation of the German Police. With this step, the Schutzstaffeln of the N.S.D.A.P., which have been under the Reichs fuehrer S.S. and Chief of the German Police up to now, have entered into close connection with the duties of the German Police."

Upon his appointment, Himmler immediately proceeded to reorganise the entire police force, designating two separate branches. (i) The regular uniformed police force (Ordnungspolizei or Orpo as they were called by their abbreviated title) ; and (2) the so-called Security Police, or as they became to be known by their abbreviated title Sipo. The Security Police was composed of all the Criminal Police in the Reich and all the Gestapo. This reorganisation was achieved by the decree assigning functions to the Office of the Chief of the German Police, published in the Reichsministerialblatt for 1936, Pages 946-948, our Document 1551-PS- Of that decree I assume the Court will take judicial notice.

To be head of the Sipo, that is, of the Criminal Police and the Gestapo, Himmler appointed Reinhard Heydrich, who was at that time the Chief of the S.D., the S.S. Intelligence Agency to which I have already referred. Thus, through Himmler's dual capacity as Reichsfuehrer S.S. and as Chief of the German Police, and through Heydrich's dual capacity as head of the S.D. and of the Security Police, a unified personal command of the S.S. and Security Police Forces was achieved.

.But further steps towards unification were taken. In 1939 the Security Police and the S.D., which up to that time had been only an agency of the S.S., were both combined in a single department: the Reich Security Main Office, commonly referred to as R.S.H.A. An important point to be observed is this: This newly created department, R.S.H.A., was not a mere department of the Government. It was a dual thing. It was simultaneously an agency of the Government, organisationally placed in the Ministry of the Interior, and, at the same time, one of the principal departments of the S.S., organisationally placed in the Supreme Command of the S.S. This division in the S.S. is shown by the chart before you, R.S.H.A. being indicated by the sixth block from the left of the chart. But it was not merely the Gestapo and Criminal Police which came under the sway of the S.S. The regular uniformed police as well were affected. Like the R.S.H.A., the department of the Regular Police, the Ordnungspolizei, was also not merely a department in the Ministry of the Interior, but also simultaneously in the Supreme Command of the S.S. Its position in the S.S. is indicated by the seventh block on the chart, on the left.

Now this unity of command between S.S. and Police was not a mere matter of the highest headquarters. It extended down to the operating level. The Court will observe from the chart that the Higher S.S. and Police Leader in each region, who was directly subordinate to Himmler, had under his command both the Security Police, Sipo, and the regular uniformed police, Ordnungspolizei; and also that these forces, Sipo and Orpo, were not only under the command of the Higher S.S. and the Police Leader, but as indicated by the blue line, were also under the command of the R.S.H.A., and the Department of the Ordnungspolizei and the S.S. Thus, you have organisationally, a unity of command over the S.S. and the Police. This organisation was not the only way by which unity was achieved. Unity of personnel was also achieved. Vacancies occurring in the police forces were filled by S.S. members. Police officials who were in the force were able to join the S.S., and schools were operated by the S.S. for the police, as well as for the S.S. officials.

These measures are described in Himmler's article " Organisation and Obligations of the S.S. and the Police," our Document 1992-A-PS. They are also described in an authoritative book on the Police, entitled, " The German Police," the book published in 1940, written by Dr. Werner Best, Ministerial Director in the Ministry of the Interior, and a department head in the Security Police. It bears on its fly-leaf the imprimatur of the Nazi Party, and the book is listed in the official list of National Socialist bibliography. Chapter 7 from that book is our Document 1852-PS. I offer this book in evidence as Exhibit USA 449.

Through this unity of organisation and personnel, the S.S. and the Police became identified in structure and in activity. The resulting situation was described in Best's book, which I have just offered in evidence, our Document 1852-PS, as follows. I quote from Page 7 of that document, paragraph 5 ; from the original book, Page 95, paragraph 3:

"Thus the S.S. and the Police form one unit, both in their structure and in their activity, although their individual organisations have not lost their true individuality and their position in the larger units of the Party and State administration which are concerned with other points of view."

Through the Police, the S.S. was in a position to carry out a large part of the functions assigned to it. The working partnership between the Gestapo, the Criminal Police and the S.D. under the direction of the Reichsfuehrer S.S. resulted in the end in repressive and unrestrained police activity. That will be dealt with in the case against the Gestapo. In considering that evidence, the Tribunal will bear in mind that the Police activities there shown were one aspect of S.S. functions, one part of the whole criminal S.S. scheme. I shall not, therefore, consider here evidence relating strictly to the police functions of the S.S.

Control over the police was not enough. Potential sources of opposition could be tracked down by the S.D. Suspects could be seized by the Criminal Police and the Gestapo, but these means alone would not assure the complete suppression of all opponents and potential opponents of the regime. For this purpose, concentration camps were invented. The evidence already presented to the Tribunal has shown what the concentration camp system involved, and the final result of that system was graphically illustrated in the moving pictures shown about io, days ago. The responsibility of the S.S. in that system is a topic to which I now turn.

The first requirement for the camps was guard and administrative personnel. Part-time volunteer members of the Allgerneine S.S. were originally utilised as guards; but part-time volunteers could not adequately serve the needs of the extensive, long-range programme that was planned. So beginning in 1933 full-time professional guards units, the Death Head Units which I have already described, were organised. During the war, members of the General S.S. resumed the function of guarding camps, which they had initially undertaken when the camps were created. The Tribunal will recall the provisions of the Hitler order which I read a few moments ago, directing the replacement of Death Head Units by General S.S. members in the event of mobilisation. It is unnecessary to repeat the evidence of wholesale brutality, torture and murder committed by S.S. guards. They were not the sporadic crimes committed by irresponsible individuals, but a part of a definite and calculated policy, a policy necessarily resulting from S.S. philosophy, a policy which was carried out from the initial creation of the camps.

Himmler bluntly stated the S.S. view as to the inmates of the camps in his article, " Organisation and Obligations of the S.S. and the Police," Exhibit USA 439, our Document 1992-A-PS. I quote from Page 7 of the translation, last paragraph; from Page 148 of the original, third paragraph.

THE PRESIDENT: Did you say 439?

MAJOR FARR: It was Exhibit 439- It is our Document 1992-A-PS. I quote from Page 7 of the translation, last paragraph:

"It would be extremely instructive for everyone-some members of the Wehrmacht had already been able to do so-to inspect such a concentration camp. Once they have seen it, they are convinced of the fact that no one has been sent there unjustly ; that it is the offal of criminals and freaks. No better demonstration of the laws of in heritance and race, as set forth by Doctor Guett, exists than such a concentration camp. There you can find people with hydrocephalus, people who are cross-eyed, deformed, half-Jewish, and a number of racially inferior products. All that is assembled there. Of course, we distinguish between those inmates who are only there for a few months for the purpose of education, and those who are to stay for a very long time. On the whole, education consists of discipline, never of any kind of instruction on an ideological basis, for the prisoners have, for the most part, slave-like souls; and only very few people of real character can be found there."

Then, omitting the next two sentences, he continues with this striking remark:

"The discipline thus means order. The order begins with these people living in clean barracks. Such a thing can really only be accomplished by us Germans, hardly another nation would be as human as we are. The laundry is frequently changed. The people are taught to wash themselves twice daily, and to use a toothbrush, a thing with which most of them have been unfamiliar."

Having heard the evidence and seen the pictures as to conditions in concentration camps, this Tribunal can appreciate how grim and savage that callous jest was. He made no such pretence in his speech to his own Grupperifuehrers at Posen, our Document 1919-PS, Exhibit USA 170. I quote from Page 43 of the original, last paragraph; from Page 2 of the translation, the first full paragraph. That is 1919-PS.

"I do not believe the Communists could attempt any action, for their leading elements, like most criminals, are in our concentration camps. And here I must say this: that we shall bp able to see after the war what a blessing it was for Germany that, in spite of all the silly talk about humanitarianism, we imprisoned all this criminal sub stratum of the German people in concentration camps. I will answer for that."

But he is not here to answer.

Certainly there was no " silly humanitarianism " in the manner in which S.S. men performed their tasks. Just as an illustration, I should like to examine their conduct, not in 1944 or 1945, but in 1933- 1 have four reports, relating to the deaths of four different inmates of the concentration camp Dachau between 16th and 27th May, 1933. Each report is signed by the Public Prosecutor of the District Court in Munich and is addressed to the Public Prosecutor of the Supreme Court in Munich. These four reports show that during that two-week period in 1933, at the time when the concentration camps had barely started, S.S. men had murdered - a different guard each time - an inmate of the camp.

Now, I do not want to take the time of the Tribunal to read that evidence if it feels that it is a minor point. The significance of it is this: It is just an illustration of the sort of thing that happened in the concentration camps at the earliest possible date, in 1933. I am prepared to offer those four reports in evidence and to quote from them, if the Tribunal thinks that the point is not too insignificant.

THE PRESIDENT: Where are they?

MAJOR FARR: I have them here. I will offer them in evidence. The first is our Document 641-PS. It is a report dated 1st June, 1933, and relates to the death of Dr. Alfred Strauss, a prisoner in protective custody, in Dachau. I offer it in evidence as Exhibit USA 450. I shall read a few paragraphs from that report, beginning with paragraph one:

"On 24th May, 1933, the 30-year-old, single, attorney-at-law, Dr. Alfred Strauss from Munich, who was in the concentration camp Dachau as a prisoner under protective custody, was killed by two pistol shots from S.S. man Johann Kantschuster who escorted him on a walk prescribed to him by the camp doctor, outside the fence part of the camp.

Kantschuster gives the following report: 'He himself had to urinate; Strauss proceeded on his way. Suddenly Strauss broke away towards the bushes located at a distance of about 6 m. from the line. When he (Kantschuster) noticed it, he fired two shots at the fugitive from a distance of about 8 m.; whereupon Strauss collapsed dead.'

On the same day, 24th May, 1933, a judicial inspection of the locality took place. The corpse of Strauss was lying at the edge of the wood. Leather slippers were on his feet. He wore a sock on one foot, while the other foot was bare, obviously because of an injury to it. Subsequently an autopsy was performed. Two bullets had entered the back of the head. Besides, the body showed several black and blue spots and also open wounds."

Passing now to the last paragraph of that report:

"I have charged Kantschuster to-day with murder and have made application for the opening and execution of a judicial preliminary investigation as well as for the issuance of a warrant of arrest against him."

That is the first of the four reports. The significance is that you have four murders one after the other, committed within a short space of time, and in each instance, an official report by the camp commander or the guard as to the cause of death, which was completely disproved by the facts.

The second report, a report dated 1st June, 1933, relates to the death of Leonhard Hausmann, another prisoner in Dachau. It is our Document 642-PS, and I offer it in evidence as Exhibit USA 451.

THE PRESIDENT: I do not think you need read the details.

MAJOR FARR: I will offer it without reading it.

The third report which I shall offer is dated 22nd May, 1933. It relates to the death of Louis Schloss, an inmate of Dachau, and is our Document 644-PS. I offer it in evidence as Exhibit USA 452.

The fourth document, our Document 645-PS, dated ist June, 1933, relates to the death of Sebastian Nefzger, 'another Dachau prisoner. I offer this in evidence as Exhibit USA 453.

These four murders, committed within the short space of two weeks in the spring of 1933, each by a different S.S. guard, are merely examples of S.S. activities in the camps at that very early date. Many similar examples from that period and later periods could be produced.

Indeed, that sort of thing was officially encouraged. I call the Tribunal's attention to the Disciplinary Regulation for the Dachau Concentration Camp, our Document 778-PS, which has already been introduced in evidence as Exhibit USA 247- 1 want to read the fourth paragraph of the introduction to those rules, a passage which was not read when the document was originally introduced. The fourth paragraph on the first page of the translation and of the original is as follows:

"Tolerance means weakness. In the light of this conception, punishment will be mercilessly handed out whenever the interests of the Fatherland warrant it.

The fellow countryman who is decent but misled will never be affected by these regulations. But let it be a warning to the agitating politicians and intellectuals, regardless of which kind: Be on guard not to be caught, for otherwise it will be your neck and you will be hoist with your own petard."

Those regulations were issued in 1933 by S.S.-Fuehrer Eich, who, it is to be noted, was the Commandant of the S.S.-Totenkopfverbinde.

Furnishing guard and administrative personnel was not the only function of the S.S. with relation to the camps. The entire internal management of the camps, including the use of prisoners, their housing, clothing, sanitary conditions, the determination of their very right to live and the disposal of their remains, was controlled by the S.S. Such management was first vested in the Leader of the S.S.

Death Head Units who had the title of Inspector of the Concentration Camps. This official was originally in the S.S. Hauptamt-represented on the chart by the second box from the left. During the course of the war - in March 1942 - Control of concentration camps was transferred to another of the departments of the S.S. Supreme Command - the S.S. Economic and Administration Department - commonly known as W.V.H.A. That department is indicated on the chart by the third box from the left. The Court will note under the top box the break down into " Concentration Camps " which in turn is broken down into " Prison, Labour, Medical and Administration."

That change was announced in a letter to Himmler dated 3oth April, 1942, from the Chief of W.V.H.A. The letter is our Document R-129 and it has already been received in evidence as Exhibit USA 217. 1 shall not quote from that letter now.

This shift of control to WN.H.A., the economic department of the S.S., coincided with a change in the basic purposes of the concentration camps. Political and security reasons, which previously had been the ground for confinement, were abandoned, and the camps were frankly made to serve the slave-labour programme. The Tribunal will recall the evidence relating to that programme which was presented last week by Mr. Dodd. I shall not deal at any length with the matter again, except to summarise the principal facts bearing on S.S. responsibility which were demonstrated by that evidence.

To satisfy the increased demands for manpower it was not enough to work the inmates of the camp harder. More inmates had to be obtained. The S.S., through its police arm, was prepared to satisfy this demand, as through the W.N.H.A. it was prepared to work those who were already in the camp.

THE PRESIDENT: Have you got any figures you can give the Tribunal as to the total numbers in the S.S. and the total numbers who were employed on concentration camps ? If you gave us the total number of the S.S. and the total number employed in concentration camps, we should see what the proportion was.

MAJOR FARR: I think I can only give you the following figures. I earlier quoted some figures from d'Alquen in his book published in 1939, in which he said that the total strength of the General S.S. was about 240,000. That is the General S.S., which was not at that time engaged in the guarding of concentration camps. The Totenkopfverbiinde, the Death Head Units, at that time, consisted of somethree or four regiments at the most. They were the guards; so that of the personnel who were employed in actual guard duty there were, in 1939, about three or four regiments.

The Court will recall that after the war had started, the TotenkopfverbInde were no longer employed in that duty and that the members of the General S.S. took it up. How many were employed is something that is difficult to estimate. The concentration camp programme was constantly expanding and, of course, as more camps were added more personnel was needed. I cannot give the Tribunal the figures of the number of persons involved in guarding the camps, but one of the matters I think significant is this: we have not only guards, we have administrative personnel, we have the whole of the WN.H.A. which, as I want to show by evidence, had complete control of the management of the concentration camps. The members of the staff office, WN.H.A., were derived from the General S.S. ; so you have on the one hand the guard personnel, Death Head Units, up to 1939, and then you have after 1939 more guards from the Allgemeine S.S. You have, after 1939, more guards from the General S.S. and also administrative personnel from W.V.H.A.

I have no figures showing how many persons were engaged. in one or another phase of the concentration camp activities. You have, of course, the S.D. and Security

Police involved in it, in so far as they went out and seized victims. You have W.V.H.A., the entire administrative personnel of that section involved in it, in so far as they handled, administrative matters.

Some conception of the number of persons who must have been engaged in the activity may be gained from noting the number of persons involved in a camp. I have a document, a report by W.V.H.A., in August 1944, which reports the number of prisoners who were then on hand in the camps and the recent arrivals who were expected. That document is our Document I I 66-PS, which I will now offer in evidence as Exhibit USA 458.

THE PRESIDENT: I do not think we had better go into that to-night. What will you be dealing with to-morrow?

MAJOR FARR: To-morrow, Sir, I intend to offer evidence showing how. W.V.H.A. and other S.S. personnel were involved in the control of every phase of the concentration camp programme. That is the first thing. The second thing is to point out the role that the S.S. played in the persecution of the Jews and their extermination, not with a view to repeating the substantive evidence to show that such acts took place, but to show how many components, how many parts of the organisation were involved in that programme.

Then I shall consider the role of the S.S. with respect to Preparations for Aggressive War and the Crimes Against Peace-a relatively brief dis cussion-and then pass on to the role that the S.S. played in War Crimes and Crimes Against Humanity, set out in Counts 3 and 4 of the Indictment, and finally, the role of the S.S. in the colonisation programme.

THE PRESIDENT: Colonisation?

MAJOR FARR: That may be an unfortunate word. Perhaps I should have said Germanisation programme, a programme of resettlement, evacuation, colonisation, and exploitation of the conquered territories.

Those, I think, are the four main functions of the S.S. which remain to be considered, and I shall endeavour not to go again into substantive crimes which have already been shown to the Tribunal, but to try to show how almost every department- in fact, every department of the S.S. and every component-was involved in one or more, and mostly more, of these crimes.

THE PRESIDENT: The Tribunal hopes that you will be able to confine yourself to the reading of evidence which is not cumulative.

MAJOR FARR: I have that in mind and I do not intend to do anything more than to show the figures and components of the S.S. which were involved in various programmes.

THE PRESIDENT: Very well.

(The Tribunal adjourned until 1000 hours on 20th December, 1945)

Twenty-Fourth Day: Thursday, 20th December, 1945

MAJOR FARR: May it please the Tribunal, when the Tribunal rose yesterday, we were discussing the number of persons who might be involved in the concentration camp programme with which the S.S. was concerned nothing better illustrates the integrated character of the whole organisation than that programme.

W.V.H.A., one of the departments of the Supreme Command, handled the administration and control of that camp programme and dealt with the victims once they were in the camp. They were assisted by the Death Head Units, who furnished the guard personnel for the camps, and subsequently by the " Allgemeine S.S.," which took over guard duties during the war.

R.S.H.A. - the police arm of the S.S. - played a part in the concentration camp programme, because through it the victims were apprehended and taken to the camps. Thus the S.D. appears in the picture, the personal staff, the first department of the Supreme Command, the top office so to speak of the whole organisation, and naturally had much to do with the work of all subordinate departments.

Thus when the question is asked how many persons in the S.S. had something to do with the concentration camp programme, it is a question which I think it is impossible to answer. You might point out how many persons were involved in the Death Head Units, who originally furnished the guard details. You might estimate how many persons were in the " Allgemeine S. S.," but to say just what percentage of the whole organisation was involved in that programme is something which I find myself unable to do.

I had just pointed out -

THE PRESIDENT: Can you say that one or other branch of the S.S. provided the whole of the staff of the concentration camps?

MAJOR FARR: By the staff, I take it, you mean guards at the camp, the guard personnel. You cannot do that. For example, the Death Head Units originally started off as being the units which furnished all the guard personnel. Subsequently, their task was taken over by members of the "Allgemeine S.S."

THE PRESIDENT: Those are both branches of the S.S.?

MAJOR FARR: Both are branches, yes. Now with respect to the camp commandants, for instance, normally all high ranking officers in the S.S. were members of the " Allgemeine S.S.," so doubtless such personnel would be drawn from that branch. It is certainly not impossible that some members of the " Waffen S.S." may have been called on to act as guards in certain camps. I do not think you can say that there is no component of the S.S. which may not have had some of its personnel involved in the programme.

THE PRESIDENT: That was not exactly what I meant. What I meant was: could you say that one or other branches of the S.S. furnished the whole staff of the concentration camps?

MAJOR FARR: I do not think I can say that. I think I could say this -

THE PRESIDENT: What other organisation was it that furnished a part of the staff of the concentration camps?

MAJOR FARR: You mean an organisation other than the S.S.

THE PRESIDENT: Yes.

MAJOR FARR: I know of none.

THE PRESIDENT: Then the answer would be "Yes"?

MAJOR FARR: I thought your Honour was referring to any one branch of the S.S., which was concerned alone with that. The S.S., so far as I know, is the only organisation which played a part in the concentration camp picture, except at the very end of the war when I think, as Colonel Storey said yesterday, some members of the S.A. were also involved as guard personnel of concentration camps.

THE TRIBUNAL (Mr. BIDDLE): Do you know the total personnel at the end of the war?

MAJOR FARR: Of the entire S.S.

THE TRIBUNAL (Mr. BIDDLE): Yes.

MAJOR FARR: That is something you would have to estimate. I quoted to the Tribunal yesterday the figures that d'Alquen gave as the strength of the " Allgemeine S.S." in 1939. He said then that there were about 240,000 men in the AllgemeineS.S." There were, at that time, about four regiments of Death Head Units, several other regiments of the " Verfilgungstruppe," a few thousand personnel involved in the S.D., so that I should say in 1939 you had about 250,000 to 300,000 members of the S.S. With the outbreak of the war, the " Waffen S.S." was built up from a few regiments of the Verfflgungstruppe to about 31 divisions at the end of the war, which probably would mean that the " Waffen S.S." by 1941, had had some 400,000 to 500,000 persons involved. I take it that 400,000 to 500,000 members of the " Waffen S.S." would be in addition to personnel of the "Allgemeine S.S.," who were subject to compulsory military service in the Wehrmacht. So that, if I had to estimate, I would say that probably some 750,000 persons would be the top figure of personnel who had been involved in the S.S. from the beginning, but that is only an estimate.

THE TRIBUNAL (Mr. BIDDLE): Then you have no break down to show how many of those were civilians, clerks, stenographers, soldiers and so on ?

MAJOR FARR: No. When we are talking about S.S. members, we are not talking about stenographers who worked in the office, who were not members of the S.S. By S.S. members, we mean personnel who took the oath and appeared on the membership list, either as a member of the " Allgemeine S.S.," the Death Head Units, or the " Waffen S.S." I would think that my figure Of 750,000 was a figure including members of the S.S., " Allgemeine S.S.," the " Totenkopfverbande," and the " Waffen S.S."

I was pointing out the shift of control of concentration camps to W.V.H.A. in 1942, which was coincident with the shift in the basic purpose of the camps, which heretofore had been concerned with custody of individuals for political and security reasons. The basic purpose of the camps was to furnish manpower, and 1 now want to point out to the Court the agencies of the S.S. which were involved in that manpower drive.

The Tribunal has already received evidence of an order, which was issued in 1942, shortly after the transfer to W.V.H.A. of concentration camp control, directing Security Police to furnish at once 35,000 prisoners qualified for work in the camps. That order is our Document 1063-PS, and was received in evidence as Exhibit USA 219.

35,000 prisoners were, of course, merely the beginning. The S.S. dragnet was capable of catching many more slaves. I offer in evidence a carbon typewritten copy of a directive to all the departments of the S.S. Supreme Command, issued from

Himmler's field headquarters on the 5th and 6th August, 1943. It is Document 744-PS. I offer it as Exhibit USA 455. That directive appears on Page 2 of the translation. It implements an order signed by the defendant Keitel, directing the use of all males, captured in guerilla fighting in the East, for forced labour. The Keitel directive appears on Page 1 of the translation.

I shall read only the Himmler directive appearing on Page 2 of the translation. The Tribunal will note that it is addressed to every main office of the S.S. Supreme Command. I read that list of addresses of the directive:

1. Chief of the personnel staff of Reichsfuehrer S.S.
2. S.S. Main Office.
3. Reich Security Main Office (R.S.H.A.).
4. Race and Resettlement Main Office S.S.
5. Main Office, Ordinary Police.
6. S.S. Economic Administrative Main Office.
7. S.S. Personnel Main Office.
8. Main Office S.S. Court.
9. S.S. Supreme Command - Headquarters of the 'Waffen S.S.'
10. Staff Headquarters of the Reich Commissar for the Consolidation of Germanism.
11. Main Office Centre for Racial Germans.
12. Office of S.S. Obergruppenfuehrer Heissmeyer.
13. Chief of the Guerilla-fighting Units."

I point out to the Court that every one of the main offices appearing on the chart is a recipient of that directive. The next addresses are the Higher S.S. and Police Leaders in the various regions. .

I continue to quote the body of the directive

" To figure 4 of the above-mentioned order I direct, that all young female prisoners capable of work are to be sent to Germany, through the agency of Reich Commissioner Sauckel.

Children, old women and men are to be collected and employed in the women's and children's camps, established by me on estates as well as on the border of the evacuated area."

In April 1944 the S.S. was called on to produce even more labourers this time 100,000 Jews from Hungary. The Tribunal will recall the minutes of the defendant Speer's discussion with Hitler on the 6th and 7th of April, 1944, which were found in our Document R-124 at page 36, and were read to the Court, in evidence as Exhibit USA 179, minutes in which Speer referred to Hitler's statement that he would call on the Reichsfuehrer S.S. to produce 100,000 Jews from Hungary.

The last source of man-power had not been tapped. To Jews, deportees, women and children, there was added the productive power of prisoners of war. It was through the S.S. that the conspirators squeezed the last drop of labour from such prisoners.

I refer to statement by the defendant Speer, which appears in our Document R-124 at Page 13 of the translation, the document itself having already been introduced in evidence as Exhibit USA 179. The statement is found at Page 7, last paragraph of the original, Page 13 of the Document R-124, the next to the last paragraph on Page 13. That appears in volume 2 of the document book. I quote:

"Speer: We have to come to an arrangement with the Reichsfuehrer S.S. as soon as possible so that P.W.'s he picks up are made available for our purposes.

The Reichsfuehrer S.S. gets from thirty to forty thousand men per month."

In order to insure S.S. control over the labour of prisoners of war, the Reichsfuehrer S.S. was finally appointed as head of all prisoner- of-war camps on 25th September, 1944. I offer in evidence the letter referring to his appointment. It is our Document 058-PS. It is Exhibit USA 456. It will be found in Volume 1 of the document book. That letter is a circular letter from the Director of the Party Chancellery, dated the 30th of September, 1944, and signed "M. Bormann." I quote, beginning with the first paragraph:

"1. The Fuehrer has ordered under the date 25 September, 1944:

The custody of all prisoners of war and interned persons, as well as prisoner-of-war camps and institutions with guards, are transferred to the Commander of the Reserve Army from October 1, 1944."

Passing to paragraph 2 of the letter, I shall read sub-paragraphs (a) and (c), I quote:

2. The Reichsfuehrer S.S. has commanded:

(a) In my capacity as Commander of the Reserve Army, I transfer the affairs of prisoners of war to Gottlieb Berger S.S.-Lieut- General Chief of Staff of the Volksturrn."

Passing now to sub paragraph (c):

"(c) The mobilisation of labour of the prisoners of war will be organised with the present labour mobilisation office in joint action between S. S. -Lieut.-General Berger and S.S.-Lieut.- General Pohl.

The strengthening of security in the field of prisoners of war affairs is to be accomplished between S.S.-Lieut.-General Berger and the Chief of the Security Police, S.S.-Lieut.-Gen. Dr. Kalteribrunner."

Thus the S.S finally took over direction and control of prisoner-of- war camps.

So impressive were the results obtained from S.S. concentration camp labour, that in 1944 the defendant Goering called on Himmler for more inmates for use in the aircraft industry. The Tribunal will recall his teletype to Himmler, our Document 1584-PS, Part 1, which was read in evidence by Mr. Dodd, as Exhibit USA 221. Let me now read Himmler's reply to that teletype. It is our Document 1584-PS, Part 3, and will be found on Page 2 of Part 3 Of 1584-PS. I offer it in evidence as Exhibit USA 457. 1 quote the beginning of that letter:

"Most Honoured Reichsmarshal:

Following my teletype letter of 18 February 1944 1 herewith transmit a survey on the employment of prisoners in the aviation industry.

This survey indicates that at the present time about 36,000 prisoners are employed for the purposes of the Air Force. An increase to a total of 90,000 prisoners is contemplated.

The production is being discussed, established and executed between the Reich Ministry of Aviation and the Chief of my Economic Administrative Main Office, S.S. Obergruppenfuehrer and General of the Waffen S.S. Pohl respectively:

We assist with all the forces at our disposal.

The task of my Economic Administrative Main Office, however, is not completely fulfilled with the delivery of the prisoners to the aviation industry, as S.S.-Obergruppenfuehrer Pohl and his assistants take care of the required working speed through constant control and supervision of the work-groups (Kommandos) and therefore have some influence on the resulting production. In this respect I may suggest consideration of the fact that in enlarging our responsibility through a speeding-up of the total work, better results can definitely be expected."

I pass now to the last two paragraphs of the letter, which will be found on the next page of the translation:

"The movement of manufacturing plants of the aviation industry to subterranean locations requires further employment of about 100,000 prisoners. The plans for this employment on the basis of your letter of 14 February 1944 are already under way.

I shall keep you, most honoured Reichsmarshal, currently informed on this subject."

Incidentally, I might call to the Tribunal's attention the fact that S.S. Obergruppenfuehrer Pohl, who was head of the W.V.H.A., was also a General of the "Waffen S.S.," which goes to show that there is no manner in which you can characterise functions in the S.S.

The extent to which the number of prisoners was increased through S.S. efforts is illustrated by our Document 1166-PS, which I offered in evidence yesterday as Exhibit USA 458. This document is a report from Office Group D of W.V.H.A., dated the 15th of August, 1944. I shall read the first page of that report, beginning:

"With reference to the above-mentioned telephone call, I am sending herewith a report on the actual number of prisoners for 1 August, 1944 and of the new arrivals already announced, as well as the clothing report for 15 August, 1944.

"1. The actual number on 1 August 1944, consisted of:

(a) Male prisoners 379,167
(b) Female prisoners 45,119

In addition, there are the following new arrivals:

1. From the Hungary programme (anti-Jewish action) - 90,000
2. From Litzmannstadt (Police prison and Ghetto) - 60,000
3. Poles from the Government General - 15,000
4. Convicts from the Eastern Territories - 10,000
5. Former Polish officers - 17,000
6. From Warsaw (Poles) - 400,000
7. Continued arrivals from France, approx. - 15,000 -20,000

Most of the prisoners are already on the way and will be received into the concentration camps within the next few days,"

This intensive drive for manpower to some extent interfered with tne programme which W.V.H.A. had already undertaken to exterminate certain classes of individuals in the camps. I offer a photostatic copy of a letter from W.V.H.A., dated 27th April, 1943, our Document 1933-PS. It is Exhibit USA 459. The letter is addressed to a number of concentration camp commanders, is signed by Gluecks, S.S. Brigade Fuehrer and Major General of the "Waffen S.S." I read it:

"The Reichsfuehrer-S.S. and Chief of the German Police has decided after consultation, that in the future only mentally sick prisoners may be selected for action 14-F-13 by the medical commissions appointed for this purpose.

All other prisoners incapable of working (tubercular cases, bed- ridden cripples, etc.) are to be basically excepted from this action. Bed-ridden prisoners are to be drafted for suitable work which they can perform in bed.

The order of the Reichsfuehrer S.S. is to be obeyed strictly in future.

Requests for fuel for this purpose are therefore out of the question."

The action "14-F-13" is not defined in the letter but it is perfectly apparent what it means. Every human being, bedridden, crippled, no matter what his physical condition, from whom any work at all could be extracted, was to be excepted from the action. Only the insane, from whom nothing could be expected, were to suffer the action. What could the action be? It is perfectly apparent. The action was extermination.

The S.S., however, was to some degree enabled to achieve both goals that of increased production and of elimination of undesirables. The Tribunal will recall the agreement between Minister of Justice Thierack and Himmler on 18th September, 1942, our Document 654-PS, which was read in evidence by Mr. Dodd as Exhibit USA 218. I am not going to quote again from that document, but will remind the Tribunal that the agreement provided for the transfer of anti-social elements from the prison to the Reichsfuehrer S.S. for extermination through work.

The conditions under which such persons worked in the camps were well calculated to lead to their death. Those conditions were regulated by the W.V.H.A. As an illustration of W.V.H.A. management, I call the Court's attention to our Document 2189-PS, which I offer in evidence as Exhibit USA 460. It is an order directed to commandants of concentration camps, dated 11th August, 1942, and bearing the facsimile signature, which does not appear on the translation, but does appear on the original, of S.S. Brigade Fuehrer and General of the Waffen S.S. Gluecks, who was Chief of Office Group D of W.V.H.A. That is Document 2189-PS. I read the body of that letter:

> "The Reichsfuehrer S.S. and Chief of the German Police has ordered that punishment by beating will be executed in concentration camps for women by prisoners under supervision, as ordered.
>
> In accordance with this order the Main Office Chief of the Main S.S. Economic Administration Office, S.S.-Obergruppenfuehrer and General of the Waffen S.S. Pohl, has ordered, to be effective immediately, that punishment by beating will also be executed by prisoners in concentration camps for men.
>
> It is forbidden that foreign prisoners should execute the punishment on German prisoners."

Even after their death, the prisoners did not escape the management of W.V.H.A. I refer the Court to our Document 2199-PS, a letter to commanders of concentration camps, dated 12th September, 1942, and signed by the Chief of the Central Office of Office Group D of W.V.H.A., S.S. Obersturmbannfuehrer Leibehenschel. I offer this as Exhibit USA 461. I shall read the body of that directive, which appears on Page 1 of the translation of 2199-PS. I quote:

> "According to a communication of the Chief of the Security Police and the S.D., and conforming to a report of the Chief of Security Police and S.D., in Prague, urns of deceased Czechs and Jews were sent for burial to the home-cemeteries within the Protectorate.
>
> In view of different events (demonstrations, placing posters inimical to the Reich on urns of deceased inmates in the halls of the home town cemeteries, of pilgrimages to the graves of deceased inmates, etc.) within the Protectorates, the delivery of urns with the ashes of deceased nationals of the Protectorate and of Jews is henceforth prohibited. The urns shall be kept within the concentration camps. In case of doubt about keeping the urns oral instructions shall be obtained from this agency."

The S.S. indeed regarded the inmates of concentration camps as its own personal property to be used for its own economic advantage. The Tribunal will recall that as early as 1942, the defendant Speer recognised that the S.S. was moved by the desire for further profits, when he suggested to Hitler that the S.S. receive a share of the war equipment produced by concentration camp labour, in ratio to the working hours of the prisoners. I refer to our Document R-124, at page 136, which was read into evidence by Mr. Dodd as Exhibit USA 179. The Fuehrer agreed that a 3 to 5 per cent share should satisfy the S.S. commanders. Himmler himself frankly admitted his intention to derive profits for S.S. purposes from the camps, in his mass-speech to the officers of the S.S. Leibstandarte "Adolf Hitler," our Document 1918, Exhibit USA 364-the passage in question being found at the top of Page 3 of the English translation and on Page 10 of the original German, seven lines from the bottom. The passage begins:

> "The apartment-building programme which is the prerequisite for a healthy and social basis of the entire S.S., as well as of the entire Fuehrercorps, can be carried out only when I get the money for it from somewhere. Nobody is going to give me the money. It must be earned, and it will be earned by forcing the scum of mankind, the prisoners, the professional criminals, to do positive work. The man guarding those prisoners serves just as hard as the one on close-order drill. The one who does this and stands near these utterly negative people, will learn within three to four months, and we shall see: in peacetime, I shall form guard battalions and put them on duty for three months only to fight the inferior beings, and this will not be a boring guard duty, but if the officers handle it right, it will be the best indoctrination on inferior beings and inferior races.
>
> This activity is necessary, as I said: (i) to eliminate these negative people from German people; (2) to exploit them once more for the great folk community, by having them break stones and bake bricks, so that the Fuehrer can again erect his grand buildings ; and (3) in turn to invest the money, earned soberly this way, in houses, in land, in settlements, so that our men can have houses in which to raise large families, and have lots of children. This in turn is necessary because we stand or die with this leading blood of Germany, and if the good blood is not reproduced, we will not be able to rule the world."

One final aspect of S.S. control over concentration camps remains to be mentioned. That is its direction of the programme of biological experiments on human beings, which was carried on in the camps. Just a few days ago, another military tribunal passed judgment on some of those who participated in the experiments at Dachau.

THE PRESIDENT: There is no date on that document you just read, is there?

MAJOR FARR: There appears to be no date on the English translation. The original document bears the notation of a speech in April, 1943.

At a later stage in this case, evidence of some of the details of this programme of experiments will be presented. It is not my purpose to deal with those experiments from the substantive aspect. I shall show only that they were the result of S.S. direction, and that the S.S. played a vital part in their successful execution.

The programme seems to have originated in a request by a Dr. Signiund Rascher to Himmler, for permission to utilise persons in concentration camps as material for experiments with human beings, in connection with some research he was conducting on behalf of the Luftwaffe. I refer to our Document 1602-PS, a photostatic copy of a letter, dated 15th. May, 1941, addressed to the Reichsfuehrer S.S., and signed "S. Rascher. " I offer it as Exhibit USA 454. I shall quote from the second paragraph of the translation, the fourth paragraph of the original letter. I quote:

"For the time being I have been assigned to the Luftgaukommando VII, Munich, for a medical course. During this course, where researches on high-altitude flights play a prominent part (determined by the somewhat higher ceiling of the English fighter planes) considerable regret was expressed at the fact that no tests with human material had yet been possible for us, as such experiments are very dangerous and nobody volunteers for them. I put, therefore, the serious question: can you make available two or three professional criminals for these experiments? The experiments are made at 'Bodenstaendige Phuestelle fuer Hoehenforschung der Luftwaffe, Munich.' The experiments, in which the subjects may, of course, die, would take place with my co-operation. They are essential for researches on high-altitude flight and cannot be carried out, as has been tried, with monkeys, who offer entirely different test-conditions. I have had a very confidential talk with a representative of the Air Force, Burgeon, who makes these experiments. He is also of the opinion that the problem in question could only be solved by experiments on human persons. (Feebleminded could also be used as test material)."

Dr. Rascher promptly received assurance from the S.S. that he would be allowed to utilise concentration camp inmates for his experiments.

I refer to our Document 1582-PS, a letter dated the 22nd of May, 1941, addressed to Dr. Rascher, and bearing the stamp of the Personal Staff of the Reichsfuehrer S.S., and the initials, "K Br," which initials are those of S.S. Sturmbannfuehrer Karl Brandt. I offer this letter as Exhibit USA 462.

"Dear Dr. Rascher:

Shortly before flying to Oslo, the Reichsfuehrer S.S. gave me your letter of 15 May 1941, for partial reply.

I can inform you that prisoners will of course be readily made available for the high-flight researches. I have informed the Chief of the Security Police of this agreement of the Reichsfuehrer S.S., and requested that the competent official be instructed to get in touch with you."

The altitude experiments were conducted by Rascher, and in May 1942, General Field Marshal Milch, on behalf of the Luftwaffe, expressed his thanks to the S.S. for the assistance it furnished in connection with the experiments.

I refer to our Document 343-PS, and I offer in evidence an original letter, dated the 20th of May, 1942, addressed to S.S. Obergruppenfuehrer Wolff, and signed E. Milch, as exhibit USA 463. That letter, which appears on Page 2 of the translation, and on Page 1 of the original German, is as follows:

Dear Wolff - (the German says, 'Liebes Woelffchen') -

In reference to your telegram of 12 May, our sanitary inspector reports to me that the altitude experiments carried out by the S.S. and Air Force at Dachau have been finished. Any continuation of these experiments seems materially unjustifiable. However, the carrying out of experiments of some other kind, in regard to perils on the high seas, would be important. These have been prepared in immediate agreement with the proper offices ; Major (MC) Weltz will be charged with the execution and Capt. (M.C.) Rascher will be made available until further orders in addition to his duties within the Medical Corps of the Air Corps. A change of these measures does not appear necessary, and an enlargement of the task is not considered pressing at this time.

The low-pressure chamber would not be needed for these low temperature experiments. It is urgently needed at another place and therefore can no longer remain in Dachau.

I convey the special thanks from the Supreme Commander of the Air Corps to the S.S. for their extensive co-operation.

I remain with best wishes for you in good comradeship and with Heil Hitler!
Always yours
E. Milch."

THE PRESIDENT: Major Farr, had you not better read the letter on the preceding page? It may be capable of an explanation.

MAJOR FARR: The letter on the preceding page, dated the 31st of August, 1942, is also from General Field Marshal Milch, and is addressed to the Reichsfuehrer S.S. It reads as follows:

"Dear Himmler:

I thank you very much for your letter of the 25th of August. I have read with great interest the reports of Dr. Rascher and Dr. Romberg. I have been informed about the current experiments. I shall ask the two gentlemen to give a lecture, combined with the showing of motion pictures, to my men in the near future. Hoping that it will be possible for me to see you on the occasion of my next visit to Headquarters, I remain with best regards and

Heil Hitler!
Yours
E. Milch."

Having finished his high altitude experiments, Dr. Rascher proceeded to experiments with methods of re-warming persons who had been subjected to extreme cold. I refer to our Document 1618-PS, which is an intermediate report on intense chilling experiments which had been started in Dachau on the 15th of August, 1942. That report, signed by Dr. Rascher, I offer in evidence as Exhibit USA 464. I shall read only a few sentences from the report, beginning with the first paragraph:

"Experimental procedure.

Persons subjected to experiments were placed in the water, dressed in complete flying uniform, winter or summer combination, and with an aviator's helmet. A life jacket made of rubber or kapok was to prevent submerging. The experiments were carried out at water temperatures varying from 2.5 degrees to 12 degrees. In one experimental series, occiput and brain stem were above the water, while in another series of experiments, the neck (brain stem) and the back of the head were submerged in the water.

Electrical measurement gave low temperature readings of 26.4 degrees in the stomach and 26.5 degrees in the rectum. Fatal casualties occurred only when the brain stem and the back of the head were also chilled. Autopsies of such fatal cases always revealed large amounts of free blood, up to one-half litre, in the cranial cavity. The heart regularly showed extreme dilation of the right chamber. As soon as the temperature in these experiments reached 28 degrees, the experimental subjects died invariably, despite all reviving attempts."

I pass now to the last paragraph of the report. I quote:

"During attempts to save severely chilled persons, it was evident that rapid re-warming was in all cases preferable to slow re-warming, because after removal from the cold water, the body temperature continued to sink rapidly. I think that, for this reason, we can dispense with the attempt to save intensely chilled subjects by means of animal warmth.

Re-warming by animal warmth - animal bodies or women's bodies - would be too slow."

Although Rascher was thus of the preliminary opinion that re-warming by women's bodies would be too slow, means for conducting such experiments were nevertheless placed at his disposal. I refer to our Document 1583-PS, a photostatic copy of a letter from Reichsfuehrer S.S. Himmler, addressed to Lieutenant General Pohl, dated the 16th of November, 1942. I offer it as Exhibit USA 465. I shall read just the first two paragraphs of that letter:

"Dear Pohl:

The following struck me during my visit to Dachau on the 13th of November 1942, regarding the experiments conducted there for the saving of people whose lives are endangered through exposure in ice, snow or water, and who are to be saved by the employment of every method or means.

I had ordered that suitable women are to be set aside from the concentration camp for these experiments for the warming of those who were exposed. Four girls were set aside who were in the concentration camp for loose morals, and because as prostitutes they were a potential source of infection."

I think it is unnecessary for me to go on with the rest of the paragraph, in which he expresses his dissatisfaction that a German prostitute should be used for this purpose.

To insure the continuance of Rascher's experiments, Himmler arranged for his transfer to the "Waffen S.S." I offer in evidence a letter which appears as our Document 16I7-PS. It is a letter from Reichsfuehrer S.S. addressed to "Dear Comrade Milch " - General Field Marshal Milch - dated November, 1942. I offer it as Exhibit USA 466. I will now read the first paragraphs of that letter, our Document 16I7- PS. I quote:

Dear Comrade Milch:

You will recall that through General Wolff I particularly recommended to you for your consideration the work of a certain S.S. Fuehrer, Dr. Rascher, who is a physician of the Air Force Reserve.

These researches which deal with the reaction of the human organism at great heights, as well as with symptoms caused by prolonged cooling of the human body in cold water, and similar problems which are of vital importance to the Air Force in particular, can be performed by us with particular efficiency because I personally assumed the responsibility for supplying asocial elements and criminals who only deserve to die, from concentration camps, for these experiments."

I shall omit the next four paragraphs, in which Himmler reflects upon the difficulties of conducting such experiments, because Christian medical circles were opposed, and pass on to the last paragraph on the first page of the translation. That is the seventh paragraph of the letter:

"I beg you to release Dr. Rascher, Stabsarzt in reserve, from the Air Force and to transfer him to me to the 'Waffen S.S.' I would then assume the sole responsibility for having these experiments made in this field, and would put the results, of which we in the S.S. need only a part for the first injuries in the East, entirely at the disposal of the Air Force. However, in this connection, I suggest that with the liaison between you and Wolff a non-Christian physician should be charged, who should be at the same time honourable as a scientist and not prone to intellectual thrift and who could be informed of the results. This physician should also have good contacts with the administrative authorities, so that the results would really attract attention.

I believe that this solution to transfer Dr. Rascher to the S.S., so that he could carry out the experiments under my responsibility and under my orders, is the best way. The experiments would not be stopped; we owe that to our men. If Dr. Rascher remained with the Air Force, there would certainly be much annoyance, because then I would have to bring a series of unpleasant details to you, because of the arrogance and presumption which Professor Dr. Holzloehner has displayed in his position at Dachau, where, although under my command, he made remarks about me to S.S. Colonel Sievers. In order to save both of us this trouble, I suggest again that Dr. Rascher should be transferred to the Waffen S.S. as quickly as possible."

THE PRESIDENT: Is that letter from Himmler?

MAJOR FARR: That letter is from Himmler.

Now Rascher's experiments were by no means the only experiments in which the S.S. was interested. Without attempting even to outline the whole extent of the experimental programme, I shall give just one further illustration of this type of S.S. activity. I refer to our Document L-103, which is a report prepared by the Chief Hygienist in the Office of the Reich Surgeon of the S.S. and Police, dated 12th September, 1944. I offer it as Exhibit USA 467. (Parenthetically I might note that the office of the Reich Surgeon S.S. and Police will be found in the personal staff department, as indicated by the second box on the right-hand side of the line leading down from the personal staff.)

I shall read a few paragraphs from this report, which is a report prepared by the Chief Hygienist in the office of the Reich Surgeon of S.S. and Police, and signed S.S. Oberfuehrer Dr. Murgowsky. It relates to experiments with poison bullets. Beginning with the first paragraph, I quote:

"On 11th September, 1944, in the presence of S.S. Sturmbannfuehrer Dr. Ding, Dr. Widmann and the undersigned, experiments with Conotine-nitrate bullets were carried out on five persons who had been sentenced to death. The calibre of the bullets used was 7.65 millimetres, and they were filled with poison in crystal form. Each subject of the experiment received one shot in the upper part of the left thigh, while in a horizontal position. In the case of two persons, the bullets passed clean through the upper part of the thigh. Even later no effect from the poison could be seen. These two subjects were therefore rejected."

I omit the next few sentences and proceed beginning with paragraph 2 of the report:

"The symptoms shown by the three condemned persons were surprisingly the same. At first, nothing special was noticeable. After 20 to 25 minutes, a disturbance of the motor nerves and a light flow of saliva began, but both stopped again. After 40 to 44 minutes, a strong flow of saliva appeared. The poisoned persons swallowed frequently, later the flow of saliva was so strong that it could no longer be controlled by swallowing. Foamy saliva flowed from the mouth. Then a sensation of choking, and vomiting started."

The next three paragraphs describe in coldly scientific fashion the reactions of the dying persons. The description then continues - and I want to quote the two paragraphs before the conclusion. It is the last paragraph on Page 1 of the translation, the sixth paragraph of the report:

"At the same time there was acute nausea. One of the poisoned persons tried in vain to vomit. In order to succeed he put four fingers of his hand, up to the main joint, right into his mouth. In spite of this, no vomiting occurred. His face became quite red.

The faces of the other two subjects had already become pale at an early stage. Other symptoms were the same. Later on the disturbances of the motor nerves increased so much that the persons threw themselves up and down and rolled their eyes and made aimless movements with their hands and arms. At last the disturbance subsided, the pupils were enlarged to the maximum, the condemned lay still. Massetercramp and loss of urine were observed in one of them. Death occurred 121, 123 and 129 minutes after they were shot."

The fact that S.S. doctors engaged in such experiments was no accident. It was consistent with an ideology and racial philosophy which, to use Himmler's words, regarded human beings as lice and offal. But the most important factor was that the S.S. alone was in a position to supply necessary human material. It did supply such material through W.V.H.A. I refer to our Document 1751-PS, which is a letter from the Chief of Office Group D of W.V.H.A, dated 12th May, 1944. I offer it as Exhibit USA 468, I quote that letter. It appears in the original file on the last page.

"There is cause to call attention to the fact that in every case permission for assignment has to be requested before assignment of prisoners is made for experimental purposes.

To be included in this request are number, kind of custody, and in case of Aryan prisoners, exact personal data, file number in the Reich Security Main Office and the reason for detention in the concentration camp.

Herewith, I explicitly forbid assignment of prisoners for experimental purposes without permission."

The translation says that the signature is illegible, but I think it appears from the original that it is the signature of Gluecks, since he was the department chief of Department D of W.V.H.A It was on the basis of being able to supply such material that the Reich Ministry of Finance was prepared to subsidise the S.S. experimental programme. I offer in evidence a series of letters between the Ministry of Finance, the Reich Research Department and the Reich Surgeon of the S.S. and Police. They are our Document 002-PS, which I offer in evidence as Exhibit USA 469. The first letter from which 1 quote appears on Page 4 of our Document 002-PS, and is from the Head of the Security Council of the Reich Research Department, addressed to the Surgeon of S.S. and Police. It is dated 19th February, 1943. I read the first three paragraphs of that letter:

"The Reich Minister of Finance told me that you requested 53 leading positions for your office, partly for a new research institute.

After the Reichsmarschall of the Greater German Reich had, as President of the Reich Research Department, himself taken charge of all German research, he issued directives, among other things, that in the execution of important military scientific tasks, the available institutions, including equipment and personnel, should be utilised to the utmost, for reasons of necessary economy of resources.

The foundation of new institutes comes therefore in question only in as far as there are no outstanding institutes available for the furtherance of important war research tasks."

I omit the rest of the letter.

To this letter the Reich Surgeon of the S.S. and Police replied on the 26th February, 1943. The reply will be found on Page z of the English translation. It is a letter from the Reich Surgeon S.S. and Police to the Head of the Security Council of the Reich

Research Department, dated 26th February, 1943. I quote the first three paragraphs of that letter. It begins:

"In acknowledgment of your letter of the 19th February, 1943, I am able to reply today as follows:

The suggested creation of 53 key positions in my department which you made the basis of your memorandum is a veritable peace-time set-up.

The special institutes of the S.S. which were to have a part of these positions would have to serve the purpose of establishing and making accessible for the entire realm of scientific research possibilities of research only open to the S.S."

Omitting the next two paragraphs, I continue:

"I will gladly be at your disposal at any time to discuss the particular research aims in connection with the S.S., which I would like to bring up upon the direction of the Reichsfuehrer S.S."

An interview between the Reich Surgeon and Mentzel, the author of the original letter, took place, and on 25th March, 1943, Mentzel wrote a letter to the Reich Minister of Finance, which is found on Page 1 of the translation. It is a letter from the President of the Reich Research Department, Head of the Security Council to the Reich Minister of Finance, dated 25th March, 1943. The letter begins:

"In regard to your letter of 19th December " - and then follow the serial numbers of the letter - to which I gave you a. preliminary answer on 19th February, I finally take the following position:

The Reich Surgeon S.S. and Police in a recent conversation with me maintained that the establishment demands made by him basically affect the purely military sector of the Waffen S.S. As these demands have to some extent been made in order to enlarge the scope of scientific research work, they exclusively refer to such matters as can only be carried out with the material at the disposal of the Waffen S. S. (prisoners) and therefore cannot be handled by any other research office. I cannot therefore, on behalf of the Reich Research Council, object to the establishment demands of the Reich Surgeon S.S. and Police."

The letter is signed, "Mentzel, Bureau Chief."

Thus it was because the S.S. was in a position to supply material for the programme of experiments that it took the lead in that field of endeavour.

THE PRESIDENT: Does the letter on Page 4 mean that the defendant Goering was president of the Reich Research Department ?

MAJOR FARR: Page 4 of the translation? Yes, that I understand is the case, the point of the letter being that Goering had laid down the rule that during the war there was to be no duplication of experimental facilities. Therefore, the Reich Research Department to which the Minister of Finance had turned for an opinion, asked the Reich Surgeon, "Why do you want to carry out this programme of experiments?"

THE PRESIDENT: I was only asking whether the President of the Reich Research Department was the defendant Goering?

MAJOR FARR: That is what is stated in the letter. I understand that to be the case.

THE PRESIDENT: Then what do the words, "President of the Reich Research Department" on Page 1 mean? Does that mean that the letter went to the defendant Goering?

MAJOR FARR: No. The letterhead bears the notation "President of the Reich Research Department," and the letter proceeds from an office of that department, Head of the Security Council. The letter was addressed to the Reich Minister of Finance.

THE PRESIDENT: I see.

MAJOR FARR: I have concluded the concentration camp phase.

THE PRESIDENT: We will recess now for ten minutes.

(A recess was taken.)

THE PRESIDENT: It will perhaps be convenient that I should announce that the Tribunal will adjourn today at four o'clock.

MAJOR FARR: Through its activities with respect to concentration camps, the S.S. performed part of its mission to safeguard the security of the Nazi regime. But another specialised aspect of that mission must not be forgotten. The Tribunal will recall Himmler's definition of that task - a definition I referred to earlier - the prevention of a Jewish-Bolshevist revolution of subhumans. In plain words, participation in the Nazi programme of Jewish persecution and extermination.

It would be idle for me to refer again at any length to the evidence relating to that programme which the Tribunal heard a day or so ago from Major Walsh. I want to call attention to just a few documents showing how the programme involved every branch and component of the S.S.

The racial philosophy of the S.S., which I dealt with at the very outset, made that organisation a natural agency for the execution of all types of anti-Semitic measures. The S.S. position on the Jewish question was publicly stated in the S.S. newspaper "Das Schwarze Corps" the issue of 8th August, 1940, by its editor, Gunter d'Alquen, in an article which has already been read into evidence as Exhibit USA 269. It is our Document 2668-PS. I shall not repeat that quotation, in which d'Alquen says that the Jewish question will not be solved until the Last Jew has been deported, and that the German peace which awaits Europe must be a peace without Jews.

The attempted solution of the Jewish question through the "spontaneous" demonstrations in Germany following the murder of von Rath in November, 1938, has been presented to the Tribunal. In those demonstrations all branches of the S.S. were called on to play a part. I refer to the teletype message from S.S. Gruppenfuehrer Heydrich, Chief of the Security Police and S.D., issued on 10th November, 1938. It is our Document 3051-PS. Portions of that teletype have already been read into evidence as Exhibit USA 240. I wish to read one further paragraph, which has not been read. It appears on Page 2 of the translation, the fourth paragraph.

> "The direction of the measures of the Security Police concerning the demonstrations against Jews is vested with the organs of the State Police (by which he means the Gestapo) inasmuch as the inspectors of the Security Police are not issuing their own orders. In order to carry out the measures of the Security Police, officials of the Criminal Police, as well as members of the S.D., of the Verfuegungstruppe and the Allgemeine S.S. may be used."

With the outbreak of the war and the march of Nazi armies over Europe, the S.S. participated in solving the Jewish question in other countries in Europe. The solution was nothing short of extermination. To a large degree these wholesale murders were disguised under the name of "anti-partisan" or "anti-guerilla" actions, and as such included as victims not merely Jews but Soviets, Poles and other Eastern peoples. With this antipartisan activity I shall deal in a few moments.

I want to refer now to a few actions confined essentially to Jews. To take one example - the mass annihilation of Jews in gas vans - described in our Document 501-PS, which was read into the record by Major Walsh as Exhibit USA 288. I simply want to point out that these gas vans, as appears from the letters, were operated by the Security Police and S.D. under the direction of R.S.H.A. Or to take another example - the report entitled "Solution of the Jewish Question in Galicia," our Document L-18, prepared by S.S. Gruppenfuehrer and Lt.- General of the Police Katzmann and rendered to S.S. Obergruppenfuehrer and General of the Police Krueger - that report has already been received in evidence as Exhibit USA 277. The Tribunal will recall that the solution, which consisted in the evacuation and extermination of all the Jews in Galicia, and the confiscation of their property, was carried out under the energetic direction of the S.S. and Police Leaders, with the assistance of S.S. Police Units. I wish to read three short items in the report, which has not yet been read. The first is a text under a photograph which appears on Page 3 of the translation and on Page 3 (a) of the original report. It is the first item on Page 3 of the translation. I quote:

"Great was the joy of the S.S. men when the Reichsfuehrer S.S. in person, in 1942 visited some camps along the Rollbahn."

The second is a balance sheet, which appears on Page 11 of the translation and Page 17 of the report. I read item 3 on the balance sheet:

"3. Amount paid over to the S.S. cashier:
   a. Camps - .6,867,251,00 zlotys
   b. W& R Factories - 6,556,513,69 zlotys
   Total - 13,423,764,69 zlotys

Further payments to the S.S. cashier are effected every month."

The third item I desire to read is the last two paragraphs of the report found on Page 20 of the translation and on Page 64 of the original document. I read the last two paragraphs of the report:

"Despite the extraordinary burden heaped upon every single S.S. Police Officer during these actions, the mood and spirit of the men were extraordinarily good and praiseworthy from the first to the last day.
Thanks only to the sense of duty of every single leader and man have we succeeded in getting rid of this plague in so short a time."

The final example of S.S. participation in Jewish extermination to which I shall call the Tribunal's attention is the infamous report by S.S. Brigadefuehrer and Major-General of the Police, Stroop, on the destruction of the Warsaw Ghetto, our Document 1061-PS. That report was introduced in evidence by Major Walsh as Exhibit USA 275, and the Tribunal indicated that it would take the whole report in evidence without the necessity of reading it in full. I shall not, therefore, read any further passages, but I do want to point out specifically two sections dealing with the constitution of the forces which participated in that fearful action. On Page 1 of the translation is a table of the units used.

THE PRESIDENT: Is it here?

MAJOR FARR: Our Document 1061-PS. I am just going to call your attention to the table of units which were employed in this action, indicating the average number of officers and men from each unit employed per day. It will be observed that among the units involved were the staff of the S.S. and Police Leader, two battalions of the "Waffen S.S.," two battalions of the 22nd S.S. Police Regiment, and members of the Security Police. The part played by the "Waffen S.S." came in for high praise from the writer of the report. The Tribunal will recall the passage which was read by Major Walsh in which reference was made to the toughness of the men of the

"Waffen S.S.," the Police and the Wehrmacht, and in which the writer said that "considering that the greater part of the men of the Waffen S.S. had been trained for only three or four weeks before being assigned to this action, high credit should be given for the pluck, courage, and devotion which they showed."

The Tribunal has already heard Himmler's proud boast of the part that the S.S. played in the extermination of the Jews. It occurs in his Posen Speech, our Document 1919-PS, and was read into the record in the presentation of the case dealing with concentration camps. The passage to which I refer appears on about the middle of Page 4 of the translation and on Page 65 of the original. Since that passage has already been read, it is unnecessary for me to quote it again ; but I do want the Tribunal to note that Himmler stated that only the S.S. could have carried out this extermination programme of the Jews, and that its participation in that programme was a page of glory in its history which could never be fully appreciated.

I now turn to the manner in which the S.S. fitted into the aggressive war programme of the conspirators, and, also, its responsibility for the Crimes Against Peace which were alleged in the Indictment. From its very beginning, it made prime contributions to the conspirators' aggressive war aims.

First, it served as one of the para-military organisations under which the conspirators disguised their building up of an army in violation of the Versailles Treaty. Second, through affiliated S.S. organisations in other countries and through some of the departments in its own Supreme Command, it fostered Fifth Column movements outside Germany and prepared the way for aggression. Third, through its militarised units, it participated in aggressive actions which eventually were carried out.

The Tribunal has just heard the evidence against the S.A., which demonstrated that from 1933 to 1938 they were militarised and were in fact nothing but a camouflaged army. Some of that evidence related to the S.S. as well. The paramilitary character of the "Allgemeine S.S." is apparent. I have already described the military character of its structure, the military discipline required of its members, and the steps it took to enlist in its ranks young men of military age. In addition to this volunteer army, the S.S. created as early as 1933 fully armed professional units. These were the "S.S. Verfuegungstruppe" and the Death Head Units with which I dealt yesterday.

While building up the S.S. as a military force within Germany, the conspirators also utilised it in other countries to lay the groundwork for aggression. The evidence presented by Mr. Alderman of the preparations for the seizure of Austria showed the part played by the S.S. Standarte 89 in the murder of Dollfuss, and described the memorial plaque which was erected in Nuremberg as a tribute to the S.S. men who participated in that murder. I refer to Exhibits USA 59 and 60, our Documents L-273 and 2968-PS, which were introduced by Mr. Alderman. The Tribunal will recall the subsequent story of the events of the night of 11th March, 1938, when the S.S. marched into Vienna and occupied all government buildings and important posts in the city - a story unfolded in Exhibit USA 61, our Document 212-PS, the report of Gauleiter Rainer to Reich Commissioner Buerckel (which was read in evidence by Mr. Alderman), and in our Document 2949-PS, Exhibit USA 76, the record of the telephone conversation between the defendant Goering and Dambrowski, which appears on Page 451 of the transcript of the record.

The same pattern was repeated in Czechoslovakia. Henlein's Free Corps played in that country the part of Fifth Column which the Austrian S.S. had played in Austria, and it was rewarded by being placed under the jurisdiction of the Reichsfuehrer S.S., in September, 1938. I refer to our Document 388-PS, which was read in evidence by Mr. Alderman as Exhibit USA 26. The items touched are 37 and 38 of the so- called

Schmundt file. Moreover, as shown by item 26 of that file, which Mr. Alderman read into the record, the S.S. had its own armed units - four battalions of the "Totenkopf Verbaende " - actually operating in Czechoslovakia before the Munich Pact was signed. S.S. preparations for aggression in Czechoslovakia were not confined to military forces. One of the departments of the S.S. Supreme Command - the "Volksdeutsche Mittelstelle" - which is represented on the chart by the third box from the top at the extreme right - was a centre for Fifth Column activity. The Tribunal may recall the secret meeting between Hitler and Henlein in March, 1938, described in notes of the German Foreign Office, Exhibit USA 95, at which the line to be followed by the Sudeten German Party was determined. The "Volksdeutsche Mittelstelle" was represented at that meeting by Professor Haushofer and S.S. Obergruppenfuehrer Lorenz. And when the Foreign Office, in August, 1938, awarded further subsidies to Henlein's Sudeten Party, the memorandum of that recommendation for further subsidies contained the significant footnote "Volksdeutsche Mittelstelle will be informed." I refer to Exhibit USA 96, our Document 3059, which was read into the record by Mr. Alderman, at Pages 631 and 632 of the record.

When at last the time came to strike, the S.S. was ready. I quote from the National Socialist Yearbook for 1940, our Document 2164-PS, Exhibit USA 255, on Page 1, paragraph 2, of the translation ; Page 365 of the original, paragraph 3:

"When the march into the liberated provinces of the Sudetenland began, on that memorable 1st October, 1938, the emergency forces (Verfuegungstruppe) as well as the Death Head Units (Totenkopf Verbaende) were with those in the lead."

I omit the remainder of the paragraph and continue with the next paragraph:

"The 15th March, 1939, brought a similar utilisation of the S.S. when it served to establish order in the collapsing Czechoslovakia. This action ended with the founding of the Protectorate Bohemia-Moravia.

Only a week later, on 29th March, 1939, Memel also returned to the Reich upon the basis of an agreement with Lithuania. Again it was the S.S., here particularly the East-Prussian S.S., which played a prominent part in the liberation of this Province."

In the final act in setting off the war - the attack on Poland in September, 1939 - the S.S. acted as a sort of stage manager. The Tribunal will recall the oral testimony of Erwin Lahousen with relation to the simulated attack on the radio station at Gleiwitz, by Germans dressed in Polish uniforms - what Lahousen referred to as one of the most mysterious things which uniforms and equipment together, he said at Page 620 of the transcript:

"These articles of equipment had to be prepared, and one day some man from the S.S. or the S.D. (the name is on the official diary of the War Department) fetched them."

The war broke out and the "Waffen S.S." again took its place in the van of the attacking forces.

During the war great use was made of the peculiar qualities possessed by the S.S., qualities not only of its combat forces but of its other components as well. 1 turn now to a consideration of some of the tasks in which the S.S. was engaged during the war - tasks which embraced the commission of War Crimes and Crimes Against Humanity described in the Indictment.

The Tribunal has already received in evidence a directive, our Document 447-PS, as Exhibit USA 135. It is a directive issued by the defendant Keitel, on 13th March,

1941, covering some of the preparations made three months in advance for the attack on Russia. Paragraph 2b of that directive, which was read into the record, provided that in the area of operations the Reichsfuehrer S.S. was entrusted with special tasks for the preparation of the political administration, tasks which would result from the struggle about to commence between two opposing political systems.

One of the steps taken by the Reichsfuehrer S.S. to carry out those "special tasks" was the formation and use of so-called "anti-partisan" units. They were discussed by Himmler in his Posen Speech, our Document 1919-PS, at Page 3 of the translation, paragraph 5, Page 57 of the original, last paragraph. I read those two paragraphs in which he discusses the anti-partisan units:

"In the meantime, I have also set up the Chief of the anti-partisan units. Our comrade S.S. Obergruppenfuehrer von dem Bach is Chief of the anti-partisan units. I considered it necessary for the Reichsfuehrer S.S. to be in authoritative command in all these battles, for I am convinced that we are in the best position to take action against this enemy struggle, which is decidedly a political one. Except where units, which had been supplied, and which we had formed for this purpose, were taken from us to fill in gaps at the front, we have been very successful.

It is notable that by setting up this department, we have gained for the S.S. in turn, a division, a corps, an army, and the next step - which is the High Command of an army or area of a group - if you wish to call it that."

What the S.S. did with its divisions, corps and army out of which the anti-partisan units were formed, is illustrated in the reports rendered as to the activities of such units. I offer in evidence activity and situation report No. 6 of the Task Forces of the Security Police and S.D. in the U.S.S.R., covering the period from the 1st to the 31st October, 1941. It is our Document R-102, and will be found in Volume 2 of the document book. It is Exhibit USA 470. The report shows that so-called "anti-partisan" activity was actually nothing but a name for extermination of persons believed politically undesirable and of Jews. The report is a very carefully organised and detailed description of such extermination. Section I describes the stations of the various Task Forces involved, Section II their activities. The latter section is divided into parts, each dealing with a different geographical region - the Baltic area, White Ruthenia, and the Ukraine.

Under each area the report of activities is classified under three headings:
(a) Partisan activity and counteraction;
(b) arrests and execution of Communists and officials; and
(c) Jews. I shall read only a few typical paragraphs, selected almost at random.

First, to show the units involved, I quote the second and third paragraphs of Page 4 of the translation and this also appears on Page 1 of the original:

"The present stations are:
Task Force A: since 7th October, 1941, Krasnogwardeisk.
Task Force B: continues in Smolensk.
Task Force C: since 27th September, 1941, in Kiev.
Task Force D: since 27th September, 1941, in Nikilaiev.
The action and Special Commandos (Einsatz-und-Sonderkommandos) which are attached to the Task Force continue on the march with the advancing troops to the sectors which have been assigned to them."

I shall now read from the section headed "Baltic area" and subsection labelled Jews", beginning with the first paragraph on Page 5 of the translation, Page 8 of the original, second paragraph.

"The male Jews over 16 were executed, with the exception of doctors and the elders. At the present time this action is still in progress. After completion of this action there will remain Only 500 Jewesses and children in the Eastern territory."

I pass now to the section headed "White Ruthenia," the subsection headed, "Partisan activity and counteraction." The paragraph I shall read begins on Page 6, paragraph 5 of the translation, found on Page 11, paragraph 1 of the original. I quote:

"In Wultschina 8 juveniles were arrested as partisans and shot. They were inmates of a children's home. They had collected weapons which they hid in the woods. Upon search the following were found: 3 heavy machine guns, 15 rifles, several thousand rounds of ammunition, several hand grenades, and several packages of poison gas Ebrit.

Arrests and executions of Communists, Officials and Criminals.

A further large part of the activity of the Security Police was devoted to the combating of Communists and criminals. A special Commando in the period covered by this report executed 63 officials, N.K.V.D. agents and agitators."

The subsection on arrests and executions of Communists, officials and criminals in White Ruthenia, ends as follows, and I read from Page 6 of the translation, paragraph 14, Page 12 of the original, paragraph 5:

"The liquidations for the period covered by this report have reached a total of 37,180 persons."

The final item I shall quote is from the section headed " Ukraine," under the subsection "Jews." It will be found on Page 8 of the translation, paragraph io, Page 18 of the original, next to the last paragraph:

"In Zhitomir 3,145 Jews had to be shot, because from experience they have to be regarded as bearers of Bolshevik propaganda and saboteurs."

This report, the Tribunal will recall, deals with the activities of four Task Forces - A, B, C and D. The more detailed report of Task Force A up to 15th October, 1941, is our Document L-180. It has already been introduced in evidence as Exhibit USA 276 and some paragraphs were read from it. It will be referred to again in the case against the Gestapo. I desire to read only two paragraphs which show the great variety of S.S. components in such a task force.

I might point out to the Court that this elaborately bound report *(Major Farr here handed in Document L-180)* which the Court has already seen, has a sort of pocket-part supplement, in which appears a break down of the personnel engaged in this action, in graphic form. I shall read the component parts which appear on this chart in a moment. First, I will quote from Page 5 of the translation, fourth paragraph:

THE PRESIDENT: Does that book you just put in refer to the extermination of the Jews in Galicia ?

MAJOR FARR: This is the report of Action Group A, an anti-partisan task force which operated in the Baltic States in 1941.

THE PRESIDENT: It is not L-180 ?

MAJOR FARR: It is L-180.

The passage I will read appears on Page 5 of the translation, paragraph 4, and on Page 12 of the original, first paragraph, I quote:

"This description of the over-all situation showed and shows that the members of the Gestapo (the Secret State Police), Kripo (that is the Criminal Police) and the S.B. (Security Service) who are attached to the Action Group, are active mainly in Lithuania, Latvia, Esthonia, White Ruthenia and, to a smaller part, in front of Leningrad. It shows further that the forces of the uniformed police and the Waffen S.S. are active mainly in front of Leningrad, in order to take measures against the returning population, and this under their own officers. This is so much easier because the task forces in Lithuania, Latvia and Esthonia have at their disposal native police units, as described in enclosure 1, and because so far 150 Latvian reinforcements have been sent to White Ruthenia.

The distribution of the leaders of Security Police and S.D. during the individual phases can be gathered from enclosure 2, the advance and activities of the task force Group and the various task forces from enclosure 3. It should be mentioned that the leaders of the armed S.S. and of the uniformed police, who are on the reserve, have declared their wish to stay with the Security Police and the S.D."

I quote now from enclosure 1a, which was referred to, showing the constitution of the force. This will be found on Page 14 of the translation. It was the graphic chart which I showed the Court a few moments ago, the translation having simply the break down of the components. I quote:

"Total Strength of Task
Force Group A:
Total - 990

Waffen S.S.	340	34.4%
Motor-bicycle Riders	172	17.4%
Administration	18	1.8%
Security Service (S.D.)	35	3.5%
Criminal Police (Kripo)	41	4.1%
State Police (Gestapo)	89	9.0%
Auxiliary Police	87	8.8%
Order Police	133	13.4%
Female Employees	13	1.3%
Interpreters	51	5.1%
Teleprinter Operators	3	0.3%
Wireless Operators	8	0.8%

The Tribunal will observe that in that list there appears the Waffen S.S., the S.D., Criminal Police, the Gestapo and the Order Police, all of which were part of the S.S. or under S.S. jurisdiction.

One final report of anti-partisan activity may be referred to. It is a report from the General Commissar for White Ruthenia to the Reich Minister for Occupied Eastern territories. It is our Document R-135, which I think is in the Document Book under 1475-PS, two document numbers have been combined. I think you will find it under 1475. That document was introduced into evidence by Major Walsh as Exhibit USA 289 and he read into the record the letter from the Reich Commissar of the Eastern territories, transmitting the report in question. The letter he read appears on Page 1 of the translation. I desire to read a paragraph or two from the report itself, which is found on Page 3 of the translation. It deals with the results of the police operation "Cottbus." I quote the first paragraph:

"S.S. Brigadefuehrer, Major General of Police von Gottberg reports that the operation 'Cottbus' had the following result during the period mentioned:
Enemy dead - 4,500

Dead suspected of belonging to bands - 5,000

German dead - 59"

I think it is unnecessary to continue further with the list. I skip to the fourth paragraph of the report:

"The figures mentioned above indicate that again a heavy destruction of the population must be expected. If only 492 rifles are taken from 4,500 enemy dead, this discrepancy shows that among these enemy dead were numerous peasants from the country. The battalion Dirlewanger especially has a reputation for destroying many human lives. Among the 5,000 people suspected of belonging to bands, there were numerous women and children.

By order of the Chief of anti-partisan units, S.S. Obergruppenfuehrer von dem Bach, units of the Armed Forces have also participated in the operation."

This is as far as I will quote.

The Tribunal will recall that S.S. Obergruppenfuehrer von dem Bach was referred to in the Posen speech by Himmler as "our comrade " whom he had placed in charge of anti-partisan activity.

The activities I have just dealt with were joint activities, in which the - the "Waffen S.S." and S.S. Police Regiments, Gestapo, Order Police, were all involved. But these units were also used individually, to carry out tasks of such a nature.

I offer in evidence a letter from the Chief of the Command Office of the Waffen S.S., our Document 1972-PS, as Exhibit USA 471. It is a letter from the Chief of the Command Office of the "Waffen S.S." to the Reichsfuehrer S.S., dated 14th October, 1941, subject: Intermediate report on civilian state of emergency. I shall read that letter. I quote:

"I deliver the following report regarding the commitment of the Waffen S.S. in the Protectorate Bohemia and Moravia during the civil state of emergency:

All battalions of the Waffen S.S. in the Protectorate Bohemia and Moravia will in rotation be employed on shootings and the supervision of hangings respectively.

Up until now there occurred:

In Prague-

  99 shootings.

  21 hangings.

In Bruenn

  54 shootings.

  17 hangings.

Total - 191 executions (including 16 Jews).

A complete report regarding other measures and on the conduct of the officers, N.C.O.'s and men will be made following the termination of the civil state of emergency."

It is not surprising that units of the "Waffen S.S." and the branch which had thus been employed in extermination actions and the executions of civilians are also to be found violating the laws of warfare when carrying on ordinary combat operations. I offer in evidence a supplementary report of the Supreme Headquarters Allied Expeditionary Force Court of Inquiry re shooting of allied prisoners- of-war by the 12th S.S. Panzer Division in Normandy, France, between 7th and 21St June, 1944. It is our Document 2997-PS, Exhibit USA 472. Extracts from that report consist of the formal record of the proceedings of the Court of Inquiry and the statement of its findings are included in the Document Book under that document number. They have been translated into German. Under Article 21 of the Charter, this Tribunal is directed to take judicial notice of the documents of committees set up in various Allied countries for the investigation of War Crimes, and also of the records and findings of military or other Tribunals of any of the United Nations. This report falls squarely within that provision. Therefore, without reading portions of the document, I shall summarise the findings of the Court of Inquiry which are set out on Pages 8 to 10 of the document. The Court concluded that there occurred between the 7th and 17th June, 1944, in Normandy, seven cases of violations of the laws of war.

THE PRESIDENT: What page?

MAJOR FARR: I am not quoting, I am summarising what appears on Pages 8 to 10 of the translation.

There occurred seven cases of violations of the laws of war, involving the shooting of 64 unarmed Allied prisoners-of-war in uniform, many of whom had been previously wounded and none of whom had resisted or attempted to escape ; that the perpetrators were members of the 12th S.S. Panzer Division, the so-called Hitler Jugend Division ; that enlisted men of the 15th Company of the 25th Panzer Grenadier Regiment of that Division were given secret orders to the effect that S.S. troops shall take no prisoners and that prisoners are to be executed after having been interrogated; that similar orders were given to men of the 3rd Battalion of the 26th Panzer Grenadier Regiment of the Division and of the 12th S.S. Engineering and Reconnaissance Battalions; and that the conclusion was irresistible that it was understood throughout the Division that a policy of denying quarter or executing prisoners after interrogation was openly approved the S.S. I refer to the execution of Allied flying personnel, of commandos and paratroopers, and of escaped prisoners-of-war who were turned over to the S.D. to be destroyed. Evidence of these actions will be presented in the case against the Gestapo.

Combatants who were taken prisoner encountered the S.S. in another form. In the case against the Gestapo, evidence will be presented of commando groups stationed in prisoner-of-war camps to select prisoners for what the Nazis euphemistically called "special treatment." Finally, the entire control of prisoners-of-war was turned over to the Reichsfuehrer S.S.

I have read in evidence this morning, our Document 058-PS, which provided for the direction of all prisoner-of-war camps by Himmler.

The final, but vital, phase of the conspiracy in which the S.S. played a leading role must be mentioned. The permanent colonisation of conquered territories, the destruction of their national existence, and the permanent extension of the German frontier were fundamental objects of the conspirators' plans.

The Tribunal received evidence, a day or so ago, of the manner in which these objectives were attained through the forcible evacuation and resettlement of inhabitants of conquered territories, confiscation of their properties, denationalisation and re-education of persons of German blood, and the colonisation of conquered territories by Germans.

The S.S. was the logical agency to formulate and carry out the programme. I have read into the record already the numerous statements made by Himmler as to the training of the S.S., which played the role of the aristocracy of the New Europe. He put those theories into practice when he was appointed, on 7th October, 1939, as Reich Commissioner for the Consolidation of German Folkdom. The decree by which he was appointed to that office - our Document 686-PS - has already been introduced into evidence as Exhibit USA 305. I shall not, therefore, read it.

To make and carry out plans for the programme of evacuation and resettlement, a new department of the S.S. Supreme Command was created; Staff Headquarters of the Reich Commissioner for the Consolidation of German Nationality. That is indicated on the chart by the fourth box from the top, on the extreme right-hand side.

The functions of this office are described in the Organisation Book of the N.S.D.A.P. for 1943, our Document 2640-PS, which has already been introduced in evidence as Exhibit USA 323. I shall read the description of the functions of that department appearing on Page 3 of the translation, the last paragraph, and Page 421 of the original.

I quote:
> "The main office of the staff of the Reich Commissioner for the Consolidation of German Nationality is entrusted with the whole settlement and constructive planning, and with its execution within the Reich and all those territories under the authority of the Reich, including all administrative and economic questions in connection with the settlement, especially the deployment of manpower for this purpose."

The colonisation programme had two principal objectives: First, the destruction of the conquered peoples by exterminating them, deporting them, and confiscating their property ; second, the settlement of racial Germans on the newly acquired land.

The extermination actions conducted by the S.S., as to which I have just introduced evidence, contributed in part to clearing the conquered territories of persons who were deemed dangerous to the Nazi Plan. But not every undesirable could be liquidated. Mass deportations accomplished the twin purpose of providing labour and of freeing the land for German colonists.

I have already introduced evidence as to the participation of S.S. agencies in deporting persons to concentration camps.

The evacuation and resettlement programme required the use of further deporting agencies. I quote from our Document z163-PS, the National Socialist Year Book for 1941, Exhibit USA 444. The passage in question appears at Page 3 of the translation, paragraph 5, and at Page 195 of the original. I quote:

> "For some time now, the Reichsfuehrer S.S. has had at his disposal an office under the management of S.S.- Obergruppenfuehrer Lorenz, the National German Central Office (Volksdeutsche Mittelstelle - VM). This office has the task to deal with national German questions and to gather the necessary documents.
>> In addition to the VM, Immigration Centre Offices, with the Chief of the Security Police and the Security Service of the S.S., under the management of S.S.-Obersturmbannfuehrer Dr. Sandberger, and the Settlement Staff with the Reich Commissioner were created, which, in co-operation with the National Socialist Welfare Organisation and the Reich Railroad Agency, took charge of the re-emigration of national Germans."

I also offer in evidence the affidavit of Otto Hoffmann, S.S. Obergruppenfuehrer and General of the Waffen S.S. and Police, our Document L-49. I offer it as Exhibit USA 473. Hoffmann was Chief of the Main Office for Race and Settlement in the S.S. Supreme Command, until 1943. This affidavit was taken on the 4th of August, 1945, at Freising, Germany. I shall read paragraph 2 of that affidavit:

> "2. The executive power, in other words the carrying out of al [sic] so-called resettlement actions, that is to say, the sending away of Polish and Jewish settlers and those of non-German blood from a territory in Poland destined for Germanisation, was in the hands of the Chief of the R.S.H.A. Heydrich, and later of Kaltenbrunner, since the end of 1942. The Chief of the R.S.H.A. also supervised and issued orders to the so-called immigration centre, which classified the Germans living abroad who returned to Germany and directed

them to the individual farms, already freed. The latter was done in agreement with the chief office of the Reichsfuehrer S.S."

Other S.S. agencies were involved in the programme for deportation. The Tribunal has already received in evidence our Document 1352-PS, as Exhibit USA 176. It is a report relating to the confiscation of Polish agricultural enterprises, dated the 22nd of May, 1940, and signed "Kusche." Portions of that document dealing with the confiscation of Polish agricultural enterprises and the deportation of Polish owners of the land to Germany were read into the record. I shall read only one further paragraph, showing S.S. personnel involved in this action. It appears on Page 2 of the translation, the first full paragraph; and on Page 10 of the original, paragraph 2.

Referring to the deportation of Polish farmers the report says and I quote:

"Means of transportation to the railroad can be provided:

By the enterprises of the East German Corporation of Agricultural Development.

2. By the S.S . N.C.O. School in Lublinitz and the concentration camp of Auschwitz.

These two latter places will also detail the necessary S.S. men for the day of the confiscation, and so forth."

The extent to which almost all departments of the Supreme Command of the S.S. were concerned with the evacuation programme is shown by the minutes of a meeting on the 4th of August, 1942, dealing with the deportation of Alsatians. It is our Document R-114, and was received in evidence as Exhibit USA 314. I shall read only the list of persons and offices represented at that conference, since the body of the report has been read, in part, into the record.

I start at the beginning of the document, Page 1 of R-114

"Memo on meeting of 4/8/42.

Subject General directions for the treatment of deported Alsatians.

Present:

S.S. Hauptsturmfuehrer Dr. Stier; S.S. Hauptsturmfuehrer Petri; R.R. Hoffman ; Dr. Scherler; S.S. Untersturmuehrer Foerster."

There is a notation next to their names of "Staff Headquarters."

Then: "S.S. Obersturinfuehrer Dr. Hinrichs, Chief of Estate Office and Settlement Staff, Strasbourg.

S.S. Sturmbannfuehrer Brueckner, National German Central Office (Volksdeutsche Mittelstelle).

S.S. Hauptsturmuehrer Hummisch, Reich Security Main Office (Reichssicherheitshauptamt).

S.S. Untersturmfuhrer Dr. Sieder, Main Office for Race and Settlement (R.U.S.-Hauptamt).

Dr. Labes, D.U.T."

The S.S. not only destroyed and deported conquered peoples and confiscated their property, but also repopulated the conquered regions with so-called racial Germans. Not all Germans were deemed reliable colonists, however. Those who were not were returned to Germany for re-Germanisation and re-education along Nazi lines.

A typical instance of the fate of such Germans is told in our Document R-112, which has already been introduced in evidence as Exhibit USA 309. It is a decree of the Reich Commissioner for the Consolidation of German Folkdorn. That decree, as the Tribunal will recall, dealt with the treatment to be accorded so-called "Polonised" Germans. By the terms of that decree these organisations were charged with the responsibility for the re-Germanisation programme, the Higher S.S. and Police Leaders, and the Gestapo.

I think it is unnecessary for me to quote from that report, since portions have already been read into evidence. I will refer the Court specifically to Section III of the decree, which appears on Page 7 of the translation, and to Section IV of the decree, which appears on the same Page, both of which indicate that the Higher S.S. and Police Leaders and the Gestapo were responsible for the re-Germanisation actions.

In the final state of the process, the resettlement of the conquered lands by racially and politically desirable Germans, still other S.S. agencies participated. I quote again from our Document 2163-PS, the Nat~onal Socialist Year Book for 1941, Exhibit USA 444. The passage appears on Page 3 of the translation, paragraph 7, and on Page 195 of the original. I quote:

> "Numerous S.S. leaders and S.S. men helped with untiring effort in bringing about this systematic migration of peoples, which has no parallel in history.
>
> There were many authoritative and administrative difficulties which, however, were immediately overcome, due to the unbureaucratic working procedure. This was especially guaranteed, above all, by the employment of the S.S.
>
> The procedure called 'Durchschleusung' takes three to four hours as a rule. The re-settler is passed through eight to nine offices, following each other in a definite order ; registration office, card-index office, certificate and photo office, property office, and biological, hereditary, and sanitary test offices. The latter was entrusted to doctors and medical personnel of the S.S. and of the Armed Forces. The S.S. Corps Areas Alpenland, North-West, Baltic Sea, Fulda-Werra, South and South East, the S.S. Main Office, the N.P.E.A. - National Political Education Institution - Vienna, and the S.S. Cavalry School in Hamburg, provided most of the S.S.-Officers and S.S.-Non-Coms who worked at this job of resettlement."

I omit the next three paragraphs and continue with the Year Book's conclusion as to the S.S. participation in the colonisation scheme:

> "The settlement, establishment and care of the newly-won peasantry in the liberated Eastern territory will be one of the most cherished tasks of the S.S. in the whole future."

THE PRESIDENT: This might be a good time to break off until 2 o'clock.

MAJOR FARR: Yes, sir.

(A recess was taken until 1400 hours.)

MAJOR FARR: In the course of its development from a group of strong, armed body guards, some 200 in number, to a complex organisation participating in every field of Nazi endeavour, the S.S. found room for its members in high places - and persons in high places found themselves a position in the S.S.

Of the defendants charged in this Indictment, seven were high ranking officers in the S.S. They are the defendants Ribbentrop, Hess, Kaltenbrunner, Bormann, Sauckel, Neurath and Seyss-Inquart. The vital part that the defendant Kaltenbrunner played in the S.S., the S.D. and the entire Security Police system, will be shown by evidence to be presented at the conclusion of the case on the Gestapo. With respect to the other six defendants whom I have named, I desire to call the Tribunal's attention to the fact of their membership in the S.S. This fact is a matter rather of judicial notice than of proof. Evidence of the fact is to be found in two official publications which I now offer the court. The first is this black book - the membership list of the S.S. as of ist December, 1936. This book contains a list of the members of the S.S. arranged according to rank. I offer it in evidence as Exhibit USA 474.

Turning to Page 8 of this publication we find at line 2 the name "Hess, Rudolf" followed by the notation "By authority of the Fuehrer the right to wear the uniform of an S.S. Obergruppenfuehrer". I now offer the 1937 edition of the same membership list as Exhibit USA 475. Turning to Page 10, line So, we find the name "Bormann, Martin " - and in line with his name on the opposite page under the column headed "Gruppenfuehrer", the following date, 30/1/37.

In the same edition on Page 12, line 56, appears the name "von Neurath, Konstantin", and on the opposite page under the column headed "Gruppenfuehrer " the date "18/9/37". The other publication to which I refer is "Der Grossdeutsche Reichstag" for the fourth voting period, edited by E. Kienast, Ministerial Director of the German Reichstag. This is an official handbook containing biographical data as to membership of the Reichstag. It is Document 2381-PS, and I offer it in evidence as Exhibit USA 476. On Page 349 the following appears: "von Ribbentrop, Joachim, Reichsminister des AuswArtigen, S.S. Obergruppenfuehrer". On Page 360 the following appears: "Sauckel, Fritz, Gauleiter und Reichsstatthalter in Thueringen, S.S. Obergruppenfuehrer ". On Page 389 the following appears: "Seyss-Inquart, Artur, Dr. jur., Reichsminister, S.S. Obergruppenfuehrer".

THE PRESIDENT: What was the date of that book ?

MAJOR FARR: This book covers the fourth voting period beginning on ioth April, 1938, covering the period up to 13th January, 1947 - that is, the voting period covers that course of years. The edition, I think, was in 1943. 1 might point out that the rank of the defendants mentioned in the 1936 and 1937 editions of the membership list of the S.S. may not be the final rank they held. They were "Gruppenfuehrer" at that time, but they were members of the S.S., as shown by the book.

It is our contention that the S.S., as defined in Appendix B, Page 36 of the Indictment, was an unlawful organisation. As an organisation founded on the principle that persons of "German blood" were a "master race", it exemplified a basic Nazi doctrine. It served as one of the means through which the conspirators acquired control of the German Government. The operations of the S.D., and of the "S.S. Totenkopf Verbaende" in concentration camps, were means used by the conspirators to secure their regime and terrorise their opponents, as alleged in Count 1. All branches of the S.S. were involved from the very beginning, in the Nazi programme of Jewish extermination. Through the Allgemeine S.S. as a para-military organisation, and the "S.S. Verfuegungstruppe" and "S.S. Totenkopf Verbaende", as professional combat forces, and the "Volksdeutsche Mittelstelle" as a Fifth Column agency, the S.S. participated in the military preparations for aggressive war, and through its militarised units in the waging of aggressive war in the West and in the East as set forth in Counts One and Two of the Indictment. In the course of such war all components of the S.S. participated in the War Crimes and Crimes against Humanity, set forth in Counts Three and Four of the Indictment - the murder and ill-treatment of civilian populations in occupied territory, the murder and ill-treatment of prisoners of war, and the Germanisation of occupied territories.

The evidence has shown that the S.S. was a single enterprise - a unified organisation. Some of its functions were, of course, performed by one branch or department or office, some by another. No single branch or department participated in every phase of its activity, but every branch and department and office was necessary to the functioning of the whole. The situation is much the same as in the case of the individual defendants at the bar. Not all participated in every act of the conspiracy - but all, we contend, performed a contributing part in the whole criminal scheme.

The evidence has shown that though the S.S. was an organisation of volunteers, applicants had to meet the strictest standards of selection. It was not easy to become an S.S. member. That was true of all branches of the S.S. We clearly recognise, of course, that during the course of the war, as the demands for man-power increased and the losses of the "Waffen S.S." grew heavier and heavier, there were occasions when men drafted for compulsory military service were assigned to units of the "Waffen S.S." rather than to the "Wehrmacht." Those instances were relatively few. Evidence of recruiting standards of the "Waffen S.S." in 1943, which I quoted yesterday, has shown that membership in that branch was as essentially voluntary and highly selective as in other branches. Doubtless some of the members of the S.S., or of other of the organisations alleged to be unlawful, might desire to show that their participation in the organisation was a small or innocuous one, that compelling reasons drove them to apply for membership, that they were not fully conscious of its aims or that they were mentally irresponsible when they became members. Such facts might or might not be relevant if such persons were on trial. But, in any event, this is not the forum to try out such matters.

The question before this Tribunal is simply this, whether the S.S. was or was not an unlawful organisation. The evidence has finally shown what the aims and activities of the S.S. were. Some of those aims were stated in publications which I have quoted to the Court. The activities were so widespread and so notorious, covering so many fields of unlawful endeavour, that the illegality of the organisation could not have been concealed. It was a notorious fact, and Himmler, himself, in 1936, in a quotation which I read to the Tribunal yesterday, admitted that, when he said, "I know that there are people in Germany now who become sick when they see these black coats. We know the reason and we do not expect to be loved by too many."

It was, we submit, at all times the exclusive function and purpose of the S.S. to carry out the common objectives of the defendant conspirators. Its activities in carrying out those objectives involved the commission of the crimes defined in Article 6 of the Charter. By reason of its aims and the means used for the accomplishment thereof, the S.S. should be declared a criminal organisation in accordance with Article 9 of the Charter.

COLONEL STOREY: If the Tribunal please, the next presentation will be the Gestapo, and it will take just a few seconds to get the material here.

We are now ready to proceed if your Honour is.

THE PRESIDENT: Yes.

COLONEL STOREY: We first pass to the Tribunal Document Books marked "Exhibit AA," Your Honour will notice they are in two volumes, and I will try each time to refer to the appropriate volume. They are separated into the D Documents, the L Documents, the PS Documents, etc.

The presentation of evidence on the criminality of the Geheime Staatspolizei (Gestapo) includes evidence on the criminality of the Sicherheitsdienst (S.D.) and of the Schutzstaffeln (S.S.), which has been discussed by Major Farr, because a great deal of the criminal acts were so inter-related. In the Indictment, as your Honour knows, the S.D. is included by special reference as a part of the S.S., since it originated as a part of the S.S. and always retained its character as a Party organisation, as distinguished from the Gestapo, which was a State organisation. As will be shown by the evidence, however, the Gestapo and the S.D. were brought into very close working relationship, the S.D. serving primarily as the information gathering agency and the Gestapo as the executive agency of the police system established by the Nazis for the purpose of combating the political and ideological enemies of the Nazi regime.

In short, I think we might think of the S.D. as the intelligence organisation and the Gestapo the executive agency, the former a Party organisation and the latter a State organisation, but merged together for all practical purposes.

The first subject: The Gestapo and S.D. were formed into a powerful, centralised political police system that served Party, State and Nazi leadership.

The Geheime Staatspolizei, or Gestapo, was first established in Prussia on 26th April, 1933, by the defendant Goering, with the mission of carrying out the duties of political police, with or in place of, the ordinary police authorities. The Gestapo was given the rank of a higher police authority and was subordinated only to the Minister of the Interior, to whom was delegated the responsibility of determining its functional and territorial jurisdiction. That fact is established in the "Preussische Gesetzsammlung," of 26th April, 1933, Page 122, and it is our Document 2104-PS.

Pursuant to this law, and on the same date, the Minister of the Interior issued a decree on the reorganisation of the Police, which established a State Police Bureau in each governmental district of Prussia subordinate to the Secret State Police Bureau in Berlin, and 1 cite as authority, the Ministerial-Blatt for the Internal Administration of Prussia, 193 3, Page 503, and it is Document 2371-PS.

Concerning the formation of the Gestapo, the defendant in " Aufbau einer Nation," 1934, Page 87, which is our Document 2344-PS-I quote from the English translation a short paragraph, of which your Honour will take judicial notice, unless you wish to turn to it in full-the defendant Goering said:

> "For weeks I had been working personally on the reorganisation, and at last I alone and upon my own decision and my own reflection created the office of the Secret State Police. This instrument, which is so feared by the enemies of the State, has contributed most to the fact that to-day there can no longer be talk of a Communist or Marxist danger in Germany and Prussia."

THE PRESIDENT: What was the date?

COLONEL STOREY: The date? 1934, sir.

On 30th November, 1933, Goering issued a decree for the Prussian State Ministry and the Reich Chancellor, placing the Gestapo under his direct supervision as chief. The Gestapo was thereby established as an independent branch of the administration of the Interior, responsible directly to Goering as Prussian Prime Minister. This decree gave the Gestapo jurisdiction over the political police matters of the general and interior administration and provided that the district, county, and local police authorities were subject to its directives, and that cites the Prussian laws of 30th November, 1933, Page 413, and Document 2105-PS.

In a speech delivered at a meeting of the Prussian State Council on 18th June, 1934, which is published in "Speeches and Essays of Hermann Goering, 1939," Page 102, our Document 3343-PS, Goering said, and I quote one paragraph:

> "The creation of the Secret State Police was also a necessity. You may recognise the importance attributed to this instrument of State security from the fact that the Prime Minister has made himself head of the department of the administration, because it is precisely the observation of all currents directed against the new State which is of fundamental importance."

By a decree of 8th March, 1934, the Regional State Police Offices were separated from their organisational connection with the District Government and established as independent authorities of the Gestapo. That cites the "Preussische Gesetzsammlung" of 8th March, 1943, Page 143, our Document 2 11 3-PS.

I now offer in evidence Document 1680-PS, Exhibit USA 477. This is an article entitled "Ten Years Security and S.D.", published in the German Police Journal, the magazine of the Security Police and S.D., of 1st February, 1943. I quote one paragraph from this article on Page 2 of the English translation, Dociiment 1680, which is the third main paragraph:

"Parallel to that development in Prussia, the Reichsfuehrer S.S. Heinrich Himmler, created in Bavaria the Bavarian Political Police, and also suggested and directed in the other Federal States outside Prussia the establishment of political police. The unification of the political police of all the Federal States took place in the spring of 1934 when Minister President Hermann Goering appointed Reichsfuehrer S.S. Heinrich Himmler, who had meanwhile become Commander of the Political Police of all the Federal States outside Prussia, to the post of Deputy Chief of the Prussian Secret State Police."

The Prussian law about the Secret State Police, dated 10th February, 1936, then summed up the development to that date and determined the position and responsibilities of the Secret State Police in the executive regulations issued the same day.

On 10th February, 1936, the basic law for the Gestapo was promulgated by Goering as Prussian Prime Minister. I refer to Document 2107-PS. This law provided that the Secret State Police had the duty of investigating and combating, in the entire territory of the State, all tendencies inimical to the State, and declared that orders and matters of the Secret State Police were not subject to the review of the administrative courts. That is the Prussian State law of that date, cited on Pages 21-22 of the publication of ihe laws of 1936.

Also on that same date, 10th February, 1936, a decree for the execution of the law was issued by Goering, as Prussian Prime Minister, and by Frick, as Minister of the Interior. This decree provided that the Gestapo had authority to enact measures valid in the entire area of the State and measures affecting that area-by the way, that is found in 2108-PS and is also a published law-that it was the centralised agency for collecting political intelligence in the field of political police, and that it administered the concentration camps. The Gestapo was given authority to make police investigations in cases of criminal attacks upon the Party as well as upon the State.

Later, on 28th August, 1936, a circular of the Reichsfuehrer S.S. and Chief of the German Police provided that as on 1st October, 1936, the Political Police Forces of the German provinces were to be called the "Geheime Staatspolizei". That means the Secret State Police. The regional offices were still to be described as State Police.

The translation of that law is in Document 2372- PS, Reichsministerial-Gesetzblatt of 1936, No. 44, Page 1344.

Later, on 20th September, 1936, a circular of the Minister of the Interior, Frick, commissioned the Gestapo Bureau in Berlin with the supervision of the duties of the Political Police Commanders in all the States of Germany. That is, Reichsministerial-Gesetzblatt, 1936, Page 1,343, our Document L-297.

The law regulating and relating to financial measures in connection with the police, of igth March, 1937, provided that the officials of the Gestapo were to be considered direct officials of the Reich, and that their salaries, in addition to the operational expenses of the whole State Police, were to be borne from 1st April, 1937, by the Reich. That is shown in Document 2243-PS, which is a copy of the law of 19th March, 1937, Page 325.

Thus, through the above laws and decrees, the Gestapo was established as a uniform political police system operating throughout the land and serving Party, State, and Nazi leadership.

In the course of the development of the S.D., it came into increasingly close co-operation with the Gestapo and also with the "Reichskriminalpolizei", the Criminal Police, known as Kripo, shown up there under A.M.T. V. The S.D. was called upon to furnish information to various State authorities. On iith November, 1938, a decree of the Reich Minister of the Interior declared the S.D. to be the intelligence organisation for the State as well as for the Party, to have the particular duty of supporting the Secret State Police, and to become thereby active on a national mission. These duties necessitated a closer co-operation between the S.D. and the authorities for the general and interior administration. That law is translated in Document 1638-PS.

The Tribunal has already received evidence concerning the decrees of 17th and 26th June, 1936, under which Himmler was appointed Chief of the German Police, and by which Heydrich became the first Chief of the Security Police and S.D. Even then Goering did not relinquish his position as Chief of the Prussian Gestapo. Thus, the decree of the Reichsfuehrer S.S. and Chief of German Police which was issued on 28th August, 1936, which is our Document 2372-PS, was distributed "to the Prussian Minister President as Chief of the Prussian Secret State Police", that is, to Goering.

On 27th September, 1939, by order of Hirmnler in his capacity as Reichsfuehrer S.S. and Chief of the German Police, the Central Offices of the Gestapo and S.D., and also of the Criminal Police, were merged in the office of the Chief of the Security Police and S.D. under the name of R.S.H.A., which your Honour has heard described by Major Farr. Under this order the personnel and administrative sections of each agency were co-ordinated in Amt. I and II of the chart shown here, of the R.S.H.A. The operational sections of the S.D. became Amt. Ill, shown in the box Amt. III, except for foreign intlligence which was placed over in Amt. VI. The operational sections of the Gestapo became Amt. IV, as shown on the chart, and the operational sections of the Kripo, that is, the Criminal Police, became Amt. V, as shown on the chart.

Ohlendorf was named the Chief of Amt. Ill, the S.D. inside Germany; Mueller was named Chief of Amt. IV, and Nebe was named Chief of Amt. V, the Kripo.

On 27th September, 1939, Heydrich, the Chief of the Security Police and S.D., issued a directive pursuant to the order of Himmler in which he ordered that the designation and heading of R.S.H.A. was to be used exclusively in internal relations of the Reich Ministry of the Interior, and the heading "The Chief of the Security Police and S.D." in transactions with outside persons and offices. The directive provided that the Gestapo would continue to use the designation and heading "Secret State Police" according to the particular instructions.

This order is Document L-361, Exhibit USA 478, which we now offer in evidence, and refer your Honour to the first paragraph L-361. That is found in the first volume. I just direct your Honour's attention to the date and to the subject, which is the amalgamation of the " Zentral Arnter " of the Sicherheitspolizei and the S.D., and the creation of the four sections, and then to the words will be joined to the R.S.H.A. in accordance with the following directives . . This amalgamation carries with it no change in the position of the ' Ainter ' in the Party nor in their local administration."

I might say here parenthetically, if the Tribunal please, that we like to think of the R.S.H.A. as being the so-called administrative office through which a great many of these organisations were administered, and then a number of these organisations, including the Gestapo, maintaining their separate identity as an operational organisation. I think a good illustration, if your Honour will recall, is that during the war there may be a certain division or a certain air force which is administratively under a certain headquarters, but operationally, when they had an invasion, may be under the general supervision of somebody else who was operating a task force. So the R.S.H.A. was really the administrative office of a great many of these alleged criminal organisations.

The Gestapo and the S.D. were therefore organised functionally on the basis of the opponents to be combated and the matters to be investigated.

I now invite the attention of the Tribunal to this chart which has already been identified, and I believe it is Exhibit 53. This chart - I am in error; that is the original identification number. This chart shows the main chain of command from Himmler, who was the Reich Leader of the S.S. and Chief of the German Police, to Kaltenbrunner, who was Chief of the Security Police and S.D., and from Kaltenbrunner to the various field offices of the Gestapo and the S.D.

We now formally offer in evidence this chart, Document L-219, as Exhibit USA 479.

This chart, from which the one on the wall is taken, has been certified by Otto Ohlendorf, Chief of Amt III of the R.S.H.A., and by Walter Schellenberg, Chief of Amt VI of the R.S.H.A., and has been officially identified by both of those former officials.

The chart shows that the principal flow of command in police matters came from Himmler as Reich Leader of the S.S. and Chief of the German Police directly to Kaltenbrunner, who was Chief of the Security Police and S.D., and as such was also head of the R.S.H.A., which is the administrative office to which I have referred.

Kaltenbrunner's headquarters organisation was composed of seven Aemter, plus a military office; the seven Aemter shown here.

Under subsection D was Obersturmbannfuehrer Rauff, who handled technical matters, including motor vehicles of the Sipo and the S.D., to which we will refer later.

Amt III was the S.D. inside Germany and was charged with investigations into spheres of German national life. It was the Internal Intelligence Organisation of the police system and its interests extended into all areas occupied by Germany during the course of the war. In 1943 it contained four sections. I would like to mention them briefly. It shows their scope of authority.

Section A dealt with questions of legal order and structure of the Reich.

Section B dealt with nationality, including minorities, race, and health of the people.

Section C dealt with culture, including science, education, religion, Press, folk culture, and art.

Section D dealt with economics, including food, commerce, finance, industry, labour, colonial economics, and occupied regions.

Now, Amt IV, with which we are dealing here, was the Gestapo, and was charged with combating opposition. In 1945, as identified by these two former officials, it contained six subsections.

1. Subsection A dealt with opponents, sabotage, and protective service, including Communism, Marxism, Reaction and Liberalism.

2. Subsection B dealt with political churches, sects and Jews, including political Catholicism, political Protestantism, other Churches, Freemasonry, and a special section, B-4, that had to do with Jewish affairs, matters of evacuation, means of suppressing enemies of the people and State, and dispossession of rights of German citizenship. The head of this office was Eichmann.

3. Subsection C dealt with protective custody.

4. Subsection D dealt with regions under German domination.

5. Subsection E dealt with security.

6. Subsection F dealt with passport matters and alien police.

Now, Amt V, which will be referred to as the Kripo was charged with combating crime. For example, Subsection D was the criminological institute for the: Sipo and handled matters of identification, chemical and biological investigations, and technical research.

Amt VI was the S.D. outside Germany and was concerned primarily with foreign political intelligence. In 1944, the "Abwehr," or Military Intelligence, was joined with Amt VI as military "Amt." Your Honour will recall that the witness Lahousen was in the "Abwehr." Amt VI maintained its own regional organisation.

And finally, Amt VII handled ideological research among enemies such as Freemasonry, Judaism, Political Churches, Marxism and Liberalism.

Within Germany there were regional offices of the S.D., the Gestapo, and the Kripo, shown on the chart at the right. The Gestapo and Kripo offices were often located in the same place and were always collectively referred to as the Sipo. You see that shaded line around the Secret Police, and kripo the Criminal Police. These regional offices all maintained their separate identity and reported directly to the section of the R.S.H.A., that is, under Kaltenbrunner, which had the jurisdiction of the subject matter. They were, however, co-ordinated by .Inspectors of the Security Police and S.D., as shown at the top of the chart. The Inspectors were also under the supervision of Higher S.S. and Police Leaders appointed for each "Wehrkreis." The Higher S.S. and Police Leaders reported to Himmler and supervised not only the Inspectors of the Security Police and S.D., but also the Inspectors of the Order Police and various sub-divisions of the S.S.

In the occupied territories, the organisation developed as the German armies advanced. Combined operational units of the Security Police and the S.D., known as Einsatz Groups, about which your Honour will hear in a few minutes, operated with and in the rear of the army. These groups were officered by personnel of the Gestapo, Kripo and the S.D., and the enlisted men were composed of Order Police and "Waffen S.S." They functioned with various Army groups.. The Einsatz Groups - and, if your Honour will recall, they are simply task force groups for special projects - were divided into "Einsatzkornmandos," "Sonderkonunandos," and "Teilkommandos," all of which performed the functions of the Security Police and the S.D., with or closely behind the Army.

After the occupied territories had been consolidated, these Einsatz Groups and their subordinate parts were formed into permanent combined offices of the Security Police and S.D. within the particular geographical location. These combined forces were placed under the Kornmandeurs of the Security Police and S.D., and the offices were organised in sections similar to this R.S.H.A. headquarters. The Konimandeurs of the Security Police and S.D. reported directly to Befehlshaber of the Security Police and S.D. who in turn reported directly to the Chief of the Security Police and S.D.

In the occupied countries, the Higher S.S. and Police Leaders were more directly controlled by the Befehlshabers and the Kornmandeurs of the Security Police and S.D. than within the Reich. They had authority to issue direct orders so long as they did not conflict with the Chief of the Security Police and S.D. who exercised controlling authority.

The above chart and the remarks concerning it are based upon two documents which I now offer in evidence. They are Document L-219, which is the organisation plan of the R.S.H.A. of 1st October, 1943, and document 2346-PS, which is Exhibit USA 480.

Now the primary mission of the Gestapo and the S.D. was to combat the actual and ideological enemies of the Nazi regime and to keep Hitler and the Nazi leadership in power as specified in Count 1 of the Indictment. The tasks and methods of the Secret State Police were well described in an article which is translated in Document 1956-PS, Volume 2 of the document book, which is an article published in January, 1936, in Das Archiv, at Page 1342, which I now offer in evidence and quote from. It is on Page 1 of the English translation, 1956. I will first read the first paragraph and then the third and fourth paragraphs. That is in January 1936:

"In order to refute the malicious rumours spread abroad, the Voelkischer Beobachter published on 22nd January, 1936, an article on the origin, meaning and tasks of the Secret Police; extracts from this read as follows:"

Now passing to the third paragraph:

"The Secret State Police is an official machine on the lines of the Criminal Police, whose special task is the prosecution of crimes and offences against the State, above all the prosecution of high treason and treason. The task of the Secret State Police is to detect these crimes and offences, to ascertain the perpetrators and to bring them to judicial punishment. The number of criminal proceedings continually pending in the People's Court on account of high treasonable actions and of treason is the result of this work. The next most important field of operations for the Secret State Police is the preventive combating of all dangers threatening the State and the leadership of the State. As, since the National Socialist Revolution, all open struggle and all open opposition to the State and to the leadership of the State is forbidden, a Secret State Police as a preventive instrument in the struggle against all dangers threatening the State is indissolubly bound up with the National Socialist Leader State. The opponents of National Socialism were not removed by the prohibition of their organisations and their newspapers, but have withdrawn to other forms of struggle against the State. Therefore, the National Socialist State has to trace out, to watch over and to render harmless the underground opponents fighting against it in illegal organisations, in camouflaged associations, in the coalitions of well-meaning fellow Germans and even in the organisations of Party and State before they have succeeded in actually executing an action directed against the interest of the State. This task of fighting with all means the secret enemies of the State will be spared no Leader State, because powers hostile to the State from their foreign headquarters, always make use of some persons in such a State and employ them in underground activity against the State.

The preventive activity of the Secret State Police consists primarily in the thorough observation of all enemies of the State in the Reich Territory. As the Secret State Police cannot carry out, in addition to its primary executive tasks, this observation of the enemies of the State, to the extent necessary, there marches by its side, to supplement it, the Security Service of the Reichsfuehrer of the S.S., set up by his deputy as the Political Intelligence Service of the movement, which puts a large part of the forces of the movement mobilised by it into the service of the security of the State.

The Secret State Police takes the necessary police preventive measures against the enemies of the State on the basis of the results of the observation. The most effective preventive measure is, without doubt, the withdrawal of freedom, which is covered in the form of protective custody, if it is to be feared that the free activity of the persons in question might endanger the security of the State in any way. The employment of protective custody is so organised by directions of the Reich and Prussian Minister of the Interior and by a special arrest procedure of the Secret State Police that, as far as the preventive fight against the enemies of the State permits, continuous guarantees against the mis-use of the protective custody are also provided."

THE PRESIDENT: Have we not really got enough now as to the organisation of the Gestapo and its Objective?

COLONEL STOREY: Your Honour, I had finished with the organisation. I was just going into the question of the action of protective custody, for which the Gestapo was famous, and showing how they went into that field of activity and the authority for taking people into protective custody - alleged protective custody.

THE PRESIDENT: I think that has been proved more than once in the preceding evidence that we have heard.

COLONEL STOREY: There is one more law I would like to refer to, to the effect that that action is not subject to judicial review, ... unless that has already been established. I do not know whether Major Farr did that, or not.

THE PRESIDENT: They are not subject to judicial review?

COLONEL STOREY: Review, yes.

THE PRESIDENT: I think you have told us that already this afternoon.

COLONEL STOREY: The citation is in the Reichsgesetzblatt of 1935 Page 577, which is Document 2347-PS.

I would like, if your Honour pleases, to refer to this quotation from that law.

The decision of the Prussian High Court of Administration on 2nd May, 1935, held that the status of the Gestapo as a special Police authority removed its orders from the jurisdiction of the administrative tribunal, and the Court said in that law that the only redress available was by appeal to the next higher authority within the Gestapo itself.

THE PRESIDENT: I think you told us that, apropos of the document of 10th February, 1936, where you said the Secret State Police was not subject to review by any of the State Courts.

COLONEL STOREY: I just did not want there to be any question about the authority. I refer your Honour to Document 1825-B-PS, which is already in evidence as Exhibit USA 449, also stating that theory, and also Document 1723-PS, and that is the decree, your Honour, of 1st February, 1938, which relates to the protective custody and the issuance of new regulations, and I would like to quote just one sentence from that law-" . . . as a coercive measure of the Secret State Police against persons.who endanger the security of the people and the State through their attitude, in order to counter all aspirations of the enemies of the people and the State". The Gestapo had the exclusive right to order protective custody and that protective custody was to be executed in the State concentration camps.

Now, I pass to another phase where the S.D. created an organisation of agents and informers who operated through the various regional offices throughout the Reich and later in conjunction with the Gestapo and the Criminal Police throughout the occupied countries. The S.D. operated secretly. One of the things it did was to mark ballots secretly in order to discover the identity of persons who cast "No " and "invalid " votes in the referendum. I now offer in evidence Document R-142, second volume. I believe it is toward the end of Document R-142, Exhibit USA 481.

This document contains a letter from the branch office of the S.D. at Kochem to the S.D. at Koblenz. The letter is dated 7th May, 1938, and refers to the plebiscite of 10th April, 1938. It refers to a letter previously received from the Koblenz office and apparently is a reply to a request for information concerning the way in which people voted in the supposedly secret plebiscite. It is on Page 1 of Document R-142.

THE PRESIDENT: Colonel Storey, I am told that that has been read before.

COLONEL STOREY: I did not know it had, if your Honour pleases. We will then just offer it without reading it.

With reference to National Socialism and the contribution of the Sipo and the S.D., I refer to an article of 7th September, 1942, which is shown in Document 3344-PS. It is the first paragraph, Volume 2. It is the official journal. Quoting:

> "Even before the taking over of power, the S.D. had added its part to the success of the National Socialist Revolution. After the taking over of power, the Security Police and the S.D. have borne the responsibility for the inner security of the Reich, and have paved the way for a powerful fulfilment of National Socialism against all resistance."

In connection with the criminal responsibility of the S.D. and the Gestapo, it will be considered with respect to certain War Crimes and Crimes Against Humanity, which were in the principal part committed by the centralised political police system. The development, organisation and tasks have been considered before. In some instances the crimes were committed in co-operation or in conjunction with other groups or organisations.

Now, in order to look into the strength of these various organisations, I have some figures here that I would like to quote to your Honour. The Sipo and S.D. were composed of the Gestapo, Kripo and S.D. The Gestapo was the largest, and it had a membership of about 40,000 to 50,000 in 1934 and 1935. That is an error; it is 1943 to 1945. It was the political force of the Reich.

THE PRESIDENT: Did you say the date was wrong?

COLONEL STOREY: Yes, it is '43 to '45.

THE PRESIDENT: Very well.

THE TRIBUNAL: (MR. BIDDLE): Where are you reading from?

COLONEL STOREY: Document 3033-PS, and it is an affidavit of Walter Schellenberg, one of the former officials I referred to a moment ago.

I think, if your Honour pleases, in order to get it in the record, I will read the whole affidavit. Document 3033-PS, Exhibit USA 488:

> "The Sipo and S.D. were composed of the Gestapo, Kripo and S.D. In 1943-45 the Gestapo had a membership of about 40,000 to 50,000 ; the Kripo had a membership of about 15,000 and the S.D. had a membership of about 3,000. In common usage, and even in orders and decrees, the term 'S.D.' was used as an abbreviation for the term 'Sipo' and 'S.D.' In most cases actual executive action was carried out by personnel of the Gestapo rather than of the S.D. or the Kripo. In occupied territories, members of the Gestapo frequently wore S.S. uniforms with S.D. insignia. New members of the Gestapo and the S.D. were taken on a voluntary basis. This has been stated and sworn to by me today the 21st November, 1945." And then, " Subscribed and sworn to before Lt. Harris, 21st November, 1945."

I think I ought to say here, if your Honour pleases, that it is our information that a great many of the members of the Gestapo were also members of the S.S. We have heard various estimates of the numbers, but have no direct authority. oome autnorities say as much as 75 per cent., but still we have no direct evidence on that.

I now offer in evidence Document 2751-PS, which is Exhibit USA 482. It is an affidavit of Alfred Helmut Naujocks, dated 20th November, 1945. This affidavit particularly refers to the actual occurrences in connection with the Polish Border incident. I believe it was referred to by the witness Lahousen when he was on the stand.

"I, Alfred Helmut Naujocks, being first duly sworn, depose and state as follows:

1. I was a member of the S.S. from 1931 to igth October, 1944, and a member of the S.D. from its creation in 1934 to January, 1941. I served as a member of the 'Waffen S.S.' from February, 1941, until the middle of 1942. Thereafter, I served in the Economic Department of the Military Administration of Belgium from September, 1942 to September, 1944. 1 surrendered to the Allies on igth October, 1944,

2. On or about 10th August, 1939, the Chief of the Sipo and S.D. Heydrich, personally ordered me to simulate an attack on the radio station near Gleiwitz, near the Polish border, and to make it appear that the attacking force consisted of Poles. Heydrich said, ' Practical proof is needed for these attacks of the Poles for the foreign Press, as well as for German propaganda purposes.' I was directed to go to Gleiwitz with five or six other S.D. men and wait there until I received a code word from Heydrich indicating that the attack should take place. My instructions were to seize the radio station and to hold it long enough to permit a Polish-speaking German, who would be put at my disposal, to broadcast a speech in Polish. Heydrich told me that this speech should state that the time had come for the conflict between Germans and Poles, and that the Poles should get together and smash down any Germans from whom they met resistance. Heydrich also told me at this time that he expected an attack on Poland by Germany in a few days.

3. I went to Gleiwitz and waited there 14 days. Then I requested permission from Heydrich to return to Berlin, but was told to stay in Gleiwitz. Between 25th and 31st August, I went to see Heinrich Mueller, head of the Gestapo, who was then nearby at Oppeln. In my presence Mueller discussed with a man named Mohlhorn plans for another border incident, in which it should be made to appear that Polish soldiers were attacking German troops. Germans in the approximate strength of a company were to be used. Mueller stated that he had 12 or 13 condemned criminals who were to be dressed in Polish uniforms and left dead on the ground of the scene of the incident, to show that they had been killed while attacking. For this purpose they were to be given fatal injections by a doctor employed by Heydrich. Then they were also to be given gunshot wounds. After the incident, members of the Press and other persons were to be taken to the scene of the incident. A police report was subsequently to be prepared.

4. Mueller told me that he had an order from Heydrich to make one of those criminals available to me for the action at Gleiwitz. The code name by which he referred to these criminals was 'Canned goods '.

5. The incident at Gleiwitz in which I participated was carried out on the evening preceeding the German attack on Poland. As I recall, war broke out on 1st September, 1939. At noon on 31st August, I received by telephone from Heydrich the code word for the attack which was to take place at 8 o'clock that evening. Heydrich said, 'In order to carry out this attack, report to Mueller for Canned Goods.' I did this and gave Mueller instructions to deliver the man near the radio station. I received this man and had him laid down at the entrance to the station. He was alive but he was completely unconscious. I tried to open his eyes. I could not recognise by his eyes that he was alive, only by his breathing. I did not see the shot wounds but a lot of blood was smeared

across his face. He was in civilian clothes.

6. We seized the radio station as ordered, broadcast a speech of three to four minutes over an emergency transmitter, fired some pistol shots and left."

And that was sworn to and subscribed before Lt. Martin.

The Gestapo and the S.D. carried out mass murders of hundreds of thousands of civilians of occupied countries as a part of the Nazi programme to exterminate political and racial undesirables, by the so-called Einsatz Groups. Your Honour will recall evidence concerning the activity of these Einsatz Groups ' or Einsatzkommandos. I now refer to Document R-102.

If your Honour pleases, I understand Major Farr introduced this document this morning, but I want to refer to just one brief statement which he did not include, concerning the S.D. and the Einsatz Groups and Security Police. It is on Page 4 of R-102.: Quoting:

"During the period covered by this report the stations of the Einsatz Groups of the Security Police and the S.D. have changed only in the Northern Sector."

THE PRESIDENT: What was the document?

COLONEL STOREY: R-102, which is already introduced in evidence by Major Farr, and it is in Volume 2 toward the end of the book.

THE PRESIDENT: I have a document here. Page 4, is it?

COLONEL STOREY: Page 4, Yes, Sir. There are two reports submitted by the Chief of the Einsatz Group A available. The first report is Document L-180, which has already been received as Exhibit USA 276.

THE PRESIDENT: Colonel Storey, will you not pass quite so fast from one document to another?

COLONEL STOREY: Yes, Sir, pardon me, Sir. L-180, and I want to quote from Page 13. It is on Page 5 of the English translation. It is the beginning of the first paragraph, near the bottom of the page. Quoting:

"In view of the extension of the area of operations and of the great number of duties which had to be performed by the Security Police, it was intended from the very beginning to obtain the co-operation of the reliable population for the fight against vermin ; that is, mainly the Jews and Communists."

And also in that same document, Page 30 of the original, Page 8 of the English translation. Quoting:

"From the beginning it was to be expected that the Jewish problem could not be solved by pogroms alone."

THE PRESIDENT: I am told that that has been read already.

COLONEL STOREY: I had it checked, and we did not find that it had, your Honour. I will pass on them.

Now, if your Honour pleases, we will pass to Document 2273-PS next. I offer in evidence now just portions of Document 2273-PS, which is Exhibit USA 487. This document was captured by the U.S.S.R. and will be offered in detail by our Soviet colleagues later. But with their consent, I want to introduce in evidence a chart which is identified by that document, and we have an enlargement which we would like to put on the board, and we will pass to the Tribunal photostatic copies.

If your Honour pleases, this chart is identified by the photostatic copy attached to the original report which will be dealt with in detail later. I want to quote just one statement from Page 2 of the English translation of that document. It is the third paragraph from the bottom on Page 2 of the English translation:

"The Estonian self-protection movement formed as the Germans advanced and began to arrest Jews, but there were no spontaneous pogroms. Only by the Security Police and the S.D. were the Jews gradually executed as they became no longer required for work. Today there are no longer any Jews in Estonia."

That document is a top secret document by Einsatz Group A, which was a special projects group. This chart, of which the photostatic copy is attached to the original in the German translation on the wall, shows the progress of the extermination of the Jews in the area in which this Einsatz Kormnando Group operated.

If your Honour will refer to the top, next to St. Petersburg, or Leningrad as we know it, you will see down below the picture of a coffin, and that is described in the report as 3,600 having been killed.

Next over, at the left, is another coffin in one of the small Baltic States, showing that 963 in that area have been put in the coffin.

Then next, down near Riga, you will note that 35,238 were put away in the coffins, and it refers to the ghetto there as still having 2,500.

You come down to the next square or the next State showing 136,421 were put in their coffins, and then in the next area near Minsk, and just above it there were 41,828 put in their coffins.

THE PRESIDENT: Are you sure that they were executed, the 136,000, because there is no coffin there.

COLONEL STOREY: Here are the totals from the documents.

THE PRESIDENT: These photostatic copies are different from what you have there. In the area which is marked 136,421 there is no coffin.

COLONEL STOREY: Well, I am sorry. The one that I have is a true and correct copy.

THE PRESIDENT: Mine has not got it and Mr. Biddle's has not got it.

COLONEL STOREY: Will you hand this to the President, please ?

THE PRESIDENT: I suppose the document itself will show it.

COLONEL STOREY: I will turn to the original and verify it. Apparently there is a typographical error. If your Honour pleases, here it is, 136,421, with the coffin.

THE PRESIDENT: Mr. Parker points out it is in the document itself too.

COLONEL STOREY: Yes, sir, it is in the document itself. There is an error on that.

The 128,000 at the bottom shows that at that time there were 128,000 on hand; and the literal translation of the statement, as I understand, means "Still on hand in the Minsk area."

I next refer to Document 1104-PS, Volume 2, Exhibit USA 483, which I now offer in evidence.

THE PRESIDENT: Colonel Storey, did you tell us what the document was ? There is nothing on the translation to show what the document is.

COLONEL STOREY: If your Honour pleases, it is a report of the special purpose Group A, or the Einsatz Group A, a top secret report, in other words, making a record of their activities in these areas, and this chart was attached showing the areas covered.

THE PRESIDENT: Special group of the Gestapo?

COLONEL STOREY: The special group that was organised of the Gestapo and the S.D. in that area. In other words, a Commando Group.

As I mentioned, your Honour, they organised these special commando groups to work with and behind the armies as they consolidated their gains in occupied territories, and your Honour will hear from other reports of these "Einsatz " groups as we go along in this presentation. In other words, "Einsatz " means special action or action groups, and they were organised to cover certain geographical areas behind the immediate front lines.

THE PRESIDENT: Yes, but they were groups, were they, of the Gestapo ?

COLONEL STOREY: The Gestapo and the S.D.

THE PRESIDENT: Well, that is part of the Gestapo.

COLONEL STOREY: There were some of the Kripo in it, too.

Now, the next document is 1104-PS, dated 30th October, 1941. This document shows on that date the Commissioner of the territory of Sluzk wrote a report to the Commissioner of Minsk, in which he severely criticised the actions of the Einsatz Commandos of the Sipo and the S.D. operating in his area for the murder of the Jewish population of that area, and I quote the English translation, on Page 4 of that document beginning at the first paragraph:

"On 27th October in the morning, at about 8 o'clock a first lieutenant of the Police Battalion No. 11, from Kauen (Lithuania) appeared and introduced himself as the adjutant of the Battalion Commander of the Security Police. The first lieutenant explained that the Police Battalion had received the assignment to effect the liquidation of all Jews here in the town of Sluzk within two days. The Battalion Commander, with his battalion in strength of four companies, two of which were made up of Lithuanian partisans, was on the march here and the action would have to begin instantly. I replied to the first lieutenant that 1 had to discuss the action in any case first with the Commander. About half an hour later the Police Battalion arrived in Sluzk. Immediately after the arrival, a conference with the Battalion Commander took place according to my request. I first explained to the Commander that it would not very well be possible to effect the action without previous preparation, because everybody had been sent to work and it would lead to a terrible confusion. At least it would have been his duty to inform me a day ahead of time. Then I requested him to postpone the action one day. However, he rejected this with the remark that he had to carry out this action everywhere and in all two days, the town of Sluzk had to be cleared of Jews by all means."

That report was made to the Reich Commissioner for the Eastern Territories through Gauleiter Heinrich Lusch at Riga. Your Honour will recall that he was referred to in another presentation.

Now, skipping over to Page 5. The first paragraph, I would like to quote it:

"For the rest, as regards the execution of the action, I must point out to my deepest regret that the matter bordered on sadism. The town itself offered a picture of horror during the action. With indescribable brutality on the part of both the German Police officers, and particularly the Lithuanian partisans, not only the Jewish people, but also White Ruthenians, were taken out of their dwellings and herded together. Everywhere in the town shots were to be heard, and in different streets the corpses of shot Jews accumulated. The White Ruthenians were in the greatest distress to free themselves from the encirclement. Regardless of the fact that the Jewish people, among whom were also tradesmen were mistreated in a terribly barbarous way, in front of the White Ruthenian people, the White Ruthenians themselves were also worked over with rubber clubs and rifle butts. There was no question of an action against the Jews any more. It rather looked like a revolution."

And then I skip down to the next to the last paragraph on that same page; quoting:

"In conclusion, I find myself obliged to point out that the Police Battalion has looted in an unheard of manner during the action, and that not only in Jewish houses but just the same in those of the White Ruthenians, anything of use such as boots, leather, cloth, gold and other valuables, has been taken away. On the basis of statements of members of the Armed Forces, watches were torn off the arms of Jews in public, on the street, and rings were pulled off the fingers in the most brutal manner. A major of the Finance Department reported that a Jewish girl was asked by the police to obtain immediately 5,000 roubles to have her father released. This girl is said to have actually gone everywhere in order to obtain the money."

There is another paragraph with reference to the number of copies - on the third page of the translation - to which I would like to call your Honour's attention. The last paragraph on Page 3 of the translation, quoting:

"I am submitting this report in duplicate so that one copy may be forwarded to the Reich Minister. Peace and order cannot be maintained in White Ruthenia with methods of that sort. To bury seriously wounded people alive who worked their way out of their graves again, is such a base and filthy act that the incident as such, should be reported to the Fuehrer and Reich Marshal.

The civil administration of White Ruthenia makes very strenuous efforts to win the population over to Germany, in accordance with the instructions of the Fuehrer. These efforts cannot be brought in harmony with the methods described herein."

Signed by the Commissioner General for White Ruthenia.

And then on 11th November, 1941, he forwarded it on to the Reich Minister for Occupied Countries, in Berlin.

THE PRESIDENT: Who was that at that time?

COLONEL STOREY: The Reich Commissionere (I believe it was shown for the Easter occupied country) was the defendent Rosenberg. I think that is correct. On the same date by separate letter the Commissioner General of White Ruthenia reported to the Reich Commissioner for the Eastern Territories that he had received money, valuables, and other objects taken by the police in the action at Sluzk, and other regions, all of which had been deposited with the Reich Credit Institute, for the disposal of the Reich Commissioner.

On 21st November, 1941, a report on the Sluzk incident was sent to the personal reviewer of the permanent deputy of the Minister of the Reich with a copy to Heydrich, who was the Chief of the Security Police and the S.D. That is shown on the first page of Document 1104.

The activities of the Einsatz Groups continued throughout 1943 and 1944 under Kaltenbrunner as Chief of the Security Police and S.D. Under adverse war conditions, however, the programme of extermination was to a large extent changed to one of rounding up slave labour for Germany.

I next refer to Document 3012-PS, which has heretofore been introduced as Exhibit USA igo. This is a letter from the headquarters of one of the Commando Groups, a section known as Einsatz Group C, dated 19th March, 1943. This letter summarises the real activities and methods of the Gestapo and S.D., and I should like to refer to additional portions of the letter, to those previously quoted on Page 2, of Document 3012- PS, and I think I will read the first page beginning with the first paragraph:

"It is the task of the Security Police and of the Security Service (S.D.) to discover all enemies of the Reich, and to fight them in the interest of security and, in the zone of operations, especially to guarantee the security of the Army. Besides the annihilation of active opponents all other elements who by virtue of their convictions or their past may prove to be active enemies, favourable circumstances provided, are to be eliminated through preventive measures. The Security Police carries out this task according to the general directives of the Fuehrer, with all of the required toughness. Energetic measures are especially necessary in territories endangered by the activity of hostile gangs.

The competence of the Security Police within the zone of operations is based on the 'Barbarossa' decrees."

The Tribunal will recall the famous "Barbarossa" code, namely, the decrees that were issued in connection with the invasion of Russia:

"I deem the measures of the Security Police carried out on a considerable scale during recent times necessary for the two following reasons:

1. The situation at the front in my sector had become so serious, with the population partly influenced by Hungarians and Italians who streamed back in chaotic condition and took, openly, positions against us.

2. The strong expeditions by hostile gangs who came especially from the Forest of Bryansk were another reason. Besides that, other partisan groups formed by the population appeared suddenly in all districts. The providing of arms was evidently no difficulty at all. It would have been irresponsible if we had observed this whole activity without acting against it. It is obvious that all such measures necessitate some harshness."

I want to take up the significant point of the harsh measures.

1. Shooting of Hungarian Jews
2. Shooting of Agronoms.
3. Shooting of children.
4. Total burning down of villages.
5. "Shooting" - I quote -"while trying to escape", of Security Service (S.D.) prisoners.

"Chief of Einsatz group C confirmed once more the correctness of the measures taken, and expressed his recognition of the energetic action. With regard to the current political situation, especially in the armament industry in the Fatherland, the measures of the Security Police have to be subordinated to the greatest extent to the recruiting of labour for Germany. In the shortest possible time the Ukraine has to put at the disposal of the armament industry 1,000,000 workers, Some of whom have to be sent from the territory daily."

Your Honour, please, I believe the numbers have been quoted before by Mr. Dodd. I refer on the next page, to the first order in sub-paragraphs 1 and 2:

"1. Special treatment is to be limited to the minimum.

2. Communist functionaries, agitators, and so on, will only be listed for the time being, without being arrested. It is, for instance, no longer feasible to arrest all the close relatives of a member of the Communist Party. Also members of the Konisomolz are to be arrested only if they occupied leading positions."

The next paragraphs have been read into evidence, 3 and 4, in a previous presentation. I will read:

"No. 5. The reporting of hostile gangs, as well as drives against them, is not affected hereby. All drives against those hostile gangs can take place only after my approval has been obtained. The prisons have to be kept empty as a rule, and we have to be aware of the fact that the Slavs will interpret the soft treatment on our part as weakness, and that they will act accordingly right away. If we limit our harsh measures of the Security Police through the above orders for the time being, that is only done for the reason that the most important thing is the recruiting of workers. No check of persons to be sent into the Reich will be made. No written certificates of political reliability check, or similar things, will be issued. Signed by Christensen, S.S. Sturmbannfuehrer and commanding officer."

I understood that your Honour wanted to adjourn at four o'clock, and I believe that I can introduce one more statement. It was the Einsatz Groups of the Security Police and S.D. that operated the infamous death vans. Document 501-PS, which was received as Exhibit USA 288, has previously referred to this operation. The letter from Becker, which is a part of this exhibit, was addressed to Obersturmbannfuehrer Rauff at Berlin. We now refer to Document L-185. I simply refer to Document 501-PS as a reference to the death vans. The Document L-185, Exhibit USA 484, is the one I am now offering in evidence, Page 7 of the English translation, L- 185. It will be observed that the Chief of Amt. II D of the R.S.H.A. in charge of technical matters was Obersturmbahnfuehrer Rauff. Mr. Harris advises me that the only point to be proved by that is that Amt. II of the R.S.H.A., who made this report on technical matters, was the Obersturmbahnfuehrer Rauff, and then he refers in the same connection to Document 2348-PS, which is Exhibit USA 485. The previous one was to identify Rauff, and then to offer his affidavit, which is Document 2348-PS, second volume. Reading from the beginning of the affidavit, which was made on 19th October, 1945, in Ancona, Italy,

"I hereby acknowledge the attached letter written by Dr. Becker on 16th May, 1942, and received by me on 29th May, 1942, as a genuine letter. I did, on 18th October, 1945, write on the side of this letter a statement to the effect that it was genuine. I do not know the number of death vans being operated, and cannot give an approximate figure. The vans were built by the Saurer Works, Germany, located, I believe, in Berlin. Some other firms built these vans also. In so far as I am aware these vans operated only in Russia. In so far as I can state these vans were probably operating in 1941, and I personally believe that they were operating up to the termination of the war."

If your Honour pleases, I do not think that we will have time to go into the next exhibit.

THE PRESIDENT: Very well. Then the Tribunal will now adjourn until Wednesday, 2nd January.

(The Tribunal adjourned to 2nd January, 1946, at 1000 hours.)

Twenty-Fifth Day: Wednesday, 2nd January, 1946

THE PRESIDENT: I call on the Counsel for the United States.

COLONEL STOREY: If the Tribunal please, when your Honours adjourned on 20th December we were presenting the Gestapo, and had referred to the use of the death vans by the Einsatz Groups in the Eastern Occupied Territories and had almost concluded that phase of the presentation. Your Honours will recall that we had referred to the use of some death vans made by the Saurer Works, and the final reference that I want to make in that connection is to a telegram attached to Document 501-PS, which it is not necessary to read, establishing the fact that the same make of truck or vans was the death van used by the Einsatz Groups.

The final document in connection with the Einsatz Groups in the Eastern Occupied Territories which we desire to offer is Document 2992-PS, and I believe it is in the second volume of the Document Book. This is an affidavit made by Hermann Graebe. Hermann Gratbe is at present employed by the United States Government in Frankfurt. The affidavit was made at Wiesbaden, and I offer excerpts from Document 2992-PS, Exhibit USA 494.

This witness was at the head of a construction firm that was doing some building in the Ukraine and he was an eye-witness of the anti-Jewish actions at the town of Rowno, Ukraine, on 13th July, 1942, and I refer to the part of the affidavit which is on Page 5 of the English translation. Beginning at the first paragraph :

"From September, 1941, until January, 1944, I was manager and engineer-in-charge of a branch office in Sdolbunow, Ukraine, of the Solingen building firm of Josef Jung. In this capacity it was my job to visit the building sites of the firm. The firm had, among others, a site in Rowno, Ukraine.

During the night of 13th July, 1942, all inhabitants of the Rowno Ghetto, where there were still about 5,000 Jews, were liquidated.

I should describe the circumstances of my being a witness of the dissolution of the Ghetto and the carrying out of the pogrom during the night and morning, as follows :

I employed for the firm, in Rowno, in addition to Poles, Germans and Ukrainians, about 100 Jews from Sdolbunow, Ostrog and Mysotch. The men were quartered in a building, 5 Bahnhofstrasse, inside the Ghetto, and the women in a house at the corner of Deutsche Strasse, 98.

On Saturday, mth July, 1942, my foreman, Fritz Einsporn, told me of a rumour that on Monday all Jews in Rowno were to be liquidated. Although the vast majority of the Jews employed by my firm in Rowno were not natives of this town, I still feared that they might be included in this pogrom which had been reported. I therefore ordered Einsporn at noon of the same day to march all the Jews employed by us - men as well as women - in the direction of Sdolbunow, about 12 km. from Rowno. This was done.

The senior Jew had learned of the departure of the Jewish workers of my firm. He went to see the Commanding Officer of the Rowne, Sipo and S.D., S.S. Major (S.S. Sturmbannfuehrer) Dr. Putz. as early as Saturday afternoon to find out whether the rumour of a forthcoming Jewish pogrom - which had gained further credence by reason of the departure of Jews of my firm - was true. Dr. Putz dismissed the rumour as a clumsy lie and, for the rest, had the Polish personnel of my firm in Rowno arrested. Einsporn avoided arrest by escaping to Sdolbunow. When I learned of this incident I gave orders that all Jews who had left Rowno were to report back to work in Rowno on Monday, 13th July, 1942. On Monday morning I myself went to see the Commanding Officer, Dr. Putz, in order to learn, for one thing, the truth about the rumoured Jewish pogrom and, for another, to obtain information on the arrest of the Polish office personnel. S.S. Major Putz stated to me that no pogrom whatever was planned. Moreover, such a pogrom would be stupid because the firms and the Reichsbahn would lose valuable workers.

An hour later I received a summons to appear before the Area Commissioner of Rowno. His deputy Stabsleiter and Cadet Officer Beck, subjected me to the same questions as I had undergone at the S.D. My explanation that I had sent the Jews home for urgent delousing appeared plausible to him. He then told me - making me promise to keep it a secret - that a pogrom would, in fact, take place in the evening of Monday, 13th July, 1945. After lengthy negotiation I managed to persuade him to give me permission to take my Jewish workers to Sdolbunow - but only after the pogrom had been carried out. During the night it would be up to me to protect the house in the Ghetto against the entry of Ukrainian Militia and S.S. As confirmation of the discussion he gave me a document, which stated that the Jewish employees of Messrs. Jung were not affected by the pogrom."

And this original which I hold in my hand, I will now pass to the translator for reading. I call the attention of your Honour to the fact that it has the letterhead of "Der Gebietskommissar in Rowno," and it is dated 13th July, 1942, and is signed by this area commissioner. I now read this document :

"The Area Commissioner" - which means Gebietskommissar - Rownno.

"Secret.

Addressed : Messrs. Jung, Rowno.

The Jewish workers employed by your firm are not affected by the pogrom " - in parenthesis "Aktion."

As I understand, that means action.

"You must transfer them to their new place of work by Wednesday, 15th July, 1942, at the latest."

Signed by the Area Commissioner Beck. And then the stamp - the official stamp of the area commissioner at Rowno.

Now, just the following paragraph on the original, Page 5 or 6, I believe it is, one more paragraph I would like to read after the reference "Original attached ":

"On the evening of this day I drove to Rowno and posted myself with Fritz Einsporn in front of the house in the Bahnhoffstrasse in which the Jewish workers of my firm slept. Shortly after 22.00 hours the Ghetto was encircled by a large S.S. detachment and about three times as many members of the Ukrainian Militia. Then the electric arclights which had been erected in and around the Ghetto were switched on. S.S. and Militia squads of 4 to 6 men entered or at least tried to enter the house. Where the doors and windows were closed and the inhabitants did not open at the knocking, the S.S. men and Militia broke the windows, forced the doors with beams and crowbars and entered the houses. The people living there were driven into the street just as they were, regardless of whether they were dressed or in bed. Since the Jews in most cases refused to leave their houses and resisted, the S.S. and Militia applied force. They finally succeeded, with strokes of the whip, kicks and blows with rifle butts in clearing the houses. The people were driven out of their houses in such haste that in several instances, small children in bed had been left behind. In the streets women cried out for their children and children for their parents. That did not prevent the S.S. from driving the people along the road, at running pace, and hitting them, until they reached a waiting freight train. Car after car was filled, and the screaming of women and children, and the cracking of whips and rifle shots resounded unceasingly.

Since several families or groups had barricaded themselves in especially strong buildings and the doors could not be forced with crowbars or beams, these houses were now blown open with hand grenades. Since the Ghetto was near the railroad tracks in Rowno, the younger people tried to get across the tracks and over a small river, to get away from the Ghetto area. As this stretch of country was beyond the range of the electric lights, it was illuminated by signal rockets. All through the night these beaten, hounded and wounded people moved along the lighted streets. Women carried their dead children in their arms, children pulled and dragged their dead parents by their arms and legs down the road toward the train. Again and again the cries 'Open the door!' ' Open the door!' echoed through the Ghetto."

1 will not read any more of this affidavit. It is a very long one. There is also a second affidavit, but the part I wanted to emphasise is the fact that the original exemption was signed by the Area Commissioner, and that the S.D. and the S.S. participated in this action.

THE PRESIDENT: Ought you not to read the rest of that page, Colonel Storey?

COLONEL STOREY: All right, sir. I really had eliminated that because I thought it might be cumulative.

"About 6 o'clock in the morning I went away for a moment, leaving behind Einsporn and several other German workers who had returned in the meantime. I thought the greatest danger was past and that I could risk it. Shortly after I left, Ukrainian Militia men forced their way into 5 Bahnhoffstrasse and brought seven Jews out and took them to a collecting point inside the Ghetto. On my return I was able to prevent further Jews from being taken out. I went to the collecting point to save these seven men. I saw dozens of corpses of all ages and both sexes in the streets I had to walk along. The doors of the houses stood open, windows were smashed. Pieces of clothing, shoes, stockings, jackets, caps, hats, coats, etc., were lying in the street. At the corner of a house lay a baby, less than a year old, with his skull crushed. Blood and brains were spattered over the house wall and covered the area immediately around the child. The child was dressed only in a little shirt. The commander, S.S. Major Putz, was walking up and down a row of about 80 - 100 male Jews who were crouching on the ground. He had a heavy dog whip in his hand. I walked up to him, showed him the written permit of Stabsleiter Beck, and demanded the seven men whom I recognised among those who were crouching on the ground. Dr. Putz was furious about Beck's concession and nothing could persuade him to release the seven men. He made a motion with his hand encircling the square and said that anyone who was once here would not get away. Although he was very angry with Beck, he ordered me to take the people from 5 Bahnhofstrasse out of Rowno by 8 o'clock at the latest. When I left Dr. Putz, I noticed a Ukrainian farm cart with two horses. Dead people with stiff limbs were lying on the cart. Legs and arms projected over the side boards. The cart was making for the freight train. I took the remaining 74 Jews who had been locked in the house to Sdolbunow.

Several days after 13th July, 1942, the Area Commissioner of Sdolbunow, Georg Marschall, called a meeting of all firm managers, railroad superintendents, and leaders of the Organisation Todt and informed them that the firms etc. should prepare themselves for the 'resettlement' of the Jews which was to take place almost immediately. He referred to the pogrom in Rowno where all the Jews had been liquidated, i.e., had been shot near Kostolpol."

Finally, his signature is sworn to on 10th November, 1945.

THE PRESIDENT: What nationality is Graebe ?

COLONEL STOREY: He is German. Graebe is a German, and is now in the employ of the Military Government at Frankfurt - the United States Military Government.

Your Honour, in that connection there is another separate affidavit, which I will not attempt to read, attached to this, a part of the same document. But it has to do with the execution of some people in another area and is along the same line. I am not reading it because it would be cumulative, but it is a part of this same document.

I now pass from that subject to the next one.

The Gestapo and S.D. stationed special units in prisoner-of-war camps for the purpose of screening racial and political undesirables and executing those who were screened. The programme of mass murder of political and racial undesirables carried on against civilians was also applied against prisoners of war who were captured on the Eastern Front. In this connection I call the attention of the Tribunal to the testimony of General Lahousen, which your Honours will recall, of the 30th November, 1945. Lahousen testified to a conference which took place in the summer of 1941, shortly after the beginning of the campaign against the Soviet Union, which he attended ; and I want to emphasise this, because we will later have a document that emanated from this conference, attended by Lahousen himself, General Reinecke, Colonel Breuer, and Mueller, the Head of the Gestapo. At this conference the command to kill Soviet functionaries and Communists among the Soviet prisoners-of-war was discussed. The executions were to be carried out by Einsatz Commandos of the Sipo and the S.D.

Lahousen further recalled that Mueller, who was the head of the Gestapo, insisted on carrying out the programme, and that the only concession he made was that, in deference to the sensibilities of the German troops, the executions would not take place in their presence. Mueller also made some concessions as to the selection of the persons to be murdered ; but, according to Lahousen, the selection was left entirely to the commanders of these screening units. I refer to Page 281 of the transcript.

Now I offer Document 502-PS as the next exhibit, Exhibit USA 486. This document is a Gestapo directive of 17th July, 1941.

If you will recall, Lahousen said this conference was in the summer of 1941.

It is addressed to commanders of the Sipo and S.D. stationed in camps and provides in part as follows, and I read from the first page of the English translation.

Now, if the Tribunal please, our colleagues, the Soviet prosecutors, will present most of that document, and I am only going to read enough to show that the Gestapo were the ones that took part in it. From the beginning :

"The action of commandos will take place in accordance with the agreement of the Chief of the Security Police and Security Service and the Supreme

Command of the Armed Forces as of 16th July, 1941. Enclosure I.

The commandos will work independently according to special authorisation and according to the general directive given to them in the limits of the camp regulations. Naturally the commandos will keep close contact with the camp commander and the intelligence officer assigned to him.

This mission of the commandos is the political investigation of all camp inmates, the elimination and further treatment:

(a) of all political, criminal, or in some other way undesirable elements among them;

(b) of those persons who could be used for the reconstruction of the occupied countries."

Now I pass to the beginning of the fourth paragraph:

"The commandos must use for their work as far as possible now, and even later, the experiences of. the camp commanders, which the latter have gathered from observation of the prisoners and examination of the camp inmates. Further, the commandos must make efforts from the beginning to seek out among the prisoners elements which would appear reliable, regardless whether there are communists concerned or not, in order to use them for intelligence purposes inside the camp, and, if advisable, later in the occupied territories also.

By using such informers, and by use of all other existing possibilities, the discovery of all elements to be eliminated among the prisoners must follow step by step. The commandos must learn for themselves in every case by means of short questioning of the informer and possible questioning of other prisoners. The information of one informer is not sufficient to designate a camp inmate to be a suspect without further proof. It must be confirmed in some way, if possible."

Now I pass to Page 4, the 3rd paragraph of the English translation, quoting:

"Executions are not to be held in the camp or in the immediate vicinity of the camp. If the camps in the Government General are in the immediate vicinity of the border, then the prisoners are to be taken for special treatment, if possible, into the former Soviet territory."

And then the 5th paragraph:

"In regard to executions to be carried out and to the possible removal of reliable civilians and the removal of informers for the Einsatzgruppe in the occupied territories, the leader of the Einsatzkommandos must make an agreement with the nearest State Police Office, as well as with the commandant of the Security Police unit and Security Service, and beyond these, with the Chief of the Einsatzgruppe concerned in the occupied territories."

Proof that persons so screened out of the prisoner of war camps by the Gestapo were executed is to be found in Document 1165-PS, from which I do not intend to quote, and which has been previously introduced as Exhibit USA 244. Document 1165-PS shows that those that had been screened out were executed.

The first page of that document, is a letter from the Camp Commandant of the concentration camp Gross-Rosen to Mueller, who was the Chief of the Gestapo, dated the 23rd of October, 1941, referring to a previous oral conference with Mueller and setting forth the names of 20 Soviet prisoners of war executed the previous day.

The second page - I am still referring to Document 1165 but not reading from it, because it has already been quoted from - is a directive issued by Mueller on the 9th of November, 1941, to all Gestapo offices, in which he ordered that all diseased prisoners of war should be excluded from transports to concentration camps for execution, because 5 to 10 per cent. of those destined for execution were arriving in the camps dead or half dead.

I now offer Document 3542-PS, Exhibit USA 489, which is in the second volume. This is an affidavit of Kurt Lindow, a former Gestapo official, which was taken on the 30th of September, 1945, at Oberursel, Germany, in the course of an official military investigation by the United States Army, and I quote from that document from the begininng:

"I was Kriminaldirektor in Section IV of the R.S.H.A." -

I call your Honour's attention to the chart on the board that he was Director of Section IV and head of the Sub-section IV A I -

"From the middle of 1942 until the middle of 1944. I had the rank of S.S.-Sturmbannfuehrer.

From 1941 until the middle of 1943, there was attached to Subsection IV A i (which is not shown on this chart, but was described in the beginning) a special department that was headed by the Regierungsoberinspektor, later Regierungsamtmann, and S.S.-Hauptsturmbannfuehrer Franz Koenigshaus. In this department were handled matters concerning prisoners of war. I learned from this department that instructions and orders by Reichsfuehrer Himmler, dating from 1941 to 1942, existed, according to which captured Soviet political Commissars and Jewish soldiers were to be executed. As far as I know, proposals for execution of such P.W's. were received from the various P.W. camps. Koenigshaus had to prepare the orders for execution and submitted them to the Chiet of Section IV, Mueller, for signature (Milller being the Head of the Gestapo). These orders were made out so that one order was to be sent to the agency making the request, and a second one to the concentration camp designated to carry out the execution. The P.W's. in question were at first formally released from P.W. status, then transferred to a concentration camp for execution.

The Department Chief, Koenigshaus, was under me in disciplinary questions from the middle of 1942 until about the beginning of 1943, and worked, in matters of his department, directly with the chief of Group IV A, Regierungsrat Panzinger. Early in 1943 the department was dissolved, and absorbed into the departments in Sub-section IV B. The work concerning Russian P.W's. must then have been done by IV B 2a. Head of Department IV B 2a was Regierungsrat and Sturmbannfuehrer Hans Helmut Wolf.

There existed in the PM. camps on the Eastern Front small screening teams (Einsatzkommandos), headed by a lower ranking member of the Secret Police or Gestapo. These teams were assigned to the camp commandos and had the job of segregating the P.W's. who were candidates for execution, according to the orders that had been given, and to report them to the Office of the Secret Police."

I will not read the remainder of that affidavit.

Passing from that phase of the case : The Gestapo and S.S. sent re-captured prisoners of war to concentration camps, where they were executed, that is, prisoners of war who had escaped and were recaptured. The Tribunal will recall that in a document heretofore introduced, 1650-PS, was an order in which the Chief of the Security Police and S.S. instructed regional Gestapo offices to take certain classes of recaptured officers from camps, and to transport them to Mauthausen. Concentration Camp, under the operation known as "Kugel." That, if your Honour recalls, means "Bullet." That is the famous "Bullet" Decree that has been previously introduced. On the journey the prisoners of war were to be placed in irons. The Gestapo officers were to make semi-annual reports, giving numbers only, of the sending of these prisoners of war to Mauthausen. On the 27th of July, 1944, an order was issued from the VI Corps Area Command on the treatment of prisoners of war. That is Document 1514-PS in the second volume, which I offer as Exhibit USA 491. This document provided that prisoners of war were to be discharged from prisoner of war status and transferred to the Gestapo under certain circumstances, and I quote from the first page:

"Subject : Delivery of prisoners of war to the Secret State Police."

Enclosed is the decree (I) referred to :

"The following summarising ruling is issued with respect to the delivery to the Secret State Police :

1. (a) According to the decrees (2) and (3), the commander of the camp has to deliver Soviet prisoners of war in case of punishable offences to the Secret State Police and to dismiss them from imprisonment of war, if he does not believe that disciplinary functions are sufficient to prescribe punishment for violations committed. Report of the facts is not necessary.

(b) Recaptured Soviet prisoners of war have to be delivered first to the nearest police office in order to ascertain whether punishable offences have been committed during the escape. The dismissal from imprisonment of war takes place upon suggestion of the police office (Section A6 of the decree No. 4) regarding the compilation of all regulations on the Arbeitseinsatz of prisoners of war who have been recaptured and refuse to work.

(c) Recaptured Soviet officers who are prisoners of war have to be delivered to the Gestapo and to be dismissed from imprisonment of war. (Section C1 of Decree No. 4 and Decree No. 5.)

(d) Soviet officer prisoners of war who refuse to work and those who distinguish themselves as agitators and have an unfavourable influence upon the willingness to work of the other prisoners of war, have to be delivered by the responsible Stalag to the nearest State Police office and to be dismissed from imprisonment of war. (Section C1 of Decree No. 4 and Decree No. 5.)

(e) Soviet enlisted prisoners of war refusing to work who are ringleaders and those who distinguish themselves as agitators and therefore have an unfavourable influence upon the willingness to work of the other prisoners of war, have to be delivered to the nearest State Police Office and to be dismissed from imprisonment of war. (Section C2 of Decree No. 4.)

(f) Soviet prisoners of war (enlisted men and officers), who with respect to their political attitude have been sifted out by Einsatzkonimando of the Security Police and the Security Service, have to be delivered upon request by the camp commander to the Einsatzkonimando and to be dismissed from imprisonment of war. (Decree No. 6.)

(g) Polish prisoners of war have to be delivered, if acts of sabotage are proven, to the nearest State Police Office and to be dismissed from imprisonment of war. The decision rests with the camp commander. Report on this is not necessary. (Decree No. 7.)

2. A report on the delivery and dismissal from imprisonment of war in the cases mentioned under paragraph 1of this decree to the Mil. District Command VI, Dept. of Prisoners of War, is not necessary.

3. Prisoners of war from all nations have to be delivered to the Secret State Police and to be dismissed from imprisonment of war, if a special order of the O.K.W. or of the Mil. District Command VI, Dept. for Prisoners of War, is issued.

4. Prisoners of war under suspicion of participating in illegal organisations and resistance movements have to be left to the Gestapo, upon request, for the purpose of interrogation. They remain prisoners of war and have to be treated as such. The delivery to the Gestapo and their dismissal from imprisonment of war has to take place only by order of the O.K.W. or of the Mil. District Command VI, Dept. of Prisoners of War.

In case of French and Belgian prisoners of war and interned Italian military personnel, approval of Mil. District Command VI ' Dept. of Prisoners of War, has to be obtained - if necessary by phone - before delivery to the Gestapo for the purposes of interrogation."

This decree was known as the "Bullet Decree." Prisoners of war, sent to Mauthausen Concentration Camp under the decree, were executed. I now offer in support of that statement Document 2285-PS, Exhibit USA 490. It is in the second volume. Document 2285-PS is an affidavit of Lt.-Col. Guivante de Saint Gast, and Lt. Jean Veith, both of the French Army, which was taken on the 13th May, 1945, in the course of an official military investigation by the United States Army. The affidavit discloses that Lt.-Col. Gast was confined at Mauthausen from 15th March, 1944, to 22nd April, 1945, and that Lt. Veith was confined from 22nd April, 1943 until 22nd April, 1945. I quote from the affidavit, beginning with the third paragraph of Page 1, quoting :

"In Mauthausen existed several treatments of prisoners, amongst them the 'action K or Kugel' (Bullet action). Upon the arrival of transports, prisoners with the mention 'K' were not registered, and received no numbers, and their names remained unknown except to the officials of the 'Politische Abteilung.' (Lt. Veith had the opportunity of hearing upon the arrival of a transport the following conversation between the Untersturmfuehrer Streitwieser and chief of the convoy: 'How many prisoners?' '15 but two K.' 'Well, that makes 13 ').

The prisoners were taken directly to the prison, where they were unclothed and taken to the 'Bathroom.' This bathroom in the cellars of the prison building near the crematory was specially designed for execution (shooting and gassing). The shooting took place by means of a measuring apparatus. The prisoners being backed towards a metrical measure with an automatic contraption releasing a bullet in his neck as soon as the moving plank determining his height touched the top of his head.

If a transport consisted of too many 'K' prisoners, instead of losing time for the measurement they were exterminated by gas, laid on to the bathrooms instead of water."

I now pass to another subject, namely "The Gestapo was responsible for establishing and classifying concentration camps and for committing racial and political undesirables to concentration and annihilation camps for slave labour and mass murder."

The Tribunal has already received evidence concerning the responsibility of the Gestapo for the administration of concentration camps, and the authority of the Gestapo for taking persons into protective custody to be carried out in the state concentration camps. The Gestapo also issued orders establishing concentration camps, transforming prisoner of war camps into concentration camps as internment camps, changing labour camps into concentration camps, setting up special sections for female prisoners, and so forth.

The Chief of the Security Police and S.S. ordered the classification of concentration camps according to the seriousness of the accusation and the chances for reforming the prisoners, from the Nazi viewpoint. I now refer to Documents 1063A and 1063B in the second volume, Exhibit USA 492. The concentration camps were classified as Class I, II or III. Class I was for the least serious prisoners, and Class III was for the most serious. Now Document 1063A is signed by Heydrich and it is dated 2nd January, 1941. I quote from the beginning:

Subject : Classification of the Concentration Camps.

The Reichsfuehrer S.S. and Chief of the German Police has given his approval to classify the concentration camps into various categories, which take into account the personality of the prisoner as well as the degree of his danger to the State. Accordingly, the concentration camps will be classified into the following categories :

Category I - for all prisoners charged with minor offences only and definitely qualified for correction ; also for special cases and solitary confinement - Camps Dachau, Sachsenhausen and Auschwitz 1. The latter also applies in part to Category II.

Category la - for all old prisoners unconditionally qualified for work, who could still be used in the medicinal herb gardens - the Camp Dachau.

Category II - for prisoners charged with major offences but still qualified for re-education and correction - the Camps Buchenwald, Flossenburg, Auschwitz II.

Category III - for prisoners under most serious charges, also for those who have been previously convicted for criminal offences ; at the same time for asocial prisoners, that is to say, those who can hardly be corrected - the Camp Mauthausen."

I call your Honour's attention to the fact that we have been talking about Mauthausen, where the "K" action took place.

The Chief of the Security Police and S.D. had authority to fix the length of the period of custody. During the war it was the policy not to permit the prisoners to know the period of custody and merely to announce the term as "Until further notice." That was established by Document 1531-PS, which has previously been introduced as Exhibit USA 248, and the only reason for referring to it is to show that they had the right to fix the period of custody.

The local Gestapo offices, which made the arrests, maintained a register called the "Haftbuch," and, as I understand, "Haftbuch" simply means a block or police register. In this register the names of all persons arrested were listed, together with personal data, grounds of arrest and disposition. When orders were received from the Gestapo Headquarters in Berlin to commit persons who had been arrested to concentration camps, an entry was made in the "Haftbuch" to that effect.

I now offer in evidence the original of one of these books, and it is Document L-358, Exhibit USA 495. This book was collected by the 3rd Army when it overran an area, and it was captured by the T Force on 22nd April, 1945, near Bad Sulze, Germany. This book is the original register used by the Gestapo at Tomassow, Poland, to record the names of the persons arrested, the grounds for arrest and the disposition made, of cases during the period from 1st June, 1943, to 20th December, 1944.

In the register are approximately 3,500 names of persons. Approximately 2,200 were arrested for membership in the resistance movements and partisan unit. This is a very large book, and I am going to ask the clerk to pass it to your Honours so that you might get a look at it. It is too big to photograph. And if your Honours will just turn to one of the pages, I will read what the different columns provide - just any one of the pages. There is a double column. It starts on the left and goes over to the other side. In the first column that heading is simply a number of the man when he comes in. The next column is his name. The third column is the family - a brief family history and his religion. The fourth is the domicile. The next shows the date he was arrested and by whom - that is the fifth column. The next column, the place of arrest. And then the next column, the reason for arrest. And then the next is another number which is apparently a serial number for delivery. And next to the last column is the disposition. And the final column, remarks.

Now, out of the 3,500 names that are shown in that book, your Honours will notice a number of red marks. Those apparently meant the ones that were shot. of those, 325 were shot. Only 35 of that 325 had first been tried. 950 out of this list were sent to concentration camps and 155 sent to the Reich for forced labour. According to this register, similar treatment was accorded persons who were arrested on other grounds, for instance, Communists, Jews, hostages, and persons taken in reprisal. A large number are shown to have been arrested during raids, no further grounds being stated.

I particularly refer your Honours to entries 286, 287 and 288, that is, the numbers in the first column of the register, where the crime charged to the person arrested was "als Juden" ; in other words, he was a Jew. And by that you will find a red cross mark, and the punishment given was death.

I now pass from this document and merely call attention to Document L- 215, which was heretofore introduced as Exhibit USA 243. I do not intend to read from it unless your Honours want to turn to L-215. This is a file of original dossiers on 25 Luxembourgers taken into protective custody for commitment to concentration camps. I will just refer to a sentence of the language in the document. Quoting :

"According to the finding of the State Police he endangers by his attitude the existence and security of the People and the State."

And in each case, with reference to those dossiers, that appears as the reason for the execution of these 25 Luxembourgers. And in connection -

THE PRESIDENT: : Colonel Storey, you said execution, did you not ?

COLONEL STOREY: I beg your pardon - sending to concentration camps.

THE PRESIDENT: : Yes. There is no evidence they were executed.

COLONEL STOREY: No, sir ; they were committed to concentration camps. And also in connection with that same document there is a form provided by which the Gestapo Headquarters in Berlin were notified when the persons were received by the concentration camps.

Another document - which has heretofore been received as Exhibit USA 279, Document 1472-PS, in the second volume - I am simply going to refer to it as a predicate for another. That was a telegram of 16th December, 1942, in which Mueller reported that the Gestapo could round up some 45,000 Jews in connection with the programme of obtaining additional labour in concentration camps. And with reference to the same subject there is Document 1063-D-PS, which has heretofore been offered as Exhibit USA 219, Mueller sent a directive to the commanders and inspectors of the Security Police and S.D. and to the directors of the Gestapo regional offices, in which he stated that Himmler had ordered on 14th December, ordered on 14th December, 1942, that at least 35,000 persons, who were fit for work, had to be put into concentration camps not later than the end of January.

Now, in that same connection I offer Document L-41, volume 1, as Exhibit USA 496. This document contains a further directive from Mueller dated 23rd March, 1943, and supplements the directive of 17th December, 1942, to which I referred, and in this he states that the measures are to be carried out until 30th April, 1943. And I would like to quote from the second paragraph on page 3 of the exhibit.

"Care must, however, be taken that only prisoners who are fit for work are transferred to concentration camps, and adolescents only in accordance with the given directives ; otherwise, the concentration camps would become overcrowded, and this would defeat the intended object."

In that same connection I offer Document 701-PS, Exhibit USA 497. This is a letter dated 1st April, 1943, from the Minister of Justice to the Public Prosecutors and also addressed to the Commissioner of the Reich Minister of Justice for the penal camps in Emsland. Quoting :

"Regarding Poles and Jews who are released from the penal institutions of the Department of Justice. Instructions for the independent penal institutions.

1. With reference to the new guiding principles for the application of Article 1, Section 2, of the decree of 11th June, 1940, Reich Legal Gazette I S. 887 - Attachment I of decree (RV) of 27th January, 1943 - 913-2 enclosure I-IIIa 2-2629 - the Reich Chief Security Office has directed by the decree of 11th March, 1943 - 11 A 2 number 100-43-176:

(a) Jews, who in accordance with number VI of the guiding principles are released from a penal institution, are to be taken by the State Police (Chief) Office competent for the district in which the penal institution is located, to be detained for the rest of their lives in the concentration camps Auschwitz or Lublin in accordance with the regulations for protective custody that have been issued.

The same applies to Jews who in future are released from a penal institution after serving sentence of confinement.

(b) Poles, who in accordance with Number VI of the guiding principles are released from a penal institution, are to be taken by the State Police (Chief) Office competent for the district in which the penal institution is located, to be placed for the duration of the war in a concentration camp in accordance with the regulations on protective custody that have been issued.

The same applies in the future to Poles, who after serving a term of imprisonment of more than six months, are to be discharged by a penal institution.

Conforming to the request of the Chief Office for Reich Security, I ask that in the future :

(a) All Jews to be discharged;

(b) All Poles to be discharged;

who have served a sentence of more than six months, be transferred for further confinement to the State Police (Chief) Office competent for the district, and are to be placed promptly at its disposal before the end of sentence, for collection."

And the last paragraph states that this ruling replaces the hitherto ordered return of all Polish prisoners undergoing imprisonment in the Old Reich condemned in the annexed Eastern territory.

The next subject: "The Gestapo and the S.D. Participated in Deportation of Citizens of Occupied Countries for Forced Labour and Handled the Disciplining of Forced Labour."

With reference to the presentation heretofore made concerning forced labour, I do not intend to repeat this. However, there were several references to the important position played by the Gestapo and the S.D. in rounding up persons to be brought into the Reich for forced labour, and references in two or three documents that were introduced. I simply want to cite those documents as showing the part that the Gestapo and S.D. played. Document L-61, Exhibit USA 177. It is set out in this document book - I am simply citing it - it is a letter of the 26th of November, 1942, from Fritz Sauckel, in which he stated that he had been advised by the Chief of the Security Police and S.D. under date of 26th October, 1942, that during the month of November the evacuation of Poles in the Lublin district would begin, in order to make room for the settlement of persons of the German race. The Poles who were evacuated as a result of this measure were to be put into concentration camps for labour, so far as they were criminal or anti-social.

The Tribunal will also recall the Christensen letter, which is our Document 3012-PS, Exhibit USA 190. In that letter it is stated that during the year 1943 the programme of mass murder carried out by the Einsatz Groups in the East should be modified in order to round up hundreds of thousands of persons for labour in the armament industry. That was in 3012-PS, which has heretofore been introduced as Exhibit USA 190. And that force was to be used when necessary. Prisoners were to be released so that they could be used for forced labour. When villages were burned down the whole population was to be placed at the disposal of the labour commissioners.

Now in that connection the direct responsibility of the Gestapo for disciplining forced workers is shown in our next exhibit, Document 1573-PS, Exhibit USA 498. This is a secret order signed by Mueller himself to the regional Gestapo Offices on the 18th June, 1941, and I quote from the document from the beginning. It is addressed:

"To all State Police Administrative Offices, attention S.S. Sturmbahnfuehrer Nosske or representative at Aachen.

Subject: Measures to be taken against emigrants and civilian workers who came from the great Russian areas and against foreign workers.

Reference: None.

To prevent the unauthorised and arbitrary return of Russian, Ukrainian, White Ruthenian, Cossack, and Caucasian emigrants and civilian workers from the territory of the Reich to the East, and to prevent attempts at disorder by foreign workers in the German production, I decide as follows:

(1) The managers of the branch offices of the Russian, Ukrainian, White Ruthenian, and Caucasian trustee office, as well as the relief committee and the leading members of the Russian, Ukrainian, White Ruthenian, Cossack, and Caucasian emigration organisations are to be notified immediately that, until further notice, they are not allowed to leave their domicile without permission of the Security Police. Also

they are to be told to apply the same measures to the members who are under their care. Their attention is to be called to the fact that they will be arrested in case of unauthorised leaving place of work and domicile. I request to have a check on the presence of branch office leaders if possible by daily inquiries under pretext.

(2) Emigrants and foreign workers are to be arrested if it is warranted by the situation, in case they were charged with similar offences previously and are under the suspicion of having been active as informers for the U.S.S.R. This measure has to be prepared. It should, however, not be taken before the pass word ' Fremdvoelker' has been transmitted by means of 'urgent' telegram."

THE PRESIDENT: Do you think you should read the rest of that ?

COLONEL STOREY: Sir?

THE PRESIDENT: Is it necessary to read the rest of that ?

COLONEL STOREY: I do not think so, your Honour.

THE PRESIDENT: We will adjourn now for ten minutes.

(A recess was taken.)

COLONEL STOREY: If the Tribunal please, I next offer in evidence Document 3330-PS, Exhibit USA 499, the second volume. Before I hand this document to the translator I should like to exhibit it to your Honours. It is an original telegram that was sent to the Gestapo office at Nuremberg. It was discovered by the C.I.C., by a Lieutenant Stevens, near Herzburg, Germany, and your Honours will notice that parts of it have been burned. It was in connection with some documents that had been buried and they were partially burned when they were buried. This is one of the telegrams. It is from the Secret State Police, the State Police Station at Nuremberg and Furth, and it is dated the 12th February, 1944. I quote from the telegram:

"R.S.H.A. IV F1 45-44.

The Border Inspector General.

Urgent - Submit immediately.

Treatment, of recaptured escaped eastern labourers (Ostarbeiter).

By order of the R.F.S.S. all recaptured escaped Eastern labourers without exception are to be sent to concentration camps, effective immediately. In regard to reporting to R.F.S.S., I request only one report by teletype to Section IV D (Foreign labourers) on 10th March, 1944, as to how many of such male or female Eastern labourers were turned over to a concentration camp, between to-day and 10th March, 1944.')"

By these methods the Gestapo and S.D. maintained control over forced labour brought into the Reich.

The next subject I go into is that the Gestapo and S.D. executed captured commandos and paratroopers and protected civilians who lynched Allied fliers.

On 4th August, 1942, Keitel issued an order which provided that the Gestapo and S.D. were responsible for taking counter-measures against single parachutists or small groups of them with jspecial missions. In substantiation I offer now Document 513-PS as the exhibit next in order, Exhibit USA 500. I read from the first page of the translation, the first part of paragraph 3:

"Single parachutists captured by members of the Armed Forces are to be delivered to the nearest agency of the Chief of the Security Police and S.D. without delay."

Now, if the Tribunal please, to digress from the text: Colonel Taylor will present the

Nazi High Command and a few of their orders. This is one thing and there is also another one, with which he is going to deal extensively. My purpose in introducing these orders now is to show the part that the Gestapo and S.D. played in connection with them.

The next order that I introduce is Document 498-PS, in the first volume, Exhibit USA 501. That is the celebrated commando order signed by the Fuehrer himself on 18th October, 1942. There were only 12 copies of this made and it bears the original personal signature of Adolf Hitler. One copy was sent to the Reichsfuehrer S.S. and Chief of the Security Police. That order, without reading it, and getting down to the part from which I want to quote, simply provides that all commandos, whether or not in uniform or unarmed, are to be slaughtered to the last man. I want to read down at the bottom, the beginning of paragraph 4, to show the part of the S.D.:

"If individual members of such commandos, such as agents, saboteurs, etc., fall into the hands of the military forces by some other means, through the police in occupied territories for instance, they are to be handed over immediately to the S.D."

Another one of those orders is Document 526-PS, Exhibit USA 502, to which I would like to refer. That document has to do with some alleged saboteurs landing in Norway. It is dated the 10th May, 1943, and is Top Secret. I quote the first paragraph as identifying a crew:

"On the 30th March, 1943, on Toftefjord (70 deg. lat.) an enemy cutter was sighted. Cutter was blown up by the enemy. Crew two dead men, 10 prisoners."

That is the crew. Near the bottom of that order, the third sentence from the bottom, is this statement

"Fuehrer order executed by S.D. (Security Service)."

We have heretofore introduced Document R-110, Exhibit USA 333, and that was the Himmler order of 10th August, 1943, which was sent to Security Police. That order provided that it was not the task of the Police to interfere in clashes between Germans and English and American terror fliers who had baled out. It was personally signed by Himmler and here is the signature. It has already been introduced in evidence, but I wanted to call the attention of the Court to it again.

May I next go to the subject where the Gestapo and the S.D. took civilians of occupied countries to Germany for secret trial and punishment. That is the so-called "Night and Fog Decree," issued on 7th December, 1941, by Hitler. That decree has not been introduced in evidence.

I now refer to Document L-90, in the first volume, Exhibit USA 503. Under that decree persons who committed offences against the Reich or occupation forces in occupied territory, except where death sentence was certain, were to be taken secretly to Germany and surrendered to the Security

Police and S.D. for trial or punishment in Germany itself. And this is the original from which we quote, beginning on the first page of the translation. It is on the stationery of the Reichsfuehrer S.S. and Chief of German Police, Munich, 4th February, 1942. Subject: Prosecution of Offences against the Reich or the Occupation Forces.

"1. The following regulations published by the Chief of the Armed Forces High Command, dated 12th December, 1941, are being made known herewith:

(1) The Chief of the Armed Forces High Command.

After thoughtful consideration, it is the will of the Fuehrer that the measures taken against those who are guilty of offences against the Reich or against the occupation forces in occupied areas should be altered. The Fuehrer thinks that in the case of such offences life imprisonment, even life imprisonment with hard labour, is regarded as a sign of weakness. An effective and lasting deterrent can be achieved only by the death penalty or by taking measures which will leave the family and the population uncertain as to the fate of the offender. The deportation to Germany serves this purpose.

The directives for the prosecution of offences as outlined below correspond with the Fuehrer's conception. They have been examined and approved by him. (Signed) Keitel."

And then follow some of the directives and descriptions.

This is a very long document, with enclosures, and we next turn to Page 4 of the English translation, near the bottom:

"In so far as the S.S. and the police are the competent authorities for dealing with offences committed under 1, they should proceed accordingly."

Next, in connection with the same document, on Page 20, Part II of the English translation, which is the secret letter addressed to the "Abwehr," I quote from Page 2. It is the letter dated 2nd February, 1942, passing down to the words "Enclosed please find:

"1. Decree of the Fuehrer and Supreme Commander of the Armed Forces of 7th December, 1941.

2. Executive order of the same date.

3. Communication of the Chief of the High Command of the Armed Forces of 12th December, 1941.

The decree introduces a fundamental innovation. The Fuehrer and Supreme Commander of the Armed Forces orders that offences committed by civilians in the occupied territories and of the kind mentioned above, are to be dealt with by the competent Military Courts in the occupied territories only if (a) the death penalty is pronounced, and (b) sentence is pronounced within eight days of the prisoner's arrest.

Unless both these conditions are fulfilled, the Fuehrer and Supreme Commander does not anticipate that criminal proceedings within the occupied territories will have the necessary deterrent effect.

In all other cases the prisoners are in future to be transported to Germany secretly, and further dealings with the offences will take place there ; these measures will have a deterrent effect because (a) the prisoners will vanish without leaving a trace, (b) no information may be given as to their whereabouts or their fate."

Now, skipping the next paragraph, to the second paragraph below:

"In case the competent Military Court, and the Military Commander respectively are of the opinion that an immediate decision on the spot is impossible, and the prisoners are therefore to be transported to Germany, the Counter Intelligence Offices have to report this fact directlyto the R.S.H.A. in Berlin, SW11, PrinzAlbrecht Street 7, c-o Dr. Fischer, Director of Criminal Police, stating the exact number of prisoners and of the group or groups which belong together as the case may be. Isolated cases, where the superior commander has an urgent interest in the case being dealt with by a military court, are to be reported to the R.S.H.A. Copy of the entire report has to be sent to Office Foreign Countries Intelligence Department, Abwehr III.

The R.S.H.A., on the basis of available accommodation, will determine which office of the State Police has to accept the prisoners. The latter office will communicate with the competent Counter Intelligence Office and determine with it the particulars of the removal, particularly whether this will be carried out by the Secret Field Police, the Field Gendarmerie, or the Gestapo itself, as well as on the place and the manner of the actual handing over."

After the civilians arrived in Germany no word of the disposition of their cases was permitted to reach the country from which they came or their relatives.

I now offer Document 668-PS, Exhibit USA 504. This is a letter of the Chief of the Security Police and the S.D., dated 24th June, 1942, and I quote from the first page of the English translation:

"It is the intent of the directive of the Fuehrer and Commander-in-Chief of the Wehrmacht concerning prosecution of criminal acts against the Reich or the occupation forces in occupied territories, dated 7th December, 1941 " - that is the order that I first referred to - "to create, for deterrent purposes, uncertainty over the fate of prisoners among their relatives and acquaintances, through the deportation into Reich territory of persons arrested in occupied areas on account of activity inimical to Germany. This goal would be jeopardised if the relatives were to be notified in cases of death. Release of the body for burial at home is inadvisable for the same reason, and beyond that also because the place of burial could be misused for demonstrations.

I therefore propose that the following rules be observed in the handling of cases of death:

(a) Notification of relatives is not to take place.

(b) The body will be buried at the place of decease in the Reich.

(c) The place of burial will, for the time being, not be made known."

Now passing to the next activity of the S.D. and Gestapo, which was that they arrested, tried and punished citizens of occupied countries under special criminal procedure and by summary methods. And I next offer in evidence Document 674-PS, Exhibit USA 505.

The Gestapo, under certain circumstances, arrested, placed in protective custody, and executed civilians of occupied countries. Even where there were courts capable of handling emergency cases the Gestapo conducted its own proceedings without regard to normal judicial processes.

This document, 674-PS, Exhibit USA 505, is a letter from the Chief Public Prosecutor at Kattowitz, dated 3rd December, 1941, and it is addressed to the Reich Minister of Justice, attention Chief Councillor to the Government Stadermann or representative in office, Berlin. The subject is "Executions by the Police and Expediting of Penal Procedure, without Order; Enclosure: 1 copy of report." I quote from the beginning:

"About three weeks ago, six ringleaders (some of them German) were hanged by the Police, in connection with the destruction of a treasonable organisation of 350 members in Tarnowitz, without notification to the Ministry of Justice. Such executions of criminal agents have previously taken place also in the Bielitz district without the knowledge of the public prosecutor. On 2nd December, 1941, the head of the State Police at Kattowitz, chief councillor to the government Mildner, reported orally to the undersigned that he had ordered, with authority from the Reichsfuehrer of the S. S., as necessary immediate action, these executions by public hanging at the place of the crime, and that deterrents would also have to be continued in future until the criminal and actively anti-German elements in the occupied Eastern territories have been destroyed, or until other immediate actions, perhaps also by the courts, would guarantee equally deterrent effect. Accordingly, six leaders of another Polish organisation guilty of high treason in the district in and around Sosnowitz were to be hanged publicly to-day as an example.

About this procedure the undersigned expressed considerable concern.

Besides the fact that such measures have been withdrawn from the jurisdiction of the ordinary courts and are contradictory to laws still in force, a justified emergency for the exceptional proceedings by the police alone cannot, in our opinion, be lawfully recognised.

The penal justice in our district within the limits of our jurisdiction is quite capable of fulfilling its duty of immediate penal retribution by means of a special form of special judicial activity established by a so-called ' Rapid Special Court.' Indictment and trial could be speeded up in such a way that between turning the case over to the public prosecutor and the execution no more than three days would elapse, if the practice of reprieve is simplified and if the decision, if necessary, can be obtained by telephone. This was expressed yesterday to the head of the State police at Kattowitz by the undersigned.

We cannot believe that execution by the police of criminals, especially German criminals, can be considered more effective in view of the shaken sense of justice of many Germans. In the long run they might, in spite of public deterrent, lead even more to further brutality of mind, which is contrary to the intended purpose of pacification. These deliberations, however, do not apply to future legal competence of a drumhead court-martial for Poles and Jews."

I next refer to document 654-PS, Exhibit USA 218, which has previously been introduced in evidence, but it bears on this subject, and I will merely summarise in a word what it provided.

It states that on 18th of September, 1942, Thierack, the Reich Minister of Justice, and Himmler came to an understanding by which anti-social elements were to be turned over to Himmler to be worked to death. That is in Document 654-PS, and a special criminal procedure was to be applied by the police to the Jews, Poles, Gypsies, Russians, and Ukrainians, who were not to be tried in ordinary criminal courts.

I refer to that document merely as bearing on the same subject.

Another document from which I will not quote, but will cite to your Honour, is the order of 5th November, 1942, issued by the R.S.H.A., and that is Document L-316, Exhibit USA 346. I do not think it is necessary to quote from that except to state that that letter provides that the administration - in fact, the last statement in it just before the signature provides:

"The administration of penal law for persons of alien race must be transferred from the hands of the administrators of justice into the hands of the police."

That is the part that connects the police with it, and I will not quote from the document otherwise.

Now I next come to the subject where the Gestapo and the S.D. executed or confined persons in concentration camps for crimes allegedly committed by their relatives and in that connection I offer Document L-37 in the first volume, Exhibit USA 506.

That is a letter dated 19th July, 1944. I call your Honour's attention to the fact that it is dated in 1944, sent by the Commander of the Sipo and S.D. for the District of Radom to the Foreign Service Office in Tomassow.

Parenthetically, that big Haftbuch that we introduced in evidence has a number of cases in connection with the District of Radom, and your Honour will remember that it is a list of the people in the District of Tomassow.

The subject of this letter is "Collective responsibility of members of families of assassins and saboteurs." I will read after the word "precedents."

> "The Higher S.S. and Police Fuehrer Ost has issued on 28th June, 1944, the following order:
>
> The security situation in the Government General has in the last nine months grown so much worse that from now on the most radical means and the harshest measures must be enforced against the alien assassins and saboteurs. The Reichsfuehrer S.S., in agreement with the Governor General, has ordered that, in all cases where assassinations of Germans or attempts at such have occurred, or saboteurs have destroyed vital installations, not only the perpetrators who are caught are to be shot but also all male relatives are to be executed and their female relatives who are over 16 years are to be put into concentration camps. It is of course strictly understood that, if the perpetrator or the perpetrators are not apprehended, their names and addresses must be correctly ascertained. Among male relatives can be considered for example: the father, sons (in so far as they are over 16 years of age), brothers, brothers-in-law, cousins and uncles of the perpetrator. Proceedings must take place in the same manner against the women. By this procedure it is intended to secure collective responsibility of all men and women relatives of the perpetrator. It furthermore affects. to the utmost the family circle of the political criminal. This practice has already shown, for example, by the end of 1939, the best results in the new Eastern territories, especially in the Warthe district. As soon as this new method for combating assassins and saboteurs becomes known to these foreign people - this may be achieved by oral propaganda - the female members of a family to which members of the resistance movement or bands belong, as shown by experience, will exert a curbing influence."

Now the S.D. and Gestapo also conducted third degree interrogations of prisoners of war, and I refer to Document 1531-PS, Exhibit USA 248. This document contains an order of 12th June, 1942, signed by Mueller, which authorised the use of third degree methods in interrogations where preliminary investigation indicated that the prisoners could give information on important facts such as subversive activities, but did not authorise their use to extort confessions of the prisoner's own crimes.

Now I quote from Page 2 of the English translation, paragraph 2:

> "Third degree may, under this supposition, only be employed against Communists, Marxists, Jehovah's Witnesses, saboteurs, terrorists, members of resistance movements, parachute agents, anti-social elements, Polish or Soviet-Russian loafers or tramps. In all other cases, my permission must first be obtained."

Then I pass to paragraph 4 at the end:

> "Third degree can, according to the circumstances, employ, among other methods:
>
> Very simple diet (bread and water) ; hard bunk; dark cell; deprivation of sleep ; exhaustive drilling; also flogging (for more than 20 strokes a doctor must be consulted)."

On 24th February, 1944, the Commander of the Sipo and the S.D. for the district of Radom published an order issued by the Befehlshaber of the Sipo and the S.D. at Cracow, which is Document L-89, Exhibit U.S.A. 507, in the first volume. This followed closely the provisions of the previous decree that I have just quoted from, and I quote the first paragraph after the list of offices on the first page:

"In view of the variety of methods used to date in intensified interrogations and in order to avoid excesses, also to protect officials against eventual criminal proceedings, the Befehlshaber of the Security Police and of the S.D. in Cracow has issued the following order for the Security Police in the Government General, which is based on the regulations in force for the Reich."

And then the regulations are quoted. The significance of this document is that it proves that as late as 1944 third degree interrogations were still being conducted by the Gestapo.

I next pass to the activity of the Gestapo and the S.D. as being primary agencies for the persecution of the Jews, and I do not intend to go into any of the evidence previously introduced, except to refer to the participation of these organisations.

The responsibility of the Gestapo and S.D. for the mass extermination programme carried out by the Einsatz Groups of the Sipo and S.D. annihilation camps to which Jews were sent by the Sipo and S.D. has already been considered, and I simply cite to the Tribunal the Document 2615-PS, which has previously been introduced, and in which the number of Jews executed was referred to by Eichmann. I simply recall to your attention the fact that Eichmann was head of Section B 4 of the Gestapo. That section of the Gestapo dealt with Jewish affairs, including matters of evacuation, means of suppressing enemies of the People and the State, and the dispossession of rights of German citizenship.

The Gestapo was also charged with the enforcement of discriminatory laws, which have heretofore been introduced.

I now invite your Honour's attention to Document 3058-PS, Exhibit USA 508. I should like to point out to your Honour that it is a red-bordered document signed by Heydrich himself and addressed to the defendant Goering. It is dated 11th November, 1938. I pass this to the reporter, and before it is passed to the reporter it is to be noted that there is an appendix attached to it to the effect that the matter had been called to the attention of the defendant Goering.

Now this concerns a report of activities of the Gestapo in connection with the anti-Jewish demonstrations which you will recall were in the fall of 1938. This is a report from Heydrich personally to the defendant Goring. It is addressed to the Prime Minister, General Field-Marshal Goering, and is dated 11th November, 1938, and the previous documents showed that these activities occurred just before, and the order for it in connection with the Jewish uprooting or extermination:

"The extent of the destruction of Jewish shops and houses cannot yet be verified by figures. The figures given in the reports: 815 shops destroyed, 171 dwelling houses set on fire or destroyed, only indicate a fraction of the actual damage caused, as far as arson is concerned. Due to the urgency of the reports, those received to date are entirely limited to general statements such as 'numerous' or 'most shops destroyed.' Therefore the figures given must have been exceeded considerably.

191 synagogues were set on fire and another 76 completely destroyed. In addition, 11 parish halls, cemetery chapels and similar buildings were set on fire and 3 more completely destroyed.

Twenty thousand Jews were arrested, also seven Aryans and three foreigners. The latter were arrested for their own safety.

Thirty-six deaths were reported and those seriously injured were also numbered at thirty-six. Those killed and injured are Jews. One Jew is still missing. The Jews killed include one Polish national, and those injuries include two Poles."

I want to call your Honour's special attention to the paper appended to that document:

"The General Field Marshal" - that is Goering - "has been informed.

No steps are to be taken. By order."

It is dated 15th November, 1938, and signed. The signature is illegible.

Now in that same connection Heydrich was charged by the defendant Goering with this entire programme, and we next offer in evidence the original of that order, Document 710-PS, Exhibit USA 509. That is an order dated 31st July, 1941. It is written on the stationery of the Reich Marshal of the Greater German Reich, Commissioner for the Four Year Plan, Chairman of the Ministerial Council for National Defence, and it is dated at Berlin 31st July, 1941, and directed to the Chief of the Security Police and the Security Service, S.S. Gruppenfuehrer Heydrich.

"Complementary to the task that was assigned to you on 24th January, 1939, which dealt with arriving at - through furtherance of emigration and evacuation - a solution of the Jewish problem, as advantageous as possible, I hereby charge you with making all necessary preparations in regard to organisational and financial matters for bringing about a complete solution of the Jewish question in the German sphere of influence in Europe.

Wherever other Government agencies are involved, these are to co- operate with you.

I charge you furthermore to send me, before long, an overall plan concerning the organisational, factual and material measures necessary for the accomplishment of the desired solution of the Jewish question."

Signed, "Goering."

The Tribunal has already received the evidence as to what was the final solution of the Jewish problem as conceived by Heydrich, and executed by the Security Police and S.D. under him and under the defendant Kaltenbrunner. It was enslavement and mass murder.

Now, finally, in this presentation the last activity of the Gestapo and S.D. to which I will refer is that these organisations were the primary agencies for the persecution of the churches. Already evidence has been received concerning the persecution of the churches. In this struggle the Gestapo and the S.D. played a secret but very highly significant part.

Section C2 of the S.D. dealt with education and religious life. Section Bi of the Gestapo dealt with political Catholicism, Section B2 with political Protestantism, and Section B3 with other churches and Freemasonry.

The Church was one of the enemies of the Nazi State, and it was a peculiar function of the Gestapo to combat it. It issued restrictions against church activities, dissolved church organisations, and placed clergymen in protective custody.

I now want to offer in evidence Document 1815.-PS, Exhibit USA 510. This is a very large file, this original document, and I want to quote only portions of it. This was a file of the Gestapo regional office at Aachen. It discloses that the purpose of the Gestapo in combating the churches was to destroy them, and I want to read the first page of the English translation from the beginning.

This is dated "12th May, 1941, at Berlin, from the R.S.H.A., Section IV, B, 2, to all Staatspolizeileitsteller. For information: The S.D. Leit-Abschnitte ; the Inspectors of the Sipo and S.D."

I understand this word "Abschnitte " means sub-divisions.

The subject is "Concerning the study and treatment of political Churches.

"The chief of the R.S.H.A. has issued an order, effective immediately, in which the S.D. and Sipo Study and Treatment of Political Churches, which has hitherto been divided between the S.D.-Abschnitte and Stapostellen, shall now be taken over entirely by the Stapostellen"

- which I understand means Regional Offices of the Gestapo.

Then it refers to the plan for the division of work issued by the R.S.H.A. on 1st March, 1941.

"In addition to combating opposition, the Stapostellen thus take over the entire Gegnernachrichtendienst "

- I understand that word means counter-intelligence

"in this sphere.

In order that the Stapostellen should be in a position to take over this work, the Chief of the Sipo and S.D. has ordered that the Church Specialists, hitherto employed in the S.D.-Abschnitte, should be temporarily transferred to the same posts at the Stapo Offices and operate the "Nachrichtendienstliche Arbielt "

- which, means Intelligence Service in the Church. -

"On the orders of the Chief of the R.S.H.A., and in agreement with the heads of Amt III, II, and I, those Church Specialists specified in the attached list " -

THE PRESIDENT: Is it necessary to give us the details of this?

COLONEL STOREY: No, Sir, I do not think so.

At any rate, if your Honour pleases, we quote from it, and it is simply a direction as to how they will proceed.

Now then, later, on 22nd and 23rd September, 1941, they called a conference of these so-called Church Specialists attached to the Gestapo Regional Offices which I have mentioned. This was held in the lecture hall of the R.S.H.A. in Berlin. Notes were taken, and this same document contains notes of that conference. The programme is shown and the plan worked out, in connection with the churches. I will just read the closing statement to these so-called Church Specialists; it is very short:

"Each one of you must go to work with your whole heart and a true fanaticism. Should a mistake or two be made in the execution of this work, this should in no way discourage you, since mistakes are made everywhere. The main thing is that the enemy " - meaning the church - " should be constantly tackled with determination, will, and effective initiative."

And then, finally, the last thing I would like to refer to in this document is on the eighth page of the English translation, which sets out their immediate aim and their ultimate aim ; it is on Page 8 of the English translation:

"The immediate aim: The Church must not regain one inch of the ground it has lost.

The ultimate aim: Destruction of the Confessional Churches to be brought about by the collection of all material obtained through Nachrichtendienst activities, which will, at a given time, be produced as evidence for the charge of treasonable activities during the German fight for existence."

I understand that long German word means intelligence activities.

Now, if your Honour pleases, this concludes the factual, documentary presentation which I shall make in connection with the S.D. and Gestapo. Closely allied with it is the case against Kaltenbrunner, as the representative of these organisations, which will be presented immediately after lunch by Lieutenant Whitney Harris. Also, there will be one or two witnesses who will be introduced in connection with these organisations and in connection with Kaltenbrunner.

There I should like to conclude, with just these remarks

The evidence shows that the Gestapo was created by the defendant Goering in Prussia in April, 1933, for the specific purpose of serving as a police agency to strike down the actual and ideological enemies of the Nazi regime, and that henceforward the Gestapo in Prussia and in the other states of the Reich carried out a programme of terror against all who were thought to be dangerous to the domination of the Conspirators over the people of Germany. Its methods were utterly ruthless. It operated outside the law and sent its victims to the concentration camps. The term "Gestapo" became the symbol of the Nazi regime of force and terror.

Behind the scenes, operating secretly, the S.D., through its vast network of informants, spied upon the German people in their daily lives, on the streets, in the shops, and even within the sanctity of the churches.

The most casual remark of the German citizen might bring him before the Gestapo where his fate and freedom were decided without recourse to law. In this government, in which the rule of law was replaced by a tyrannical rule of men, the Gestapo was the primary instrument of oppression.

The Gestapo and the S.D. played an important part in almost every criminal act of the Conspiracy. The category of these crimes, apart from the thousands of specific instances of torture and cruelty in policing Germany for the benefit of the Conspirators, reads like a page from the Devil's notebook:

They fabricated the border incidents which Hitler used as an excuse for attacking Poland.

They murdered hundreds of thousands of defenceless men, women and children by the infamous Einsatz Groups.

They removed Jews, political leaders, and scientists from prisoner of war camps and murdered them.

They took recaptured prisoners of war to concentration camps and murdered them.

They established and classified the concentration camps and sent thousands of people into them for extermination and slave labour.

They cleared Europe of the Jews, and were responsible for sending hundreds of thousands to their deaths in annihilation camps.

They rounded up hundreds of thousands of citizens of occupied countries and shipped them to Germany for forced labour and sent slave labourers to labour reformatory camps.

They executed captured commandos and paratroopers and protected civilians who lynched allied fliers.

They took civilians of occupied countries to Germany for secret trial and punishment.

They arrested, tried and punished citizens of occupied countries under special crimifial procedures which did not accord fair trails, and by summary methods.

They murdered or sent to concentration camps the relatives of persons who had allegedly committed crimes.

They ordered the murder of prisoners in Sipo and S.D. prisons to prevent their release by Allied armies.

They participated in the seizure and spoliation of public and private property.

They were primary agencies for the persecution of the Jews and churches.

In carrying out these crimes the Gestapo operated as an organisation closely centralised and controlled from Berlin headquarters. Reports were submitted to Berlin and all important decisions emanated from Berlin. The regional offices had only limited power to commit persons to concentration camps. All cases, other than short of duration, had to be submitted to Berlin for approval.

The Gestapo was organised on a functional basis. Its principal divisions dealt with groups and institutions against which it committed the worst crimes - which I have enumerated.

Thus, in perpetrating these crimes, the Gestapo acted as an entity, each section performing its parts in the general criminal enterprises ordered by Berlin. The Secret State Police should be held responsible as an organisation for the vast crimes in which it participated.

The S.D. was at all times a department of the S.S. Its criminality directly concerns and contributes to the criminality of the S.S.

And as to the Gestapo, it is submitted that it was an organisation in the sense in which that term is used in Article 9 of the Charter, that the defendants Goering and Kaltenbrunner committed the crimes defined in Article 6 of the Charter in their capacity as members and leaders of the Gestapo, and that the Gestapo, as an organisation, participated in and aided the conspiracy which contemplated and involved the commission of the crimes defined in Article 6 of the Charter.

And finally, I have in my hand here a brochure published in honour of the famous Heydrich, the former Chief of the Security Police and S.D., and I quote from a speech delivered by Heydrich on German Police Day, 1941, of which I ask the Tribunal to take judicial notice:

> "Secret State Police, Criminal Police, and S.D. are still adorned with the furtive and whispered secrecy of a political detective story. In a mixture of fear and shuddering-and yet at home with a certain feeling of security because of their presence - brutality, inhumanity bordering on the sadistic, and ruthlessness are attributed abroad to the men of this profession."

Those are the words of Heydrich, who was the former head of this organisation. Does your Honour want to go ahead?

DR. KURT KAUFMANN (Counsel for defendant Kaltenbrunner): I have just heard that during the afternoon the evidence will concern the defendant Kaltenbrunner. I therefore regard it as advisable to make a proposition regarding Kaltenbrunner immediately, before the recess, and not in the afternoon.

My suggestion is the following:

I ask that the trial against Kaltenbrunner be postponed during his absence. Kaltenbrunner, so far as the proceedings thus far have been concerned, has taken only a small part. The reason for his absence is an illness which, according to my opinion, is of a serious nature, for it is obvious that in so important a trial only a very serious illness can bring about the absence of a defendant and justify it. I have no doctor's report on his present condition. It therefore appears to me dubious whether he will be capable of attending the hearing at all in the future.

Be that as it may, my present suggestion that the trial of Kaltenbrunner be postponed is not in contradiction to paragraph 12 of the Charter. If a defendant is alive and cannot be brought to trial in person, then the trial can proceed against him in his absence. This is particularly justified if the defendant is concealing himself and if he thus is obliged to submit to the trial even in his absence.

But Kaltenbrunner is here in prison. He did not withdraw himself from the trial and he wishes nothing more than that he may be able to take a position as regards the accusation. But if such a defendant is absent through no fault of his own, it would hardly be consistent with justice if his trial were nevertheless carried out.

I should regret the procedure of the trial all the more since it is precisely now that Kaltenbrunner must have an opportunity to give me information in my capacity as his defence counsel. The particular indictment is not even known to him; it was given to him just before the Christmas recess.

I do not need to emphasise how much more difficult the defence's task is made by a continuation of the trial - indeed, it is made almost impossible.

THE PRESIDENT: The Tribunal will consider the application which has been made on behalf of counsel for the defendant Kaltenbrunner and will give its decision shortly.

The Tribunal will now adjourn until 2 o'clock.

COLONEL STOREY: If I may make just one statement in connection with that, if your Honour pleases?

THE PRESIDENT: Yes, certainly.

COLONEL STOREY: The evidence against Kaltenbrunner will be in connection with the part he played in these organisations, and we thought that, in the interest of time, the individual case against Kaltenbrunner could be presented simultaneously. Now, if it were not presented in this connection, it would be within a few days, early next week, in connection with the other individual defendants. Counsel mentions that he probably will not be able to be here for some time, and I thought I would make that statement.

THE PRESIDENT: Yes.

(A recess was taken until 1400 hours.)

THE PRESIDENT: The Tribunal has considered the motion made by counsel on behalf of Kaltenbrunner, and it considers that any evidence which you were intending to produce, which is directed against Kaltenbrunner individually and not against the organisations, ought to be postponed until the prosecution come to deal, as the Tribunal understands you do propose to deal, with each defendant individually; and the Tribunal thinks that Kaltenbrunner's case might properly be kept to the end of the individual defendants, and that the evidence which is especially brought against Kaltenbrunner might then be adduced. If Kaltenbrunner is then still unable to be in Court, that evidence will have to be given in his absence.

COLONEL STOREY: If your Honour pleases, I do not believe that the case, as we have it prepared now, can be separated as between the organisations and the individuals.

THE PRESIDENT: No, but if it bears against the organisations it can be adduced now.

COLONEL STOREY: I understand that, but if your Honour pleases, I say that the preparation that we have made is in connection both with the organisations and the individuals. In other words, it is a joint presentation. Therefore, under your Honour's ruling, as taken, it would have to go over until next week with the individual defendants' cases, because we prepared it so that it will affect the organisations as well as the defendant individually, because his acts are in connection with what he has done with the organisations included; in other words, we have not got it separated.

THE PRESIDENT: How will that affect you for this afternoon?

COLONEL STOREY: We can introduce a witness, next, but if your Honour pleases, in reference to the witness, he, of course, would affect the organisations, and incidently would affect Kaltenbrunner, too. I do not see how you could separate that, except that for the witnesses this afternoon the questions could be confined to the organisations.

THE PRESIDENT: Now, of course, all the evidence which has been given up to date, much of it in Kaltenbrunner's absence, has in one sense been against Kaltenbrunner in being evidence against the organisation of which he was the head.

COLONEL STOREY: Colonel Amen is going to examine the witness orally, and it is primarily evidence against the organisations; and, incidentally, it would affect Kaltenbrunner's individual liability.

THE PRESIDENT: I think the Tribunal would like you to go on with the evidence.

COLONEL STOREY: Yes. It has been suggested, if your Honour pleases, that we might have a few minutes to confer about the situation, about the witnesses.

THE PRESIDENT: You wish to adjourn for a few minutes?

COLONEL STOREY: Just a few minutes so that we can confer, as it changes our order of proof.

THE PRESIDENT: Very well.

COLONEL STOREY: Just ten minutes will be sufficient.

THE PRESIDENT: Yes, we will adjourn now.

(A recess was taken.)

THE PRESIDENT: The Tribunal will now hear the evidence which the prosecution desires to call, and in so far as it consists of oral testimony, the Tribunal will afford counsel for Kaltenbrunner the opportunity of cross-examining the witnesses now called, at a later stage if he wishes to do so.

DR. LUDWIG BABEL (Counsel for S.S. and S.D.): I was first appointed counsel for the members of the S.S. and S.D., who in these proceedings have asked for leave to be heard. My duties were circumscribed in such a manner that I was to present to the Court the motions in suitable form. Not until the Tribunal made its announcement of 17th December, 1945, was I appointed as defence counsel for the organisations of the S.S. and the S.D. As such I am not working on behalf of a client who could give me information or instructions for carrying on the defence. In order to obtain the necessary information I am, therefore, restricted to communicating with members of the organisations I am representing, most of which members are in prisoner of war camps or have been arrested. Thus far, because of the shortness of time, I have not been able to get the necessary information.

After 17th December, 1945, thousands of requests were submitted to me by the Court and in the short period of time, since then, I have not been able to work on all of them.

According to Article 16 of the Charter, a copy of the Indictment and of all pertaining documents - written in a language he understands - is to be handed to the defendant within a reasonable time prior to the beginning of the trial. This provision should, presumably, be also applied to the indicted organisations. To serve the Indictment on the organisations is not provided for in the rules of procedure nor has the Tribunal so far ordered it.

In view of the very extensive work involved I personally was not in a position to have copies prepared in a number sufficient for distribution to the members of the organisations in the various camps so that they could express their views and give me the needed information.

In face of these circumstances, for which neither I nor the organisaitons which I am representing are reponsible, I am not in a position to cross-examine a witness. who would be heard to-day thereby making use of the right accorded to me as defence counsel. To hear a witness against the defendant Kaltenbrunner likewise concerns the organisations which I represent, the S.S. and the S.D. To hear this witness at this point would mean limiting the defence.

I therefore submit a motion to postpone the further discussion of the charges against the organisations of the S.S. and the S.D. By visiting the camps, in which there are members of the organisations of the S.S. and S.D., and after discussions with them, I shall be able to obtain the information needed for the defence. I should like to add that thereby no delay in the proceedings would be caused and, I presume, this would in no way place a burden upon the prosecution.

THE PRESIDENT: If you will allow me to interrupt you, I understand your application to be, that you are not in a position to cross-examine these witnesses this afternoon, and that you wish for an opportunity similar to that which I have already accorded to the counsel for Kaltenbrunner, to be accorded to you. You wish for an opportunity to cross-examine these witnesses at a later stage, is that right?

DR. BABEL: Yes. At the same time, however, I should like to point out at this moment that, through the peculiarity of the task that has been allotted to me, my defence is being made so difficult that to cover questions subsequently -

THE PRESIDENT: Let us not take up time by that. Was your application that you might have an opportunity of cross-examining these witnesses at a later date?

DR. BABEL: My motion had that meaning but its purpose was also to make the defence practicable and ensure that the witnesses should not be heard at a time when I cannot make use to the fullest extent of the privileges granted me by the Charter.

THE PRESIDENT: The Tribunal is ready to give you the opportunity of cross-examining these witnesses at a later date.

LT. WHITNEY R. HARRIS: May it please the Tribunal.

We submit Document Book BB as a separate Document Book, relating to the defendant Kaltenbrunner. This book contains our documents, from which quotations will be made during this presentation. Reference will be made to three or four other documents contained in the Document Book on the Gestapo and the S.D.

During the past three Court days, the Tribunal has heard evidence of the criminality of the S.S., the S.D. and the Gestapo. The fusion of these organisations into the shock formations of the Hitler Police-State has been explained from an organisational standpoint. There is before the Tribunal a defendant who represents these organisations through the official positions which he held in the S.S. and the German Police, and whose career gives added significance to this unity of the S.S. and the Nazi Police. The name of this defendant is Ernst Kaltenbrunner.

I now offer Document 2938-PS as the Exhibit next in order, USA 511. This is an article which appeared in Die Deutsche Polizei, the magazine of the Security Police and S.D., on 15th May, 1943, at Page 193, entitled, "Dr. Ernst Kaltenbrunner, the New Chief the Security Police and S.D." and I quote the beginning of the article:

"S.S. Gruppenfuehrer Dr. jur. Kaltenbrunner was born the son of the lawyer Dr. Hugo Kaltenbrunner, on 4th October, 1903, at Ried on Inn, near Braunau. He spent his youth in the native district of the Fuehrer, with whom his kinsfolk, originally a hereditary farming clan, had been closely connected since olden times. Later he moved with his parents to the little market-town Raab, and then to Linz, on the Danube, where he attended the State Realgymnasium, and there he passed his final examination in 1921."

The next paragraph describes Kaltenbrunner's legal education, his nationalistic activities and his opposition to Catholic-Christian-Social student groups. It states that after 1928 Kaltenbrunner worked as a lawyer-candidate in Linz. The article continues, and I quote, reading the third paragraph:

"As early as January, 1934, Dr. Kaltenbrunner was imprisoned by the Dollfuss

Government on account of his Nazi views and sent with other leading National Socialists into the concentration camp Kaisersteinbruch. He caused and led a hunger strike and forced the Government to dismiss 490 National Socialist prisoners. In the following year he was imprisoned again, because of suspicion of high treason and committed to the Court-Martial of Wels (Upper Danube). After an investigation of many months, the accusation of high treason collapsed, but he was sentenced to six months' imprisonment for conspiracy. After the spring of 1935, Dr. Kaltenbrunner was the leader of the Austrian S.S., the right to practise his profession having been suspended because of his National Socialist views. It redounds to his credit that in this important position he succeeded, through energetic leadership, in maintaining the unity of the Austrian S.S., which he had built up, in spite of all persecution, and succeeded in committing it successfully at the right moment.

After the annexation, in which the S.S. was a decisive factor, he was appointed State Secretary for Security Matters on 11th March, 1938, in the new National Socialist Cabinet of Dr. Seyss-Inquart. A few hours later he was able to report to the Reichsfuehrer S.S. Heinrich Himmler, who had landed at Aspern, the Vienna Airport, on 12th March, 1938, 3 a.m., as the first National Socialist leader, that the Movement had achieved complete victory and that " - the article quotes Kaltenbrunner - " the S.S. is in formation awaiting further orders " - closing Kaltenbrunner's statement.

"The Fuehrer promoted Dr. Kaltenbrunner on the day of the annexation, to S.S. Brigadefuehrer and leader of the S.S.- Abschnitt Ober Donau. On 11th September, 1938, this was followed by his promotion to S.S. Gruppenfuehrer."

The Tribunal will recall evidence heretofore received, and I refer to Page 254 (Part I) of the transcript of these proceedings, of the telephone conversation between Goering and Seyss- Inquart, in which Goering stated that Kaltenbrunner was to have the Department of Security.

I continue quoting the last paragraph from this article:

"During the liquidation of the Austrian National Government and the reorganisation of Austria into Alps and Danube Districts, he was appointed Higher S.S. and Police Leader with the Reich Government in Vienna, Lower Danube and Upper Danube in Corps Area 17, and in April, 1941, he was promoted to Major General of Police."

Kaltenbrunner thereby became the little Himmler of Austria.

According to Der Grossdeutsche Reichstag, Vierte Wahlperiode, 1938, published by F. Kienast, at Page 262, our Document 2892-PS, Kaltenbrunner joined the Nazi Party and the S.S. in Austria in 1932. He was Party Member 300179 and S.S. Member 13039. Prior to 1933 he was the "Gauredner" and legal adviser to S.S. Division 8. After 1933, he was the leader of S.S. Regiment 37, and later the leader of S.S. Division 8. Kaltenbrunner was given the highest Nazi Party decorations, the Golden Insignia of Honour and the Blutorden. He was a member of the Reichstag after 1938.

I now offer Document 3427-PS, as Exhibit next in order USA 512. This is also an article which appeared in Die Deutsche Polizei, the magazine of the Security Police and S.D., 12th February, 1943, at Page 65, and I quote:

"S.S. Gruppenfuehrer Kaltenbrunner Appointed Chief of the Security Police and of the S.D.

Berlin, 30th January, 1943.

Upon suggestion of the Reichsfuehrer S.S. and Chief of German Police, the

Fuehrer has appointed S.S. Gruppenfuehrer and Major General of Police Dr. Ernst Kaltenbrunner as Chief of the Security Police and of the S.D. as successor of S.S. Obergruppenfuehrer and Lieutenant General of Police Reinhard Heydrich, who passed away 4th June, 1942."

The Tribunal has heard frequent references made to the speech of Himmler delivered on 4th October, 1943, at Posen, Poland, to Gruppenfuehrers of the S.S., our Document 1919- PS, heretofore received as Exhibit USA170, in which, with unmatched frankness, Himmler discussed the barbaric programme and criminal activities of the S.S. and the Security Police. Near the beginning of the speech Himmler referred to, and I quote merely this one sentence: "Our comrade, S.S. Gruppenfuehrer Ernst Kaltenbrunner, who has succeeded our fallen friend Heydrich."

Kaltenbrunner carried out the responsibilities as Chief of the Security Police and S. D. to the satisfaction of Himmler and Hitler, for on 9th December 1944, according to the "Befehlsblatt " of the Security Police and S.D.

DR. KAUFMANN (Counsel for defendant Kaltenbrunner): May I interrupt just for a second ? I understood the decision of the Tribunal to be that the proceedings against Kaltenbrunner were to be postponed until Kaltenbrunner is fit for trial and now the matter of Kaltenbrunner is being discussed.

THE PRESIDENT: No, the decision which the Tribunal indicated before was based upon the view that the evidence could be divided between evidence which bore directly against Kaltenbrunner and evidence which bore against the organisation of the Gestapo, but, when you attended before us in closed session, it was explained that it was impossible to do that and that the evidence was so inextricably mingled that it was impossible to direct the evidence solely to the organisation and not to include that against Kaltenbrunner. Accordingly the Tribunal decided that they would go on with the evidence, which the prosecution desired to present, in its entirety, but that they would give you the opportuinty of cross-examining any witnesses who might be called, at a later date. Of course, you will, in addition to that, have the fullest opportunity of dealing with any documentary evidence which bears against Kaltenbrunner when the time comes for you to present the defence on behalf of Kaltenbrunner.

Do you follow that ?

DR. KAUMANN: Of course.

THE PRESIDENT: You will have the opportunity of cross-examining any witness who is called this afternoon or to-morrow, at a later date, a date which will be convenient to yourself. And in addition, with reference to any documentary evidence such as is now being presented by counsel for the United States, you will have full opportunity at a future date of dealing any way that it seems right to you to do.

DR. KAUFMANN: Yes. May I just say one word more? The misunderstanding from which I am suffering is probably due to the fact that I was of the opinion that witnesses were now to be heard, but now I hear that the evidence - that is to say, a vastly greater complex of evidence - is to be put forward. Now that I hear that the Tribunal is also admitting the evidence in its entirety I shall, of course, have to submit to this decision.

LT. HARRIS: Kaltenbrunner carried out the responsibilities as Chief of the Security Police and S.D. to the satisfaction of Hirmmler and Hitler, it for on 9th December, 1944, according to the " Befehlsblatt " of the Securi y Police and S.D., No. 51, Page 361, our 2770-PS, he received, as Chief of the Security Police and S.D., the decoration known as the Knight's Cross of the War Merit with Crossed Swords, one of the highest military decorations. By that time Kaltenbrunner had been promoted to the high rank of S.S. Obergruppenfuehrer and General of the Police.

I invite the attention of the Tribunal to the organisation chart entitled "The Position of Kaltenbrunner and the Gestapo and S.D. in the German Police System," Exhibit USA 493. As Chief of the Security Police and S.D., Kaltenbrunner was the Head of the Gestapo, the Kripo and the S.D. and of the R.S.H.A., which was a department of the S.S. and the Reich Ministry of the Interior. He was in charge of the regional offices of the Gestapo, the S.D. and the Kripo within Germany, and of the Einsatz Groups and Einsatz Commandos in the occupied territories.

Directly under Kaltenbrunner were the Chiefs of the main offices of the R.S.H.A., including Amt III (the S.D. within Germany), Amt IV (the Gestapo), Amt V (the Kripo), and Amt VI (Foreign Intelligence).

I offer Document 2939-PS as Exhibit next in order, Exhibit USA 513. This is the affidavit of Walter Schellenberg, who was chief of Amt VI of the R.S.H.A. from the autumn of 1941 to the end of the war. I am going to read a very small portion of this affidavit, beginning with the sixth sentence of the first paragraph:

"On or about 25th January, 1943, I went together with Kaltenbrunner to Himmler's headquarters at Loetzen in East Prussia. All of the Amt Chiefs of the R.S.H.A. were present at this meeting, and Himmler informed us that Kaltenbrunner was to be appointed Chief of the Security Police and S.D. (R.S.H.A.) as successor to Heydrich. His appointment was effective as from 30th January, 1943. 1 know of no limitation placed on Kaltenbrunner's authority as Chief of the Security Police and S.D. He promptly entered upon the duties of the office and assumed direct charge of the office and control over the Amt. All important matters of all Amter had to clear through Kaltenbrunner."

During Kaltenbrunner's term in office as Chief of the Security Police and S.D., many crimes were committed by the Security Police and S.D. pursuant to policy established by the R.S.H.A. or upon orders issued out of the R.S.H.A., for all of which Kaltenbrunner was responsible by virtue of his office. Each of these crimes has been discussed in detail in the case against the Gestapo and S.D., and reference is here made to that presentation. Evidence now will be offered only to show that these crimes continued after Kaltenbrunner became Chief of the Security Police and S.D. on 30th January, 1943.

The first crime for which Kaltenbrunner is responsible as Chief of the Security Police and S.D. is the murder and mistreatment of civilians of occupied countries by the Einsatz Groups. There were at least five Einsatz Groups operating in the East during Kaltenbrunner's term in office.

The "Befehlsblatt" of the Security Police and S.D. - and this is contained in our Document 2890-PS, of which I ask the Tribunal to take judicial notice - contains reference to Einsatz Groups A, B, D, G and Croatia during the period of August, 1943, to January, 1945.

I shall not read from the document which contains those excerpts, but the Tribunal will note those references to the name "Einsatz Groups," indicating that they were operating during the time that Kaltenbrunner was Chief of the Security Police and S.D. The Tribunal will recall Document 1104-PS, which has heretofore been received as Exhibit USA 483. I will only refer in passing to this document, which contained a lengthy and critical report on the conduct of the Security Police in exterminating the Jewish population of Sluzk, White Ruthenia. That report was submitted to Heydrich on 21st November, 1941. Yet, the same conditions of horror and cruelty continued to characterise the operations of Einsatzkornmandos in the East while Kaltenbrunner was Chief of the Security Police and S.D. I refer to Document R-135, which has heretofore been received as Exhibit USA 289, and I will not read anything from that but simply refresh the Tribunal's recollection of the report of Gunther, the prison warden at Minsk, under date of 31st May, 1943, to the General Commissioner for White Ruthenia, in which he pointed out that after 13th April, 1943, the S.D. had pursued a policy of removing all gold teeth, bridgework and fillings of Jews, an hour or two before they were murdered.

The Tribunal will also recall in this Exhibit the report of 18th June, 1943, to the Reich Minister for the occupied territories describing the practice of the police battalions of locking men, women and children into barns which were then set on fire.

The second crime for which Kaltenbrunner is responsible as Chief of the Security Police and S.D. is the execution of racial and political undesirables.

THE PRESIDENT: Lieutenant Harris, I think you are going perhaps a little bit too fast, and it is difficult for us to follow you when you are referring so quickly to these documents.

LIEUTENANT HARRIS: Thank you, sir.

The second crime for which Kaltenbrunner is responsible as Chief of the Security Police and S.D. is the execution of racial and political undesirables screened out of prisoner-of-war camps by the Gestapo. The Tribunal will recall Document 2542-PS, heretofore received as Exhibit USA 489.

I believe, you will find that document in the Gestapo Document Book. It was introduced this morning.

THE PRESIDENT: The Lindow affidavit?

LIEUTENANT HARRIS: Yes. That is the Lindow affidavit that indicates that the programme of screening prisoner of war camps continued during 1943.

The third crime for which Kaltenbrunner is responsible as Chief of the Security Police and S.D. was the taking of recaptured prisoners of war -

THE PRESIDENT: Wait a minute. You have not yet drawn our attention to any specific paragraph which shows that this programme was in operation after 1943; you are passing on to something else whilst I am looking at the document to see what I have got.

LIEUTENANT HARRIS: Referring specifically to the third paragraph, if the Tribunal please, which has heretofore been read into evidence.

THE PRESIDENT: That only says until about the beginning of 1943.

LIEUTENANT HARRIS: It says early in 1943 the department was dissolved and it went into the departments in Subsection IV B. The work concerning Russian prisoners of war must then have been done by IV B2a.

THE PRESIDENT: Yes. Well, that is all you want it for, is it not

LIEUTENANT HARRIS: Yes.

The third crime for which Kaltenbrunner is responsible as Chief of the Security Police and S.D. was the taking of recaptured prisoners-of- war to concentration camps where they were executed. I invite the attention of the Tribunal to Document 1650-PS, which has heretofore been received as Exhibit USA 246. This is the secret Gestapo order, the" Kugel Erlass," or "Bullet Decree," under which escaped prisoners-of-war were sent to concentration camps by the Security Police and S.D. for execution.

This order, dated 4th March, 1944, was signed - and I quote - "Chief of the Security Police and of the Security Service, for the Chief," (signed) " Mueller."

I now offer Document L-158 as Exhibit next in order. This is Exhibit USA 54. I am not going to read this document since it is similar to the previous document offered, but I do wish to refer to the marked passages. First: "On 2nd March, 1944, the Chief of the Security Police and S.D., Berlin, forwarded the following O.K.W. order." Then follows the statement that upon recapture certain escaped prisoners of war should be turned over to the Chief of the Security Police and S.D.

The document goes on to say - and I quote - "In this connection the Chief of the Security Police and S.D. has issued the following instructions." Detailed instructions follow concerning the turning over of such prisoners to the commandant of Mauthausen under the operation "Bullet." Further, this order states - and I quote - this is at the very end of the order - "The list of the recaptured officers and non-working N.C.O. prisoners of war will be kept here by IV A I. To enable a report to be made punctually to the Chief of the Sipo and S.D., Berlin, statements of the numbers involved must reach Radom by 20th June, 1944."

I recall the attention of the Tribunal to Document 2285-PS, which was received this morning as Exhibit USA 490.

THE PRESIDENT: Has that Document L-158 already been put in evidence?

LT. HARRIS: No, Sir, I have just put in those portions. I have just put the document in evidence at this time, Sir. The document has not been read in its entirety for the reason that the contents, other than the quoted portions, are substantially the same as Document 1650, which has been read at length.

THE PRESIDENT: You say it is the same as 1650?

LT. HARRIS: It is, Sir, substantially the same. It relates to the same subject. It was, however, addressed to a different party, and I particularly wish to place before the Tribunal the last paragraph which has been quoted and read into evidence.

THE PRESIDENT: The last paragraph does not mean very much by itself, does it?

LT. HARRIS: Very well, Sir. Then, if the Tribunal will permit it, I would like to read the document in its entirety.

THE PRESIDENT: Do you mean that 1650 has got these paragraphs 1, 2 and 3 in it?

LT. HARRIS: Yes, Sir. That is exactly what I do mean, Sir.

I will call the attention of the Tribunal to Document 2285-PS, which was received in evidence this morning as Exhibit USA 490. That was the affidavit of Lt. Colonel Gast and Lt. Veith of the French Army, who stated that during 1943 and 1944 prisoners of war were murdered at Mauthausen under the "Bullet Decree." I am sure the Tribunal will recall that document.

The fourth crime for which Kaltenbrunner is responsible as Chief of the Security Police and S.D. was the commitment of racial and political undesirables to concentration camps and annihilation camps, for slave labour and mass murder. Before Kaltenbrunner became Chief of the Security Police and S.D., on 30th January, 1943, he was fully cognisant of conditions in concentration camps and of the fact that concentration camps were used for slave labour and mass murder. The Tribunal will recall from previous evidence that Mauthausen concentration camp was established in Austria and that Kaltenbrunner was the Higher S.S. and Police Leader for Austria. This concentration camp, as shown by Document 1063A-PS, which was received this morning as Exhibit USA 492, was classified by Heydrich in January, 1941, in Category III, a camp for the most heavily accused prisoners and for asocial prisoners who were considered incapable of being reformed. The Tribunal will recall that prisoners of war to be executed under the "Bullet Decree " were sent to Mauthausen. As will be shown hereafter, Kaltenbrunner was a frequent visitor to Mauthausen concentration camp. On one such visit in 1942 Kaltenbrunner personally observed the gas chamber in action. I now offer Document 2753- PS as

Exhibit next in order, Exhibit USA515. This is the affidavit of Alois Hoellriegl, former guard at Mauthausen concentration camp. The affidavit states, and I quote:

"I, Alois Hoellriegl, being first duly sworn, declare I was a member of the Totenkopf S. S. and stationed at the Mauthausen concentration camp from January, 1940, until the end of the war. On one occasion, I believe it was in the fall of 1942, Ernst Kaltenbrunner visited Mauthausen. I was on guard duty at the time and saw him twice. He went down into the gas chamber with Ziereis, commandant of the camp, at a time when prisoners were being gassed. The sound accompanying the gassing operation was well known to me. I heard the gassing taking place while Kaltenbrunner was present.

I saw Kaltenbrunner come up from the gas cellar after the gassing operation had been completed.

(Signed) Hoellriegl"

On one occasion Kaltenbrunner made an inspection of the camp grounds at Mauthausen with Himmler and had his photograph taken during the course of the inspection. I offer Document 2641-PS as exhibit next in order, Exhibit USA 5 16.

This exhibit consists of two affidavits and a series of photographs. Here are the original photographs in my hand. The original photographs are the small ones which have been enlarged, and those in the Document Book are not very good reproductions, but the Tribunal will see better reproductions which are being handed to it.

DR. KAUFMANN (Counsel for defendant Kaltenbrunner): Since the whole accusation against Kaltenbrunner has nevertheless been brought forward, I feel bound to make a motion on a matter of principle. I could have made this motion this morning just as well. It is in reference to the question of whether affidavits may be read or not. 1 know that this question has already been the subject of consultation by the Tribunal and that the Tribunal has already decided this question in a definite manner. When I ask that this question be decided once more, it is for a special reason.

Every trial is something dynamic. What was correct at that time may at a later date be wrong. The most important and most significant trial in history rests in many important points on the mere reading of affidavits which have been taken down by the prosecution exclusively, according to its own maxims.

The reading of affidavits is not satisfactory in the long run. It is becoming more necessary from hour to hour to see, to hear for once a witness for the prosecution and to test his credibility and the reliability of his memory. There are many witnesses standing, so to speak, at the door of this Courtroom, and they need only be called in. To hear the witness at a later stage is not sufficient; nor is it certain that the Tribunal will permit a hearing on the same evidential subject. I therefore oppose the further reading of the affidavit just announced. The meaning of Article 19 of the Charter should not be killed by a literal interpretation.

THE PRESIDENT: Is your application that you want to cross-examine the witness or is your application that the affidavit should not be read ?

DR. KAUFMANN: The latter.

THE PRESIDENT: That the affidavit should not be read ?

DR. KAUFMANN: Yes.

THE PRESIDENT: Are you referring to the affidavit of Hoellriegl, Document 2753-PS ?

DR. KAUFMANN: Yes.

THE PRESIDENT: The Tribunal is of the opinion that the affidavit, which is upon a relevant point, upon a material point, is evidence which ought to be admitted under Article 19 of the Charter, but they will consider any motion which counsel for Kaltenbrunner may think fit to make for cross-examination of the witness who made the affidavit, if he is available and could be called.

LT. HARRIS: Yes, Sir. They have been offered in evidence as the exhibit next in order, and I wish to refer to the first affidavit accompanying them, which appears in the Document Book.

THE PRESIDENT: Yes.

LT. HARRIS: It being the affidavit of Alois Hoellriegl.

THE PRESIDENT: Yes. You had handed up the affidavit at the same time, had you not?

LT. HARRIS: Yes, Sir, I did, Sir. That affidavit states, and I quote:

"I was a member of the Totenkopf S.S. and stationed in the Mauthausen concentration camp from January, 1940, until the end of the war. I am thoroughly familiar with all of the buildings and grounds at Mauthausen concentration camp. I have been shown Document 2641-PS, which is a series of six photographs. I recognise all these photographs as having been taken at Mauthausen concentration camp. With respect to the first photograph I positively identify Heinrich Himmler as the man on the left, Ziereis, the commandant of Mauthausen concentration camp, in the centre, and Ernst Kaltenbrunner as the man on the right."

THE PRESIDENT: He does not say, does he, at what date the photographs were taken?

LT. HARRIS: No, Sir. I have no evidence as to what date the photographs were taken, Sir.

THE PRESIDENT: Just that Kaltenbrunner was there?

LT. HARRIS: Just that Kaltenbrunner was there, at some time, in the company of Ziereis and Himmler.

THE PRESIDENT: Yes.

LT. HARRIS: With full knowledge of conditions in and the purpose of concentration camps, Kaltenbrunner ordered or permitted to be ordered in his name, the commitment of persons to concentration camps.

I offer Document L-38 as exhibit next in order, Exhibit USA S17. This is the affidavit of Herman Pister, the former commandant of Buchenwald concentration camp, which was taken on 1st August, 1945, at Freising, Germany, in the course of an official military investigation by the United States Army, and I quote from it as follows, beginning with the second paragraph:

"With exception of the mass delivery of prisoners from the concentration camps of the occupied territory all prisoners were sent to the concentration camp Buchenwald by order of the Reichssicherheitshauptamt - Reich Security Main Office - Berlin. These orders for protective custody (red forms) were in most cases signed with the name 'Kaltenbrunner.' The few remaining protective custody orders were signed by 'Foerster'."

I now offer Document 2477-PS as exhibit next in order, Exhibit USA 5 18. This is the affidavit of Willy Litzenberg, former Chief of Department IV A Ib in the R.S.H.A. This document reads in part as follows, and I quote, beginning with the second paragraph:

"The right of summary taking into protective custody belongs to the Directors of the State Police H.Q.'s or State Police Offices; previously for a period of 21 days; later, I think, for a period of 56 days. Custody exceeding this time had to be sanctioned by the competent Office for Protective Custody in the R.S.H.A. The Regulations for Protective Custody or the signing of the Protective Custody Order could only be issued through the Director of the R.S.H.A. as Chief of the Sipo and S.D. All Regulations and Protective Custody Orders that I have seen bore a facsimile stamp of Heydrich or Kaltenbrunner. As far as I can remember, I have never seen a document of this kind with another name as signature. How far and to whom the Chief of the Sipo and S.D. possibly gave authority for the use of his facsimile stamp, I do not know. Perhaps the Chief of Amt IV possessed a similar authority.

The greater part of the Protective Custody Office was transferred to Prague. Only one staff remained in Berlin."

I now offer Document 2745-PS as exhibit next in order, Exhibit USA 519.

This is an order under date 7th July, 1943, which was found at the former office of the section of the Gestapo which handled protective custody matters in Prague. It was an order to the Prague Office to send a teletype message to the Gestapo office in Koeslin, ordering protective custody of one Racke, and her commitment to the concentration camp at Ravensbrueck for refusing to work. The order carried the facsimile signature of Kaltenbrunner and I invite the attention of the Tribunal to the original which has that facsimile for the arrest. Orders of this type were the basis for the orders actually sent out to the Prague office, which carried the teletype signature of Kaltenbrunner. At the bottom of the page the Tribunal will note the facsimile stamp of Kaltenbrunner.

I next refer to Document L-215, which has heretofore been received as Exhibit USA 243, and which contains 25 orders for arrest issued out of the Prague office of the R.S.H.A. to the Einsatz.

THE PRESIDENT: Which number are you dealing with now?

LT. HARRIS: I am dealing with Document L-215. I believe the Tribunal will recall this document, which has heretofore been received in evidence, and which contains 25 orders for arrest issued out of the Prague office of the R.S.H.A. to the Einsatz Commando of Luxembourg, all of which carry the typed signature of Kaltenbrunner. And the Court will remember, and I am holding up the original document, that these arrest orders were the red forms which the Commandant of Buchenwald referred to in his affidavit as being the forms which he saw coming from R.S.H.A. committing persons to Buchenwald.

The concentration camps to which persons were committed, according to Document L-215, by Kaltenbrunner, included Dachau, Natzweiler, Sachsenhausen, and Buchenwald.

THE PRESIDENT: What was the date of it?

LT. HARRIS: Most of these, Sir, were in 1944. I believe they are all in 1944.

THE PRESIDENT: It does not appear on the document does it?

LT. HARRIS: It does appear, Sir, on the original document. The first page of this translation is a summary of all of these. There is only one of the dossiers which has been translated in full, and the date on that one is 15th February, 1944.

THE PRESIDENT: Yes; I see.

LT. HARRIS: Among the grounds specified on these orders carrying the typed signature of Kaltenbrunner were, quoting:

"Strongly suspected of working to the detriment of the Reich; spiteful statements inimical to Germany, as well as aspersions and threats against persons active in the National Socialist Movement; strongly suspected of aiding deserters."

I now offer Document 2239-PS as exhibit next in order, Exhibit USA 52o. This is a file of 42 telegrams sent by the Prague office of the R.S.H.A. to the Gestapo office at Darmstadt, and they all carry the teletype signature of Kaltenbrunner. These commitment orders were issued during the period from 20th September, 1944, to 2nd February, 1945. The concentration camps to which Kaltenbrunner sent these people included Sachsenhausen, Ravensbruck, Buchenwald, Bergen-Belsen, Flossenburg, and Theresienstadt. Nationalities included Czech, German, French, Dutch, Italian, Corsican, Lithuanian, Greek and Jews. Grounds included refusal to work, religious propaganda, sex relations with prisoners of war, communist statements, loafing on the job, working against the Reich, spreading of rumours detrimental to morale, "action Gitter," breach of work contracts, statements against Germany, assault of foremen, defeatist statements, and theft and escape from gaol.

Not only did Kaltenbrunner commit persons to concentration camps, but he authorised executions in concentration camps. I now offer Document L-51 as exhibit next in order, Exhibit USA 521. This is the affidavit of Adolf Zutter, the former adjutant of Mauthausen concentration camp, in the course of an official military investigation of the United States Army, on 2nd August, 1945, at Linz, Austria. This affidavit states, and I am quoting from paragraph 3:

"Standartenfuehrer Ziereis, the commander of Camp Mauthausen, gave me a large number of execution orders after opening the secret mail, because I was the adjutant and I had to deliver these to Obersturmfuehrer Schulz. These orders of execution were written approximately in the following form."

There follows in the affidavit a description of the order for execution issued by the R.S.H.A. to the commander of the concentration camp Mauthausen. I omit quoting that description and continue at the next paragraph:

"Orders for execution also came without the name of the court of justice. Until the assassination of Heydrich, these orders were signed by him or by his competent deputy. Later on the orders were signed by Kaltenbrunner, but mostly they were signed by his deputy, Gruppenfuehrer Mueller.

Dr. Kaltenbrunner, who signed the above-mentioned orders, had the rank of S.S. General (S.S. Obergruppenfuehrer) and was the Chief of the Reich Security Main Office.

Dr. Kaltenbrunner is about 40 years old, height about 1.76 to 1.80 metres, and has deep fencing scars on his face. When Dr. Kaltenbrunner was only a Higher S.S. and Police Officer, he visited the camp several times, later on as the Chief of Reich Security Main Office (R.S.H.A.) he visited the camp too, though much less frequently. During these visits, the commander usually received him outside the building of the camp headquarters and reported.

Concerning the American military mission, which landed behind the German front in the Slovakian or Hungarian area in January, 1945, I remember when these officers were brought to Camp Mauthausen. I suppose the number of the arrivals was about 12 to 15 men. They wore a uniform, which was American or Canadian, brown-green colour shirt and cloth cap. Eight or ten days after their arrival the execution order came in by telegraph or teletype. Standartenfuehrer Ziereis came to me, into my office, and told me: 'Now Kaltenbrunner has given permission for the execution.' This letter was secret and had the signature ' signed Kaltenbrunner.' Then these people were shot according to martial law and their belongings were given to me by

Oberscharfuehrer Niedermeier."

The fifth crime for which Kaltenbrunner is responsible as Chief of the Security Police and S.D. was the deportation of citizens of occupied territories for forced labour and the disciplining of forced labour.

I am sure the Tribunal will recall, without referring to it, Document 3012-PS. which has heretofore been received as Exhibit USA 190. That was the letter from the head of the Sonderkommando of the Sipo and S.D., which stated that the Ukraine would have to provide a million workers for the armament industry and that force should be used where necessary. That letter was dated 19th March, 1943.

Kaltenbrunner's responsibility for the disciplining of foreign labour is shown by Document 1063B-PS, which has heretofore been received as Exhibit USA 492. No part of this letter has been read into the record. This letter dated 26th July, 1943, was addressed to Higher S.S. and Police Leaders, Commanders and Inspectors of the Sipo and S.D., and to the Chiefs of Einsatz Groups B and D.

The Tribunal will recall that Einsatz Groups A, B, C, and D, operating in the East, carried out the extermination of Jews and communist leaders. This document proves Kaltenbrunner's control over Einsatz Groups B and D. It is signed "Kaltenbrunner." The first paragraph provides as follows:

> "The Reichsfuehrer S.S. has given his consent that besides concentration camps, which come under the jurisdiction of the S.S. Economic Administration Main Office, further labour reformatory camps may be created, for which the Security Police alone is competent. These labour reformatory camps are dependent on the authorisation of the Reich Security Main Office, which can only be granted in case of emergency (great number of foreign workers, and so forth)."

I now offer Document D-473 as exhibit next in order, Exhibit USA 522. It should be right at the beginning of the Document Book. This letter signed " Kaltenbrunner " was sent by him under date of 4th December, 1944, to Regional Offices of the Criminal Police.

The Tribunal will recall that Kaltenbrunner's responsibility covered the Criminal Police as well as the Gestapo. It provides in part, and I quote, reading at the beginning of the letter:

> "According to the Decree of 30th June, 1943, crimes committed by Polish and Soviet- Russian civilian labourers are being prosecuted by the State Police (Head) Offices, and even in those cases, where for the time being the Criminal Police had, within the sphere of its competence, carried on the inquiries. For the purpose of speeding up the process and in order to save manpower, the Decree of 30th June, 1943, is altered, and the Criminal Police (Head) Offices are authorised as from now on to prosecute, themselves, the crimes they are inquiring into, within the sphere of their competence, in so far as they are cases of minor or medium crimes."

I begin with the second paragraph:

> "The following are available to the Criminal Police as a means of prosecution:
> Police imprisonment.
> Admission into a concentration camp for preventive custody as being anti-social or dangerous to the community."

And next to the last paragraph:

> "Their stay in the concentration camp is normally to be for the duration of the war. Besides this, the Criminal Police (Head) Offices are authorised to hand over Polish and Soviet-Russian civilian labourers in suitable cases and with the

agreement of the competent State Police (Head) Offices to the Gestapo's penal camps for the 'education for labour.' Where the possibilities of prosecuting an individual case are insufficient because of the peculiarity of the case, the case is to be handed over to the competent State Police (Head) Office.

Signed: Dr. Kaltenbrunner."

In addition to sending foreign workers to Gestapo labour camps, Kaltenbrunner punished foreign workers by committing them to concentration camps. I offer Document 2582-PS as the exhibit next in order, USA 523.

This is a series of four teletype orders committing individuals to concentration camps. I invite the attention of the Tribunal to the second order dated the 18th of June, 1943, under which the Gestapo at Saarbrucken was ordered to deliver a Pole to the concentration camp Natzweiler as a skilled workman, and to the third teletype dated the 12th of December, 1944, in which the Gestapo at Darmstadt was ordered to commit a Greek to the concentration camp Buchenwald because he was drifting around without occupation, and to the fourth teletype dated the 9th of February, 1945, in which the Gestapo at Darmstadt in Benslein was ordered to commit a French citizen to Buchenwald for shirking work and insubordination. All of those orders are signed, Kaltenbrunner.

I offer document 2580-PS as Exhibit next in order, USA 524. This document contains three more of these red-form orders for protective custody, all signed Kaltenbrunner. The first one shows that a citizen of the Netherlands was taken into protective custody for work sabotage, and the second one shows that a French citizen was taken into protective custody for work sabotage and insubordination, both under date 2 December, 1944.

The sixth crime for which Kaltenbrunner is responsible as Chief of the Security Police and S.D. is the executing of captured commandos and paratroopers and the protecting of civilians who lynched Allied fliers.

The Tribunal will recall, I am sure, without referring to it, the Hitler Order of 18 October, 1942, which was introduced this morning, Document 498-PS, Exhibit USA 501, to the effect that commandos, even in uniform, were to be exterminated to the last man, and that individual members captured by the police in occupied territory were to be handed over to the S.D.

I now offer document 1276-PS as Exhibit next in order, USA 525. This is an express top secret letter from the Chief of the Security Police and S.D. signed "Mueller, by order," to the Supreme Command of the Armed Forces, in which the Chief of the Security Police and S.D. states, and I quote from the third paragraph of the second page of the English translation:

"I have instructed the 'Befehlshaber' of the Security Police and the S.D. in Paris to treat such parachutists in English uniform as members of the commando operations in accordance with the Fuehrer's order of 18 October, 1942, and to inform the military authorities in France that there must be corresponding treatment at the hands of the armed forces."

This letter was dated 17th June, 1944. That executions were carried out by the S.D. pursuant to the said Hitler order of 18th October, 1942, while Kaltenbrunner was Chief of the Security Police and S.D., is indicated by Document 526-PS heretofore received as Exhibit USA 502 ; that was the order introduced this morning; I am sure the Tribunal recalls it.

The policy of the police to protect civilians who lynched Allied fliers was effective during the period that Kaltenbrunner served as Chief of the Security Police and S.D. I now offer Document 2990-PS as Exhibit next in order, USA 526. This is an affidavit of Walter Schellenberg, the former Chief of Amt VI of the R.S.H.A., and provides in paragraph 7 - this is all I am going to read from the affidavit:

> "In 1944, on another occasion but also in the course of an Amtschef conference, I heard fragments of a conversation between Kaltenbrunner and Muller. I remember distinctly the following remarks of Kaltenbrunner:
> 'All officers of the S.D. and the Security Police are to be informed that pogroms of the populace against English and American terror fliers are not to be interfered with. On the contrary, this hostile mood is to be fostered.'"

The seventh crime for which Kaltenbrunner is responsible as Chief of the Security Police and S.D. is the taking of civilians of occupied countries to Germany for secret trial and punishment and the punishment of civilians of occupied territories by "summary methods." The fact that this crime continued after the 30th of January, 1943, is shown by Document 835-PS, which is offered as Exhibit next in order, USA 527. This is a letter from the High Command of the Armed Forces to the German Armistice commission under date 2nd September, 1944. The document begins, and I quote:

> "Conforming to the decrees, all non-German civilians in occupied territories who have endangered the security and readiness for action of the occupying power by acts of terror and sabotage or in other ways, are to be surrendered to the Security Police and S.D. Only those prisoners are to be accepted who were legally sentenced to death or were serving a sentence of confinement prior to the announcement of these decrees. Included in the punishable acts which endanger the security or readiness of action of the garrison power, are those of a political nature."

The eighth crime for which Kaltenbrunner is responsible as Chief of the Security Police and S.D. is the crime of executing and confining persons in concentration camps for crimes allegedly committed by their relatives.

That this crime continued after the 30th January, 1943, is indicated by Document L-37, heretofore received in evidence as Exhibit USA 506. That was received this morning. It is the letter of the Konimandeur of Sipo and S.D. at Radom, dated the 19th of July, 1944, in which it was stated that the male relatives of assassins and saboteurs should be shot and the female relatives over 16 years of age sent to concentration camps. I refer again to Document L- 215, which has heretofore been received in evidence as Exhibit USA 243, and specifically to the case of Junker, who was ordered by Kaltenbrunner to be committed to Sachsenhausen concentration camp by the Gestapo "because as a relative of a deserter, he is expected to endanger the interest of the German Reich if allowed to go free."

The ninth crime for which Kaltenbrunner is responsible as Chief of the Security Police and S.D. is the clearance of Sipo and S.D. prisons and concentration camps. I refer the Tribunal to Document L-53, which was received in evidence as Exhibit USA 291. This was the letter from the Kommandeur of the Sipo and S.D. Radom, dated 21St July, 1944, in which it is stated that the Kommandeur of the Sipo and S.D. of the Government General had ordered all Sipo and S.D. prisons to be cleared and, if necessary, the inmates to be liquidated. I now offer Document 3462-PS as Exhibit next in order, USA 528. This is the sworn interrogation of Bertus Gerdes, the former Gaustabsanitsleiter under the Gauleiter of Munich. This interrogation was taken in the course of an official military investigation of the U.S. Army. In this interrogation Gerdes was ordered to state all he knew about Kaltenbrunner. I am only going to read a very small portion of his reply, beginning on the third paragraph of page 2:

> "Giesler told me that Kaltenbrunner was in constant touch with him because

he was greatly worried about the attitude of the foreign workers and especially inmates of concentration camps Dachau, Muehldorf and Landsberg, which were in the path of the approaching Allied armies. On a Tuesday in the middle of April 1945, I received a telephone call from Gauleiter Giesler asking me to be available for a conversation that night. In the course of our personal conversation that night, I was told by Giesler that he had received a directive from Kaltenbrunner by order of the Fuehrer, to work out a plan without delay for the liquidation of the concentration camp at Dachau and the two Jewish labour camps in Landsberg and Muehldorf. The directive proposed to liquidate the two Jewish labour camps at Landsberg and Muehldorf, by use of the German Luftwaffe, since the construction area of these camps had previously been the targets of repeated enemy air attacks. This action received the code name of ' Wolke A- I.' "

I now pass to the second paragraph on page 3, continuing quoting from this interrogation:

"I was certain that I would never let this directive be carried out. As the action 'Wolke A-I ' should already have become operational for some time, I was literally swamped by couriers from Kaltenbrunner and moreover I was supposed to have discussed the details of the Muehldorf and Landsberg actions in detail with the two Kreisleiter concerned. The couriers who were in most cases S.S. officers, usually S.S. lieutenants, gave me terse and strict orders to read and initial. The orders threatened me with the most terrible punishment, including execution, if I did not comply with them. However, I could always excuse my failure to execute the plan because of bad flying weather and lack of gasoline and bombs. Therefore, Kaltenbrunner ordered the Jews in Landsberg to be marched to Dachau in order to include them in the Dachau extermination operations, and the Muehldorf action to be carried out by the Gestapo.

Kaltenbrunner also ordered an operation - 'Wolkenbrand' - for the concentration camp at Dachau, which provided that the inmates of the concentration camp at Dachau were to be liquidated by poison with the exception of Aryan nationals of the Western Powers.

Gauleiter Giesler received this order direct from Kaltenbrunner an discussed, in my presence, the procurement of the required amounts poison with Dr. Hartfeld, the Gau Health Chief. Dr. Hartfeld promise to procure these quantities when ordered and was advised to await my further directions. As I was determined to prevent the execution this plan in any event, I gave no further instructions to Dr. Hartfeld.

The inmates of Landsberg had hardly been delivered at Dachau when Kaltenbrunner sent a courier declaring the action Wolkenbran was operational.

I prevented the execution of the Wolke A-I and Wolkenbrand by giving Giesler the reason that the Front was too close and asked him transmit this on to Kaltenbrunner.

Kaltenbrunner therefore issued directives in writing to Dachau transport all Western European prisoners by truck to Switzerland an to march the remaining inmates into the Tyrol, where the final liquidation of these prisoners was to take place without fail."

THE PRESIDENT: The Court will adjourn now.

(The Tribunal adjourned until 1000 hours on 3rd January, 1946)

Twenty-Sixth Day: Thursday, 3rd January, 1946

LT. HARRIS: If the Tribunal will recall, at the end of the last session we had finished reading a portion of the sworn interrogation of the Gaustabsamtsleiter under the Gauleiter of Munich and had touched on the point where he said that Kaltenbrunner issued directives to Dachau to transport Western European prisoners by truck to Switzerland and to march the remaining inmates into the Tyrol.

I now offer as Exhibit next in order the first five pages of the interrogation report of Gottlieb Berger, Chief of the head office of the S.S., made under oath on 20th September, 1945, in the course of these proceedings. You will find these pages at the end of the Document Book and this is offered as Exhibit US.A. 529. These pages have been translated into German and made available to the defendants.

THE PRESIDENT: Does it have a number?

LT. HARRIS: It has no PS number, Sir. It is at the very end of the Document Book. I wish to read only one question and answer from these pages; and I refer to the last question and answer Page 3 of the Exhibit:

"Q: Assuming, only for the purposes of this discussion, that these atrocities that we hear about are true, who do you think is primarily responsible?

"A: The first one, the Commandant; the second one, Gluecks; because he was practically responsible for all the interior direction of the camps. If one wants to be exact, one would have to find out how the information service between the camp Commandant and Gluecks actually operated. I want to give you the following example: During the night of the 22nd and 23rd April I was sent to Munich. As I entered the city, I met a group of perhaps 120 men dressed in the suits of the concentration camps. I asked the guard who was with them, 'What about these men?' He told me that these men were marching by foot to the Alps. Firstly, I sent him back to Dachau. Then I wrote a letter to the Commandant, to send no more people by foot to any place, but, whenever the Allies advanced any further, to give over the camp completely. I did that on my own responsibility and I told him that I came straight from Berlin and that I can be found in my service post in Munich. The Commandant, or his deputy, telephoned at about twelve o'clock and told me that he had received this order from Kaltenbrunner after he had been asked by the Gauleiter of Munich, the Reichskommissar."

The tenth crime for which Kaltenbrunner is responsible as Chief of the Security Police and S.D. is the persecution of the Jews. This crime, of course, continued after 30th January, 1943, and evidence has heretofore been received that the persecutions continued until and were accelerated toward the end of the war. Kaltenbrunner took a personal interest in such matters, as is indicated by Document 2519-PS, which is offered as Exhibit next in order, Exhibit US.A. 530. This exhibit consists of a memorandum and an affidavit, and I invite the attention of the Tribunal to the affidavit. Quoting from the affidavit:

"I, Henri Monneray, being first duly sworn, depose and say that since 12th September, 1945, I have been and I am the member of the French staff for the prosecution of Axis Criminality and have been pursuing my official duties in this connection in Nuremberg, Germany, since 12th October, 1945.

In the course of my official duties, at the instruction of the French Chief Prosecutor, I examined the personal document of the defendant-"

THE PRESIDENT: Is it necessary to read all of this? What is the object of this affidavit?

LT. HARRIS: To show that this document was derived from the personal effects of the defendant Kaltenbrunner.

THE PRESIDENT: You can leave out the immaterial parts.

LT. HARRIS: Very good, Sir. Passing to the last sentence of the affidavit:

"Said Document 2519-PS is the document which I found in the envelope containing Kaltenbrunner's personal papers."

I now read the memorandum:

"Radio message to Gruppenfuehrer S.S. Major General Fegelein, Headquarters of the Fuehrer, through Sturmbannfuehrer S.S. Major Sansoni, Berlin:

Please inform the Reichsfuehrer S.S. and report to the Fuehrer that all arrangements against Jews, political and concentration camp internees in the Protectorate have been taken care of by me personally to-day. The situation there is one of calmness, fear of Soviet successes and hope of an occupation by the Western enemies.

Kaltenbrunner."

THE TRIBUNAL (Mr. BIDDLE): That is not dated?

LT. HARRIS: This is not dated.

The eleventh crime for which Kaltenbrunner is responsible is the persecution of the Churches. It is unnecessary to present specific evidence that this crime continued after 30th January, 1943, since this was one of the fundamental purposes of the Security Police and S.D., as has already been shown.

These are the crimes for which the defendant Kaltenbrunner must answer. As to his criminal intent, there is no need to go outside the record before this Tribunal. On 1st December, 1945, in these proceedings the witness Lahousen was asked on cross-examination, "Do you know Mr. Kaltenbrunner?"

After describing his meeting with Kaltenbrunner on a day in Munich when a university student and his sister were arrested and executed for distributing leaflets from the auditorium, Lahousen said - and I wish to quote only to two sentences on Page 324 (Part I.) of the transcript:

"I can easily reconstruct that day. It was the first and last time that I saw Kaltenbrunner, with whose name was known to me. Of course, Kaltenbrunner mentioned this subject to Canaris, and witnesses were there, and everybody was under the terrible impression of what had happened, and Kaltenbrunner spoke about that to Canaris in a manner for which cynicism would be a very mild description. This is the only thing I can say to this question."

Kaltenbrunner was a life-long fanatical Nazi. He was the leader of the S.S. in Austria prior to the Anschluss and played a principal role in the betrayal of his native country to the Nazi Conspirators. As higher S.S. and Police Leader in Austria after the Anschluss, he supervised and had knowledge of the activities of the Gestapo and the S.D. in Austria. The Mauthausen concentration camp was established in his jurisdiction and he visited it several times. On at least one occasion he observed the gas chamber in action. With this knowledge and background he accepted, in January,

1943, appointment as Chief of the Security Police and S.D., the very agencies which sent such victims to their deaths. He held that office to the end, rising to great prominence in the S.S. and the German Police and receiving high honours from Hitler. Like other leading Nazis, Kaltenbrunner sought power; to gain it, he made his covenant with crime.

COL. STOREY: If the Tribunal please, next will be some witnesses and Colonel Amen will handle the interrogation.

COLONEL JOHN H. AMEN: May it please the Tribunal, I wish to call, as a witness for the prosecution, Mr. Otto Ohlendorf. Your Lordship will note that his name appears under Amt III on the chart on the wall.

THE PRESIDENT: What did you say appeared?

Q. The name of this witness appears under Amt III of the chart, R.S.H.A., the large square, the third section down.

THE PRESIDENT: I see it.

Otto Ohlendorf, will you repeat this oath after me: I swear by God, the Almighty and Omniscient, that I will speak the pure truth and will withhold and add nothing.

(The witness repeated the oath.)

BY COLONEL AMEN:

Q. Where were you born?
A. In Hohen Egelsen.
Q. How old are you?
A. Thirty-eight years old.
Q. When, if ever, did you become a member of the National Socialist Party?
A. 1925.
Q. When, if ever, did you become a member of the S.A.?
A. For the first time in 1926.
Q. When, if ever, did you become a member of the S.S.?
A. I must correct myself. I answered the first question as if I were speaking of my membership in the S.S.
Q. When did you become a member of the S.A.?
A. In the year 1923.
Q. When, if ever, did you join the S.D.?
A. In 1936.
Q. What was your last position in the S.D.?
A. Amt Chief of Amt III in the R.S.H.A..
Q. Turning to the chart on the wall behind your back, will you tell the Tribunal whether you can identify that chart in any way?
A. This chart was seen previously by me and worked on by me and I can consequently identify it.
Q. What, if anything, did you have to do with making up that chart?
A. This chart was made during my interrogation.

COLONEL AMEN: For the information of the Tribunal, the chart of which the witness speaks is Exhibit US.A. 493.

Q. Will you tell the Tribunal whether that chart correctly portrays the basic organization of the R.S.H.A., as well as the position of Kaltenbrunner, the Gestapo, and the S.D. in the German Police system?

A. The organisation, as represented in that chart, is a correct representation of the organisation of the R.S.H.A. It shows correctly the position of the S.A. as well as the

State Police, the Criminal Police, and the S.D.

Q. Referring once more to the chart, please indicate your position in the R.S.H.A. and state for what period you continued to serve in that capacity.

(At this point the witness pointed to Amt III on the chart.)

Q. *What were the positions of Kaltenbrunner, Mueller, and Eichmann in the R.S.H.A., and state for what periods of time each of them continued to serve in his respective capacity?*

A. Kaltenbrunner was Chief of the Sicherheitspolizei and the S.D.; as such, he was also Chief of the R.S.H.A., the internal organisational term for the office of the chief of the Sicherheitspolizei and the S.D.

Kaltenbrunner occupied this position from 30th January, 1943, until the end of the war. Mueller was Chief of Amt IV, the Gestapo. When the Gestapo was established, he became Deputy Chief, and as such he subsequently was appointed Chief of Amt IV of the R.S.H.A.. He occupied this position until the end of the war.

Eichmann occupied a position in Amt IV under Mueller and worked on the Jewish problem from 1940 on. To my knowledge, he also occupied this position until the end of the war.

Q. Will you tell us for what period of time you continued to serve as Chief of Amt III?

A. I was Chief of Amt III from 1939 to 1945.

Q. Turning now to the designation "Mobile Units" with the Army, shown in the lower right-hand corner of the chart, please explain to the Tribunal the significance of the terms "Einsatzgruppe" and "Einsatzkommando".

A. The concept "Einsatzgruppe" was established after an agreement between the Chiefs of the R.S.H.A., O.K.W., and O.K.H., in regard to the use of the Sipo in the area of operation. The concept "Einsatzgruppe" first appeared during the Polish campaign.

The agreement with the O.K.H. and O.K.W., however, was first arrived at before the beginning of the Russian campaign. This agreement specified that an official of the Sipo and the S.D. should be assigned to the Army Groups, or the Armies, and that this official would have at his disposal mobile units of the Sipo and the S.D. in the form of Einsatzgruppen, subdivided into Einsatzkommandos. The Einsatzkommandos should be assigned to the Army Units as needed, to the particular Army Group or Army.

Q. State, if you know, whether prior to the campaign against Soviet Russia, any agreement was entered into between the O.K.W., O.K.H., and R.S.H.A.?

A. Yes, the Einsatzgruppen, just described by me, and the Einsatzkommandos were used in the Russian campaign, according to a written agreement between the O.K.W., O.K.H., and R.S.H.A..

Q. How do you know that there was such a written agreement?

A. I was often present when the negotiations which Schellenberg conducted with the O.K.H. and OKW were being discussed, and I also had a written copy of this agreement in my own hands when I took over the Einsatzgruppen.

Q. Explain to the Tribunal who Schellenberg was. What position, if any, did he occupy?

A. Schellenberg was finally the Chief of Amt VI in the R.S.H.A.; at the time when he was conducting these negotiations as ordered by Heydrich, he belonged to the Amt.

Q. On approximately what date did these negotiations take place?

A. The negotiations took several weeks. The agreement must have been reached about one or two weeks before the beginning of the Russian campaign.

Q. Did you yourself ever see a copy of this written agreement?

A. Yes.

Q. Did you have occasion to work with this written agreement?

A. Yes.

Q. On more than one occasion?

A. Yes; and in regard to more than one question which had to do with the use of Einsatzgruppen in the Army.

Q. Do you know where the original or any copy of that agreement is located today?

A. No, I do not.

Q. To the best of your knowledge and recollection, please explain to the Tribunal the entire substance of this written agreement.

A. First of all, the agreement stated the fact that Einsatzgruppen should be set up and that Einsatzkommandos should be used for joint efforts in this operation. Up to that time the Army had completely taken over the tasks that the Sipo should have done itself.

THE PRESIDENT: What is it that you say the Einsatzkommandos did under the agreement?

A. The second was the authority of the Army in regard to the Einsatzgruppen and the Einsatzkommandos. The agreement specified that the Army Groups or Armies should be responsible for marching and maintenance so far as the Einsatzgruppen were concerned. Particular instructions came from the Chief of the Sipo and S.D.

COL. AMEN: Q. Let us understand. Is it correct that an Einsatz Group was to be attached to each Army Group or Army?

A. Every Army Group was to have attached to it an Einsatzgruppe. The Einsatzkommandos, in their turn, were to be attached to the Armies by the Army Group.

Q. And was the Army Command to determine the area within which the Einsatz Group was to operate?

A. The operational region of the Einsatzgruppe was determined by the fact that the Einsatzgruppe was attached to a specific Army Group and therefore marched with it, whereas the Einsatzkommandos functioned in territories as determined by the Army Group or Army.

Q. Did the agreement also provide that the Army Command was to direct the time during which they were to operate?

A. That was included under the concept "March."

Q. And also to direct any additional tasks they were to perform?

A. Yes. As far as the actual instructions of the Chiefs of the Sipo and S.D. were concerned, they were guided by the general practice that they could issue orders to the Army if the operational situation made it necessary.

Q. What did this agreement provide with respect to the attachment of the Einsatz Group Command to the Army Command?

A. I cannot remember whether anything specific was said about that. At any rate, an attachment was established.

Q. Do you recall any other provisions of this written agreement?

A. I believe I can state the essential content of that agreement.

Q. What position did you occupy with respect to this agreement?

A. From June, 1941, to the death of Heydrich in June, 1942, I led Einsatzgruppe D, and was the Deputy of the Chief of the Sipo and the S.D. with the 11th Army.

Q. And when was Heydrich's death?

A. Heydrich was wounded at the end of May, 1942, and died on 4th June, 1942.

Q. How much advance notice, if any, did you have of the campaign against Soviet Russia?

A. About four weeks.

Q. How many Einsatz Groups were there, and who were their respective leaders?

A. There were four Einsatzgruppen, Group A, B, C and D. Chief of Einsatzgruppe A was Stahlecker; Chief of Einsatzgruppe B was Nebe; Chief of Einsatzgruppe C Dr. Rausche, and later, Dr. Thomas; Chief of Einsatzgruppe D, Bierkamp.

Q. To which army was Group D attached?

A. Group D was not attached to any Army Group, but was attached directly to the 11th Army.

Q. Where did Group D operate?

A. Group D operated in the Southern Ukraine.

Q. Will you describe in more detail the nature and extent of the area in which Group D originally operated, naming the cities or territories?

A. The most Northern city was Czernowitz; then Southward to Mogilev-Podelsk; South-west to Odessa; North-east of that, Melitopol, Mariupol, Taganrog, Rostov and the Crimea.

Q. What was the ultimate objective of Group D?

A. Group D was held in reserve for the Caucasus. An Army Group was provided for this operation.

Q. When did Group D commence its move into Soviet Russia?

A. Group D left Duegen on 21st June, reaching Romania in 21 days. There the first Einsatzkommandos were already being demanded by the Army, and they marched at once to the goals set by the Army. The entire Einsatzgruppe was made use of at the beginning of July.

Q. You are referring to the 11th Army?

A. Yes.

Q. In what respects, if any, were the official duties of the Einsatz Groups concerned with Jews and Communist Commissars?

A. As far as the question of Jews and Communists is concerned, the Einsatzgruppen and Einsatzkommandos were orally instructed by their leaders before the march.

Q. What were their instructions with respect to the Jews and the Communist functionaries?

A. They were instructed that in the field of activity of the Einsatzgruppe in Russian territory the Jews, as well as the political Soviet Commissars, were to be liquidated.

Q. And when you say "liquidated" do you mean "killed?"

A. I mean "killed."

Q. Prior to the opening of the Soviet campaign, did you attend a conference at Pretz?

A. Yes, it was a discussion at which the Einsatzgruppen and the Einsatzkommandos were informed of the goals of their activity and were given the necessary commands.

Q. Who was present at that conference?

A. The Chiefs of the Einsatzgruppen and the leaders of the Einsatzkommandos and Streckenbach of the R.S.H.A., who transmitted the orders of Heydrich and Himmler.

Q. What were those orders?

A. Those were the general orders regarding the work of the Sipo, which aided the liquidation order which I have already mentioned.

Q. And that conference took place on approximately what date?

A. About three or four days before our march.

Q. So that before you commenced to march into Soviet Russia, you received orders at this conference to exterminate the Jews and Communist functionaries, in addition to the regular professional work of the Security Police and SD; is that correct?

A. That is right.

Q. Did you, personally, have any conversation with Himmler, respecting any communication from Himmler to the Chiefs of Army Groups and Armies concerning this mission?

A. Yes. Himmler informed me that before the beginning of the Russian campaign Hitler, in a conference with the Commander of the Army, had stated this task and had instructed the High Commander to provide the necessary support in regard to it.

Q. So that you can testify that the Chiefs of the Army Groups and the Armies had been similarly informed of those orders for the liquidation of the Jews and Soviet functionaries?

A. I believe that it is not correct in this particular form. They had no orders for liquidation. The order for the liquidation originated with Himmler, but since this liquidation took place in the operational region of the High Command, of the Army Groups or the Army, the Army was ordered to support these measures. Without these instructions to the Army, the Einsatzgruppe in this sense would not have been possible.

Q. Did you have any other conversation with Himmler concerning this order?

A. Yes, in the late summer of 1941 Himmler was in Nikolaiev. He assembled the leaders and men of the Einsatzgruppen and Kommandos and repeated to them the orders for liquidation with the remark that the leaders and men who were taking part in the liquidation bore no personal responsibility for the execution of these orders. The responsibility was his, alone, as well, of course, as that of the Fuehrer.

Q. And you yourself heard that said?

A. Yes.

Q. Do you know whether this mission of the Einsatz Group was known to the Army Group Commanders?

A. This order and the execution of these orders were known to the High Commander of the Army.

Q. How do you know that?

A. Through conferences with the Army and through instructions which were given by the Army in reference to this execution.

Q. Was the mission of the Einsatz Groups and the agreement between O.K.W., O.K.H. and R.S.H.A. known to the other leaders in the R.S.H.A.?

A. At least some of them knew, since some of the leaders were also active in the Einsatzgruppen and Einsatzkommandos in the course of time. Furthermore, the leaders who had to do with organisation also knew it.

Q. Most of the leaders came from the R.S.H.A., did they not?

A. Which leaders?

Q. Of the Einsatz Groups.

A. No, one cannot say that. The leaders in the Einsatzgruppen and Einsatzkommandos came from the entire Reich.

Q. Do you know whether the mission and the agreement were also known to Kaltenbrunner?

A. After his entry into service Kaltenbrunner had to concern himself with these questions and consequently must have known the background of the Einsatzgruppen which were dealt with in his own office.

Q. Who was the commanding officer of the 11th Army?

A. At first, Ritter von Schober; later, Von Mannstein.

Q. Will you tell the Tribunal in what way or ways the commanding officers of the 11th Army directed or supervised Einsatz Group D in carrying out its liquidation activities?

A. An order from the 1st Army came to Nikolaiev, stating that liquidations were to take place only at a distance of not less than 200 kilometers from the Headquarters of the High Commander Mannheim.

Q. Do you recall any other occasion?

A. In Simferopol, the Army High Command gave the proper Einsatzkommandos further orders to hasten the liquidation, on the grounds that in this region there was a great housing shortage.

Q. Do you know how many persons were liquidated by Einsatz Group D, under your direction?

A. In the year between June, 1941, to June, 1942, the Einsatzkommandos announced 90,000 people liquidated.

Q. Did that include men, women, and children?

A. Yes.

Q. On what do you base those figures?

A. On reports sent by the Einsatzkommandos to the Einsatzgruppen.

Q. Were those reports submitted to you?

A. Yes.

Q. And you saw them and read them?

A. I beg your pardon?

Q. And you saw and read those reports, personally?

A. Yes.

Q. And it is on those reports that you base the figures you have given the Tribunal?

A. Yes.

Q. Do you know how those figures compare with the number of persons liquidated by other Einsatz Groups?

A. The figures known to me from other Einsatzgruppen are materially larger.

Q. That was due to what factor?

A. I believe that to a large extent the figures submitted by the other Einsatzgruppen were exaggerated.

Q. Did you see reports of liquidations from the other Einsatz Groups from time to time?

A. Yes.

Q. And those reports showed liquidations exceeding those of Group D; is that correct?

A. Yes.

Q. Did you personally supervise mass executions of these individuals?

A. I was present at mass executions for purposes of inspection.

Q. Will you explain to the Tribunal in detail how an individual mass execution was carried out?

A. A local Einsatzkommando attempted to collect all the Jews in one area. The registration of the Jews was performed by the Jews themselves.

Q. On what pretext, if any, were they rounded up?

A. On the pretext that they were to be re-located.

Q. Will you continue?

A. After the registration, the Jews were collected at a certain place. From there they were later led to the place of execution. The execution was carried out in a military fashion.

Q. In what way were they transported to the place of execution?

A. They were transported to the place of execution in a wagon - always only as many as could be executed immediately. In this way the attempt was made to keep the span of time in which the victims knew what was about to happen to them until the time of their actual execution as short as possible.

Q. Was that your idea?

A. Yes.

Q. And after they were shot what was done with the bodies?

A. The bodies were buried in the trenches.

Q. What determination, if any, was made as to whether the persons were actually dead?

A. The unit leaders had the order to watch out for that and to administer the coup de grace themselves if necessary.

Q. And who would do that?

A. Either the unit leader himself or somebody designated by him.

Q. In what positions were the victims shot?

A. Standing or kneeling.

Q. What was done with the personal property and clothing of the persons executed?

A. All personal property of value was collected at the time of the shooting, confiscated and handed over to the R.S.H.A. or the Finance Minister. At first the clothing was divided up, but in the winter of 1942 it was taken by the N.S.V. and disposed of by that organisation.

Q. All their personal property was registered at the time?

A. Only the objects of value were registered. The other objects were not.

Q. What happened to the garments which the victims were wearing when they went to the place of execution?

A. They were obliged to take off their outer garments immediately before the execution.

Q. All of them?

A. The outer garments, yes.

Q. How about the rest of the garments they were wearing?

A. They were allowed to keep their underclothing.

Q. Was that true of not only your group but of the other Einsatz Groups?

A. That was the order in my Einsatzgruppe. Other Einsatzgruppen handled the matter differently.

Q. In what way did they handle it?

A. A few of the Einsatz leaders did not employ the military way of liquidation and killed the victims simply by shooting them in the back of the neck.

Q. And you objected to that procedure?

A. I was against that procedure, yes.

Q. For what reason?

A. Because for the victims as well as those who carried out the executions that was an unnecessary spiritual suffering.

Q. Now, what was done with the property collected by the Einsatzkommandos from these victims?

A. In so far as it was a question of objects of value, they were sent to the R.S.H.A. in Berlin or to the Reich Ministry of Finance. The articles which could be used in the operational area were used there immediately.

Q. For example, what happened to gold and silver taken from the victims?

A. That was, as I have just said, turned over to the Reich Ministry of Finance in Berlin.

Q. How do you know that?

A. I can remember that it was actually handled in that way in Simferopol.

Q. How about watches, for example, taken from the victims?

A. At the request of the Army watches were put at the disposal of the Front.

Q. Were all victims, including men, women, and children, executed in the same manner?

A. Until the spring of 1942, yes. Then an order came from Himmler that in the future women and children should be killed only in gas vans.

Q. How had the women and children been killed previously?

A. In the same way as the men - by shooting.

Q. What, if anything, was done about burying the victims after they had been executed?

A. At first the Kommandos filled the graves so that signs of the execution could not be seen any more, and then levelled the graves with Arbeitskommandos from the population.

Q. Referring to the gas vans which you said you received in the spring of 1942, what order did you receive with respect to the use of these vans?

A. That these gas vans should be used in the future for the killing of women and children.

Q. Will you explain to the Tribunal the construction of these vans and their appearance?

A. The actual purpose of these vans could not be recognised from the outside. They were practically closed trucks. They were so constructed that when the motor ran, the gas was conducted into the van causing death of the occupants in 10 to 15 minutes.

Q. Explain in detail just how one of these vans was used for an execution.

A. The vans were loaded with the victims and driven to the place of burial, which was usually the same as that used for the mass executions. The time needed for transportation was long enough to insure the death of the passengers.

Q. How were the victims induced to enter the vans?

A. They were told that they were to be transported to another locality.

Q. How was the gas turned on?

A. I am not familiar with the technical details.

Q. How long did it take to kill the victims ordinarily?

A. About 10 to 15 minutes, the victims did not notice what was going on.

Q. How many persons could be killed simultaneously one such van?

A. The vans were of various sizes, anywhere from 15 to 25 persons.

Q. Did you receive reports from those persons operating these vans from time to time?

A. I did not understand the question.

Q. Did you receive reports from those who were working on the vans?

A. I received the report that the Einsatzkommandos did not like to use the vans.

Q. Why not?

A. Because the burial of the occupants was a great ordeal for the members of the Einsatzkommandos.

Q. Now, will you tell the Tribunal who furnished these vans to the Einsatz Groups?

A. The gas vans did not belong to the motor pool of the Einsatzgruppen but came from a special Kommando of the Einsatzgruppe. This Kommando also had charge of the construction of the vans. These vans were assigned to the Einsatzgruppen by the R.S.H.A.

Q. Were the vans supplied to all of the different Einsatz Groups?

A. I cannot say that. I only know about Einsatzgruppe D, and indirectly about Einsatzgruppe C, both of which had such vans.

Q. Are you familiar with the letter from Becker to Rauf with respect to these gas vans?

A. I saw this letter during my interrogation.

COLONEL AMEN: May it please the Tribunal, I am referring to Document 501-PS, Exhibit USA 288, being a letter already in evidence, a letter from Becker to Rauf.

Q. Will you tell the Tribunal who Becker was?

A. As far as I recall, Becker was the builder of the vans. It was he who was in charge of the vans for Einsatzgruppe D.

Q. Who was Rauf?

A. Rauf was group leader in Amt II of the R.S.H.A. He was in charge of motor vehicles and other things at that time.

Q. Can you identify that letter in any way?

A. The contents seem to bear out my experiences and are therefore probably correct. (Document 501-PS was handed to the witness.) Yes.

Q. Will you look at the letter before you and tell us whether you can identify it in any way?

A. I recognise the external appearance of the letter as well as the sign "R" (Rauf) on it, and the reference to the man who took care of the motor vehicles under Rauf seems to testify to its authenticity. The contents bear out the experiences which I had at that time.

Q. So that you believe it to be an authentic document?

A. Yes, I do.

Q. Will you now lay it aside on the table there?

Referring to your previous testimony, will you explain to the Tribunal why you believe that the type of execution ordered by you, namely, military, was preferable to the shooting in the neck procedure adopted by the other Einsatz Groups?

A. On the one hand, the aim was that the individual leaders and men should be able to carry out the executions in a military fashion acting on order and should have to make no decision of their own. That is, it should take place only by order. On the other hand, it was known to me that in the case of individual executions emotional disturbances could not be avoided since the victims discovered too soon that they were to be executed and thereby were subjected to prolonged nervous strain. Likewise, it seemed intolerable to me that the individual leaders and men were forced in this way to form their own decisions in the killing of a large number of people.

Q. In what manner did you determine which were the Jews to be executed?

A. That was not part up to me, but the identification of the Jews was done by the Jews themselves, since the registration was carried out by a Jewish Council of Elders.

Q. Did the amount of Jewish blood have anything to do with it?

A. I cannot remember the details, but I believe that in this case half-Jews were also included in the concept "Jew."

Q. What organisations furnished most of the officer personnel of the Einsatz Groups and Einsatzkommandos?

A. I did not understand the question.

Q. What organisations furnished most of the officer personnel of the Einsatz Groups?

A. The leadership personnel was furnished by the State Police, the Kripo, and, to a lesser extent, by the S.D.

Q. Kripo?

A. Yes, the Kripo. The State Police, the Criminal Police and, and to a lesser extent, the S.D.

Q. Were there any other sources of personnel?

A. Yes; the great masses of men employed were furnished by the Waffen S.S. and the Ordinary Police. The State Police and the Kripo furnished the experts for the most part and the troops were furnished by the Waffen S.S. and the Ordinary Police.

Q. How about the Waffen S.S.?

A. The Waffen S.S. was supposed to supply the Einsatzgruppen with one company, just as was the Ordinary Police.

Q. How about the Ordinary Police?

A. The Ordinary Police [Ordnungspolizei] also furnished a company to the Einsatzgruppen.

Q. What was the size of Einsatz Group D and its operating area as compared with the other Einsatz Groups?

A. I estimate that Einsatzgruppe D was two-thirds to one- half as large as the other Einsatzgruppen. That changed in the course of time. Individual Einsatzgruppen were in the course of time greatly enlarged.

COLONEL AMEN: May it please the Tribunal, I have other questions relating to organisational matters which I think would clarify some of the evidence which has already been in part received by the Tribunal; but I don't want to take the time of the Tribunal unless they feel that they want any more such testimony. I thought, perhaps, if any members of the Tribunal had questions they would ask this witness directly, because he is the best informed on these organisational matters of anyone who will be presented in Court.

THE PRESIDENT: We will adjourn now for 10 minutes.

(A recess was taken.)

THE PRESIDENT: Colonel Amen, the Tribunal does not think that it is necessary to go further into the organisational questions at this stage, but it is a matter which must be really decided by you because you know what the nature of the evidence which you are considering is. So far as the Tribunal is concerned, they are satisfied at the present stage to leave the matter where it is. But there is one aspect of the witness's evidence which the Tribunal would like you to investigate, and that is whether the practices of which he has been speaking continued after 1942, and for how long.

BY COLONEL AMEN:

Q. Can you state whether the liquidation practices which you have described continued after 1942 and, if so, for how long a period of time thereafter?

A. I do not think that the basic order was ever lifted. But I cannot remember sufficient details to enable me to make concrete statements on this subject, at least not in reference to Russia; for very shortly thereafter the retreat began, so that the operational region of the Einsatzgruppen became smaller and smaller. I do know whether other Einsatzgruppen with similar orders were provided for other areas.

Q. The question was up to what date does your personal knowledge of these liquidation activities go.

A. As far as the liquidation of Jews is concerned, I know that appropriate withdrawals of the order were made about six months before the conclusion of the war. Furthermore, I saw a document according to which the liquidation of Soviet Commissars was to be terminated. I cannot recall a specific date.

Q. Do you know whether in fact it was so terminated?

A. Yes, I believe so.

BY THE PRESIDENT:

Q. The Tribunal would like to know the number of men in your Einsatz Group.

A. There were about five hundred people in my Einsatzgruppe, besides those who were added to the group from the country itself to help out.

Q. Including them, did you say?

A. Excluding those who were brought into the group from the land itself.

Q. Do you know how many there would be in other groups?

A. I should estimate that at the beginning, seven to eight hundred men; but, as I said before, this number changed rapidly in the course of time for this reason, that individual Einsatzgruppen themselves acquired new people or succeeded in getting additional personnel from the R.S.H.A..

Q. The numbers increased, did they?

A. Yes, the numbers increased.

THE PRESIDENT: All right.

COLONEL AMEN: Now, here are perhaps just a half dozen of these questions I would like to ask, because I do think they might clear up, in the minds of the Tribunal, some of the evidence which has gone before. I shall be very brief, if that is satisfactory to the Tribunal.

THE PRESIDENT: Yes.

BY COLONEL AMEN:

Q. Will you explain the significance of the different widths of the blue lines on the chart?

A. The thick blue line between the name Himmler, as Reichsfuehrer S.S. and Chief of the German Police and the initials R.S.H.A. is designed to show the identity of the offices of the chiefs of the Sicherheitspolizei and the S.D. and their tasks. This is a department in which ministerial questions of leadership as well as individual executive matters were treated, that is to say, the closed circle of operations of the

Sipo and the S.D. The organisational scheme, however, seen from the legal administrative point of view, represents an illegal state of affairs since the R.S.H.A. never actually had official validity.

The formal, legal situation was different from that which appears on this chart. Party and State offices were amalgamated here with different channels. Under this designation neither orders nor laws with a legal basis were issued. That is due to the fact that the State Police, in its ministerial capacity, was subordinate to the Ministry of the Interior just as before, whereas the S.D., despite this organisation, was an organ of the Party.

Therefore if I wished to reproduce this scheme legally according to the administrative situation, I should have to put, for example, in place of Amt IV the Amt Political Police of the former Sicherheitspolizei Hauptamt. This Amt Political Police existed formally to the very end and had its origin in the Police Department of the Ministry of the Interior. At the same time, the Secret State Police Amt, the Central Office of the Prussian Secret State Police, the leading organ of all the political police offices of the different provinces [Laender], continued to exist formally.

Thus, ministerial questions continued to be handled under the leadership of the Minister of the Interior; in so far as the emphasis on the formal competence of the Ministry of the Interior was necessary, it appeared under the heading "Reich Minister of the Interior" with the filing notice "Pol," the former designation of the Police Department of the Ministry of the Interior and the appropriate filing notice of the competent department of the former Sicherheitspolizei Hauptamt. For example, filing notice "Pol-S" meant Sicherheitspolizei; "V" meant Amt Verwaltung und Recht (Department Administration and Law).

The R.S.H.A. was therefore nothing more than a camouflage designation which did not correctly represent the actual conditions but gave the Chief of the Sipo and the S.D. as a collective designation for the Chief of the Sicherheitspolizei Hauptamt and the Chief of the S.D. Hauptamt (an office held until 1939) the opportunity of using one or the other letterhead at any given time.

At the same time it gave him the opportunity of an internal amalgamation of all forces and the opportunity of a division of activity-areas according to the point of view of practical effectiveness. But the fact remains that in this department State offices did remain in a way dependent on the Ministry of the Interior, and similarly the departments of the S.D. remained Party departments.

The S.D. Hauptamt, or the R.S.H.A., had formally only the significance of an S.S. Main Office, a main office in which the S.S. members of the Sipo and the S.D. belonged to the S.S. But the S.S., that is to say, Himmler, as Reichsfuehrer S.S., gave these state offices no official authority to issue orders.

BY THE PRESIDENT:

Q. I am not sure that I follow altogether what you have been saying, but is what you have been saying the reason why you are shown on the chart as concerned with Amt III, which refers, apparently, only to inside Germany, while, according to your evidence, you were the head of Einsatz Group D, which was operating outside Germany?

A. The fact that I led an Einsatzgruppe had nothing to do with the fact that I was also Chief of Amt III. I was given that as an individual, not as Chief of Amt III; and in my capacity as leader of an Einsatzgruppe I came into a completely new function and into an office completely separate from the former one.

Q. I see. And did it involve that you left Germany and went into the area invaded in the Soviet Union?

A. Yes.

BY COLONEL AMEN:

Q. Will you explain the significance of the dotted blue lines, as compared with the solid blue lines on the right hand side of the chart?

A. The solid lines indicate a direct official channels, whereas the dotted lines signify that here as a rule there were no direct channels.

Q. Was the term "S.D." ever used to include both the Sipo and the S.D.?

A. In the course of years the term "S.D." was used more and more incorrectly. It came to be established as an abbreviation for Sipo and S.D., without actually being suitable for that. "S.D." was originally simply a designation for the fact that someone belonged to the S.S.via the S.D. Main Office. When the S.D. Main Office was dissolved and was taken over into the R.S.H.A., the question arose as to whether the designation S.D., which was also worn as insignia on the sleeve of the particular S.S. man, should be replaced by another insignia or a new abbreviation, e.g. R.S.H.A.. Things did not reach that point because the camouflage of the R.S.H.A. would thereby have been endangered. But when, for example, I read in a Fuehrer order that in France people were to be turned over to the S.D., that was a case in point of the false use of the designation S.D., since there were no such offices in France, and, on the other hand, the S.D., in so far as it functioned in departments, e.g., Amt III, in offices, had no executive power but was purely an intelligence organ.

Q. Briefly, what was the relationship between the S.S. and the Gestapo?

A. The relationship between the S.S. and Gestapo was this: The Reichsfuehrer S.S., as such, took over the tasks of the police and attempted to combine more closely the State Police and the S.S., that is to say, on the one hand to employ only those members of the State Police who were eligible for the S.S., and, on the other hand, to use the institutions of the S.S., e.g., education and training of the younger generation by the Waffen-S.S., in order in this way to draw the younger generation into the State Police. This amalgamation was later extended by him in an attempt to bring about the same relationship between the S.S. and the Ministry of the Interior, i.e., the whole internal administration.

Q. About how many full-time agents and honourary auxiliary personnel did the S.D. employ?

A. One cannot use the concept SD in this connection either. It is necessary to distinguish here between Amt III and Amt VI. Amt III, as the interior intelligence service, had about three thousand main office members, including men and women. On the other hand, the interior intelligence service worked essentially with honourary personnel, that is to say, with men and women who could serve the internal intelligence services with their professional experiences and with experiences based on their surroundings. I would judge that the number of these persons was roughly thirty thousand.

Q. Will you briefly give the Tribunal a general example of how a typical transaction was handled through the channels indicated on the chart?

A. First, a general example, invented to make things clear. Himmler discovered through experience that more and more saboteurs were being dropped from planes into Germany and were endangering transportation and factory sites. He told this to Kaltenbrunner in the latter's capacity as Chief of the Sipo and instructed him to make his organisation aware of this state of affairs and to take measures to see to it that these saboteurs would be seized as soon and as completely as possible.

Kaltenbrunner instructed Amt IV, that is to say, the State Police, with the preparation of the necessary order to the regional offices. This order was drawn up by the competent office of experts in Amt IV and was either transmitted by Mueller directly to the State Police offices in the Reich or, what is more probable because of the importance of the question and because of necessity and in order to bring to the attention of the other offices and officials to this fact, was given by him to Kaltenbrunner, who signed it and issued it to the regional offices in the Reich.

On the basis of this order it was, for example, determined that the State Police offices should report the measures they were taking as well as any successes they might have. These reports went back through the same channels from the regional offices to the offices of experts in Amt IV, thence to the Chief of Amt IV, thence to the Chief of the R.S.H.A., Kaltenbrunner, and thence to the Chief of the German Police Himmler.

Q. And, finally, will you give a specific example of typical transaction handled through the channels indicated on the chart?

A. The example of the arrest of the leaders of the leftist parties after the event of the 20th of July: This order was also transmitted from Himmler to Kaltenbrunner; Kaltenbrunner passed it on to Amt IV and an appropriate draft for a decree was formulated by Amt IV, signed by Kaltenbrunner and sent to the regional offices. The reports were returned from the subordinate offices back to the higher offices along the same channels.

COLONEL AMEN: May it please the Tribunal. The witness is now available to other counsel. I understand that Colonel Pokrovsky has some questions that he wishes to ask on behalf of the Soviets.

DIRECT EXAMINATION BY COLONEL POKROVSKY:

The testimony of the witness is important for the clarification of such questions, on the report of which the Soviet Delegation is at present working. Therefore, with the permission of the Court, I would like to ask the witness Ohlendorf a number of questions.

Q. You, witness, said that you were present twice at the mass executions. On whose orders were you an inspector at the executions?

A. I was present at the executions on my own initiative.

Q. But you said that you attended as inspector.

A. I said that I attended for inspection purposes.

Q. That was your initiative?

A. Yes.

Q. Did one of your chiefs always attend the executions for purposes of inspection?

A. Whenever possible I sent some leader of the Einsatzgruppe, but this was not always possible because of the great distance from the Einsatzgruppe.

Q. For what reasons was a person sent for purposes of inspection?

A. Please repeat the question?

Q. For what purpose was an inspector sent?

A. To determine whether or not my instructions regarding the manner of the execution were actually being carried out.

Q. Am I to understand that the inspector was to make certain that the execution had actually been carired [sic] out?

A. No, that is not a correct statement of the fact. He should simply ascertain whether the conditions which I set for the execution were actually being carried out.

Q. What manner of conditions had you in mind?

A. (1) The absence of publicity; (2) The carrying out of the execution in a military fashion. (3) The arrival of the transports and the carrying out of the liquidation without any hitch, in order to avoid unnecessary excitement. (4) The control of the property, in order to prevent appropriation by any person. There may have been other details which I no longer remember. At any rate any mistreatment, whether physical or spiritual, was to be prevented by means of these measures.

Q. You wished to make sure that, according to your opinion, a more equitable distribution of this property was effected, or did you aspire to a complete acquisition of the valuables?

A. Yes. *[Note: Only the first half of the preceding question, originally spoken in Russian, was transmitted to the witness in German by the interpreter. The answer of the witness, therefore, refers only to the first half of the question.]*

Q. You spoke of ill-treatment. What did you mean by ill- treatment at the executions?

A. If, for instance, the manner in which the executions were carried out was not able to prevent excitement and disobedience among the victims and the consequent execution of the order by means of violence.

Q. What do you mean by "execution of the order by means of violence"? What do you mean by violent suppression of the excitement arising amongst the victims?

A. When, as I have already stated, in order to carry out the liquidation as ordered it was necessary, for example, to resort to beating.

Q. Was it absolutely necessary to beat the victims?

A. I myself never saw such a case, but I heard of such.

Q. From whom?

A. In conversations held with members of other Kommandos.

Q. You said that cars, auto-cars, were used for the executions?

A. Yes.

Q. Do you know where, and with whose assistance, the inventor, Becker, was able to materialise his inventions?

A. I remember only that it took place within Amt II of the R.S.H.A.; but I can no longer say definitely.

Q. How many were executed in these cars?

A. I did not understand the question.

Q. How many persons were executed by means of these cars?

A. I cannot give you any precise figures. The number was comparatively small - about a few hundred.

Q. You said that mostly women and children were executed in these vans. For what reason?

A. There was a special order from Himmler to that effect.

According to this order women and children were not to be executed in this manner in order to avoid the spiritual strain arising from other forms of execution and likewise not to force the soldiers, mostly married men, to shoot down women and children.

Q. Did anybody observe the behavior of the persons executed in these vans?

A. Yes, the doctor.

Q. Did you know that Becker had reported that death in these vans was particularly agonizing?

A. No. I only learned about Becker from the letter which was shown to me here in the Court. On the contrary, I know that according to the doctor's reports the victims felt nothing at the time of death.

Q. Did any military units - I should say, Army units - take part in these mass executions?

A. As a rule, no.

Q. And as an exception?

A. In so far as I remember, in Nikolaiev and in Simferopol an observer from the Army High Command was there for a short time.

Q. For what purpose?

A. I do not know. Probably for personal information.

Q. Were military units assigned for carrying out the executions in these towns?

A. Officially, the Army did not assign any units for this purpose, since the Army as such was opposed to the liquidation.

Q. But factually?

A. Individual units voluntarily made themselves available. However, I know of no such case in the Army itself, only in the units attached to the Army (Heeresgefolge).

Q. You were the man by whose orders people were sent to their death. Were Jews only handed over for the execution by the Einsatzgruppe or were Communists - "Communist Officials" you call them in your instructions - handed over for execution along with the Jews?

A. Yes, "Communist Officials" was the name for political commissars and for those who were politically active. The mere fact of belonging to the Communist Party was not sufficient grounds for sending a man to his death.

Q. Were any special investigations made concerning the part played by persons in the Communist Party?

A. No, I said precisely the contrary, i.e., that the fact of belonging to the Communist Party was not, in itself, a determining factor in regard to persecution or in regard to execution - unless it implied a special political function.

Q. Did you hold any conversations regarding the murder vans sent from Berlin and on their work?

A. I do not understand the question.

Q. Had you any occasion to discuss, with your chiefs and your colleagues, the fact that motor vans had been sent to your own particular Einsatzgruppe from Berlin for carrying out the executions? Do you remember any such conversations?

A. I do not remember any specific conversation.

Q. Had you any information concerning the fact that members of the execution squad in charge of the executions were unwilling to use the vans?

A. I knew that the Einsatzkommandos used these gas vans.

Q. No, I have something else in mind. I wish to discover whether you received any information whether members of the execution squads were unwilling to choose the vans or whether they preferred other means of execution?

A. In other words, that they would killing by gas vans rather than by shooting?

Q. On the contrary, that they preferred execution by shooting to rather than by the gas vans.

A. Yes, I have already said so, that the gas van-

Q. And why did they prefer execution by shooting to killing in the gas vans?

A. I have already said: because, according to the opinion of the Einsatzkommandos, the unloading of the corpses was an unnecessary spiritual strain.

Q. What do you mean "an unnecessary spiritual strain"?

A. As far as I can remember the actual conditions, for instance, the state of the bodies, certain functions of the body took place which left the corpses lying in filth.

Q. You wish to say that the sufferings endured prior to death were clearly visible on the victims? Have I understood you correctly?

A. Do you mean during that moment when the gas killed them in the van?

Q. Yes.

A. I can only repeat what the doctor told me, namely, that the victims at the time of death, felt nothing.

Q. In that case your reply to my previous question, namely, that the unloading of the bodies made a very terrible impression on the members of the execution squad, becomes entirely incomprehensible.

A. As I have already said, the terrible impression was created by the whole situation and by the fouling of the vans by excreta.

COLONEL POKROVSKY: I have no further questions to ask this witness at the present stage of the Trial.

THE PRESIDENT: Does the Prosecutor for the French Republic desire to put any questions to the witness?

M. DE MENTHON: No.

THE PRESIDENT: Does the counsel for Kaltenbrunner desire to cross-examine now or at a later date?

DR. KAUFFMANN (Counsel for defendant Kaltenbrunner): Perhaps I could ask a few questions now and request that I be allowed to make my cross-examination later after I have already spoken with Kaltenbrunner.

THE PRESIDENT: Certainly.

CROSS-EXAMINATION BY DR. KAUFFMANN:

Q. Since when have you known Kaltenbrunner?

A. May I address a request to the Tribunal? May I sit down?

Q. Yes.

THE WITNESS: I saw Kaltenbrunner for the first time on a trip from Berlin to Himmler's headquarters at the time when Kaltenbrunner was to be appointed Chief of the Sipo and S.D. Previously to that I simply knew the fact of his existence.

BY DR. KAUFFMANN:

Q. Did you come into personal contact with Kaltenbrunner through private or official conversations after he had become Chief of the R.S.H.A.?

A. Yes, of course.

Q. Do you know his attitude, as for example, on the Jewish question?

A. I am not familiar with any particular attitude of Kaltenbrunner's.

Q. How about the question of the Church?

A. The question of the church - he deplored the anti-church course taken by Germany. We agreed that an understanding should be reached with the Church.

Q. Do you know what his thoughts were on the liquidation of civilian prisoners, parachute troops, and so on?

A. No.

Q. Do you know that Kaltenbrunner made special efforts to make use of the S.D., in order to supply the Fuehrerstab with the criticism it otherwise lacked?

A. Yes, that was the duty of the S.D. and he also gave this task his official support.

Q. A little bit more slowly.

A. It was the duty of the S.D. even before Kaltenbrunner came and he supported and officially approved the direction of this work.

Q. Do you know, either directly or indirectly, that Kaltenbrunner had no authority to give executive orders, for example, that he had no authority to put people into concentration camps or to take them from concentration camps, that all these things were handled exclusively by Himmler and Mueller?

A. I believe this question is too general for me to be able to answer correctly. The question will have to be broken down, I believe.

If you ask the question whether Kaltenbrunner could bring about executive actions, I must answer in the affirmative. If you then name Himmler and Mueller to the exclusion of Kaltenbrunner, then I must point out that according to the organisation of the R.S.H.A. Mueller was a subordinate of Kaltenbrunner, and consequently orders from Himmler to Mueller were also orders to Kaltenbrunner and Mueller was obliged to inform Kaltenbrunner of them.

On the other hand, it is certain that, particularly in regard to the concentration camps, the final decision regarding entry into or departure from was determined by Himmler. I can say that I know absolutely that - I refer to the expression that often came up, namely, "to the last washerwoman" - Himmler reserved the final decision for himself. As to whether Kaltenbrunner had no authority at all in this regard, I can make no statement.

Q. Have you personally seen the original orders and original signatures of Kaltenbrunner's that ordered the liquidation of sabotage troops and so on?

A. No.

Q. Do you know, either directly or indirectly, that after Heydrich's death a change, which to be sure was not a formal change, took place and that another milder course was taken by Kaltenbrunner?

A. I could not answer that question concretely.

Q. I withdraw the question. Here is another question. Did Kaltenbrunner know that you were an Einsatz Leader in the East?

A. Yes.

Q. Who gave you this command?

A. Heydrich gave it to me.

Q. Heydrich gave it to you? That was before this time?

A. Yes, of course.

DR. KAUFFMANN: I have no further questions at this time.

BY THE TRIBUNAL (GENERAL NIKITCHENKO):

Q. Witness Ohlendorf, can you answer up to what date the Einsatzgruppe under your command was operating?

A. The staff of the Einsatzgruppe went to the Caucasus and was then led back. As far as I can remember, a Combat Command (Kampfkommando) was formed out of it under the name "Bierkamp" which was used in fighting the Partisans. Then the Einsatzgruppe was entirely disbanded, Bierkamp went into the Government General and took a large number of his men with him.

Q. What was your occupation after Bierkamp left?

A. I think I can say that the Einsatzgruppe ceased to exist after the retreat from the Caucasus. It took over tasks similar in the Wehrmacht under the immediate command of the Commander of the Ukraine and particularly under the command of the Higher S.S. and Police Leaders.

Q. In other words, you merely entered a different circle of activity, under a different leadership, and that is all there was to it. Such functions as were performed by the Einsatzgruppe in the past continued to be carried out in the new circle?

A. No, it actually became a Combat Unit.

Q. What does that mean? Against whom were the military activities directed?

A. Within the scope of the operations which were directed against the Partisan movement.

Q. Or can you say more particularly what this group was actually doing?

A. After the retreat?

Q. When you say that the function of this group had changed when it conducted operations against the Partisans.

A. I have no concrete experiences myself. It was probably used, I believe, for reconnaissance against the Partisans and also was actually used as a military fighting unit.

Q. But did it carry out any executions?

A. I cannot make any definite statement about that as regards this period of time, for it now entered into territories in which that sort of activity no longer came into question.

Q. In your testimony you said that the Einsatz Group had the object of annihilation of the Jews and the commissars; is that correct?

A. Yes.

Q. And in what category did you consider the children? For what reason were the children massacred?

A. The order was that the Jewish population should be liquidated in its entirety.

Q. Including the children?

A. Yes.

Q. Were all the Jewish children murdered?

A. Yes.

Q. But the children of those whom you considered as belonging to the category of commissars, were they also destroyed?

A. I am do not know that the families of Soviet commissars were ever inquired after.

Q. Were you sending anywhere the reports of those executions which the group carried out?

A. The reports on the executions were regularly submitted to the R.S.H.A..

Q. No; did you personally send any reports with reference to the annihilation of thousands of people effected by you? You, personally, did you submit any report?

A. Yes, the reports came from the Einsatzkommandos who carried out the actions, to the Einsatzgruppe, and the Einsatzgruppe informed the R.S.H.A.

Q. Where to?

A. They went to the Chief of the Sipo personally.

Q. Personally.

A. Yes, personally.

Q. What was the name of this police officer? Can you give his name?

A. At the time, Heydrich.

Q. After Heydrich?

A. I did not mention any time, but that was the standing order.

Q. I am asking of you whether you continued to submit reports after Heydrich left or not?

A. After Heydrich's death I was no longer in the Einsatz, but the order, of course, continued in effect.

Q. Have you any information whether the reports were continued after Heydrich left or were discontinued?

A. Yes, they were continued.

Q. Was the order concerning the annihilation of the Soviet people in conformity with the policy of the German Government or the Nazi Party or was it against it? Do you understand the question?

A. Yes. One must distinguish. The order for the liquidation came from the Fuehrer of the Reich and it was to be carried out by the Reichsfuehrer S.S. Himmler.

Q. But was it in conformity with the policy which was conducted by the Nazi Party and the German Government, or was it contrary to it?

A. Politics expresses itself in activity, in so far it was thus a policy that was determined by the Fuehrer. If you ask whether this activity was in conformity with the idea of National Socialism, then I should deny that.

Q. I am talking about the practice.

BY THE PRESIDENT:

Q. I understood you to say that objects of value were taken from the Jewish victims by the Jewish Council of Elders.

A. Yes.

Q. Did the Jewish Council of Elders settle who were to be killed?

A. No.

Q. How did they know who was to be killed?

A. The Jewish Council of Elders determined who were Jews and registered them individually.

Q. And when they registered them did they take their valuables from them?

A. That was done in various ways. As far as I remember, the Council of Elders was given the order to collect valuables at the same time.

Q. So that the Jewish Council of Elders would not know whether or not they were to be killed?

A. That is true.

THE PRESIDENT: We will adjourn now until five minutes past two.

(A recess was taken until 1405 hours.)

CROSS-EXAMINATION BY DR. KAUFFMANN:

Since when have you known Kaltenbrunner?

A. May I address a request to the Tribunal? May I sit down?

Q. Yes.

THE WITNESS: I saw Kaltenbrunner for the first time on a trip from Berlin to Himmler's headquarters at the time when Kaltenbrunner was to be appointed Chief of the Sipo and S.D. Previously to that I simply knew the fact of his existence.

BY DR. KAUFFMANN:

Q. Did you come into personal contact with Kaltenbrunner through private or official conversations after he had become Chief of the R.S.H.A.?

A. Yes, of course.

Q. Do you know his attitude, as for example, on the Jewish question?

A. I am not familiar with any particular attitude of Kaltenbrunner's.

Q. How about the question of the Church?

A. The question of the church - he deplored the anti-church course taken by

Germany. We agreed that an understanding should be reached with the Church.

Q. Do you know what his thoughts were on the liquidation of civilian prisoners, parachute troops, and so on?

A. No.

Q. Do you know that Kaltenbrunner made special efforts to make use of the S.D., in order to supply the Fuehrerstab with the criticism it otherwise lacked?

A. Yes, that was the duty of the S.D. and he also gave this task his official support.

Q. A little bit more slowly.

A. It was the duty of the S.D. even before Kaltenbrunner came and he supported and officially approved the direction of this work.

Q. Do you know, either directly or indirectly, that Kaltenbrunner had no authority to give executive orders, for example, that he had no authority to put people into concentration camps or to take them from concentration camps, that all these things were handled exclusively by Himmler and Mueller?

A. I believe this question is too general for me to be able to answer correctly. The question will have to be broken down, I believe.

If you ask the question whether Kaltenbrunner could bring about executive actions, I must answer in the affirmative. If you then name Himmler and Mueller to the exclusion of Kaltenbrunner, then I must point out that according to the organisation of the R.S.H.A. Mueller was a subordinate of Kaltenbrunner, and consequently orders from Himmler to Mueller were also orders to Kaltenbrunner and Mueller was obliged to inform Kaltenbrunner of them.

On the other hand, it is certain that, particularly in regard to the concentration camps, the final decision regarding entry into or departure from was determined by Himmler. I can say that I know absolutely that - I refer to the expression that often came up, namely, "to the last washerwoman" - Himmler reserved the final decision for himself. As to whether Kaltenbrunner had no authority at all in this regard, I can make no statement.

Q. Have you personally seen the original orders and original signatures of Kaltenbrunner's that ordered the liquidation of sabotage troops and so on?

A. No.

Q. Do you know, either directly or indirectly, that after Heydrich's death a change, which to be sure was not a formal change, took place and that another milder course was taken by Kaltenbrunner?

A. I could not answer that question concretely.

Q. I withdraw the question. Here is another question. Did Kaltenbrunner know that you were an Einsatz Leader in the East?

A. Yes.

Q. Who gave you this command?

A. Heydrich gave it to me.

Q. Heydrich gave it to you? That was before this time?

A. Yes, of course.

DR. KAUFFMANN: I have no further questions at this time.

BY THE TRIBUNAL (GENERAL NIKITCHENKO):

Q. Witness Ohlendorf, can you answer up to what date the Einsatzgruppe under your command was operating?

A. The staff of the Einsatzgruppe went to the Caucasus and was then led back. As far as I can remember, a Combat Command (Kampfkommando) was formed out of it under the name "Bierkamp" which was used in fighting the Partisans. Then the

Einsatzgruppe was entirely disbanded, Bierkamp went into the Government General and took a large number of his men with him.

Q. What was your occupation after Bierkamp left?

A. I think I can say that the Einsatzgruppe ceased to exist after the retreat from the Caucasus. It took over tasks similar in the Wehrmacht under the immediate command of the Commander of the Ukraine and particularly under the command of the Higher S.S. and Police Leaders.

Q. In other words, you merely entered a different circle of activity, under a different leadership, and that is all there was to it. Such functions as were performed by the Einsatzgruppe in the past continued to be carried out in the new circle?

A. No, it actually became a Combat Unit.

Q. What does that mean? Against whom were the military activities directed?

A. Within the scope of the operations which were directed against the Partisan movement.

Q. Or can you say more particularly what this group was actually doing?

A. After the retreat?

Q. When you say that the function of this group had changed when it conducted operations against the Partisans.

A. I have no concrete experiences myself. It was probably used, I believe, for reconnaissance against the Partisans and also was actually used as a military fighting unit.

Q. But did it carry out any executions?

A. I cannot make any definite statement about that as regards this period of time, for it now entered into territories in which that sort of activity no longer came into question.

Q. In your testimony you said that the Einsatz Group had the object of annihilation of the Jews and the commissars; is that correct?

A. Yes.

Q. And in what category did you consider the children? For what reason were the children massacred?

A. The order was that the Jewish population should be liquidated in its entirety.

Q. Including the children?

A. Yes.

Q. Were all the Jewish children murdered?

A. Yes.

Q. But the children of those whom you considered as belonging to the category of commissars, were they also destroyed?

A. I am do not know that the families of Soviet commissars were ever inquired after.

Q. Were you sending anywhere the reports of those executions which the group carried out?

A. The reports on the executions were regularly submitted to the R.S.H.A..

Q. No; did you personally send any reports with reference to the annihilation of thousands of people effected by you? You, personally, did you submit any report?

A. Yes, the reports came from the Einsatzkommandos who carried out the actions, to the Einsatzgruppe, and the Einsatzgruppe informed the R.S.H.A.

Q. Where to?

A. They went to the Chief of the Sipo personally.

Q. Personally.

A. Yes, personally.

Q. What was the name of this police officer? Can you give his name?

A. At the time, Heydrich.

Q. After Heydrich?

A. I did not mention any time, but that was the standing order.

Q. I am asking of you whether you continued to submit reports after Heydrich left or not?

A. After Heydrich's death I was no longer in the Einsatz, but the order, of course, continued in effect.

Q. Have you any information whether the reports were continued after Heydrich left or were discontinued?

A. Yes, they were continued.

Q. Was the order concerning the annihilation of the Soviet people in conformity with the policy of the German Government or the Nazi Party or was it against it? Do you understand the question?

A. Yes. One must distinguish. The order for the liquidation came from the Fuehrer of the Reich and it was to be carried out by the Reichsfuehrer S.S. Himmler.

Q. But was it in conformity with the policy which was conducted by the Nazi Party and the German Government, or was it contrary to it?

A. Politics expresses itself in activity, in so far it was thus a policy that was determined by the Fuehrer. If you ask whether this activity was in conformity with the idea of National Socialism, then I should deny that.

Q. I am talking about the practice.

BY THE PRESIDENT:

Q. I understood you to say that objects of value were taken from the Jewish victims by the Jewish Council of Elders.

A. Yes.

Q. Did the Jewish Council of Elders settle who were to be killed?

A. No.

Q. How did they know who was to be killed?

A. The Jewish Council of Elders determined who were Jews and registered them individually.

Q. And when they registered them did they take their valuables from them?

A. That was done in various ways. As far as I remember, the Council of Elders was given the order to collect valuables at the same time.

Q. So that the Jewish Council of Elders would not know whether or not they were to be killed?

A. That is true.

THE PRESIDENT: We will adjourn now until five minutes past two.

DR. RUDOLF MERKEL (Counsel for the Gestapo):

Q. Witness, do you know that in April 1933 the Gestapo was created in Prussia?

A. I do not know the month, but I do know the year.

Q. Do you know what was the purpose of creating this institution?

A. To fight political opponents potentially dangerous to the State.

Q. Do you know how this institution, which was intended originally for Prussia only, was extended to the rest of the Reich?

A. Either in 1933 or in 1934, the institution of the Political Police was created in all of the States (Laender). These political police agencies were officially subordinated, in 1934, as far as I remember, to the Reichsfuehrer S.S. as Political Police Chief of the States. The Prussian Secret State Police Office represented the first central headquarters. After the creation of the "Main Office Security Police" the command tasks were delegated by Himmler to Heydrich who carried them out through the "Main Office Security Police."

Q. Who created and instituted the Gestapo in the individual States?

A. I cannot give you an answer to this question.

Q. Do you know whether before 1933, in the area which then constituted the Reich, there had existed a similar institution, a political police force?

A. Yes, that existed, as far as I remember, at Police headquarters, Berlin, for instance, and I believe it was Department IA. At any rate political police organisations did exist.

Q. Do you know anything about the sphere of activities of this organisation which existed before 1933?

A. Yes. They were the same; at any rate their activities were fundamentally the same.

Q. Do you know anything about the recruiting of the Gestapo personnel, which, on the whole, was a new institution and consequently not constituted merely by transfer of personnel already in existence.

A. When I got acquainted with the State Police it was certainly true that the nucleus of expert personnel had been taken from the Criminal Police, and the majority of the leading men in the State Police Offices, i.e., in the regional offices of the State police, had risen from the ranks of the Department of the Interior, possibly also from the State Police Administrations, and that they had, in part, even been detailed from this Department of the Interior civil. The same was also true for the experts within Amt IV, i.e., the Gestapo.

Q. You say the majority of the officials were detailed?

A. I did not say the majority were detailed, but I said "in part."

Q. Detailed in part! Could any of these members of the Gestapo possibly resist being taken over into the Gestapo if they did not wish it, or could they not?

A. I would not affirm that a definite resistance was possible. Some of them might have succeeded, by cunning, in avoiding it had they not wanted to go. But if one was detailed to such an office from the Department of the Interior, then, as an official, one simply had to obey. As an official he had to....

Q. The members of the Gestapo evidently consisted almost exclusively, or exclusively, of officials? Do you know anything about that?

A. That probably was no longer the case during the war. But as a rule it should be assumed that they were officials in as far as the experts were concerned. Some of them, of course, while in training, were not yet officials, and others again were merely employees, especially in the Auxiliary Forces.

Q. Can you tell me the approximate number of the members of the Gestapo towards the end of the war?

A. I estimate the total organisation of the Gestapo, including the regional offices and the Occupied Territories, at about 30,000.

Q. There was therefore within the Gestapo, a considerable percentage of officials who were merely administrative officials and had nothing to do with executive powers?

A. Yes, of course.

Q. And what was the percentage of these administrative officials who performed purely administrative functions?

A. We must, in the first instance, take into consideration that this number included the auxiliaries, as well as the women, and I cannot, offhand, immediately give you any figures. But it is certain that a proportion of one expert to three or four persons not employed in an executive capacity could not be considered excessive.

Q. Do you know anything about who was responsible for the direction and administration of the concentration camps?

A. It was Obergruppenfuehrer Pohl.

Q. Did the Gestapo have anything to do with the leadership and with the administration of the concentration camps or not?

A. According to my knowledge, no.

Q. Therefore, no members of the Gestapo were active, or in any way involved in the measures carried out in the concentration camps?

A. As far as I could judge, from a distance, only investigating officials of the State Police were active in the concentration camps.

Q. Did the Gestapo in any way participate in the mass executions undertaken by your Einsatzgruppe, which you described this morning?

A. Only as much as every other person present in the Einsatzgruppe.

DR. MERKEL: I ask the Tribunal to give me the opportunity of questioning this witness again after the return of the defendant Kaltenbrunner, since I am obliged to rely exclusively on information received from Kaltenbrunner.

THE PRESIDENT: I think that the Tribunal will be prepared to allow you to put further questions at a later stage.

DR. MERKEL: Thank you.

BY DR. EXNER (Counsel for the General Staff and the O.K.W.):

Q. Witness, you mentioned the negotiations which took place in the O.K.W., which later led to an agreement between O.K.W. and O.K.H. on the one side, and the Main Security Office of the Reich (R.S.H.A.) on the other. I am interested in this point: Can you state that during the negotiations on this agreement there was any mention made regarding the extermination and the killing of Jews?

A. I cannot say anything concrete on this particular subject, but I do not believe it.

Q. You do not believe it?

A. No.

Q. In addition, you have told us that the Commander-in-Chief of the 11th Army knew about the liquidations, and I should like to ask you first of all: Do you know anything regarding the Commanders-in-Chief of the other armies?

A. In general, they must have been informed, through the speech of the Fuehrer, before the beginning of the Russian campaign.

Q. That is a conclusion that you have drawn?

A. No, it is not a conclusion that I have drawn; it is merely a report on the contents of the speech which, according to Himmler's statement, Hitler had made to the Commanders-in-Chief.

Q. Now, you have spoken about directives given by the Commander-in-Chief of the 11th Army. What kind of directives were they?

A. I once spoke about the Commander-in-Chief in the case of Nikolaiev, i.e., that the order given at that time, for the liquidations to take place 200 kilometers away from the headquarters of the Army. On the second occasion, I did not speak about the Commander-in-Chief of the Army, but about the High Command of the Army at Simferopol, because I cannot say, with any certainty, who had requested the competent Einsatzkommando at Simferopol to speed up the liquidation.

Q. That is the very question I should like to put to you: With whom in the 11th Army did you negotiate at that time?

A. I did not personally negotiate at all with anyone on this subject, since I was not the person directly concerned with these matters; but the High Command of the Army negotiated with the competent local Einsatzkommando either through the responsible army office, which at all times was in touch with the Einsatzkommandos, namely the I-C or the I-CAO, or else through the staff of the O.Q.

Q. Who gave you directives for the march?

A. The directives for the march came, as a rule, from the Chief of Staff.

Q. From the Chief of Staff? The Commander-in-Chief of the Army at the time referred to was von Manstein. Was there ever an order in this case signed by von Manstein?

A. I cannot remember any such order, but when the march was discussed there were oral consultations with von Manstein, the Chief of Staff and myself.

Q. When discussing the march?

A. Yes.

Q. You said that the Army was opposed to these liquidations. Can you state how this became evident?

A. Not the Army, but the Leaders were secretly opposed to the liquidations.

Q. Yes. But I mean, how did you recognise that fact?

A. By our conversations. Not only the leaders of the Army but also most of those who had to carry them out were opposed to the liquidations.

DR. EXNER: I thank you.

BY PROFESSOR KRAUS (Counsel for defendant Schacht):

Q. Were you acquainted with the personal records kept in your department on Reichsbank President Schacht?

A. No.

Q. Do you know why, after the 20th July, 1944, the former Reichsbank President Schacht was arrested and interned in a concentration camp?

A. Probably the occasion of the 20th of July was also favorable for a possible conviction of Reichsbank President Schacht, who was known to be inimical to the Party, whilst by means of witnesses or other methods he could be prosecuted in connection with the events of the 20th of July.

Q. Then defendant Schacht was known to your people as being inimical to the Party?

A. Yes, at least since the year 1937 or 1938.

Q. Since the year 1937 or 1938? And you also suspected him of participating in "putsches"?

A. Personally I did not suspect this, because I was not concerned with these matters at all; He was mainly under suspicion mainly because of his well-known enmity. But, as far as I know, this suspicion was never confirmed.

Q. Can you tell me, who caused Schacht to be arrested?

A. That I cannot say.

Q. Then you do not know whether the arrest was ordered by the Fuehrer, by

Himmler or by some subordinate authority.

A. I consider it impossible that it should emanate from any subordinate authority.

Q. Then you assume that it had been ordered by the Fuehrer?

A. At least by Himmler.

BY DR. STAHMER (Counsel for defendant Goering):

Q. Witness, if I have understood you correctly, you said that at the beginning of 1933, after the seizure of power by Hitler, the Gestapo was created in Prussia; but before that time there had already existed in Prussia an organisation with similar tasks; for instance at the Police Headquarters in Berlin with Department IA; only this organisation was opposed to National Socialism, whereas now the contrary is true. But you also had the task of keeping political opponents under observation and possibly of arresting them, thus protecting the State from these political opponents.

A. Yes.

Q. You said further that in 1933, after the seizure of power, a political police with identical tasks was also instituted in all the other States (Laender).

A. Yes, in the year 1933-1934.

Q. This political police, which existed in the various States was then centralised in 1934 and its direction handed over to Himmler?

A. It was not at first centralised, but Himmler did become Chief of Police of all the States.

Q. Now one more question. Did the Prussian Gestapo play a leading role, as far as the other States were concerned, as early as 1933 or only after Himmler took over the leadership in 1934?

A. I do not believe that the Prussian State Police, which after all was under the leadership of Reichsmarshal Goering, became, at that time, the competent authority for the other States as well.

BY DR. KRANZBUEHLER (Counsel for defendant Doenitz):

I am speaking as the representative of the counsel for defendant Grand Admiral Raeder.

Q. Witness, you just mentioned a speech of the Fuehrer before the Commanders-in-Chief, in which the he is supposed to have instructed the Commanders-in-Chief regarding the liquidation of Jews. Which conference do you mean by that?

A. A conference took place, shortly before the Russian campaign, with the Commanders-in-Chief of the Army Groups and the Armies, at the Fuehrer's quarters.

Q. Were the of the Commanders-in-Chief of the divisions of the Armed Forces absent?

A. I do not know that.

Q. Were you yourself present at this conference?

A. No. I have recounted this conference on the basis of a conversation I had with Himmler.

Q. Did this conversation with Himmler take place in a large circle of people or was it a private conversation?

A. It was a private conversation.

Q. Did you have the impression that Himmler stated facts, or do you consider it possible that he wished to encourage you in your difficult task?

A. No. The conversation took place much later and did not spring from such motives, but from resentment at the attitude of certain generals of the Armed Forces;

Himmler wanted to say that these generals of the Armed Forces could not disassociate themselves from the events that had taken place, as they were just as responsible as all the rest.

Q. And when did this conversation with Himmler take place?

A. In May, 1945, at Flensburg.

DR. KRANZBUHLER: Thank you.

(A recess was taken until 1405 hours.)

BY DR. SERVATIUS (Counsel for the Political Leaders and for defendant Sauckel).

Q. Witness, with regard to the command channels at the disposal of the R.S.H.A. for the execution of their orders and measures and for the transmission of these orders to tactical organisations, such as the S.D. and the concentration camps, did the R.S.H.A. possess their own official channels or did they rely on the channels of the Political Leaders Organisation, i.e., were these orders forwarded via the Gauleitung and the Kreisleitung?

A. I know nothing at all about it. I consider it entirely out of the question.

Q. You consider it entirely out of the question that the Gauleitung and the Kreisleitung had been informed? How was it, for instance...

A. One moment, please. You asked me whether the channels passed their way; you did not ask me whether they had been informed.

Q. Were these offices informed of the orders?

A. The Inspectors, the Gestapo, or the S.D. Leaders were considered as police or political reporters (Referenten) of the Gauleiter or the Reichsstatthalter, and these official chiefs had to report to the Gauleiter on their respective fields of activity. Just how extensively this was done, I am unable to judge. It depends on the activities and on the nature of the co-operation between the Gauleiter and these offices, but it is, in any case, inconceivable that the State Police could carry on these activities, for any length of time, without the knowledge of the responsible Party Organisations.

Q. Does this also refer to reports from lower to higher units, i.e., to the activities of the concentration camps?

A. The concentration camps were not subordinate to the State Police; I am convinced - since these were purely affairs of the Reich - that there was no such close connection between the Gauleiter and the concentration camps as there was between the Gauleiter and the permanent activities of the State Police.

Q. I also represent the defendant Sauckel. Do you know of the impressment of foreign workers by the S.S.? Foreign workers who, as a matter of fact, came from the concentration camps?

A. Only superficially.

BY HERR BABEL (Counsel for the S.S. and the S.D.).

Q. Witness, this morning you mentioned the figures of 3,000 and 30,000 for the Security Service. I should now like to know for certain how these figures are to be understood. Do the 3,000 members of the S.D., whom you mentioned this morning, represent the entire personnel of the S.D. at that time, or did they only represent that part of the units which were employed in the field with the mobile units also mentioned by you this morning?

A. No, the figures represent the total personnel including employees and women auxiliaries.

Q. Including employees and women auxiliaries. And the 30,000, which we also discussed, were they honorary members (ehrenamtliche Mitglieder) employed only in the interior of Germany?

A. Yes, as a rule, in any case...

Q. And who, to a considerable extent, belonged neither to the S.S. nor to the Party?

A. Yes.

Q. How large were the mobile units of the S.D. employed in these executions?

A. The S.D. had no mobile units and only individual members of the S.D. were detailed to regional offices elsewhere. The S.D., as a separate entity, did not act independently anywhere.

Q. In your opinion and judging by your own experience, what figure did this detailed personnel attain?

A. The figure was quite a low one.

Q. Will you please give an approximate figure.

A. I place the figure at an average of about two to three S.D. experts per Einsatzkommando.

Q. I should like to be informed of the total number of the S.S. Do you know anything about that?

A. No, I have no idea at all.

Q. No idea at all. Did any units of the S.S. Armed Forces (Waffen S.S.) and other subordinate S.S. Groups in any way participate in the Einsatzgruppen?

A. As I said this morning, in each Einsatzgruppe there was, or rather there should have been, one company of the S.S. Armed Forces (Waffen S.S.).

Q. One company. And what, at that time, was the exact strength of one company?

A. I do not know about the Waffen S.S. serving with the other Einsatzgruppen, but I estimate that my particular group employed approximately 100 men of the S.S. Armed Forces.

Q. Were "Death's Head Units" (Totenkopf Verbaende) also involved?

A. No.

Q. Was the "Adolf Hitler Bodyguard" (Leibstandarte Adolf Hitler) employed in any fashion?

A. That was purely a matter of chance. I cannot name a single formation from which these S.S. Armed Forces had been seconded.

Q. Another question that was touched upon this morning: When was the S.D. created and what, at first, were their duties?

A. As far as I know, the S.D. was created in 1932.

Q. And what were their duties at that time?

A. They constituted, so to speak, the I-C [Intelligence Corps] of the Party. They were supposed to give information about Party opponents and, if necessary, to deceive them.

Q. Did these duties change in the course of time. and, if so, when?

A. Yes, after the seizure of power, the combating of political opponents was, in certain spheres, one of their principal duties, and supplying the required information on certain individuals was considered their main task. At that time an Intelligence Service, in the true sense of the word, did not yet exist; the real evolution of the S.D. machine within the field of the Home Intelligence Service only followed as from 1936-1937. From that time onwards the work changed, from the observation of individuals to technical matters. With the 1939 reorganisation, when the Main Office of the S.D. was dissolved, the handling of political opponents was completely eliminated from the work of the S.D., which work was thereafter limited to technical matters. Its duties now consisted in observing the effects of the measures carried out by the leading authorities of the Reich and the States (Laender) and in determining how the circles affected reacted to them; in addition, they had to determine what shape the moods and attitude of the people and various classes of society assumed during the course of the war. It was, as a matter of fact, the only authority supplying criticism within the Reich and reporting facts on objective lines to the highest authorities. It should also be pointed out that the Party did not, at any stage, legitimise this work until 1945. The only legal recognition of this critical work came from Reichsmarshal Goering, and that only after the beginning of the war, since he could, in this way, draw the attention of the other departments, at meetings of the Reich Defence Council, to faulty developments. This unbiased and critical work became, in fact, after 1939 the main function of the S.D. Home Intelligence Service.

Q. Another question. To what extent were units of the S.D. committed for duty in the concentration camps?

A. I would ask you, at all times to distinguish between the Home Front S.D. (Inland) working under the Head Office (Amt III) and the Foreign S.D. (Ausland). I cannot give you any information about the Foreign S.D. (Ausland), but their Chief, Schellenberg, is present in this courthouse. As far as Amt III is concerned, I know of no single case in which the representatives of the Home Front S.D. (Inland) had anything at all to do with concentration camps.

Q. Now, a question concerning you personally. From whom did you receive your orders for the liquidation of the Jews and so forth? And in what form?

A. My duty was not the task of liquidation, but I did head the staff which led the Einsatzkommandos in the field, whilst the Einsatzkommandos themselves had already received this order in Berlin, on behalf of Himmler and Heydrich, from Streckenbach. This order was renewed by Himmler at Nikolaiev.

Q. You personally were not concerned with the execution of these orders?

A. I led the Einsatzgruppe, and therefore I had the task of seeing how the Einsatzkommandos executed the orders received.

Q. But did you have no scruples in regard to the execution of these orders?

A. Yes, of course.

Q. And how is it that they were carried out regardless of these scruples?

A. Because to me it is inconceivable that a subordinate leader should not carry out orders given by the Leaders of the State.

Q. This is your own opinion. But this must have been not only your point of view but also the point of view of the majority of the people involved. Did not some of the men appointed to execute these orders ask you to be relieved of such tasks?

A. I cannot remember any one concrete case. I excluded some whom I did not consider emotionally suitable for executing these tasks and I sent some of them home.

Q. Was the legality of the orders explained to these people under false pretenses?

A. I do not understand your question; since the order was issued by the superior authorities, the question of legality could not arise in the minds of these individuals, for they had sworn obedience to the people who had issued the orders.

Q. Could any individual expect to succeed in evading the execution of these orders?

A. No, the result would have been a court martial with a corresponding sentence.

THE PRESIDENT: Colonel Amen, do you wish to re-examine?

COLONEL AMEN: Just a very few questions, Your Honor.

RE-EXAMINATION BY COLONEL AMEN:

Q. What organisation furnished the supplies to the Einsatz Groups?
A. The Reichssicherheitshauptamt furnished supplies.
Q. What organisation furnished weapons to the Einsatz Groups?
A. The weapons were also furnished through the R.S.H.A.
Q. What organisation assigned personnel to the Einsatz Groups?
A. The Organisation and Personnel Department of the Reichssicherheitshauptamt.
Q. And all these activities of supplies required personnel in addition to the operating members?
A. Yes.
COLONEL AMEN: I have no more questions.
THE PRESIDENT: That will do; thank you.
(The witness withdrew.)
Q. The next witness to be called by the prosecution is Dieter Wisliceny. That witness will be examined by Lieutenant-Colonel Smith W. Brookhart, Jr.
BY THE PRESIDENT:
Q. What is your name?
A. Dieter Wisliceny.
Q. Will you repeat this oath? I swear by God, the Almighty and Omniscient, that I will speak the pure truth and will withhold and add nothing.
(The witness repeated the oath in German.)
Q. Please speak slowly and pause between each sentence.
BY LIEUTENANT COLONEL BROOKHART:
Q. How old are you?
A. I am thirty-four years old.
Q. Where were you born?
A. I was born at Regulowken in East Prussia.
Q. Were you a member of the N.S.D.A.P.?
A. Yes, I was a member of the N.S.D.A.P..
Q. Since what year?
A. I entered the N.S.D.A.P. first in 1931, was then struck off the list and finally entered in 1933.
Q. Were you a member of the S.S.?
A. Yes, I entered the S.S. in 1934.
Q. Were you a member of the Gestapo?
A. In 1934 I entered the S.D.
Q. What rank did you achieve?
A. In 1940 I was promoted to S.S. Hauptsturmfuehrer.
Q. Do you know Adolf Eichmann?
A. Yes, I have known Eichmann since 1934.
Q. Under what circumstances?
A. We joined the S.D. about the same time, in 1934. Until 1937 we were together in the same department.
Q. How well did you know Eichmann personally?
A. We knew each other very well. We used the intimate "Du," and I also knew his family very well.
Q. What was his position?

A. Eichmann was in the R.S.H.A., Chief of Department IV, Gestapo.

Q. Do you mean Section IV or a subsection, and, if so, which subsection?

A. He led Section IV-A-4. This department comprised two subsections: one for Church and another for Jewish matters.

Q. You have before you a diagram showing the position of Subsection IV-A-4-b in the R.S.H.A.

A. Yes.

Q. Did you prepare this diagram?

A. Yes, I made the diagram myself.

Q. Does it correctly portray the organisational set-up showing the section dealing with Jewish problems?

A. Yes, this was approximately the personnel of the section at the beginning of 1944.

Q. Referring to this chart and the list of leading personnel, as shown in the lower section of the paper, were you personally acquainted with each of the individuals named therein?

A. Yes; I knew all of them personally.

Q. What was the particular mission of IV-A-4-b of the R.S.H.A.?

A. This Section IV-A-4-b was concerned with the Jewish question on behalf of the R.S.H.A. Eichmann had special powers from Gruppenfuehrer Mueller, the Chief of Amt IV, and from the Chief of the Security Police. He was responsible for the so-called solution of the Jewish question in Germany and in all countries occupied by Germany.

Q. Were there distinct periods of activity affecting the Jews?

A. Yes.

Q. Will you describe to the Tribunal the approximate periods and the different types of activity?

A. Yes. Until 1940 the general policy within the section was to settle the Jewish question in Germany and in areas occupied by Germany by means of a planned emigration. The second phase, from that time on, was the concentration of all Jews in Poland and in other territories occupied by Germany in the East, by concentration in ghettos. This period lasted approximately until the beginning of 1942. The third period was the so-called "final solution" of the Jewish question, that is, the planned extermination and destruction of the Jewish race; this period lasted until October, 1944, when Himmler gave the order to stop their destruction.

(A recess was taken.)

LT. COLONEL BROOKHART:

Q. When did you first become associated with Section IV-A-4 of the R.S.H.A.?

A. That was in 1940. I accidentally met Eichmann....

Q. What was your position?

A. Eichmann suggested that I should go to Bratislava as adviser on the Jewish question to the Slovakian Government.

Q. Thereafter how long did you hold that position?

A. I was at Bratislava until the spring of 1943; then, almost a year in Greece and later, from March, 1944, until December, 1944, I was with Eichmann in Hungary. In January, 1945, I left Eichmann's department.

Q. In your official connection with Section IV-A-4, did you learn of any order which directed the annihilation of all Jews?

A. Yes, I learned of such an order for the first time from Eichmann in the summer of 1942.

Q. Will you tell the Tribunal under what circumstances, and what was the substance of the order?

A. In the spring of 1942 about 17,000 Jews were taken from Slovakia to Poland as workers. It was a question of an agreement with the Slovakian Government. The Slovakian Government further asked whether the families of these workers could not be taken to Poland as well. At first Eichmann declined this request.

In April, or at the beginning of May, 1942, Eichmann told me that henceforward whole families could also be taken to Poland. Eichmann himself was at Bratislava in May, 1942, and had discussed the matter with competent members of the Slovakian Government. He visited Minister Mach and the then Prime Minister, Professor Tuka. At that time he assured the Slovakian Government that these Jews would be humanely and decently treated in the Polish ghettos. This was the special wish of the Slovakian Government. As a result of this assurance about 35,000 Jews were taken from Slovakia into Poland. The Slovakian Government, however, made efforts to see that these Jews were, in fact, humanely treated; they particularly tried to help such Jews as had been converted to Christianity. Prime Minister Tuka repeatedly asked me to visit him, and expressed the wish that a Slovakian delegation be allowed to enter the areas to which the Slovakian Jews were supposed to have been sent. I transmitted this wish to Eichmann, and the Slovakian Government even sent a note on the matter to the German Government. Eichmann, for the time being, gave evasive answers.

Then at the end of July or the beginning of August, I went to see him in Berlin and implored him once more to grant the request of the Slovakian Government. I pointed out to him that abroad there were rumors to the effect that all Jews in Poland were being exterminated. I pointed out to him that the Pope had intervened with the Slovakian Government on their behalf. I advised him that such a proceeding, if really true, would seriously injure our prestige, i.e., the prestige of Germany, abroad. For all these reasons I begged him to permit the inspection in question. After a lengthy discussion, Eichmann told me that this request to visit the Polish ghettos could not be granted under any circumstances whatsoever. In reply to my question "Why?" he said that most of these Jews were no longer alive. I asked him who had given such instructions and he referred me to an order of Himmler's. I then begged him to show me this order, because I could not believe that it actually existed in writing. He....

Q. Where were you at that time? Where were you at the time of this meeting with Eichmann?

A. This meeting with Eichmann took place in Berlin, Kurfuerstenstrasse 116, in Eichmann's office.

Q. Proceed with the answer to the previous question. Proceed with the discussion of the circumstances and the order.

A. Eichmann told me he could show me this order in writing if it would soothe my conscience. He took a small volume of documents from his safe, turned over the pages, and showed me a letter from Himmler to the Chief of the Security Police and the S.D. The gist of the letter was roughly as follows:

The Fuehrer had ordered the "final solution" of the Jewish question; the Chief of the Security Police and the S.D. and the Inspector of the Concentration Camps were entrusted with carrying out this so-called "final solution." All Jewish men and women who were able to work were to be temporarily exempted from the so-called "final solution" and used for work in the concentration camps. This letter was signed by Himmler in person. I could not possibly be mistaken since Himmler's signature was well known to me. I....

Q. To whom was the order addressed?

A. To the Chief of the Security Police and S.D., i.e. , to the office of the Chief of the Security Police and S.D.

Q. Was there any other addressee on this order?

A. Yes, the Inspector of the Concentration Camps. The order was addressed to both these offices.

Q. Did the order bear any classification for security purposes?

A. It was classified as "Top Secret."

Q. What was the approximate date of this order?

A. This order was dated April, 1942.

Q. By whom was it signed?

A. By Himmler personally.

Q. And you personally examined this order in Eichmann's office?

A. Yes, Eichmann handed me the document and I saw the order myself.

Q. Was any question asked by you as to the meaning of the words "final solution" as used in the order?

A. Eichmann went on to explain the meaning of the concept to me. He said that the planned biological destruction of the Jewish race in the Eastern Territories was disguised by the concept and wording "final solution." In later discussions on this subject the same words "final solution" re-appeared over and over again.

Q. Was anything said by you to Eichmann in regard to the power given him under this order?

A. Eichmann told me that within the R.S.H.A. he personally was entrusted with the execution of this order. For this purpose, he had received every authority from the Chief of the Security Police; he himself was personally responsible for the execution of this order.

Q. Did you make any comment to Eichmann about his authority?

A. Yes. It was perfectly clear to me that this order spelled death to millions of people. I said to Eichmann, "God grant that our enemies never have the opportunity of doing the same to the German people," in reply to which Eichmann told me not to be sentimental; it was an order of the Fuehrer's and would have to be carried out.

Q. Do you know whether that order continued in force and under the operation of Eichmann's department?

A. Yes.

Q. For how long?

A. This order was in force until October, 1944. At that time Himmler gave a counter-order which forbade the annihilation of the Jews.

Q. Who was Chief of the Reichssicherheitshauptamt at the time the order was first issued?

A. That would be Heydrich.

Q. Did the program under this order continue with equal force under Kaltenbrunner?

A. Yes; there was no alleviation or change of any kind.

Q. State, if you know, how long Kaltenbrunner knew Eichmann.

A. From various statements by Eichmann I gathered that Kaltenbrunner and Eichmann had known each other for a long time. Both came from Linz, and when Kaltenbrunner was made Chief of the Security Police, Eichmann expressed his satisfaction. He told me at that time that he knew Kaltenbrunner very well personally, and that Kaltenbrunner was very well acquainted with Eichmann's family in Linz.

Q. Did Eichmann ever refer to his friendship or standing with Kaltenbrunner as being helpful to him?

A. Yes, he repeatedly said that, if he had any serious trouble, he could, at any time, go to Kaltenbrunner personally. He did not have to do that very often, since his relations with his immediate superior, Gruppenfuehrer Mueller, were very good.

Q. Have you been present when Eichmann and Kaltenbrunner met?

A. Yes; once I saw how cordially Kaltenbrunner greeted Eichmann. That was in February, 1945, in Eichmann's office in Berlin. Kaltenbrunner came to lunch every day at Kurfuerstenstrasse 116; there the Chiefs met for their mid- day meal with Kaltenbrunner; and it was on one such occasion that I saw how cordially Kaltenbrunner greeted Eichmann and how he inquired after the health of Eichmann's family in Linz.

Q. In connection with the administration of his Office, do you know to what extent Eichmann submitted matters to Heydrich, and later to Kaltenbrunner for approval?

A. The routine channel from Eichmann to Kaltenbrunner lay through Gruppenfuehrer Mueller. To my knowledge reports to Kaltenbrunner were drawn up at regular intervals by Eichmann and submitted to him. I also know that in the summer of 1944 he made a personal report to Kaltenbrunner.

Q. Did you have an opportunity to examine files in Eichmann's office?

A. Yes; I frequently had occasion to examine the files in Eichmann's office. I know that he handled all files pertaining to questions with this particular order very carefully. He was in every respect a definite bureaucrat; he immediately recorded in the files every discussion he ever had with any of his superiors. He always pointed out to me that the most important thing was for him to be covered by his superiors at all times. He shunned all personal responsibility and took good care to take shelter behind his superiors - in this case Mueller and Kaltenbrunner - and to inveigle them into accepting the responsibility for all his actions.

Q. In the case of a typical report going from Eichmann's department through Mueller, Kaltenbrunner to Himmler - have you seen copies of such reports in Eichmann's file?

A. Yes, such copies were naturally very often in the files. The regular channel was as follows: Eichmann had a draft made by an expert or he prepared it himself; this draft went to Gruppenfuehrer Mueller, his Chief of Department; Mueller either signed this draft himself or left the signing to Eichmann. In most cases, when reports to Kaltenbrunner and Himmler were concerned, Mueller signed them himself. Whenever reports were signed unchanged by Mueller, they were returned to Eichmann's office, where a fair copy and one carbon copy were prepared. The fair copy then went back to Mueller for his signature, and thence it was forwarded either to Kaltenbrunner or to Himmler. In individual cases where reports to Himmler were involved, Kaltenbrunner signed them himself. I myself have seen carbon copies with Kaltenbrunner's signature.

Q. Turning now to areas and countries in which measures were taken affecting the Jews, will you state as to which countries you have personal knowledge of such operations?

A. Firstly, I have personal knowledge of all measures taken in Slovakia. I also know full particulars of the evacuation of Jews from Greece and especially from Hungary. Further, I know about certain measures taken in Bulgaria and in Croatia. I naturally heard about the measures adopted in other countries, but was unable from my own observations or from detailed reports, to gain a clear picture of the situation.

Q. Considering the case of Slovakia, you have already made reference to the 17,000 Jews specially selected who were sent from Slovakia. Will you tell the Tribunal of the other measures that followed concerning Jews in Slovakia?

A. I mentioned before that these first 17,000 laborers were followed by about 35,000 Jews, including entire families. In August, or the beginning of September, 1942, an end was put to this action in Slovakia. The reasons for this were that a large number of Jews still in Slovakia had been granted - either by the President or by various Ministries - special permission to remain in the country. A further reason might have been the unsatisfactory answer I gave the Slovakian Government in reply to their request for the inspection of the Jewish camps in Poland. This state of affairs lasted until September, 1944; from August, 1942, until September, 1944, no Jews were removed from Slovakia. From 25,000 to 30,000 Jews still remained in the country.

Q. What happened to the first group of 17,000 specially selected workers?

A. This group was not annihilated, but all were employed for enforced labor in the Auschwitz and Lublin concentration Camps.

Q. How do you know this?

A. I know this detail because the Commandant of Auschwitz, Hoess, made a remark to this effect to me in Hungary, in 1944. He told me, at that time, that these 17,000 Jews were his best workers in Auschwitz.

Q. What was the name of that Commandant?

A. The Commandant of Auschwitz was Hoess.

Q. What happened to the approximately 35,000 members of the families of the Jewish workers that were also sent to Poland?

A. They were treated according to the order which Eichmann had shown me in August, 1942. Part of them were left alive if they were able to work. The others were killed.

Q. How do you know this?

A. I know that from Eichmann and, naturally, also from Hoess, during conversations in Hungary.

Q. What proportion of this group remained alive?

A. Hoess, at that time, in a conversation with Eichmann, at which I was present, gave the figure of the surviving Jews who had been put to work at about 25 to 30 per cent.

Q. Referring now to the 25,000 Jews that remained in Slovakia until September, 1944, do you know what was done with those Jews?

A. After the outbreak of the Slovakian insurrection in the fall of 1944, Huptsturmfuehrer [sic] Brunner, one of Eichmann's assistants, was sent to Slovakia. My wish to go to Slovakia was refused by Eichmann. Brunner then, with the help of German police forces and also with forces of the Slovakian Gendarmerie, assembled these Jews in several camps and transported them to Auschwitz. According to Brunner's statement, about 14,000 people were involved. A small group which remained in Camp Szered was, as far as I know, sent to Theresienstadt in the spring of 1945.

Q. What happened to these Jews after they were deported from Slovakia, this group of 25,000?

A. I assume that they also met with the so-called "final solution," because

Himmler's order to suspend this action was not issued until several weeks later.

Q. Considering now actions in Greece about which you have personal knowledge, will you tell the Tribunal of the actions there in a chronological sequence?

A. In January, 1943, I was summoned by Eichmann to Berlin, where he told me that I was to proceed to Salonika, there to solve the Jewish problem there in cooperation with the German Military Administration in Macedonia. Eichmann's permanent representative, Sturmbannfuehrer Wolf, had previously been to Salonika. My departure had been scheduled for February, 1942. At the end of January, 1942, I was told by Eichmann that Hauptsturmfuehrer Brunner had been nominated by him for the technical execution of all operations in Greece, and that he was to accompany me to Salonika. Brunner was not subordinate to me; he worked independently. In February, 1942, we went to Salonika and there contacted the Military Administration. As first action....

Q. With whom in the Military Administration did you deal?

A. War Administration Counsellor (Kriegsverwaltungsrat) Dr. Merten, Chief of the Military Administration with the Commander of the Armed Forces in the Salonika-Aegean theatre.

Q. I believe you used 1942 once or more in reference; did you at all times refer to 1943 in dealing with Greece?

A. That is an error. These events occurred in 1943.

Q. What arrangements were made through Dr. Merten and what actions were taken?

A. In Salonika the Jews were first of all concentrated in certain quarters of the city. There were, in Salonika, about 50,000 Jews of Spanish descent. At the beginning of March, after this concentration had taken place, a teletype arrived from Eichmann to Brunner, ordering the immediate evacuation of all Jews from Salonika and Macedonia to Auschwitz. Armed with this order Brunner and I went to the Military Administration; no objections were raised by the Administration and measures were prepared and executed. Brunner directed the entire action in Salonika in person. The trains necessary for the evacuation were requisitioned from the Transport Command of the Armed Forces. All Brunner had to do was to indicate the number of railway cars needed and the exact time at which they were required.

Q. Were any of the Jewish workers retained at the request of Dr. Merten or the Military Administration?

A. The Military Administration had requisitioned about 3,000 Jews for construction work on the railroad, which number was duly delivered. Once the work was ended, these Jews were returned to Brunner and were, like all the others, dispatched to Auschwitz. The work in question was carried out within the programme of the Todt Organisation.

Q. What was the number of Jewish workers retained for the Organization Todt?

A. Three to four thousand.

Q. Was there any illness among the Jews that were concentrated for transport?

A. In the camp proper, i.e., the concentration camp, there were no incidence of disease to report. However, in certain quarters of the city inhabited by the Jews there was a prevalence of typhus and other contagious diseases, especially tuberculosis of the lungs.

Q. What, if any, communication did you have with Eichmann concerning this typhus?

A. On receipt of the teletype concerning the evacuation from Salonika, I drew

Eichmann's attention over the telephone to the prevalence of typhus. He ignored my objections and gave orders for the evacuation to proceed immediately.

Q. Altogether, how many Jews were collected and shipped from Greece?

A. There were over 50,000 Jews; I believe that about 54,000 were evacuated from Salonika and Macedonia.

Q. What is the basis for your figure?

A. I myself read a comprehensive report from Brunner to Eichmann on completion of the evacuation. Brunner left Salonika at the end of May 1943. I personally was not in Salonika from the beginning of April until the end of May, so that the action was carried out by Brunner alone.

Q. How many transports were used for shipping Jews from Salonika?

A. From 20 to 25 transport trains.

Q. And how many were shipped in each transport?

A. There were at least 2,000, and in many cases 2,500.

Q. What kind of railway equipment was used for these shipments?

A. Sealed freight cars were used. The evacuees were given sufficient food to last them for about ten days, consisting mostly of bread, olives and other dry food. They also received water and various sanitary facilities.

Q. Who furnished this railway transportation?

A. Transport was supplied by the Rail Transport Command of the Armed Forces, i.e., the cars and locomotives. The food was furnished by the Military Administration.

Q. What did the Subsection IV-A-4 have to do with obtaining this transportation, and who in that sub-section dealt with transportation?

THE PRESIDENT: Colonel Brookhart, you need not go into this in such great detail.

LIEUTENANT-COLONEL BROOKHART: If Your Honour pleases, this particular question, I believe, will have a bearing on the implications involving the military; I can cut down on the other details.

THE PRESIDENT: Well, you spent some considerable time in describing how many of them were concentrated. Whether it was 60,000, or how many were kept for the Todt Organisation - all those details are really unnecessary.

LIEUTENANT-COLONEL BROOKHART: Very well, Sir.

THE PRESIDENT: I mean, you must use your own discretion about how you cut down. I do not know what details or what facts you are going to prove.

LIEUTENANT-COLONEL BROOKHART: If Your Honour pleases, this witness, as he has testified, is competent to cover practically all details in these Balkan countries. It is not our wish to add cumulative evidence, but his testimony does furnish a complete story from the Head Office of the Reichssicherheitshauptamt through the field operations to the "final solution."

THE PRESIDENT: Well, what is he going to prove about these 50,000 Jews?

LIEUTENANT-COLONEL BROOKHART: Their ultimate disposition at Auschwitz, as far as he knows.

THE PRESIDENT: Well, you can go on to what ultimately happened to them then.

LIEUTENANT-COLONEL BROOKHART: Yes, Sir.

Q. What was the destination of these transports of Jews from Greece?

A. In every case to Auschwitz.

Q. And what was the ultimate disposition of the Jews sent to Auschwitz from

Greece?

A. They were without exception destined for the so-called "final solution."

Q. During the collection period were these Jews called upon to furnish their own subsistence?

A. I did not understand the question exactly.

THE PRESIDENT: Colonel Brookhart, does it matter, if they were "brought to the "final solution"" which I suppose means death?

LIEUTENANT-COLONEL BROOKHART: Your Honour, this witness will testify that 280,000,000 drachmas were deposited in the Greek National Bank for the subsistence of these people and that this amount was later appropriated by the German Military Administration. That is all I have hoped to prove by this question.

LIEUTENANT-COLONEL BROOKHART (to the Witness): Is that a correct statement of your testimony?

A. Yes. The cash which the Jews possessed was taken away and put into a common account at the Bank of Greece. After the Jews had been evacuated from Salonika this account was taken over by the German Military Administration. About 280,000,000 drachmas were involved.

Q. When you say the Jews taken to Auschwitz were submitted to the "final solution," what do you mean by that?

A. By that I mean what Eichmann had explained to me under the term "final solution," that is, they were destroyed biologically. As far as I could gather from my conversations with him, this annihilation took place in the gas chambers and the bodies were subsequently destroyed in the crematories.

LIEUTENANT-COLONEL BROOKHART: If Your Honour pleases, this witness is able to testify as to actions in Hungary, involving approximately 500,000 Jews.

THE PRESIDENT: Go on, then. You must use your own discretion. I cannot present your case for you.

LIEUTENANT-COLONEL BROOKHART: I have no desire to submit cumulative evidence.

Q. Turning to actions in Hungary, will you briefly outline the actions taken there and your participation?

A. After the entry of the German troops into Hungary, Eichmann went there personally with a large command. By an order signed by the head of the Security Police, I was assigned to Eichmann's Command. Eichmann began his activities in Hungary at the end of March 1944. He contacted members of the then Hungarian Government, especially Secretaries of State Endre and von Baky. The first measures adopted by Eichmann in co-operation with these Hungarian Government officials were the concentration of the Hungarian Jews in special places and special localities. These measures were carried out zone-wise, beginning in Ruthenia and Transylvania. The action was initiated in mid-April 1944.

In Ruthenia over 200,000 Jews were affected by these measures. In consequence, impossible food and housing conditions developed in the small towns and rural communities where the Jews were assembled. On the strength of this situation Eichmann suggested to the Hungarians that these Jews be transported to Auschwitz and other camps. He insisted, however, that a request to this effect be submitted to him either by the Hungarian Government or by a member thereof. This request was submitted by Secretary of State von Baky. The evacuation was carried out by the Hungarian Police.

Eichmann appointed me Liaison Officer to Lieutenant-Colonel Ferency, charged by the Hungarian Minister of the Interior with this operation. The evacuation of Jews from Hungary began in May, 1944, and was also carried out zone by zone, first starting in Ruthenia, then in Transylvania, Northern Hungary, Southern, and Western Hungary. Budapest was to be cleared of Jews by the end of June. This evacuation, however, was never carried out, as the Regent, Horthy, would not permit it. This operation affected some 450,000 Jews. A second operation was then...

Q. Before you go into that, please, will you tell the Tribunal what, if anything, was done about organising an Einsatz Group to act in Hungary on the Jewish question?

A. At the beginning of March, 1944, a so-called Einsatzgruppe consisting of Security Police and S.D., was formed at Mauthausen near Linz. Eichmann himself headed a so- called "Sondereinsatz-Kommando" (Execution Squad) to which he detailed everybody who, in his department, had occupied some position or other. This "Sondereinsatz-Kommando" was likewise assembled at Mauthausen. All questions of personnel devolved on the then Standartenfuehrer, Dr. Geschke, Leader of the Einsatzgruppe. In technical matters Eichmann was subordinate only to the Chief of the Security Police and the S.D.

Q. What was the meaning of the designation "Special Action Commando Eichmann" in relation to the movement into Hungary?

A. Eichmann's activities in Hungary comprised all matters connected with the Jewish problem.

Q. Under whose direct supervision was Special-Action Commando Eichmann organised?

A. I have already said that in all matters of personnel and economy Eichmann was subordinate to Standartenfuehrer, Dr. Geschke, Leader of the Einsatzgruppe. In technical matters he could give no orders to Eichmann. Eichmann likewise reported direct to Berlin on all the special operations undertaken by him.

Q. To whom?

A. Either to Gruppenfuehrer Mueller, or, in more important cases, to the Chief of the Security Police and S.D., i.e., to Kaltenbrunner.

Q. During the period in which Hungarian Jews were being collected, what, if any, contact was made by the Joint Distribution Committee for Jewish Affairs with Eichmann's representative?

A. The Joint Distribution Committee made efforts to contact Eichmann and to try to ward off the fate of the Hungarian Jews. I myself established this contact with Eichmann, since I wanted to discover some means of protecting the half million Jews in Hungary from the measures already in force. The Joint Distribution Committee made certain proposals to Eichmann and, in return, requested that the Jews should remain in Hungary. These proposals were particularly of a financial nature. Eichmann felt himself, much against his will, obliged to forward these proposals to Himmler. Himmler thereupon entrusted a certain Standartenfuehrer Becher with further negotiations. Standartenfuehrer Becher then continued the negotiations with Dr. Kastner, Delegate of the J.D.C. But Eichmann, from the very first, endeavored to wreck the negotiations. Before any concrete results were obtained he attempted to face us with a fait accompli: in other words, he tried to transport as many Jews as possible to Auschwitz.

THE PRESIDENT: Need we go into all these conferences? Can you take us on to the conclusion of the matter?

LIEUTENANT-COLONEL BROOKHART: The witness is inclined to be lengthy in his answers. That has been true in his pre-trial examination I will try...

THE PRESIDENT: You are examining him.

LIEUTENANT-COLONEL BROOKHART: Yes, Sir.

Q. Was there any money involved in the meeting between Dr. Kastner and Eichmann?

A. Yes.

Q. How much?

A. In the first conversation Dr. Kastner gave Eichmann about 3,000,000 pengoes. What the sums mentioned in further conversations amounted to, I do not exactly know.

Q. To whom did Dr. Kastner give this money and what became of it?

A. It was given to Eichmann, who then turned it over to his trustee; the sum was, in turn, handed to the Commander of the Security Police and the S.D. in Hungary.

Q. These actions that you have described involving approximately 450,000 Jews being moved from Hungary - were there any official communications sent to Berlin concerning these movements?

A. Yes, as each transport left, Berlin was informed by teletype. From time to time Eichmann also dispatched a comprehensive report to the R.S.H.A. and to the Chief of the Security Police.

Q. Now, with reference to the Jews that remained in Budapest, what, if any, action was taken against them?

A. After Szalasi had taken over the Government of Hungary.

THE PRESIDENT: Colonel Brookhart, we have not yet heard have we, what happened to these Jews from Hungary? If we have, I have missed it.

LIEUTENANT-COLONEL BROOKHART: I will ask that question now, Sir.

Q. What became of the Jews to whom you have already referred - approximately 450,000?

A. They were, without exception, taken to Auschwitz and brought to the "final solution".

Q. Do you mean they were killed?

A. Yes, with the exception of perhaps 25 to 30 per cent. who were used for labour purposes. I here refer to a previously mentioned conversation on this matter between Hoess and Eichmann in Budapest.

Q. Turning now to the Jews remaining in Budapest, what happened to them?

A. In October-November, 1944, about 30,000 of these Jews, perhaps a few thousand more, were removed from Budapest and sent to Germany. They were to be used to work on the construction of the so-called South-East-Wall, a fortification near Vienna. They were mostly women.

They had to walk from Hungary to the German border - almost 200 kilometers. They were assembled in marching formations and followed a route specially designated for them. Their shelter and nutrition on this march was extremely bad. Most of them fell ill and lost strength. I had been ordered by Eichmann to take over these groups at the German border and direct them further to the "Lower Danube" Gauleitung for labour purposes. In many cases I refused to take over these so-called workers, because the people were completely exhausted and emaciated by disease. Eichmann, however, forced me to take them over and in this case even threatened to turn me over to Himmler to be put into a concentration camp if I caused him further political difficulties. For this same reason I was later removed from Eichmann's department.

A large proportion of these people then died in the so-called "Lower Danube" Work Camp from exhaustion and epidemics. A small percentage, perhaps 12,000, were taken to Vienna and the surrounding area, and a group of about 3,000 were taken to Bergen-Belsen, and from there to Switzerland. Those were Jews who had been released from Germany as a result of the negotiations with the "Joint."

Q. Summarising the countries of Greece, Hungary, and Slovakia, approximately how many Jews were affected by measures of the Secret Police and S.D. in those countries about which you have personal knowledge?

A. In Slovakia there were about 66,000, in Greece about 64,000, and in Hungary more than half a million.

Q. In the countries of Croatia and Bulgaria, about which you have some knowledge, how many Jews were thus affected?

A. In Bulgaria, to my knowledge, about 8,000; in Croatia I know of only 3,000 Jews who were brought to Auschwitz from Agram in the summer of 1942.

Q. Were meetings held of the specialists on the Jewish problem from Amt IV-A, for the names which appear on this sheet, to which we made reference earlier?

A. Yes. Eichmann was accustomed to calling a large annual meeting of all his experts in Berlin. This meeting was usually in November. At these meetings all the men who were working for him in foreign countries had to report on their activities In 1944, to my knowledge, such a meeting did not take place, because in November, 1944, Eichmann was still in Hungary.

Q. In connection with the Jews about whom you have personal knowledge, how many were subjected to the "final solution", i.e., to being killed?

A. The exact number is extremely hard for me to determine. I have only one basis for a possible estimate, that is a conversation between Eichmann and Hoess in Vienna, in which he said that only a very few of them had been fit for work. Of the Slovakian and Hungarian Jews about 20 to 30 per cent. have been able to work. It is, therefore, very hard for me to give a reliable total.

Q. In your meetings with the other specialists on the Jewish problem and Eichmann did you gain any knowledge or information as to the total number of Jews killed under this program?

A. Eichmann personally always talked about at least 4,000,000 Jews. Sometimes he even mentioned 5,000,000. According to my own estimate I should say that at least 4,000,000 must have been affected by the so-called "final solution". How many of those actually survived, I am not in a position to say.

Q. When did you last see Eichmann?

A. I last saw Eichmann towards the end of February, 1945, in Berlin. At that time he said that if the war were lost he would commit suicide.

Q. Did he say anything at that time as to the number of Jews that had been killed?

A. Yes, he expressed this in a particularly cynical manner. He said "he would leap laughing into the grave because the feeling that he had 5,000,000 people on his conscience would be, for him, a source of extraordinary satisfaction."

LIEUTENANT-COLONEL BROOKHART: The witness is available for other counsel.

THE PRESIDENT: Do any of the other prosecuting counsel wish to examine the witness?

MR. ROBERTS: My Lord, I have no desire to ask any questions.

THE PRESIDENT: Does the Soviet prosecutor wish to ask any questions?

COLONEL POKROVSKY: At this stage the Soviet Union does not wish to ask any questions.

THE PRESIDENT: Does the French prosecutor?

(No response.)

CROSS-EXAMINATION BY DR. SERVATIUS (Counsel for the defendant Sauckel.):

Q. Witness, you mentioned the labour impressment of the Jews and named two cases, one of Jews from Slovakia, who were brought to Auschwitz and of whom those fit for work were so used; the other when, later, you spoke of such Jews who were brought from Hungary to the "South-East Wall." Do you know whether the Plenipotentiary for Labor, Sauckel, had any connection with these actions, whether this happened on his orders and whether he otherwise had anything to do with these matters?

A. As far as the Jews from Slovakia were concerned, the Plenipotentiary for Labor had nothing to do with these matters. It was a purely internal affair for the Inspector of Concentration Camps who committed these Jews for his own purposes. Concerning the impressment of Jews for the construction of the "South-East Wall," I cannot definitely answer this question. I do not know to what extent the construction of the "South-East Wall" was directed by the Plenipotentiary for Labor. The Jews who came up from Hungary for this construction work were turned over to the "Lower Danube" Gauleitung.

DR. SERVATIUS: I have no further questions to ask the witness.

THE PRESIDENT: Any other?

BY DR. BABEL (Counsel for S.S. and S.D.):

Q. Witness, you mentioned measures taken by the Security Police and the S.D., and you spoke about these organisations several times in your testimony. Is this merely an official designation or are we justified in concluding from your statement that the Security Service, the S.D., was participating in any way?

A. The actions mentioned were executed by Amt IV, i.e., the Gestapo. If I mentioned the Chief of the Security Police and the S.D., I did so because it was the correct designation of thier office and not because I wished mention the S.D. as such.

Q. Did the S.D. therefore participate, in any way, in the measures against the Jews mentioned by you: (1) numerically, and (2) with regard to the execution of these measures?

A. The S.D. as an organisation, was not involved. Some of the leaders, including myself, had risen from the S.D., but they had been detailed to Amt IV, i.e., the Gestapo.

Q. Did former members of the S.S. and S.D., who later became active in the Gestapo, still remain members of their original organisation, or were they exclusively members of the Gestapo?

A. No, they still remained with the S.D.

Q. And were they acting as members of the S.D. or actually by order of the Gestapo?

A. We belonged to the Gestapo for the duration of the detail. We merely remained on the S.D. payroll and were taken care of as members of their personnel. Orders were received exclusively from the Gestapo, i.e., Amt IV.

Q. In this connection I should like to ask one more question. Could an outsider ever know his way about in this maze of offices?

A. No; that was practically impossible.

THE PRESIDENT: Is there any other of the defendants' counsel who wishes to cross-examine this witness? Colonel Amen? Do you wish, or Colonel Brookhart, does he wish to re- examine the witness?

COLONEL AMEN: No further questions, Your Lordship.

THE PRESIDENT: Very well. That will do.

(The witness withdrew.)

COLONEL AMEN: It will take about 10 minutes, sir, to get the next witness up. I had not anticipated we would finish quite so quickly. Do you still want me to get him up this afternoon?

THE PRESIDENT: Have you any other witnesses on these subjects?

COLONEL AMEN: Not on this subject, Sir. I have two very short witnesses: one on the written agreement, as to which testimony was given this morning, between the O.K.W., and O.K.H. and the R.S.H.A., a witness who can answer the questions which the members of the Tribunal asked this morning, very briefly; and one other witness who is on a totally different subject.

THE PRESIDENT: On what subject is the other witness?

COLONEL AMEN: Well, he is on the subject of identifying two of the defendants at one of the concentration camps. I prefer not to mention these names to the defence unless you wish me to.

THE PRESIDENT: Very well. Then you will call those two witnesses to-morrow?

COLONEL AMEN: Yes, Your Lordship. I do not think either of them will take more than twenty minutes.

THE PRESIDENT: Very well. Then you will go on with the evidence against the High Command?

COLONEL AMEN: Yes, Sir.

THE PRESIDENT: We will adjourn now.

(The Tribunal adjourned until 4th January, 1946, at 1000 hours.).

Twenty-Seventh Day: Friday, 4th January, 1946

COL. AMEN: I would like to call as a witness for the prosecution Walter Schellenberg.

THE PRESIDENT: Is your name Walter Schellenberg?

THE WITNESS SCHELLENBERG: My name is Walter Schellenberg.

THE PRESIDENT: Will you take this oath: I swear to God, the Almighty and Omniscient, that I will speak the pure truth and will withhold and add nothing.

(The witness repeated the oath in German.)

COL. AMEN:

Q. Where were you born?

A. In Saarbruecken.

Q. How old are you?

A. Thirty-five years.

Q. You were a member of the N.S.D.A.P.?

A. Yes.

Q. And of the S.S.?

A. Yes ; the S.S. also.

Q. And of the Waffen S.S.?

A. And the Waffen S.S.

Q. And of the S.D.?

A. And the S.D.

Q. What rank did you hold?

A. The highest rank that I held was that of S.S. Brigadefuehrer in the S.S. and of Major-General in the Waffen S.S.

Q. You were Chief of Amt VI?

A. I was Chief of Amt VI and ...

Q. During what period of time?

A. I was Deputy Chief of Amt VI in July, 1941, and the final confirmation of my appointment as Chief was in June of 1942.

Q. State briefly the functions of Amt VI of the R.S.H.A.

A. Amt VI was the political secret service of the Reich and worked basically in foreign countries.

Q. Do you know of an agreement between O.K.W., O.K.H. and the R.S.H.A. concerning the use of Einsatz Groups and Einsatz Commandos in the Russian campaign?

A. At the end of May, 1941, conferences took place between the then head of the Security Police and the Quartermaster-General, General Wagner.

Q. And who?

A. The Quartermaster-General of the Army, General Wagner.

Q. Did you personally attend those conferences?

A. Yes. I kept the minutes of the final meetings.

Q. Have you given us the names of all persons present during those negotiations?

A. The conferences took place principally between Obergruppenfuehrer Heydrich, who was then the Chief of the Security Police and, the S.D., and the Quartermaster-General of the Army.

Q. Was anyone else present during any of the negotiations?

A. Not during the conferences themselves, but at a later meeting other persons took part.

Q. And did those negotiations result in the signing of an agreement?

A. A written agreement was concluded.

Q. Were you there when the written agreement was signed?

A. I kept the minutes and was present when both gentlemen signed.

Q. By whom was this agreement signed?

A. It was signed by the then Chief of the Security Police, S.S. Obergruppenfuehrer Heydrich, and the Quartermaster-General of the Army, General Wagner.

Q. Do you know where the original agreement, or any copy thereof, is located today?

A. No, that I cannot say. I know nothing about that.

Q. But you are familiar with the contents of that written agreement?

A. Yes ; for the most part I recollect that.

Q. To the best of your knowledge and recollection, please tell the Tribunal exactly what was contained in that written agreement.

A. The first part of this agreement began with the quotation of a basic decree by the Fuehrer. It read somewhat as follows:

"For the safety of the fighting troops in the Russian campaign that is now at hand, all means are to be used to keep the rear safe and protected. On the basis of this consideration every resistance is to be broken by every means. In order to support the fighting unit of the Army, the Security Police and the Security Service are also to be called in for this task."

If I remember correctly, as a special example of something to be protected, the safeguarding of the so-called great routes of supply, also called "Rollbahnen," was mentioned.

Q. Do you recall anything else contained in that agreement?

A. In the second part of this agreement the organisation of the Army Groups was mentioned . . .

Q. And what was said about that?

A. . . . and the corresponding organisation of the Einsatz Groups and the Einsatzkonimandos of the Security Police and the S.D. Four different spheres of activity were distinguished.

I remember the following: first, the front area; second, the operational zone - it was also divided into an Army area and a rear Army area; third, the rear Army area; and fourth, the area for the Civil Administration "Reichskommissariate" to be set up.

To cover these different spheres, questions of subordination and command were settled exactly. In the front areas or fighting areas, the Einsatzkornmandos of the Security Police and the S.D. were tactically and operationally under the command of the Army, that is, they were completely under the command of the Army.

In the operational zones only subordination in respect to operations should apply and this same rule should apply in the rear Army area. In the zone intended for the Civil Administration (Reichskommissariate) the same conditions of subordination and command were to apply as in the area of the Reich.

In a third part was explained what was meant by tactical and operational, or rather only the concept "operational" was explained in detail.

By "operational " was meant the subordination to the Army in respect to discipline and provisions. Special mention was made of the fact that the operational subordination also included all supplies - especially supplies of petrol, food and the making available of technical routes of intelligence transmission.

Q. Have you now told us everything which you can recall about that agreement?

A. Yes; I cannot remember anything else contained in the agreement.

COL. AMEN: If your Honour pleases, that is all.

THE PRESIDENT: Has the English prosecution any questions to ask?

SIR DAVID MAXWELL FYFE: No.

THE PRESIDENT: Has the Russian prosecution any questions to ask?

COL. POKROVSKY: No.

THE PRESIDENT: Has the French prosecution any questions to ask?

(There was no response.)

THE PRESIDENT: Do the defendants' counsel wish to ask any questions?

CROSS-EXAMINATION BY DR. KAUFFMANN (Counsel for defendant Kaltenbrunner)

Q. Is it correct that Dr. Kaltenbrunner was your superior?

A. Dr. Kaltenbrunner was my immediate superior.

Q. During what time?

A. From the 30th January, 1943, until the end.

Q. Do you know his attitude towards the important views of life entertained by National Socialism, for instance, towards the question of the treatment of the Jews or the question of the treatment of the Church?

A. I personally did not have a chance to converse with him on these problems. What I know about him is the result of my own few personal observations.

Q. Did you see original orders from Kaltenbrunner dealing with the execution of saboteurs, the confinement of people in concentration camps and the like?

A. No. I had only oral orders from him in respect to this - commands which he gave to the Chief of the State Police, the Chief of Amt IV of the R.S.H.A.

Q. Did Kaltenbrunner ever indicate to you that he had agreed with Himmler that everything concerning concentration camps and the entire executive power was to be taken away from him, and that only the S.D., as an Intelligence Service, was to be entrusted to you and him, and that he wanted to expand this Intelligence Service, in order to supply the criticism that was otherwise lacking?

A. I never heard of any such agreements. and what I found out later to be the fact is to the contrary.

Q. Now, since you have given a negative answer, I must ask you the following question, in order to make this one point clear: What fact do you mean?

A. I mean, for instance, the fact that, after the Reichsfuehrer S.S., persuaded by me, had very reluctantly agreed not to evacuate the concentration camps, Kaltenbrunner, in direct contact with Hitler, circumvented this decree of Himinler's and broke his word in respect to international promises.

Q. Were there any international decisions in respect to this, decisions which referred to existing laws, or decisions which referred to international agreements?

A. I would like to explain that, if in regard to internationally known persons the then Reichsfuehrer S.S. promised the official Allied authorities not to evacuate the concentration camps in case of emergency, this promise was humanly binding.

Q. What do you mean by evacuate?
A. Arbitrarily to evacuate the camps before the approaching enemy troops and to transplant them to other parts of Germany still unoccupied by the enemy troops.

Q. What was your opinion?
A. That no further evacuation should take place, because human right simply did not allow it ; that the camps should therefore be surrendered to the approaching enemy.

Q. Did you know that your activity could also contribute to the suffering caused to many people who were innocent?
A. Yes.

Q. Did you know that your activity, too, could bring suffering to many people, to people who were per se innocent?
A. I did not understand the question. Will you please repeat it?

Q. Did you ever think that your activity, too, and the activity of your fellow workers, was a cause for the great suffering of many people - let us say Jews - even though these people were innocent?
A. I cannot imagine that the activity of my office could cause any such thing. I was merely in an information service.

Q. Then your information service had no connection at all with such crimes?
A. No.

Q. Then Kaltenbrunner too would not be guilty in regard to this point?
A. But he was, at the same time, the Chief of Amt IV of the State Police.

Q. I asked in regard to this point, and by that I meant your sector.
A. I only represented the sector Amt VI and Amt Mil.

Q. But Kaltenbrunner, at the same time, was Chief of Amt VI?
A. Kaltenbrunner was the Chief of the R.S.H.A. Eight departments were under him. One or two of them I headed, namely, Amt VI and Amt Mil. These two offices had nothing to do with the executive power of the State Police.

THE PRESIDENT: What I understood you to say was that you were only in a branch which was an information centre ; is that right?

THE WITNESS: Yes.

THE PRESIDENT: And that Kaltenbrunner was your immediate chief; is that right?

THE PRESIDENT: Yes, he was the Chief not only of your branch but of the whole organisation.

THE WITNESS: Yes, this is correct.

DR. KAUFMANN: I should like to question this witness later on. I should like to reserve these important questions for later on, after I have talked with Kaltenbrunner.

BY DR. KUBUSCHOF (Counsel for defendant von Papen)

Q. In the summer of 1943 were you in Ankara, and did you then pay a visit to the German Embassy?
A. Yes.

Q. Did you during this visit criticise German foreign policy in various respects, and did you in this regard mention that it was absolutely advisable to establish better relations with the Holy See? Did Herr von Papen then answer: "That would be possible only if, in accordance with the demands that I have made repeatedly, the Church policy is revised completely and the persecution of the Church ceases"?
A. Yes, that is the correct gist of the conversation, and I spoke with the then

Ambassador von Papen to that effect.

BY DR. THOMA (Counsel for defendant Rosenberg)

Q. You said a little while ago that the same regulations applied in the area of the Civil Administration as in the Reich.

A. I said they were to apply.

Q. Please answer my question again.

A. I will repeat: I described the agreement which contained the pro vision that in the areas intended for Civil Administration (Reichskommissariate) the same relations to the Security Police and the S.D., in regard to subordination and command, were applicable as in the Reich.

Q. Do you know how that was done in practice?

A. No, later on I did not concern myself with these questions any more.

Q. Thank you.

BY DR. BABEL (Counsel for S.S. and S.D.):

Q. You were a member of the S.S. and of the S.D., and in leading positions ...

THE PRESIDENT: Will you state, for the purposes of the record, on behalf of which organisation you appear?

DR. BABEL: I represent the organisations of the S.S. and S.D.

Q. In the R.S.H.A. there were departments of the Security Police and the S.D. How were these two departments related, and what was the purpose of the S.D.?

A. That is a question that I cannot answer in one sentence.

Q. I can withdraw the question for the moment and ask a concrete one:

Was the S.D. used with the "Einsatzgruppen" in the East? To what extent? And with what tasks?

A. I believe that the largest employment of personnel in the East was undertaken by the Security Police, that is, by the Secret State Police and the Criminal Police, and that from the personnel of the S.D. only supplementary contingents were formed.

Q. How large were these contingents? How large was the S.D.

A. I believe that I can estimate the figures: excluding female help, the State Police - perhaps 40,000 to 45,000; the Criminal Police - 15,000 to 20,000; the S.D. of the Interior, that is, Amt III with its organisational subsidiaries - 2,000 to 2,500; and the S.D. outside Germany, that is my Amt VI - about 400.

Q. And how was the S.D. used in the East with the Einsatz Groups?

A. I cannot give you the particulars, since that was a concern of the Personnel Administration, and subject directly,to the instructions of the then Chief of the Security Police.

Q. Did the figures you mentioned include male members of the S.D. exclusively, or was female help also included?

A. Only male members. I excluded the female help.

Q. Yesterday a witness gave us approximately the same figure of 3,000, but he included the female help in this figure.

A. I mentioned a figure of 2,000 to 2,500 for the S.D. in the Interior.

Q. What was the organisational structure of the Waffen S.S.?

A. As for the organisational structure of the Waffen S.S., I cannot give you a detailed reply that is reliable.

Q. You were a member of the Waffen S.S. and of the S.D.

A. I was appointed a member of the Waffen S.S. only in January, 1945, by higher orders, so to speak. There I had more military units under my command through the

Amt Mil and had to have a military rank to justify my activities.

Q. Do you know whether that also happened to a large extent in other cases?

A. That question is beyond me to answer.

DR. BABEL: Thank you.

RE-EXAMINATION BY COLONEL AMEN:

Q. Do you know of any particular case in which Kaltenbrunner had ordered the evacuation of any one concentration camp, in direct contradiction to Himinler's wishes?

A. Yes.

Q. Will you tell the Tribunal about that?

A. I cannot give you the exact date, but I believe it was in the beginning of April, 1945. The son of the former Swiss President, Muesi, who had taken his father to Switzerland, returned by car to the Buchenwald Concentration Camp, in order to call for a Jewish family which I myself had set free. He found the camp in complete evacuation and under the most deplorable conditions. As he had, three days previously, driven his father to Switzerland, with the final decision that the camps would not be evacuated, and since this declaration was also intended for General Eisenhower, he was doubly disappointed at this breach of promise. Muesi Jr. called on me personally at my office. He was deeply offended and reproached me bitterly. I could not understand the situation and at once contacted Himmler's secretary, protesting against this sort of procedure. Shortly after the truth of the facts, as depicted by Muesi Jr., was confirmed, although it was still incomprehensible, since Himinler had not given these orders. An immediate halt to the evacuations by every available method was assured. This was certified personally by Himmler by telephone a few hours later. I believe it was on the same day, after a meeting of office chiefs, that I informed Kaltenbrunner of the situation and expressed my profound concern at this new breach of international assurances. As I paused in the conversation, the Chief of the State Police, Gruppenfuehrer Mueller, interrupted and explained that he had started the evacuation of the more important internees of the individual camps, three days ago at Kaltenbrunner's orders. Kaltenbrunner replied with these words:

> "Yes, that is correct, it was an order of the Fuehrer which was also recently confirmed by the Fuehrer in person. All the important internees are to be evacuated at his order to the South of the Reich."

He then turned to me mockingly and, speaking in dialect, said:

> "Tell your old gentleman (i.e., Muesi Jr.) that there are still enough left in the camps. With that you, too, can be satisfied."

I think this was on the 10th April, 1945.

COL. AMEN: That is all, may it please the Tribunal.

QUESTIONS BY THE TRIBUNAL (GENERAL NIKITCHENKO):

Q. Can you say what the functions of the Chief Amt of the Security Police were?

A. That I cannot answer in one sentence. I believe . . .

Q. Be brief, be brief! What were the aims?

A. The R.S.H.A. was a comprehensive grouping of a Security Police, that is, a State Police . . .

Q. We know about this organisation on the basis of the documents which are at the disposal of the Court, but what were its functions?

A. I just wanted to explain its functions. Its functions consisted of security, that is, State Police activity, of Criminal Police activity, and of intelligence activity at home and abroad.

Q. Would it be correct to formulate the functions as follows : to suppress those whom the Nazi Party considered its enemies?

A. No, I think that statement is too one-sided.

Q. But these functions were included?

A. They were, perhaps, a certain part of the activities of the State Police.

Q. Had this part of the functions, then, been changed after Kaltenbrunner took office?

A. No, there was no change.

Q. Had those functions, to which you referred just now, been changed since the time that Kaltenbrunner took office as Chief of the Security Police?

A. The functions, as I formulated them, did not change after Kaltenbrunner assumed office.

Q. I have one more question : What were the aims and purposes of the operation groups which were to have been created on the basis of the agreement between the S.D. and the High Command?

A. As far as the agreement was covered at that time, the first part, as I mentioned before, referred to the task laid down of protecting the rear of the troops, and using all means against opposition and against resistance.

Q. To repress or to crush resistance?

A. The words were: "All resistance is to be crushed with every means."

Q. By what means was the resistance suppressed?

A. The agreement did not mention nor discuss this in any way.

Q. But you know what means were used for that suppression, do you not?

A. Later I heard that because of the bitterness of the struggle, harsh means were chosen, but I know this only by hearsay.

Q. What does it mean more exactly?

A. That in Partisan fighting and in the treatment of the civilian population many shootings took place.

Q. Including the children?

A. That I did not hear.

Q. You have not heard it?

A. (No response.)

Q. That is all.

SIR DAVID MAXWELL FYFE: Since your Lordship was good enough to ask me whether I wanted to put any questions, I have had some further information and I should be very grateful if you would be good enough to allow me to ask one or two questions.

RE-EXAMINATION BY SIR DAVID MAXWELL FYFE:

Q. Would you direct your mind to a conversation between the defendant Kaltenbrunner, Gruppenfuehrer Nebe and Gruppenfuehrer Mueller, in the Spring of 1944, in Berlin at Wilhelmstrasse 102?

A. Yes.

Q. With what was that conversation concerned?

A. That conversation, as far as I could gather - since I took no part in it - concerned the subsequent invention of excuses for the shooting of about 50 English and American prisoners of war. The conversation in its particulars and to the best of my recollection, was as follows: there had evidently been a request from the International Red Cross inquiring as to the whereabouts of 50 English and American prisoners of war. This request for information by the International Red Cross appears to have been passed on to the Chief of the Security Police and the S.D. via the Foreign Office. From the conversation I could ...

Q. Just one moment: was it already in the form of a protest against the shooting of prisoners of war?

A. I believe it was lodged in the form of a protest, since from fragments of this conversation I gathered that there was a discussion as to how the shooting of these prisoners of war, which had already taken place, could be covered up or disguised.

Q. How this could be done?

A. Or had been done.

Q. Did Kaltenbrunner discuss this with Mueller and Nebe?

A. Kaltenbrunner discussed this matter with Mueller and Nebe, but I merely heard fragments of the conversation. I heard, incidentally, that they meant to discuss the details in the course of the afternoon.

Q. Did you hear any suggestion put forward as to what explanations should be offered to explain away the shooting of these prisoners?

A. Yes, Kaltenbrunner himself offered these suggestions.

Q. What were the suggestions?

A. That the greatest part be treated as individual cases, as "having perished in air raids"; some, I believe, because they "offered resistance" i.e., "physical resistance", while others were "pursued when escaping".

Q. You mean - shot while trying to escape?

A. Yes, shot in flight.

Q. And these were the excuses which Kaltenbrunner suggested?

A. Yes. these were the excuses that Kaltenbrunner suggested.

Q. Now, I want you to try and remember as well as you can about these prisoners. Does any number remain in your mind? Can you remember any number of prisoners that they were discussing or how these explanations arose? About how many?

A. I remember only that the number 50 was mentioned over and over again, but how the particulars went I cannot say because I just followed fragments of the conversation, I could not follow the exact conversation.

Q. But the number 50 remains in your mind?

A. Yes, I heard 50.

Q. Can you remember anything of the place or the camp in which these people had been, who were said to have been shot?

A. I cannot tell you under oath. There is a possibility that I might add a little bit. I believe it was Breslau, but I cannot state it exactly, as a fact.

Q. Can you remember anything of what service the people belonged to? Were they Air Force or Army? Have you any recollection on that point?

A. I believe they were all officers.

Q. Were officers?

A. Yes.

Q. But you cannot remember what service?

A. No, that I cannot tell you.

SIR DAVID MAXWELL FYFE: I am very grateful to the Tribunal for letting me ask these questions.

COLONEL AMEN: That is all for this witness.

THE PRESIDENT: Very well, the witness can go then.

(The witness withdrew.)

COLONEL AMEN: I wish to call as the next witness Alois Hoellriegel.

THE PRESIDENT: What is your name?

THE WITNESS: Alois Hoellriegel.

THE PRESIDENT: Will you take this oath?

I swear by God, the Almighty and Omniscient, that I will speak the pure truth and will withhold and add nothing.

(The witness repeated the oath in German.)

THE PRESIDENT: You can sit down if you want to.

DIRECT EXAMINATION BY COLONEL AMEN:

Q. What position did you hold at the end of the war?

A. At the end of the war I was Unterscharfuehrer at Mauthausen.

Q. Were you a member of the Totenkopf S.S.?

A. Yes; in the year 1939 I was drafted into the S.S.

Q. What were your duties at the Mauthausen Concentration Camp?

A. I was, until the winter of 1942, with a guard company and I stood guard. From 1942 until the end of the war I was detailed to the inner service of the concentration camp.

Q. And you therefore had occasion to witness the extermination of inmates of that camp by shooting, gassing and so forth?

A. Yes, I saw that.

Q. And did you make an affidavit in this case to the effect that you saw Kaltenbrunner at that camp?

A. Yes.

Q. And that he saw and was familiar with the operation of the gas chamber there?

A. Yes.

Q. Did yuou also have occasion to see nay other important personages visiting that concentration camp?

A. I remember Pohl, Gluecks, Kaltenbrunner, Schirach and Gauleiter of the Steyermark, Uiberreuther.

Q. And did you personally see Schirach at that concentration camp at Mauthausen?

A. Yes.

Q. Do you remember what he looks like so that you could identify him

A. I think that he has probably changed a little in recent times, but I would certainly remember him.

Q. How long ago was it that you saw him there

A. It was in the fall of 1942. Since then I have not seen him.

Q. Will you look around the Courtroom and see whether you can see Schirach in the Courtroom?

A. Yes.

Q. Which person is it?

A. In the second row, the third person from the left.

COLONEL AMEN: The affidavit to which I referred was Exhibit USA 515.

THE PRESIDENT: What is the PS number?

COLONEL AMEN: 2753-PS.

BY COLONEL AMEN:

Q. I now show you a copy of Document 2641-PS and ask you whether you can recognise the place where those individuals are standing?

A. As far as I can recognise it at a glance, it is a quarry; whether it is at Mauthausen or not one cannot determine exactly, because the view is too small.

Q. Would you repeat that answer please?

A. Certainly, as far as can be seen from this picture, I cannot see clearly if this is the Wiener-Graben quarry near Mauthausen. It might easily be another quarry. A larger range of vision is required. But I think that visits were often made there. I assume that this is the Wiener-Graben quarry.

Q. Very good. Just lay the picture aside for the time being.

Did you have occasion to observe the killing of inmates of the concentration camp by their being pushed off a cliff?

A. Yes.

Q. Will you tell the Tribunal what you saw with respect to that practice?

A. I remember it was in 1941. At that time I was with a guard company on the tower which closed off the area of the quarry. I was able to observe in the morning about six to eight prisoners who came with two S.S. men of my acquaintance. One was Spatzenecker and the other, Unterscharfuehrer Eichenhofer; they moved ...

THE PRESIDENT: Wait, you are going too fast. You should go slower.

A. I saw that they were approaching the precipice near the quarry. I saw, from my watch-tower, that these two S.S. men were beating the prisoners and I realised immediately that they intended to force them to throw themselves over the precipice or else to push them over. I noticed how one of the prisoners was kicked while lying on the ground, and the gestures showed that he was supposed to throw himself down the precipice. This the prisoner promptly did under the pressure of the blows - presumably in despair.

A. I estimate that it was 30 to 40 metres.

Q. Was there a term used amongst you guards for this practice of having the prisoners fall from the top of the precipice?

A. Yes. In Mauthausen Camp they were called paratroopers.

COLONEL AMEN: The witness is available to other counsel.

THE PRESIDENT: Has the Russian Prosecutor or the French Prosecutor or any defence counsel any questions?

CROSS-EXAMINATION BY DR. SAUTER (Counsel for defendant von Schirach):

Q. Witness, I am interested in the following points.

You said previously that in 1939 you were taken into the S.S.?

A. That is true, on 6th September....

Q. One moment, please repeat your answer.

A. That is right. On 6th September, 1939, I was taken into the S.S. at Ebersberg near Linz.

Q. Had you no connection at all with the Party before then?

A. Yes. In April, 1938, I enlisted in the Civilian S.S., because I was out of work and without any support, and I thought, I will join the Civilian S.S.; there I will get work, in order to be able to marry.

Q. Then, if I understood you correctly, you were drafted into the S.S. in 1939, because you had already enlisted in the Civilian S.S. in the spring of 1938?

A. I cannot say that exactly. Many were drafted into the Armed Forces, into the Air

Force and into the General S.S.

Q. Are you an Austrian?
A. Yes.
Q. Then at that time you lived in Austria
A. Yes, at Graz.
Q. I am interested in a certain point in regard to the defendant von Schirach. You saw the defendant von Schirach at Mauthausen. How often did you see him there?
A. I cannot remember so exactly - once.
Q. Once?
A. Yes.
Q. Was von Schirach alone at Mauthausen, or was he with other people?
A. He was accompanied by other gentlemen. There was a group of about ten people, and among them I recognised von Schirach and Gauleiter Niberreuter.
Q. There are supposed to have been 20 persons at least and not 10, on that occasion.
A. I did not know at that time that I might have to give these figures I did not count them.
Q. This point is important to me, because the defendant Schirach told me it was a, visit of inspection, an official inspection tour of the concentration camp Mauthausen, occasioned by a meeting of the Economic Advisors of all six Gaue of the Ostmark.
A. Yes, I naturally did not know why he came to the camp, but I remember that this group came with von Schirach and Schutzhaftlagerfuehrer (Protective Custody-Camp Leader) Bachmeyer. At any rate I could see that it looked like an inspection.
Q. Did you know that this inspection was announced in we camp severai days before and that certain preparations were made in the camp because of it?
A. I cannot remember any specific preparations, but I do remember it was during the evening hours. I cannot tell you the exact hour ; it was the time of the evening roll-call. The prisoners had assembled for roll-call and all the troops on duty also had to fall in. Then this group came in.
Q. Did you or your comrades not know on the day before that this inspection would take place the very next day?
A. I cannot remember that.
Q. And did it not strike you that certain definite preparations had been made in this camp?
A. I cannot remember that any preparations were made.
DR. SAUTER: I have no further questions to ask this witness.
BY DR. STEINBAUER (Counsel for defendant Seyss-Inquart):
Q. Witness, you described an incident which, according to the conception entertained by civilised people, cannot be designated anything but murder - i.e., the hurling of people over the side of the quarry. Did you report this incident to your superiors?
A. These incidents happened frequently and it is to be assumed with a 100 per cent. degree of accuracy, that the superiors knew about them
Q. In other words, you did not report this. Is it true that on pain of death not only the internees but also the guards were forbidden to report incidents of this sort to a third person?
A. Yes.
DR. STEINBAUER: I have no other question.

RE-EXAMINATION BY COLONEL AMEN:

Q. Would you just look at that picture again?
A. Yes.
Q. Will you look at it carefully and tell me whether that is the quarry underneath the cliff which you have just described?
A Yes, as far as I can tell from this picture, I assume with a 100 per cent. degree of accuracy that it is the quarry Wiener-Graben ; but one would have to see more, more background, to decide whether it is really this quarry. One sees too little, but I think quite certainly . . .
Q. Do you recognise the individuals whose faces appear in the picture?
A. Yes.
Q. Will you tell the Tribunal the ones whom you recognise?
A. I recognise of course Reichsfuehrer S.S. Himmler first of all, next to him the Commandant of Mauthausen Concentration Camp and away to the right I recognise Kaltenbrunner.
COLONEL AMEN: That is all, may it please the Tribunal.
THE PRESIDENT: The witness can go and we will adjourn for ten minutes.
(A recess was taken.)
COLONEL STOREY: If the Tribunal please, the next and final subject of the criminal organisations is the General Staff and High Command, to be presented by Colonel Taylor.
COLONEL TELFORD TAYLOR: Your Lordship and members of the Tribunal: The Indictment seeks a declaration of criminality under Articles 9 to i i of the Charter against six groups or organisations, and the last one listed in the Indictment is a group described as the General Staff and High Command of the German Armed Forces.

At first sight these six groups and organisations seem to differ rather widely one from another, both in their composition and in their functions. But all of them are related and we believe that they are logically indicted together before the Tribunal because they are the primary agencies and the chief tools by means of which the Nazi conspirators sought to achieve their aims. All six of them were either established by, controlled by, or became allied with the Nazis, and they were essential to the success of the Nazis. They were at once the principal and indispensable instruments : the Party, the Government, the Police and the Armed Forces. It is my task to present the case in chief against the General Staff and High Command group.

Now, in one respect this group is to be sharply distinguished from the other groups and organisations against which we have sought this declaration. For example, the Leadership Corps of the Nazi Party, of the N.S.D.A.P., is the Leadership Corps of the Party itself, the Party which was the embodiment of Nazism, and was the instrument primarily through which Hitlerism rode to full power and tyranny in Germany. The S.A. and the S.S. were branches - to be sure, large branches - of the Nazi Party. The German Police did indeed have certain roots and antecedents which antedated Hitlerism, but it became 99 per cent. a creature of the Nazi Party and the S.S. The Reich Cabinet was in essence merely a committee or series of committees of Reich Ministers, and when the Nazis came to power, quite naturally these ministerial positions were filled for the most part by Nazis. All these groups and organisations, accordingly, either owe their origin and development to Nazism or automatically became Nazified when Hitler came to power.

Now, that is not true of the group with which we are now concerned. I need not remind the Tribunal that German armed might and the German military tradition antedate Hitlerism by many decades. One need not be a greybeard to have very vivid personal recollections of the war of 1914 to 1918, of the Kaiser and of the scrap of paper. For these reasons I want to sketch very briefly, before going into the evidence, the nature of our case against this group, which is unique in the particulars I have mentioned.

As a result of the German defeat in 1918 and the Treaty of Versailles. the size and permissible scope of activities of the German Armed Forces were severely restricted. That these restrictions did not destroy or even seriously undermine German militarism, the last few years have made abundantly apparent. The full flowering of German military strength came about through collaboration, collaboration between the Nazis on the one hand and the career leaders of the German Armed Forces, the professional soldiers, sailors, and airmen on the other.

When Hitler came to power, he did not find a vacuum in the field of military affairs. He found a small Reichswehr and a body of professional officers with a morale and outlook nourished by German military history. The leaders of these professional officers constitute the group named in the indictment, the General Staff and High Command of the German Armed Forces. This part of the case concerns that group of men.

Now, needless to say, the prosecution does not take the stand that it is a crime to be a soldier or a sailor or to serve one's country as a soldier or sailor in time of war. The profession of arms is an honourable one and can be honourably practised. But it is too clear for argument that a man who commits crimes cannot plead in his defence that he committed them in uniform.

It is not in the nature of things and the prosecution does not take the stand that every member of this group was a wicked man or that they were all equally culpable. But we will show that this group not only collaborated with Hitler and supported the essential Nazi objectives but we will show that they also furnished the one thing which was essential and basic to the success of the Nazi programme for Germany, and that thing was skill and experience in the development and use of armed might.

Why did this group support Hitler and the Nazis? I think your Honours will see, as the proof is given, that the answer is very simple. The answer is that they agreed with the truly basic objectives of Hitlerism and Nazism and that Hitler gave the generals the opportunity to play a major part in achieving these objectives. The generals, like Hitler, wanted to aggrandise Germany at the expense of neighbouring countries and were prepared to do so by force or threat of force. Force, armed might, was the keystone of the arch, the thing without which nothing else would have been possible.

As they came to power and when they had attained power, the Nazis had two alternatives, either to collaborate with and expand the small German army known as the Reichswehr, or to ignore the Reichswehr and build up a separate army of their own. The generals feared that the Nazis might do the latter and accordingly were the more inclined to collaborate. Moreover, the Nazis offered the generals the chance of achieving much that they wished to achieve by way of expanding German armies and German frontiers, and so, as we will show, the generals climbed on to the Nazi bandwagon. They saw it was going in their direction at the time. No doubt they hoped later to take over the direction themselves. In fact, as the proof will show, ultimately it was the generals who were taken for a ride by the Nazis.

Hitler, in short, attracted the generals to him with the glitter of conquest, and then succeeded in submerging them politically and, as the war proceeded, they became his tools. But if these military leaders became the tools of Nazism, it is not to be supposed that they were unwitting, or that they did not participate fully in many of the crimes which we will bring to the notice of the Tribunal. The willingness and, indeed, the eagerness of the German professional officer corps to become partners of the Nazis, will be fully developed.

Your Lordship, there will be three principal parts to this presentation. There will be first a description of the composition and functioning of the General Staff and High Command group as defined in the Indictment; next, the evidence in support of the charges of criminality under Counts 1 and 2 of the Indictment; finally, the evidence in support of the charges under Counts 3 and 4.

The members of the Tribunal should have before them three document books which have been given the designation CC. The first of these books is a series of sworn statements or affidavits which are available to the Tribunal in English, in Russian and in French, and which have been available to the document books, separated merely for convenience of handling. The second book contains documents in the C and L series, and the third book, in the PS and R series. For the convenience of the Tribunal we have had handed up a list of these documents in the order in which they will be referred to.

The Tribunal should also have one other document, and that is a short mimeographed statement entitled "Basic Information on the Organisation of the German Armed Forces" That has also been handed up in English, Russian and French and has been made available to the defendants' Information Centre in German.

So I turn first to the description of the group as defined in the Indictment.

During the First World War there was an organisation in the German Armed Forces known as the Great General Staff. This name, the German General Staff or Great General Staff, persists in the public mind, but the "Grosse Generalstab " no longer exists in fact. There has been no such single organisation, no single German General Staff, since 1918, but there has, of course, been a group of men responsible for the policy and the acts of the German Armed Forces, and the fact that these men have no single collective name does not prevent us from collecting them together. They cannot escape the consequences of their collective acts by combining informally instead of formally. The essence of a general staff or a high command lies not in the name you give it, but in the functions it performs and the men comprised within the group as we have defined it in the Indictment, constituted a functional group, welded together by common responsibility, of those officers who had the principal authority and responsibility under Hitler for the plans and operations of the German Armed Forces.

Let us examine first the general structure and organisation of the German Armed Forces and then look at the composition of the group as specified in the Indictment. As I just mentioned, we have prepared a very short written exposition of the organisation of the German Armed Forces, which we have handed up to the Tribunal. That document contains a short sketch setting forth the basic history and development of the Supreme Command of the German Armed Forces since 1933, and the structure as it emerged after its reorganisation in 1938. It also contains a simple chart, which in a few moments will be displayed at the front of the Courtroom. It also contains a short glossary of German military expressions and a comparative table of ranks in the German Army and in the S.S., showing the equivalent ranks in the American Army and the equivalent ranks for the German Navy and the British Navy. I may say that although military and naval ranks differ slightly among the principal nations, by and large they follow the same general pattern and terminology.

When the Nazis came to power in 1933, the German Armed Forces were controlled by a Reich Defence Minister, who at that time was Field Marshal Werner von Blomberg. Under von Blomberg were the chief of the Army Staff, who at that time was von Fritsch, and of the Naval Staff, the defendant Raeder. Owing to the limitations imposed on Germany by the Treaty of Versailles, the German Air Force at that time had no official existence whatever. The Army and Navy Staffs were renamed "High Command" - Oberkornmando der Heeres and Oberkornmando der Kriegs Marine - from which are derived the initials by which they are generally known - O.K.H. and O.K.M. In May, 1935, at the time that military conscription was introduced in Germany, there was a change in the titles of these officers but the structure remained basically the same. Field Marshal von Blomberg remained in supreme command of the Armed Forces, with the title of Reich Minister for War and Commander-in-Chief of the Armed Forces. Von Fritsch assumed the title Commander-in-Chief of the Army, and Raeder, Commander-in-Chief of the Navy.

The German Air Force came into official and open existence at about this same time, but it was not put under von Blomberg. It was an independent institution under the personal command of the defendant Goering, who had the double title of Air Minister and Commander-in-Chief of the Air Force.

I will now ask that the chart be displayed.

This chart, your Honour, has been certified and sworn to by three principal German generals, and the affidavits with reference to it will be introduced in a few moments. It shows the organisation, the top organisation, of the Armed Forces as it emerged in 1938 after the reorganisation which I will now describe.

In February, 1938, von Blomberg and von Fritsch were both retired from their positions, and Blomberg's ministry, the War Ministry, was wound up. The War Ministry had contained a division or department called the Wehrmacht Amt, meaning the Armed Forces Department, and the function of that department had been to co-ordinate the plans and operations of the Army and Navy. From this Armed Forces Department was formed a new overall Armed Forces authority known as the High Command of the German Armed Forces-that is the box in the centre, right under Hitler-known in German as Oberkommando der Wehrinacht, and usually known by the initials O.K.W.

Since the Air Force as well as the Army was subordinated to O.K.W., co-ordination of all Armed Forces matters was vested in the O.K.W., which was really Hitler's personal staff for these matters. The defendant Keitel was appointed Chief of the O.K.W. The most important division of the O.K.W., shown just to the right, was the Operations Staff, of which the defendant Jodl became the chief. Now, this reorganisation and the establishment of O.K.W. was embodied in a decree issued by Hitler on 4th February, 1938. This decree appeared in the Reichsgcsetzblatt, and I invite the Court's attention to it by way of judicial notice. Copies are available, and I would like to read the decree, which is very short, into the transcript. I quote:

> "Command authority over the entire Armed Forces is from now on exercised directly by me personally."

THE PRESIDENT: Where do we find it?

COLONEL TAYLOR: That is not a document, your Honour, because it is a decree from the Reichsgesetzblatt and subject to judicial notice, but copies are available here if the Tribunal cares to look at it.

I will continue with the second paragraph of this decree:

> "The Armed Forces Department in the Reich War Ministry with its functions becomes the High Command of the Armed Forces and comes directly under my command as my military staff.

The head of the Staff of the High Command of the Armed Forces is the Chief of the former Armed Forces Department, with the title of Chief of the High Command of the Armed Forces. His status is equal to that of a Reich Minister.

The High Command of the Armed Forces also takes over the affairs of the Reich War Ministry. The Chief of the High Command of the Armed Forces, as my representative, exercises the functions hitherto exercised by the Reich War Minister. The High Command of the Armed Forces is responsible in peace-time for the unified preparation of the defence of the Reich in all areas according to my directives."

Dated at Berlin, 4th February, 1938. Signed by Hitler, by Lammers, and by Keitel.

Underneath the O.K.W. come the three supreme commands of the three branches of the Armed Forces: O.K.H., O.K.M., and the Air Force. The Air Force did not receive the official designation O.K.L. until 1944. The defendant Raeder remained after 1938 as Commander-in-Chief of the Navy, but von Fritsch, as well as Blomberg, passed out of the picture, von Fritsch being replaced by von Brauchitsch as Commander-in-Chief of the Army, while Goering continued as Commander-in-Chief of the Air Force. In 1941 von Brauchitsch was replaced as Commander-in-Chief of the Army - that is the first box in the left column - by Hitler himself, and in 1943 Raeder was replaced as Commander-in-Chief of the Navy by the defendant Doernitz, but the defendant Goering continued as Commander-in- Chief of the Air Force until the last month of the war.

O.K.W., O.K.H., O.K.M. and O.K.L. each had its own staff. These four staffs did not have uniform designations. The three staffs of the Army, Navy and Air Force are the three boxes in a horizontal line next to the bottom. The staff of the O.K.W. is the little box to the right at the top, bearing the names of Jodl and Warlimont.

In the case of O.K.H. - that is the Army - the staff was known as the Generalstab or the General Staff. In the case of O.K.W., it was known as the Fuehrungsstab or Operations Staff, but in all cases the functions were those of a general staff in military parlance.

It will be seen, therefore, that in this war there was no single German General Staff but, rather, that there were four, one for each branch of the Service and one for the O.K.W. as the overall inter-Service Supreme Command.

So we come to the bottom line on the chart. Down to the bottom line we have been concerned with the central staff organisation at the centre of affairs. Now we pass to the field. Under O.K.H., O.K.M. and O.K.L. come the various fighting formations of the Army, Air Force and Navy, respectively.

In the Army the largest Army field formation was known to the Germans, as indeed it is among the nations generally, as an Army Group, or in German "Heeresgruppe." These are shown in the box in the lower left-hand corner. An army group or Heeresgruppe controls two or more armies - in German, Armeen. Underneath the armies come the lower field formations, such as corps, divisions and regiments, which are not shown on the chart.

In the case of the German Air Force, the largest formation was known as an air fleet or Luftflotte, and the lower units under the air fleet were called corps, Fliegerkorps or Jagdkorps, or divisions, Fliegerdivisionen or Jagddivisionen. These lower formations again we have not shown on the chart.

Under the O.K.M. were the various naval group commands, which controlled all naval operations in a given area, with the exception of the high seas fleet itself and submarines. The commanders of the fleet and the submarines were directly under the German Admiralty.

So we may now examine the group as defined in the Indictment, the group against which the prosecution seeks the declaration of criminality. It is defined in Appendix B of the Indictment. The group comprises firstly, German officers who held the top positions in the four supreme commands which I have just described and, secondly, the officers who held the top field commands.

Turning first to the officers who held the principal positions in the supreme commands, we find that the holders of nine such positions are included in the group. Four of these are positions of supreme authority: the Chief of the O.K.W., Keitel; the Commander-in-Chief of the Army, von Brauchitsch, later Hitler; Commander-in-Chief of the Navy, Raeder, and later, Doenitz; Commander-in- Chief of the Air Force, Goering, and later, von Greim.

Four other positions are those of the chiefs of the staffs to those four commanders-in-chief : the Chief of the Operations Staff of the O.K.W., Jodl; the Chief of the General Staff of the Army, Halder, and later others ; the Chief of the General Staff of the Air Force, Jeschannek, and later others; and the Chief of the Naval War Staff.

The ninth position is that of Deputy Chief of the Operations Staff of O.K.W. Throughout most of the war that was General Warlimont, whose name is shown under Jodl's on the chart. The particular responsibility of Jodl's deputy was planning, strategic planning, and for that reason, his office has been included in the group as defined in the Indictment.

The group named in the Indictment includes all individuals who held any of those nine staff positions between February, 1938, and the end of the war in May, 1945. February, 1938, was selected as the opening date because it was in that month that the top organisation of the German Armed Forces was reorganised, and assumed substantially the form in which you see it there and in which it persisted until the end of the war.

Twenty-two different individuals occupied those nine positions during that period, and of those twenty-two, eighteen are still living. Turning next to the officers who held the principal field commands, the Indictment includes, as members of the group, all commanders-in-chief in the field who had the status of OberbefehIshaber in the Army, Navy or Air Force. The term "OberbefehIshaber " rather defies literal translation into English. Literally, the components of the word mean "Over-command-holder," and we can perhaps best translate it as "Commander-in-Chief."

In the case of the Army, commanders of the army groups and armies always had the status and title of "OberbefehIshaber." In the Air Force the commanders-in-chief of air fleets (Luftwaffe) always had the status of "OberbefehIshaber," although they were not formally so designated until 1944. In the Navy the officers holding the senior regional commands and, therefore, in control of all naval operations in a given sector, had the status of "Oberbefehlshaber."

Roughly one hundred and ten individual officers had the status of "OberbefeWshaber " in the Army, Navy or Air Force during the period in question. All but approximately a dozen of them are still alive. The entire General Staff and High Command group, as defined in the Indictment, comprises about one hundred and thirty officers, of whom one hundred and fourteen are believed to be still living. These figures, of course, are the cumulative total of all officers who at any time belonged to the group during the seven years and three months, from February, 1938, to May, 1945.

The number of active members of the group at any moment is, of course, much smaller. It was about twenty at the outbreak of the war and it rose to about fifty in 1944 and 1945. That is to say, that at any one moment of time in 1944, the group, the active group, would have consisted of the nine individuals occupying the nine staff positions and about forty- one Naval, Air Force or Army Commanders-in-Chief.

The structure and the functioning of the German General Staff and High Command group has been described in a series of affidavits by some of the principal German field marshals and generals. These affidavits are included in Document Book 1. I want to state briefly how these statements were obtained.

In the first place two American officers who were selected for their ability and experience in interviewing high-ranking German prisoners-of-war were briefed by an Intelligence Officer and by the trial counsel on the particular problems presented by this part of the case, the organisational side of the German Armed Forces. These officers were already well versed in military intelligence and were fluent in German. It was emphasised that the function of these interrogating officers was merely to inquire into and establish the facts with respect to the organisation of the Armed Forces, to establish facts on which the prosecution wanted to be accurately informed.

The German generals to be interrogated were selected on the basis of the special knowledge which they could be presumed to possess by reason of the positions which they had held in the past. After each interview the interrogator prepared a report, and from this report such facts as appeared relevant to the issues before the Tribunal were extracted and a statement embodying them was prepared. This statement was then presented to the German officer at a later interview in the form of a draft, and the German officer was asked whether it truly reproduced what he had said, and was invited to alter it in any way he saw fit. The object was to procure the most accurate testimony that we could on organisational matters.

I will take up these affidavits one by one, and I think the members of the Tribunal will see that they fully support the prosecution's description of the group, and conclusively establish that this group of officers was, in fact, the group which had the major responsibility for planning and for directing the operations of the German Armed Forces.

The Soviet and French judges have copies in French and Russian, and the defence has copies in German.

The first of these affidavits is that of Franz Halder who held the rank of "Generaloberst " or Colonel-General - the equivalent of a four-star general in the American Army. His affidavit will be Exhibit USA 531- Halder was Chief of the General Staff of O.K.H. That would be the box second from the bottom on the left-hand side. He was Chief of the General Staff of the O.K.H. from September, 1938, to September, 1942. He is, accordingly, a member of the group and well qualified by his position to testify as to the organisation. His statement is short, and I will read it in full:

> "Ultimate authority and responsibility for military affairs in Germany was vested in the Head of the State, who prior to 2nd August, 1934, was Field Marshal von Hindenburg and thereafter, until 1945, was Adolf Hitler.
>
> Specialised military matters were the responsibility of the three branches of the Armed Forces subordinate to the Commander-in-Chief of the Armed Forces (at the same time Head of the State), that is to say, the Army, Navy and the Air Force. In practice, supervision within this field was exercised by a relatively small group of high- ranking officers. These officers exercised such supervision in their official capacity and by virtue of their training, their positions, and their mutual contacts. Plans for military operations of the German Armed Forces were prepared by members of this group according to the instructions of the O.K.W. in the name of their respective commanding

officers, and were presented by them to the Commander-in-Chief of the Armed Forces (at the same time the Head of the State).

The members of this group were charged with the responsibility of preparing for military operations within their competent fields, and they actually did prepare for any such operations as were to be under- taken by troops in the field.

Prior to any operation, members of this group were assembled and given appropriate directions by the Head of the State. Examples of such meetings are the speech by Hitler to the Commanders-in-Chief on 2znd August, 1939, prior to the Polish campaign, and the consulta- tion at the Reich Chancellery on 14th June, 1941, prior to the Russian campaign. The composition of this group and the relationship of its members to each other were as shown in the attached chart. This was, in effect, the General Staff and High Command of the German Armed Forces.

(Signed) Halder."

The chart to which reference is made is the chart which is at the front of the room and which was attached to the affidavit. The two meetings referred to in the last paragraph of the affidavit are covered by documents which will be introduced subsequently.

I next offer a substantially identical statement by von Brauchitsch, which will be Exhibit USA 532. Von Brauchitsch held the rank of Field Marshal and was Commander-in-Chief of the Army from 1938 to 1941, and therefore was also a member of the group. I need not read his statement, since it is practically the same as that given by Halder, but I will ask that it be set forth in full in the transcript at this point. The only difference between the two statements is in the last sentence of each. Halder states that the group described in the Indictment "was, in effect, the General Staff and High Command of the German Armed Forces," whereas von Brauchitsch puts it a little differently, saying, "In the hands of those who filled the positions shown in the chart lay the actual direction of the Armed Forces." Otherwise, the two statements are identical.

(The document referred to above is as follows.)

"Ultimate authority and responsibility for military affairs in Germany was vested in the Head of State who, prior to 2nd August, 1934, was Field Marshal von Hindenburg, and thereafter until 1945 was Adolf Hitler.

Specialised military matters were the responsibility of the three branches of the Armed Forces subordinate to the Commander-in-Chief of the Armed Forces (at the same time Head of State), that is to say, the Army, the Navy and the Air Force. In practice, supervision within this field was exercised by a relatively small group of high-ranking officers. These officers exercised such supervision in the official capacity and by virtue of their training, theirpositions and their mutual contracts. Plans for military operations of the German Armed Forces were prepared by members of this group according to the instructions of the O.K.W. in the name of their respective Commanding Officers and were presented by them to the Commander-in-Chief of the Armed Forces (at the same time Head of State).

The members of this group were charged with the responsibility of preparing for military operations within their competent fields and they actually did prepare for any such operations as were to be undertaken by troops in the field.

Prior to any operation, members of this group were assembled and given appropriate directions by the Head of State. Examples of such meetings are the speech by Hitler to the Commanders-in-Chief on 22nd August, 1939, prior to the Polish campaign, and the consultation at the Reich Chancellery on 14th June, 1941, prior to the Russian campaign. The composition of this group and the relationship of its members to each other were as shown in the attached chart. In the hands of those who filled the positions shown in the chart lay the actual direction of the Armed Forces.

(Signed) von Brauchitsch."

COLONEL TAYLOR: Now, the Tribunal will see from these affidavits that the chart, which is on display at the front of the Court and which is contained in the short expository statement, has been laid before von Brauchitsch and Halder, and that these two officers have vouched for it under oath as an accurate picture of the top Organisation of the German Armed Forces. The statements by von Brauchitsch and Halder also fully support the prosecution's statement that the holders of the positions shown on this chart constitute the group in whom lay the major responsibility for the planning and execution of all Armed Forces matters.

I would now like to offer another affidavit by Halder which sets forth some of the matters of detail to which I referred in describing the group. It is quite short. It is Affidavit Number 6, which becomes Exhibit USA 533, and I shall read it. in full into the transcript :

"The most important department in the O.K.W. was the Operations Staff, in much the same way as the General Staff was in the Army and Air Force and the Naval War Staff in the Navy. Under Keitel there were a number of departmental chiefs who were equal in status with Jodl, but in the planning and conduct of military affairs, they and their departments were less important and less influential than Jodl and Jodl's staff.

The O.K.W. Operations Staff was also divided into sections. Of these the most important was the section of which Warlimont was chief. It was called the National Defence Section and it was primarily con- cemed with the development of strategic questions. From 1941 onwards, Warlimont, though charged with the same duties, was known as Deputy Chief of the O.K.W. Operations Staff.

There was, during World War II, no unified General Staff such as the Great General Staff which operated in World War I.

Operational matters for the Army and Air Force were worked out by the group of high-ranking officers described in my statement of 7th November (in the Army, General Staff of the Army, and in the Air Force, the General Staff of the Air Force).

Operational matters of the Navy were, even in World War I, not worked out by the Great General Staff but by the Naval Staff,

(Signed) Halder."

The Tribunal will note that this affidavit is primarily concerned with the functions of the General Staffs of the four commands of O.K.W., O.K.L., O.K.H. and O.K.M., and fully supports the inclusion in the group of the Chiefs of Staff of the four services, as well as the inclusion of Warlimont as Deputy Chief of the O.K.W. staff because of his strategic planning responsibilities.

I have just one other very short affidavit covering a matter of detail. The Tribunal will remember that the highest fighting formation in the German Air Force was known as an air fleet or Luftflotte, and that all commanders-in-chief of air fleets are included in this group. That is the box in the lower right-hand corner. The commanders of air fleets always had the status of " Oberbefehlshaber," but they were not formally so designated until 1944. These facts are set forth in an affidavit by the son of Field Marshal von Brauchitsch. His son had the rank of Oberst, or colonel, in the German Air Force, and was personal aide to the defendant Goering as Commander-in-Chief of the Air Force. His affidavit is Number 9 and becomes Exhibit USA 534. It reads as follows:

> "Luftflottenchefs have the same status as the 'Oberbefehlshaber' of an army. During the war they had no territorial authority and, accordingly, exercised no territorial jurisdiction.
>
> They were the highest troop commanders of the Air Force units subordinate to them, and were directly under the command of the Commander-in-Chief of the Air Force.
>
> Until the summer of 1944 they bore the designation 'Befehlshaber' and from then on that of 'Oberbefehlshaber.' This change of designa- tion carried with it no change from the functions and responsibilities that they previously had."

Your Honour, that concludes the description of the composition of the group and its personnel. The staff of the Tribunal have referred to me two inquiries which have been addressed to the Tribunal by counsel for the group, and it seemed to me it might be appropriate if I disposed of these inquiries now, as to the composition of the group. The letters were turned over to me two days ago.

> The first is from Hofrat Dullmann, and he has asked whether the group, as defined in the Indictment, is contingent upon rank; whether it includes officers holding a definite rank such as field marshal or "Generaloberst."

The answer to that is clearly "No." As has been pointed out, the criterion of membership in the group is whether one held one of the positions on the chart up there, and one would be in the group if one held one of the positions, no matter what one's rank. Rank is no criterion. In point of fact, I suppose, everybody in the group held at least the rank of general in the German Army, which is the equivalent of lieutenant-general in ours.

He has also asked whether the group includes officers of the so-called General Staff Corps." The answer to that is "No." There was in the German Army a war academy, and graduates of the war academy were in the branch of service described as the General Staff Corps. They signed themselves, for example, "Colonel in Generalstab." They functioned largely as adjutants and assistants to the chief staff officers. I suppose there were some thousands of them - two or three thousand, but they are not included in the group. Many of them were officers of junior rank. They are not named in the Indictment, and there is no reason and no respect in which they are comprehended within the group as defined.

The other letter of inquiry is from Dr. Exner, who states that he is in doubt as to the meaning of " Oberbefehlshaber," and goes on to state that he believes that "Oberbefehlshaber " includes commanders-in-chief in theatres of war, the commanders-in-chief of army groups, and the com- manders-in-chief of armies. That is quite right. Those are the positions as shown on the chart.

Let us now spend a few minutes examining the way this group worked. In many respects, of course, the German military leaders functioned in the same general manner as obtained in the military establishments of other large nations. General plans were made by the top staff officers and their assistants, in collaboration with the field generals or admirals who were entrusted with the execution of the plans. A decision to wage a particular campaign would be made, needless to say, at the highest level, and the making of such a decision would involve political and diplomatic questions, as well as purely military considerations. When, for example, the decision was made to attack Poland, the top staff officers in Berlin and their assistants would work out general military plans for the campaign. These general plans would be transmitted to the commanders of the army groups and armies who would be in charge of the actual campaign, and then there would follow consultation between the top field commanders and the top staff officers of O.K.W. and O.K.H., in order to revise and perfect and refine the plans.

The manner in which this group worked, involving as it did the inter- change of ideas and recommendations between the top staff officers of O.K.W. and O.K.H. on the one hand and the principal field commanders on the other hand, is graphically described in two statements by Field Marshal von Brauchitsch. That is Affidavit No- 4, which will be Exhibit USA 535. I invite the Tribunal's attention to these and will read them into the transcript. The statement of 7th November, 1945 :

> "In April, 1939, 1 was instructed by Hitler to start military preparations for a possible campaign against Poland. Work was immediately begun to prepare an operational and deployment plan. This was then presented to Hitler and approved by him, after an amendment which he desired. After the operational and deployment orders had been given to the two commanders of the army groups and the five commanders of the armies, conferences took place with them about details, in order to hear their wishes and recommendations. After the outbreak of the war I continued this policy of keeping in close and constant touch with the commanders-in-chief of army groups and of armies, by personal visits to their headquarters, as well as by telephone, teletype, or wireless.
>
> In this way I was able to obtain their advice and their recommendations during the conduct of military operations. In fact, it was the accepted policy and common practice for the commander-in-chief of the army to consult his subordinate commanders-in-chief and maintain a constant exchange of ideas with them.
>
> The commander-in-chief of the army and his chief of staff communi- cated with army groups and through them, as well as directly, with the armies ; through army groups on strategic and tactical matters; directly on questions affecting supply and administration of conquered territory occupied by the armies. An army group had no territorial jurisdiction. It had a relatively small staff, which was concerned only with military operations. In all territorial matters it was the commander-in-chief of the army, and not of the army group, who exercised jurisdiction.
>
> (Signed) von Brauchitsch."

There follows a supplement to the statement of 7th November :

> "When Hitler had made a decision to support the realisation of his political objectives through military pressure or through the application of military force, the commander-in-chief of the army, if he were at all involved, generally first received an appropriate oral briefing or an appropriate oral command. Operational and deployment plans were next worked out in the O.K.H. After these plans had been presented to Hitler, generally by word of mouth, and had been approved by him, there followed a written order from the O.K.W. to the three branches of the Armed Forces. In the meanwhile the O.K.H. began to transmit the operational and deployment plans to the army groups and armies involved.
>
> Details of the operational and deployment plans were discussed by the O.K.H.

with the commanders-in-chief of the army groups and armies and with the chiefs of staff of these commanders. During the operations the O.K.H. maintained a constant exchange of ideas with the army groups by means of telephone, radio, and courier. The commander- in-chief of the army used every opportunity to maintain a personal exchange of ideas with the commanders of army groups, armies, and lower echelons by means of personal visits to them.

In the war against Russia the commanders of army groups and armies were individually and repeatedly called in by Hitler for consultation. Orders for all operational matters went from the O.K.H. to army groups, and for all matters concerning supply and territorial jurisdiction from the O.K.H. directly to the armies.

(Signed) von Brauchitsch."

The Oberbefehlshabers in the field therefore - and in the case of the army that means the commanders-in-chief of army groups and armies - participated in planning and directing the execution of the plans, as those affidavits show. The Oberbefehlshabers were also the repositories of general executive powers in the areas in which their army groups and armies were operating. In this connection I invite the Court's attention to 447-PS, which is already in evidence as Exhibit USA 135 ; Document 447-PS, this being a directive of 13th March, 1941, signed by Keitel and issued by the Supreme Command of the Armed Forces. This directive sets out various regulations for the operations against the Soviet Union which were actually begun a few months later on 22nd June

The documents, your Honour, are in numerical order in Document Books 2 and 3. Document Book 2 contains C and L; Document Book 3 contains PS; and this, being 447-PS, will be in Document Book 3 in numerical order within the PS's. And within that document, under paragraph 1, the paragraph entitled "Area of Operations and Executive Power" ("Vollziehende Gewalt"), the Tribunal will find sub-paragraph 1, in which the following appears. That is Page 1 of the translation, paragraph 2:

"It is not intended to declare East Prussia and the Government-General an area of operations. However, in accordance with the unpublished Fuehrer orders from 19th and 21st Octover, 1939, the commander-in-chief of the Army shall be authorised to take all measures necessary for the execution of his military aim and for the safeguarding of the troops. He may transfer his authority to the commanders-in-chief" - that, in the original german is "Oberbefehlshaber" - "of the army groups and armies. Orders of that kind have priority over all orders issued by civilian agencies."

Your Honour will see that this executive power, with priority over civilian agencies, was vested in the commander-in-chief of the army, with authority to transfer it to commanders-in-chief of army groups or armies - to the members of the group as defined in the Indictment.

Further on in the document, under sub-paragraph 2a, the document states - that is the fourth paragraph, on Page 1 of the document:

"The ares of operations created through teh advance of the army beyond the frontiers of the Reich and the neighbouring countries is to be limited in depth as far as possible. The commander-in-chief of the army has the right to exercise the executive pwer (Vollziehende Gewalt) in this area, and may transfer his authority to the commanders-in-chief (Oberbefehlshaber) of the army groups and armies."

THE PRESIDENT: This would be a convenient time to break off.

(A recess was taken until 1400 hours.)

THE PRESIDENT: The Tribunal will sit to-morrow in closed session to consider matters of procedure, and there will therefore be no public session to-morrow.

COLONEL TAYLOR: Your Lordship, I have just one more document dealing with this subject of this structure of the group before passing on to the substantive charges of criminality.

This document is C-78, which is already in evidence as Exhibit USA 139. That will be found in Document Book 2. This document is the official command invitation to participate in the consultation at the Reich Chancellery on 14th June, 1941, eight days prior to the attack on the Soviet Union. This is one of the meetings that was referred to in the last paragraph of the affidavits by Halder and von Brauchitsch, which were read into the record this morning. It is signed by Colonel Schmundt, the Chief Wehrmacht Adjutant to Hitler, and is dated at Berchtesgaden, 9th June, 1941. It begins:

"In re: Conference 'Barbarossa ' " - that being the code word for the attack on the Soviet Union - "The Fuehrer and Supreme Commander of the Armed Forces has ordered reports on 'Barbarossa' by the Commanders of Army Groups and Armies and Naval and Air Commanders of equal rank."

That is, as the Tribunal will see once again, the very group specified in the bottom line of the chart on the wall, Army Groups, Armies, Army, Naval and Air Commanders of similar rank.

This document likewise includes a list of the participants in this conference, and I would just like in closing on this subject to run through that list to show who the participants in this conference were, and how closely they parallel the structure of the group as we find it in the Indictment. The Tribunal will see that the list of participants begins at the foot of Page 1 of the translation:

General Field Marshal von Brauchitsch, who was then Commander-in-Chief of the Army and a member of the group; General Halder, who was Chief of the Army Staff and a member of the group; then three subordinates, who were not members of the group; Paulus, Hausinger, and Guldenfeldt.

Navy: Captain Wagner, who was chief of the Operations Staff, Operations Division of the Naval War Staff, not a member of the group. On the air side: Goering, a member of the group; General Milch, State Secretary and Inspector of the Air Force, again not a member of the group; General Jeschomiek, Chief of the General Staff of the Air Force and a member of the group; and two of his assistants.

Passing over the page to the O.K.W., High Command of the Armed Forces, we find Keitel, Jodl, Warlimont, all members of the group, were present, with an assistant from the General Staff.

Then four officers from the office of the adjutant, who were not members of the group.

Then we pass to the officers from the Field Commands: General von Falkenhorst, Army High Command, Norway, member of the group; General Stumpff, Air Fleet 5, member of the group; Rundstedt, Reichenau, Stillpnagel, Schobert, Kleist, all from the Army, all members of the group.

Air Force: General Loehr, Air Fleet 4, member of the group.

General Fromm and General Udet were not members. Fromm was director of the Home Forces, commander of the Home Forces, and Udet the Director General of Equipment and Supply.

The Navy: Raeder, a member of the group; Fricke, chief of the Naval War Staff, and a member of the group; and an assistant who was not a member; Karls, Navy

Group North, member of the group.

Then from the Army: Leeb, Busch, Kuhler, all members of the group as Oberbefehlshaber. From the Air Force, Keller, a member of the group.

Bock, Kluge, Strauss, Guderian, Hoth, Kesselring, all members of the group.

It will accordingly be seen that except for a few assisting officers of relatively junior rank, almost all the participants in these consultations were members of 'the group as defined in the Indictment, and that in fact the participants included almost all the members of the group who were concerned in the impending operations against the Soviet Union.

I have now concluded the first part of the presentation, to wit, the description of the General Staff and High Command Group and its composition and structure and general manner of functioning. I turn now to the charges levelled against this group in the Indictment.

Appendix B charges that this group had a major responsibility for the planning, preparation, initiation and waging of the illegal wars set forth in Counts 1 and 2 and for the War Crimes and Crimes Against Humanity detailed in Counts 3 and 4.

In presenting the evidence in support of these charges we must keep in mind that under the Charter the group may be declared criminal in connection with any acts of which an individual defendant who was a member of the group may be convicted.

The General Staff and High Command group is well represented among the individual defendants in this case. Five of the individual defendants, or one-quarter of the individuals here, are members of the group.

Taking them in the order in which they are listed, the first is defendant Goering. Goering is a defendant in this case in numerous capacities. He is a member of the General Staff and High Command group by reason of having been Commander-in-Chief of the Air Force from the time when the Air Force first came into the open and was officially established, until about one month prior to the end of war. During the last month of the war he was replaced in this capacity by von Greim, who committed suicide shortly after his capture at the end of the war. Goering is charged with crimes under all counts of the Indictment.

The next listed defendant who is a member of the group is Keitel. He and the remaining three defendants are, all four of them, in this case primarily or solely in their military capacities, and all four of them are professional soldiers or sailors.

Keitel was made Chief of the High Command of the German Armed Forces, or O.K.W., when the O.K.W. was first set up in 1938 and remained in that capacity throughout the period in question. He held the rank of field marshal throughout most of this period, and in addition to being the Chief of the O.K.W., he was a member of the Secret Cabinet Council and of the Council of Ministers for the Defence of the Reich. Keitel is charged with crimes under all four counts.

The defendant Jodl was a career soldier. He was an Oberstleutnant, or Lieutenant Colonel, when the Nazis came to power and ultimately attained the rank of Generaloberst or Colonel General. He became the Chief of the Operations Staff of the Welirmacht and continued in that capacity throughout the war. He also is charged with crimes under all four counts.

The other two defendants who are members of this group are on the nautical side. The defendant Raeder is in a sense the senior member of the entire group, having been commander-in-chief of the German Navy as early as 1928. He attained the highest rank in the German Navy, Grossadmiral. He retired from the Supreme Command of the Navy in 1943, in January, and was replaced by Donitz. Raeder is charged under Counts 1, 2 and 3 of the Indictment.

The last of the five defendants, Donitz, was a relatively junior officer when the

Nazis came to power. During the early years of the Nazi regime, he specialised in submarine activities and was in command of the U-boat arm when the war broke out. He rose steadily in the Navy and was chosen to succeed Raeder when the latter retired in 1943, became commander-inchief of the Navy and attained the rank of Grossadmiral. When the German Armed Forces collapsed near the end of the war, Doernitz succeeded Hitler as head of the German Government. He is charged under Counts 1, 2 and 3 of the Indictment.

Four of these five defendants are reasonably typical of the group as a whole. We must except the defendant Goering, who is primarily a Nazi party politician nourishing a hobby for aviation as a result of his career in 1914-18. But the others made soldiering or sailoring their life-work. They collaborated with and joined in the most important adventures of the Nazis, but they were not among the early party members. They differ in no essential respects from the other 125 members of the group. They are, no doubt, abler men in certain respects. They rose to the highest positions in the German Armed Forces, and all but Jodl attained the highest rank.

But they will serve as excellent case studies and as representatives of the group, and we can examine their ideas as they have expressed them in these documents, and their actions, with fair assurance that these ideas and actions are characteristic of the other group members.

I turn first to the criminal activities of the General Staff and High Command group under Counts 1 and 2 of the Indictment, their activities in planning and conspiring to wage illegal wars. Here my task is largely one of recapitulation. The general body of proof relating to aggressive war has already been laid before the Tribunal by my colleague, Mr. Alderman, and the distinguished members of the British delegation.

Many of the documents to which they drew the Tribunal's attention showed that the defendants here who were members of the General Staff and High Command group participated knowingly and wilfully in crimes under Counts 1 and 2. I propose to avoid referring again to that evidence so far as I possibly can, but I must refer to one or two of them again to focus the Tribunal's attention on the part which the General Staff and High Command group played in aggressive War Crimes.

Now it is, of course, the normal function of a military staff to prepare military plans. In peacetime military staffs customarily concern themselves with the preparation of plans for attack or defence based on hypothetical contingencies. There is nothing criminal about carrying on these exercises or preparing these plans. That is not what the defendants and this group are charged with.

We will show that the group agreed with the Nazi objective of aggrandising Germany by threat of force or force itself, and they joined knowingly and enthusiastically in developing German armed might for this purpose. They were advised in advance of the Nazi plans to launch aggressive wars. They laid the military plans and directed the initiation and carrying on of the wars. These things we believe to be criminal under Article 6 of the Charter.

Aggressive war cannot be prepared or waged without intense activity on the part of all branches of the Armed Forces, and particularly by the high-ranking officers who control these forces. To the extent, therefore' that German preparation for and the waging of aggressive war are historicai facts of common knowledge, or are already proved, it necessarily follows that the General Staff and High Command group, and the German Armed Forces, participated therein.

This is so notwithstanding the effort on the part of certain German military leaders to insist that until the troops marched they lived in an ivory tower unwilling to see the direction to which their work led.

The documents to which I shall refer fully refute this, and moreover some of these men now fully admit they participated gladly with the Nazis because the Nazi aims coincided closely with their own.

I think that the documents which Mr. Alderman read into the transcript already adequately reflect the purposes and objectives of the German General Staff and High Command Group during the period prior to the absorption of Austria. During this period occurred, as is charged in the Indictment, firstly, secret rearmament, including the training of military personnel, the production of war munitions and building of an Air Force; secondly, the Goering announcement on 10th March, 1933, that Germany was building a military Air Force; thirdly, the law for compulsory military service of 16th March, 1935, fixing the peace-time strength of the German Army at 500,000; and finally, and fourthly, the reoccupation of the Rhineland on 7th March, 1936, and the refortification of that area.

Those particular facts do not require judicial proof. They are historical facts, and likewise the fact that it would have been impossible for the Nazis to achieve these things without co-operation by the Armed Forces is indisputable from the very nature of things.

Mr. Alderman described to the Tribunal and read from numerous documents which illustrate these events. He included numerous documents concerning the secret expansion of the German Navy in violation of treaty limitations, under the guidance of the defendant Raeder.

He also read the secret Reich Defence Law, Document 2261-PS, already in the record as Exhibit USA 24, which was adopted on the same day that Germany unilaterally renounced the armament provisions of the Versailles Treaty. He read von Blomberg's plan, dated 2nd May, 1935, for the reoccupation of the Rhineland - that is Document C-159, Exhibit USA 54 and Blomberg's orders under which the reoccupation was actually carried out.

All these events, by obvious inference, required the closest collaboration between the military leaders and the Nazis. I need not labour that point further.

But it is worth while, I think, to re-examine one or two of the documents which show the state of mind and the objectives of the German military leaders during this early period. One document, read from by Mr. Alderman, which reflects the viewpoint of the German Navy on the opportunities which Nazism accorded for rearmament so that Germany could achieve its objectives by force or threat of force, is a memorandum published by the High Command of the German Navy in 1937, entitled "The Fight of the Navy Against Versailles." That is Document C-156, Exhibit USA 41. The Tribunal will recall that this memorandum, this official publication of the German Navy, stated that only with the assistance of Hitler had it been possible to create the conditions for rearmament. The defendant Jodl has stated this better than I could possibly put it, in his speech to the Gauleiters on 7th November, 1943. That is in Document L-172, Exhibit USA 34, from which Mr. Alderman read at length.

Nor were the high-ranking German officers unaware that the policies and objectives of the Nazis were leading Germany in the direction of war. I invite the Court's attention to Document C-23, which is already in the record as Exhibit USA 49. This consists of some notes made by Admiral Carls of the Germany Navy in September, 1938, These notes were written by Admiral Carls by way of comment on a "Draft Study of Naval Warfare Against England," and they read in part as follows. That will be found your Lordship, on Page 3 of the translation of Document C-23:

"There is full agreement with the main theme of the study.

1. If, according to the Fuehrer's decision, Germany is to acquire a position as a world power, she needs not only sufficient colonial possessions but also secure naval communications and secure access to the sea.

2. Both requirements can only be fulfilled in opposition to Anglo-French interests and would limit their position as world powers. It is unlikely that they can be achieved by peaceful means. The decision to make Germany a world power therefore forces upon us the necessity of making the corresponding preparations for war.

3. War against England means at the same time war against the Empire, against France, probably against Russia as well and a large number of countries overseas; in fact, against one half to one third of the whole world.

It can only be justified and have a chance of success if it is prepared economically as well as politically and militarily and waged with the aim of conquering for Germany an outlet to the ocean."

Let us turn to the Air Force, having seen what the viewpoint of the Navy was. Parts of the German Air Force during this pre-war period were developing even more radically aggressive plans for the aggrandisement of the Reich. Document L-43, GB-29, is a study prepared by the Chief of a branch of the General Staff of the Air Force called the "Organisation Staff." The study in question is a recommendation for the organisation of the German Air Force in future years up to 1950. The recommendation is based on certain assumptions, and one assumption was that by 1950 the frontiers of Germany would be as shown on the map which was attached as an enclosure to this study. There is only one copy of the map available, your Honour.

The Court will note on this map that Austria, Czechoslovakia, Hungary, Poland and the Baltic coast up to the Gulf of Finland are all included within the borders of the Reich. The Court will also note, at Page 2 of the document itself - that is L-43 - that the author envisaged the future peacetime organisation of the German Air Force as comprising seven group commands, four of which lie within the borders of Germany proper at Berlin, Braunschschweig, Munich and Koenigsberg, but the three others are proposed to be at Vienna, Budapest and Warsaw.

Before turning to particular acts of aggression by the German Armed Forces, I want to stress once more the basic agreement and harmony between the Nazis and the German military leaders. Without this agreement on objectives there might never have been a war. In this connection I want to direct the Tribunal's attention to an affidavit - No. 3, which will be Exhibit USA 536 - by von Blomberg, formerly Field Marshal, Reich War Minister, and Commander-in-Chief of the German Armed Forces until February, 1938. I will read the affidavit into the transcript:

"From 1919, and particularly from 1924, three critical territorial questions occupied attention in Germany. These were the questions of the Polish Corridor, the Ruhr and Memel.

I myself, as well as the whole group of German staff officers, believed that these three questions, outstanding among which was the question by force of arms. About go per cent. of the German people were of the same mind as the officers, on the Polish question. A war to wipe. out the desecration involved in the creation of the Polish Corridor and to lessen the threat to separated East Prussia, surrounded by Poland and Lithuania, was regarded as a sacred duty, though a sad necessity. This was one of the chief reasons behind the partially secret rearmament which began about ten years before Hitler came to power and was accentuated under Nazi Rule.

Before 1938-1939 the German generals were not opposed to Hitler. There was no reason to oppose Hitler, since he produced the results which they desired. After this time some generals began to condemn his methods, and lost confidence in the power of his judgment. However, they failed as a group to take any definite stand against him, although a few of them tried to do so and as a result had to pay for this with their lives or their positions.

Shortly before my removal from the post of Commander-in-Chief of the Armed Forces, in January, 1938, Hitler asked me to recommend a successor. I suggested Goering, who was the senior ranking officer, but Hitler objected because of his lack of patience and diligence. I was replaced as Commander-in-Chief of the Armed Forces by no officer, but Hitler personally took over my function as Commander. Keitel was recommended by me as a Chef de Bureau. As far as I know, he was never named Commander of the Armed Forces but was always merely a 'Chief of Staff' under Hitler and, in effect, conducted the administrative functions of the Ministry of War.

At my time Keitel was not opposed to Hitler and therefore was qualified to bring about a good understanding between Hitler and the Armed Forces, a thing which I myself desired and had furthered as Reichswehrminister and Reichskriegsminister. To do the opposite would have led to a civil war, for at that time the mass of the German people supported Hitler. Many are no longer willing to admit this. But it is the truth.

As I heard, Keitel did not oppose any of Hitler's measures. He became a willing tool in Hitler's hands for every one of his decisions.

He did not measure up to what might have been expected of him."

The statement by von Blomberg which I have just read is paralleled closely in some respects by an affidavit by Colonel General Blaskowitz. That is Affidavit No. 5 in Document Book 1 and will be Exhibit USA 537. Blaskowitz commanded an army in the campaign against Poland and the campaign against France. He subsequently took command of Army Group G in Southern France and held command of Army Group H, which retreated beyond the Rhine at the end of the war. The first three paragraphs of his affidavit are substantially identical with the first three paragraphs of von Blomberg's, and since they are available in all languages, for expedition I will start reading with paragraph 4, where the affidavitjs on a different subject:

"After the annexation of Czechoslovakia we hoped that the Polish question would be settled in a Peaceful fashion through diplomatic means, since we believed that this time France and England would come to the assistance of their ally. As a matter of fact, we felt that if political negotiations came to nothing the Polish question would unavoidably lead to war, that is, not only with Poland herself but also with the Western Powers.

When in the middle of June I received an order from the O.K.H. to prepare myself for an attack on Poland, I knew that this war came even closer to the realm of possibility. This conclusion was only strengthened by the Fuehrer's speech on 22nd August, 1939, at the Obersalzberg when it clearly seemed to be an actuality. Between the middle of June, 1939, and 1st September, 1939, the members of my staff who were engaged in preparations, participated in various dis cussions which went on between the O.K.H. and the army group. During these discussions such matters of a tactical, strategical and general nature were discussed as had to do with my future position as Commander-in-Chief of the Eighth Army during the planned Polish campaign.

During the Polish campaign, particularly during the Kutno operations, I was repeatedly in communication with the Commander-in-Chief of the Army, and he, as well as the Fuehrer, visited my headquarters. In fact, it was common practice for commanders-in-chief of army groups and of armies to be asked from time to time for estimates of the situation, and for their recommendations by telephone, teletype or wireless, as well as by personal calls. These front line commanders-in-chief thus actually became advisers to the O.K.H. in their own field, so that the positions shown in the attached chart embrace that group which was the actual advisory council of the High Command of the German Armed Forces."

The Tribunal will note that the latter part of this affidavit, like those of Halder and Brauchitsch, vouches for the accuracy of the structure and organisation of the General Staff and High Command group as described by the prosecution. The Tribunal will also note that the von Blomberg affidavit and the first part of the Blaskowitz affidavit make it clear beyond question that the military leaders of Germany knew of, approved, supported, and executed plans for the expansion of the Armed Forces beyond the limits set by treaties. The objectives they had in mind are obvious from the affidavits and documents to which reference has been made. In these documents and affidavits we see the Nazis and the Generals in agreement upon the basic objective of aggrandising Germany by force or threat of force and collaborating to build up the armed might of Germany, in order to make possible the subsequent acts of aggression. We turn to an examination of those particular acts of aggression which have already been described to the Tribunal in general, with the particular purpose of noting participation in these criminal acts by the General Staff and High Command group.

I may say, your Lordship, that in going over this matter, I propose, in order to save time, to read from very few of the large numbers of documents. Accordingly, when I cite them I think there is probably no need for the Tribunal to try to find them in the documents before it. Most of them are in evidence and I propose to cite them for purposes of recapitulation, without reading very much.

The Tribunal will recall that Mr. Alderman read into the transcript portions of a document, 386-PS, Exhibit USA 25, consisting of notes by Colonel Hoszbach on a conference which was held in the German Chancellery in Berlin on 5th November, 1937. Hitler presided at this conference, which was a small and highly secret one, and the only other participants were the four principal military leaders and the Minister of Foreign Affairs, the defendant Neurath. The four chief leaders of the Armed Forces - Blomberg, who was then Reich Minister of war, and the Commander-in-Chief of the three branches of the Armed Forces, von Fritsch for the Army, Raeder for the Navy, and Goering for the Air Force - were present. Hitler embarked on a general discussion of Germany's diplomatic and military policy and stated that the conquest of Austria and Czechoslovakia was an essential preliminary "for the improvement of our military position" and "in order to remove any threat from the flanks."

The military and political advantages envisaged included the acquisition of a new source of food, shorter and better frontiers, the release of troops for other tasks, and the possibility of forming new divisions from the population of the conquered territories. Blomberg and von Fritsch joined in the discussion and von Fritsch stated "that he was making a study to investigate the possibilities of carrying out operations against Czechoslovakia with special consideration of the conquest of the Czechoslovakian system of fortifications."

The following spring, in March, 1938, the German plans with respect to Austria came to fruition. Mr. Alderman has already read into the record portions of the diary kept by the defendant Jodl. The portion here in question, Document 1780-PS,

Exhibit USA 72, of this diary shows the participation of the German military leaders in the absorption of Austria. As is shown by Jodl's diary entry for 11th February, 1938, the defendant Keitel and other generals were present at the Obersalzberg meeting between von Schuschnigg and Hitler, and the purpose is shown clearly by the entry which recites that "in the evening and on 12th February General Keitel with General von Reichenau and Sperrle at the Obersalzberg. Schuschnigg together with G. Schmidt are again being put under heaviest political and military pressure. At 2300, hours Schuschnigg signs protocol." The General von Reichenau referred to was at that time the head commander of Wehrkreis 7, one of the military districts into which Germany was divided. He subsequently commanded the Tenth Army in Poland and the Sixth Army in France and was a member of the group as defined in the Indictment. Sperrle who was in Spain during the Civil War and then commanded Luftflotte 3, the Third German Air Fleet, practically throughout the war, was also a member of the group. Two days later Keitel and other military leaders were preparing proposals to be submitted to Hitler which would give the Austrian Government the impression that Germany would resort to force unless the Schuschnigg agreement was ratified in Vienna.

These proposals are embodied in Document 1775-PS, dated 14th February, 1938, Exhibit USA 73, and signed by Keitel. Portions of Keitel's proposals to the Fuehrer are as follows:

"To take no real preparatory measures in the Army or Luftwaffe. No troop movements or redeployments. Spread false but quite credible news which may lead to the conclusion of military preparations against Austria, (a) through V-men" - that means agents - "in Austria; (b) through our customs personnel at the frontier; (c) through travelling agents."

Going down the document to 4, Keitel proposed:

"Order a very active make-believe wireless exchange in Wehrkreis VII and between Berlin and Munich; (5) real manoeuvres, training flights and winter manoeuvres of the Mountain Troops near the frontier; (6) Admiral Canaris has to be ready, beginning on 14th February in the Service Command Headquarters, in order to carry out measures given by order of the Chief of the O.K.W."

As Jodl's diary shows under the entry for 14th February, these deceptive manceuvres were very effective and created in Austria the impression that these threats of force might be expected to create. About a month later armed intervention was precipitated by von Schuschnigg's decision to hold a plebiscite in Austria. Hitler ordered mobilisation in accordance with the pre-existing plans for the invasion of Austria, these plans being known as "Case Otto," in order to absorb Austria and stop the plebiscite. Jodl's diary under the entry for ioth March, 1938, tells us as follows on Page 2:

"By surprise and without consulting his ministers Schuschnigg ordered a plebiscite for Sunday, 13th March, which should bring a strong majority for the Legitimists in the absence of plan or preparation.

Fuehrer is determined not to tolerate it. The same night, 9th to 10th March, he calls for Goering. General von Reichenau is called back from Cairo Olympic Committee, General von Schobert is ordered to come as well as Minister Glaise-Horstenau, who is with Gauleiter Burckel in the Palatinate."

The General von Schobert referred to succeeded General von Reichenau as Commander of Wehrkreis 7 and later was Commander of the Eleventh Army in Russia and was a member of the group as defined in the Indictment.

The invasion of Austria differs from the other German acts of aggression in that the invasion was not closely scheduled and timed in advance. This is the case simply because the invasion was precipitated by an outside event - von Schuschnigg's order for the plebiscite. But, although for this reason the element of deliberately timed planning was lacking, the foregoing documents make clear the participation of the military leaders at all stages.

At the small policy meeting of November, 1937, when Hitler's general programme for Austria and Czechoslovakia was outlined, the only others present were the four principal military leaders and the Foreign Secretary. In February, Keitel, Reichenau and Sperrle were present to help subject von Schuschnigg to the heaviest military pressure. Keitel and others immediately thereafter worked out and executed a programme of military threat and deception to frighten the Austrian Government into acceptance of the Schuschnigg protocol. When the actual invasion took place, it was, of course, directed by the military leaders and executed by the Armed Forces, and we are indebted to the defendant Jodl for a clear statement of why the German military leaders were only too delighted to join with the Nazis in bringing about the end of Austrian independence.

In his lecture in November, 1943, to the Gauleiters, which appears in Document L-172, which is Exhibit USA 34, Jodl explained:

"The Austrian Anschluss in its turn, not only brought with it fulfilment of an old national aim, but also had the effect both of reinforcing our fighting strength and of materially improving our strategic position. Whereas up till then the territory of Czechoslovakia had projected in a most menacing way right into Germany (a wasp waist in Russia), Czechoslovakia herself was now enclosed by pincers. Her own strategic position had now become so unfavourable that she was bound to fall a victim to any attack pressed home with vigour before effective aid from the West could be expected to arrive."

The foregoing extract from Jodl's speech makes a good transition to the case of Czechoslovakia - "Case Green," or "Fall Gruen," which I propose to treat very briefly, as Mr. Alderman has covered the general story of German aggression against Czechoslovakia very fully, and the documents he read from are full of evidence showing the knowing participation in this venture by Keitel, Jodl, and other members of the group.

Once again the Hoszbach minutes of the conference between Hitler and the four principal military leaders, Document 386-PS, Exhibit USA 25 may be called to mind. Austria and Czechoslovakia were listed as the nearest victims of German aggression. After the absorption of Austria, Hitler, as head of the State, and Keitel, as Chief of all the Armed Forces, lost no time in turning their attention to Czechoslovakia. From this point on nearly the whole story is contained in the Schmundt file (Document 388-PS, Exhibit USA 26) and Jodl's diary, both of which have been read from extensively. These two sources of information go far, I think, to demolish what is urged in defence of the military defendants and the General Staff and High Command Group. They seek to create the impression that the German generals were pure military technicians, that they were not interested in, or not informed about political and diplomatic considerations, that they prepared plans for military attack or defence on a purely hypothetical basis. They say all this in order to suggest that they did not share and could not estimate Hitler's aggressive intentions, that they carried out politically-conceived orders like military automatons, with no idea whether the wars they launched were aggressive or not.

When these arguments are made, your Honour, may I respectfully suggest that you read the Schumndt file and General Jodl's diary. They make it abundantly clear that aggressive designs were conceived jointly between the Nazis and the generals, that the military leaders were fully posted on the aggressive intentions, and informed on the political and diplomatic developments. Indeed, German generals had a strange habit of turning up at diplomatic foregatherings, and, surely, if the documents did not show these things, a moment's thought must show them to be true.

A highly successful programme of conquest depends on armed might. It cannot be executed by an unprepared, weak, or recalcitrant military leadership. It has, of course, been said that war is too important a business to be left to soldiers alone; and this is, no doubt, true, but it is equally true that an aggressive diplomacy is far too dangerous a business to be conducted without military advice and support, and no doubt some of the German generals had qualms about Hitler's timing and the boldness of some of his moves. Some of these doubts are rather interestingly reflected in an entry from Jodl's diary which has not yet been read.

That is Document 1780-PS again - the entry for 10th August, 1938. It appears on Page 4 of the translation of 1780-PS:

"10th August, 1938. The Army Chiefs and the Chiefs of the Air Forces Groups, Lieut.-Colonel Jeschonnek and I - are ordered to the Berghof. After dinner the Fuehrer makes a speech lasting for almost three hours, in which he develops his political thoughts. The subsequent attempts to draw the Fuehrer's attention to the defects of our preparations, which are undertaken by a few generals of the army, ar rather unfortunate. This applies especially to the remark of General Wietersheim, in which, to cap it, he claims to quote from Genera Adams that the Western fortifications can be held for only three weeks. The Fuehrer becomes very indignant and flares up, bursting into th remark that in such a case the whole Army would not be good fo anything. 'I assure you, General, the position will be held not only for three weeks, but for three years.' The cause of this despondent opinion, which unfortunately enough is held very widely within th Army General Staff, is based on various reasons. First of all, it (the General Staff) is restrained by old memories; political consideration play a part as well, instead of obeying and executing its military mission That is certainly done with traditional devotion, but the vigour of th soul is lacking, because in the end they do not believe in the genius of the Fuehrer. One does perhaps compare him with Charles XII. And since water flows downhill, this defeatism may not only possibly cause immense political damage, for the opposition between the generals' opinion and that of the Fuehrer is common talk, but may also constitute a danger for the morale of the troops. But I have no doubt that th Fuehrer will be able to boost the morale of the people in an unexpecte way when the right moment comes."

THE PRESIDENT: Shall we break off now for ten minutes?

(A recess was taken.).

COLONEL TAYLOR: The extract from the Jodl diary from which I have just read may indeed show that some of the German generals at that time were cautious with respect to Germany's ability to take on Poland and the Western Powers simultaneously; but nevertheless the entry shows no lack of sympathy with the Nazi aims for conquest. And there is no evidence in Jodl's diary or elsewhere that any substantial number of German generals lacked sympathy with Hitler's objectives. Furthermore, the top military leaders always joined with and supported his decisions, with formidable success in these years from 1938 to 1942.

So, if we are told that German military leaders did not know that German policy toward Czechoslovakia was aggressive or based on force or threat of force, let us remember that on 30th May, 1938, Hitler signed a most secret directive to Keitel - already in the transcripts, Document 388-PS, Exhibit USA 26 - in which he stated clearly his unalterable decision to smash Czechoslovakia by military action in the near future.

The defendant Jodl was in no doubt what that directive meant. He noted in his diary, the same day, that the Fuehrer had stated his final decision to destroy Czechoslovakia soon, and had initiated military preparation all along the line.

And the succeeding evidence, both in the Schmundt file and in the Jodl diary, shows how these military preparations went forward. Numerous examples of discussions, plans, and preparations during the last few weeks before the Munich Pact, including discussions with Hungary and the Hungarian General Staff, in which General Halder participated, are contained in the Jodl diary and the later items in the Schmundt file. The day the Munich Pact was signed, the 29th September, Jodl noted in his diary - 1780-PS, the entry for 29th September:

> "The Munich Pact is signed. Czechoslovakia as a power is out. Four zones as set forth will be occupied between the 2nd and 7th of October. The remaining part, of mainly German character, will be occupied by the 10th of October. The genius of the Fuehrer and his determination not to shun even a World War have again won the victory without the use of force. The hope remains that the incredulous, the weak and the doubtful people have been converted and will remain that way."

Plans for the liquidation of the remainder of Czechoslovakia were made soon after Munich. Ultimately the absorption of the remainder was accomplished by diplomatic bullying, in which the defendant Keitel participated, for the usual purpose of demonstrating that German armed might was ready to enforce the threats - as shown by two documents already in, which I need not read: Document 2802-PS, Exhibit USA 107; and Document 2798-PS, Exhibit USA 118. And once again the defendant Jodl in his 1943 lecture, Document L 172, Exhibit USA 34 - tells us clearly and in one sentence why the objective of eliminating Czechoslovakia lay as close to the hearts of the German military leaders as to the hearts of the Nazis:

> "The bloodless solution of the Czech conflict in the autumn of 1938 and the spring of 1939 and the annexation of Slovakia rounded off the territory of Greater Germany in such a way that it then became possible to consider the Polish problem on the basis of more or less favourable strategic premises."

And this serves to recall the affidavits by Blomberg and Blaskowitz, from which I have already read. "The whole group of German staff and front officers believed that the question of the Polish Corridor would have to be settled some day, if necessary by force of arms," they told us, and "Hitler produced the results which all of us warmly desired."

I turn now to Poland. The German attack on Poland is a particularly interesting one from the standpoint of the General Staff and High Command. The documents which show the aggressive nature of the attack have already been introduced by Colonel Griffith Jones of the British Delegation. I propose to approach it from a slightly different angle, inasmuch as these documents serve as an excellent case-study of the functioning of the General Staff and High Command Group as defined in the Indictment.

> This attack was carefully timed and planned, and in the documents one can observe the staff work step by step. Colonel Griffith Jones read from a series of directives from Hitler and Keitel, embodied in Document C-120, GB 41,

involving "Fall Weiss," which was the code word for the plan of attack on Poland. That is a whole series of documents, and the series starts - C 120 - with a re-issuance of a document called "Directive for the Uniform Preparation for War by the Armed Forces."

We have encountered this periodically re-issued directive previously. That was a sort of form of standing instructions to the Armed Forces laying out what their tasks during the coming period would be.

In essence these directives are, firstly, statements of what the Armed Forces must be prepared to accomplish in view of political and diplomatic policies and developments and, secondly, indications of what should be accomplished diplomatically in order to make the military tasks easier and the chances of success greater. They constitute, in fact, a fusion of diplomatic and military thought and they strongly demonstrate the mutual inter-dependence of aggressive diplomacy and military planning.

Note the limited distribution of these documents, early in April, 1939, in which the preparation of the plans for the Polish war is ordered. Five copies only are distributed by Keitel: one goes to Brauchitsch, O.K.H.; one to Raeder, O.K.M.; one to Goering at O.K.L.; and two to Warlimont in the Planning Branch of O.K.W.

Hitler lays down that the plans must be capable of execution by 1st September, 1939, and, as we all well remember, that target date was adhered to. The fusion of military and diplomatic thought is clearly brought out by a part of one of these documents which has not previously been read; that is Document C 120, sub-division D, and it is to be found at Page 4.

The sub-heading is: "Political Requirements and Aims.

> German relations with Poland continue to be based on the principle of avoiding any quarrels. Should Poland, however, change her policy towards Germany, based up to now on the same principles as our own, and adopt a threatening attitude towards Germany, a final settlement might become necessary, notwithstanding the pact in effect with Poland.
>
> The aim, then, will be to destroy Polish military strength and create in the East a situation which satisfies the requirements of national defence. The free State of Danzig will be proclaimed a part of the Reich territory at the outbreak of the conflict at the latest.
>
> The political leadership considers it its task in this case to isolate Poland if possible, that is to say, to limit the war to Poland only.
>
> The development of increasing internal crises in France and the resulting British cautiousness might produce such a situation in the not too distant future.
>
> Intervention by Russia, so far as she would be able to do this, cannot be expected to be of any use for Poland, because this would imply Poland's destruction by Bolshevism.
>
> The attitude of the Baltic States will be determined wholly by German military exigencies.
>
> On the German side Hungary cannot be considered a certain ally. Italy's attitude is determined by the Berlin-Rome Axis."

Sub-heading 2: "Military Conclusions.

> The great objectives in the building up of the German Armed Forces will continue to be determined by the antagonism of the Western Democracies. ' Fall Weiss' constitutes only a precautionary complement to these preparations. It is not to be looked upon in any way, however, as the necessary prerequisite for a military settlement with the Western opponents.

The isolation of Poland will be more easily maintained, even after the beginning of operations, if we succeed in starting the war with heavy, sudden blows, and in gaining rapid successes.

The entire situation will require, however, that precautions be taken to safeguard the Western boundary and the German North Sea coast, as well as the air over them."

Let no one suggest that these are hypothetical plans or that the General Staff and High Command Group did not know what was in prospect. The plans show on their face that they are no war game. But, to clinch this point, let us refer briefly to Mr. Alderman's " pin-up " document on Poland, Document L-79, Exhibit USA 27. These are Schmundt's notes on the conference in Hitler's study at the Reich Chancellery, Berlin, on 23rd May, 1939, when Hitler announced - and I quote just one sentence - "There is, therefore, no question of sparing Poland, and we are left with the decision to attack Poland at the first suitable opportunity."

Note who was present besides Hitler and a few military aides: the defendant Goering, Commander-in-Chief of the Luftwaffe; the defendant Raeder, Navy; the defendant Keitel, O.K.W.; von Brauchitsch, Cornmander-in-Chief of the Army; Colonel General Milch, who was State Secretary of the Air Ministry and Inspector General of the Luftwaffe; General Bodenschatz, Goering's personal assistant; Rear Admiral Schniewindt, Chief of the Naval War Staff; Colonel Jeschonnek, Chief of the Air Staff; Colonel Warlimont, Planning Staff. All of them, except Milch, Bodenschatz, and the adjutants, are members of the Group.

So far these documents have shown us the initial and general planning of the attack on Poland. These general plans, however, had to be checked, corrected and perfected by the field commanders who were to carry out the attack.

I offer Document C-1142, which will be Exhibit USA 538. This document was issued in the middle of June, 1939, and in it von Brauchitsch, as Commander-in-Chief of the Army, passed on the general outlines of the plan for the attack on Poland to the field commanders- in-chief-to the Oberbefehlshaber of army groups and armies - so that the field commanders could work out the actual preparation and deployment of troops in accordance with the plans.

This is from Page 1 of the translation, and I quote:

> "The object of the operation is to destroy the Polish Armed Forces. High policy demands that the war should be begun by heavy surprise blows in order to achieve quick results. The intention of the Army High Command is to prevent a regular mobilisation and concentration of the Polish Army by a surprise invasion of Polish territory, 'and to destroy the mass of the Polish Army which is to be expected to be West of the Vistula-Narve Line."

I pass to the next paragraph:

> "The Army Group Commands and the Army Commands will make their preparations on the basis of surprise of the enemy. There will be alterations necessary if surprise should have to be abandoned. These will have to be developed simply and quickly on the same basis; they are to be prepared mentally to such an extent that in case of an order from the Army High Command they can be carried out quickly."

THE PRESIDENT: What is the date of that document?

COLONEL TAYLOR: The date of that document is the middle of June, 1939; I believe it is the 15th or 14th of June, 1939. The date is on the original.

The next document is 2327-PS, which will be Exhibit USA 539, signed by Blaskowitz. It is dated 14th June, 1939, and it shows us an Oberbefehlshaber at work in the field, planning an attack. Blaskowitz at that time was Commander of the Third Army Area Command and he became Commander-in-Chief of the German Eigth Army during the Polish campaign. I read some extracts trom this document - found on Page 1 of the translation:

> "The Commander-in-Chief of the Army has ordered the working out of a plan of deployment against Poland, which takes into account the demands of the political leadership for the opening of war by surprise and for quick success.
>
> The order of deployment by the High Command, known as 'Fall Weiss,' authorises the Third Army Group - in Fall Weiss Eighth Army Headquarters - to give necessary directions and orders to all commands subordinated to it for ' Fall Weiss'."

I pass to paragraph 7 on Page 1.

> "The whole correspondence on 'Fall Weiss' has to be conducted under the classification 'Top Secret.' This is to be disregarded only if the contents of a document, in the judgment of the chief of the responsible command, is harmless in every way - even in connection with other documents.
>
> For the middle of July a conference is planned where details of the execution will be discussed. Time and place will be ordered later on. Special requests are to be communicated to Third Army Group before 10th July."

That is signed: "The Commander-in-Chief of Army Area Command 3, F. Blaskowitz."

I pass to paragraph 2 to read one further extract under the title - at the top of Page 2 of the translation - " Aims of Operation 'Fall Weiss '."

> "The operation, in order to forestall an orderly Polish mobilisation, is to be opened by surprise with forces which are, for the most part, armoured and motorised, placed on alert in the neighbourhood of the border. The initial superiority over the Polish frontierguards and surprise, both of which can be expected with certainty, are to be maintained by quickly bringing up other parts of the Army, as well as by counteracting the marching up of the Polish Army. Accordingly, all units have to keep the initiative against the foe by acting quickly and attacking ruthlessly."

Finally, a week before the actual attack on Poland, and when all the military plans have been laid , we find the Group as defined in the Indictment all in one place, in fact, all in one room. On 23rd August the Oberbefehlshaber assembled at the Obersalzberg to hear Hitler's explanation of the timing of the attack, and for political and diplomatic orientation from the head of the State. This speech has already been read from at length. It is found in Document 798-PS, Exhibit USA 29, and I pass over it, except to note and emphasise that it is addressed to the very group defined in the Indictment as the General Staff and High Command group. It is, incidentally, the second of the two examples referred to in the affidavits by Halder and Brauchitsch, numbers 1 and 2, which I read previously.

We have now come to the point where Germany actually launched the war. Within a few weeks, and before any important action on the Western Front, Poland was overrun and conquered; German losses were insignificant.

The three principal territorial questions mentioned in the Blomberg and Blaskowitz affidavits were all solved. The Rhineland had been reoccupied and fortified; Memel was annexed; the Polish Corridor had been annexed. There was a good deal more, too: Austria a part of the Reich; Czechoslovakia occupied; and all of Western Poland in German hands. Germany was superior in arms and in experience to her Western enemies, France and England.

Then came the three black years of the war - 1939, 1940 and 1941 - when German armed might swung like a great scythe from North to South to East: Norway and Denmark; the Low Countries; France; Italy became an ally of Germany; Tripoli and Egypt; Yugoslavia and Greece; Roumania, Hungary and Bulgaria became allies; the Western part of the Soviet Union was overrun.

I would like to deal as a whole with the period from the fall of Poland in October, 1939, to the attack against the Soviet Union in June of 1941. In this period occurred the aggressive wars in violation of treaties, as charged in the Indictment, against Norway, Denmark, Holland, Belgium, Luxembourg, Jugoslavia, and Greece.

I cannot improve on or add much to the presentation of these matters by the British Delegation. From the standpoint of proving Crimes Against Peace, our case is complete. But I would like to review this period briefly from the military standpoint and view it as the German military leaders viewed it. Of one thing we may be sure: Neither the Nazis nor the Generals thought during this period in terms of a series of violations of neutrality and treaties. They thought in terms of a war, a war of conquest, a war for the conquest of Europe. Neutrality, treaties, non-aggression pacts - these were not the major consideration. They were annoying obstacles, and devices had to be formed and excuses manufactured to fit the circumstances.

Von Blomberg has told us in his affidavit, which I have read, that after 1939 some generals began to condemn Hitler's methods and lost confidence in his judgment. Which particular Hitler method some of the generals condemned is not stated, but I think the Tribunal will not hear any substantial evidence that many of the generals condemned the march of conquest during the years 1939 to 1941.

In fact the evidence is, rather, that most of the generals were having the time of their lives during those years. Six weeks after the outbreak of the war and upon the successful termination of the Polish campaign, on 9th October, 1939, there was issued a memorandum and directive for the conduct of the war in the West. That is Document L-52, and becomes Exhibit USA 540. It is not signed. It was distributed only to the four service chiefs, Keitel, Brauchitsch, Goering and Raeder. From the wording there is every indication that it was issued by Hitler. I will read an extract starting with Page 2 of the document, about two-thirds of the way down in the first paragraph, beginning from the words "The aim of the Anglo-French conduct of war":

"The aim of the Anglo-French conduct of war is to dissolve or disintegrate the 80-million- State again so that in this manner the European equilibrium, in other words, the balance of power, which serves their ends, may be restored. This battle, therefore, will have to be fought out by the German people one way or another. Nevertheless the very great successes of the first month of war could serve, in the event of an immediate signing of peace, to strengthen the Reich psychologically and materially to such an extent that from the German viewpoint there would be no objection to ending the war immediately, in so far as the present achievement with arms is not jeopardised by the peace-treaty.

It is not the object of this memorandum to study the possibilities in this direction, or even to take them into consideration. In this paper I shall confine myself exclusively to the other case: the necessity to continue the fight, the object of which, as already stressed, consists, in so far as the enemy is concerned, in the dissolution or destruction of the German Reich. In opposition to this the German war aim is the final military dispatch of the West, i.e., destruction of the power and ability of the Western Powers ever again to be able to oppose the State consolidation and further development of the German people in Europe. As far as the outside world is concerned, however, this internal aim will have to undergo various propaganda adjustments, necessary from a psychological point of view. This does not alter the war aim. It is and remains the destruction of our Western enemies."

I now pass to Page 3 of the translation, paragraph 2, and the sub-heading "Reasons":

"Reasons.

The successes of the Polish campaign have made possible first of all a war on a single front, awaited for past decades without any hope of realisation ...

That is to say, Germany is able to enter the fight in the West with all her might, leaving only a few covering troops. The remaining European States are neutral, either because they fear for their own fates, or lack interest in the conflict as such, or are interested in a certain outcome of the war which prevents them from taking part at all, or at any rate too soon.

The following is to be firmly borne in mind ... "

And at this point I interpolate a succession of references to countries, and then pass to Belgium and Holland at the foot of page 3:

"Belgium and Holland. Both countries are interested in preserving their neutrality but incapable of withstanding prolonged pressure from England and France. The preservation of their colonies, the maintenance of their trade, and thus the securing of their interior economy, even of their very life, depend wholly upon the will of England and France. Therefore in their decisions, in their attitude, and in their actions both countries are dependent in the highest degree upon the West. If England and France promise themselves a successful result at the price of Belgian neutrality, they are at any time in a position to apply the necessary pressure. That is to say, without covering themselves with the odium of a breach of neutrality, they can compel Belgium and Holland to cease to be neutral. Therefore, in the matter of the preservation of Belgo-Dutch neutrality, time is not a factor which might promise a favourable development for Germany."

The final paragraph to be read is as follows:

"The Nordic States: Provided no completely unforeseen factors appear, their neutrality in the future is also to be assumed. The con tinuation of German trade with these countries appears possible even in a war of long duration."

Six weeks later, on 23rd November, 1939, our group as defined in the Indictment - The Oberbefehlshaber - again assembled, as found in Document 789-PS, already in the record as Exhibit USA 23, and heard from Hitler much of what he had said previously to the four service chiefs. This speech, part of which is already in the record, contains other portions not previously read from and now of interest, and the first extract which I would like to read is on Page 2 of the translation, about half- way down in paragraph 1, starting with the words "For the first time in history we have to fight on only one front." I quote:

"For the first time in history we have to fight on only one front, the other front is at present free. But no one can know how long that will remain so. I have doubted for a long time whether I should strike in the East and then in the West. Basically I did not organise the Armed Forces in order not to strike. The decision to strike was always in me. Earlier or later, I wanted to solve the problem. Under pressure it was decided that the East was to be attacked first. If the Polish war was won so quickly, it was due to the superiority of our

Armed Forces. The most glorious appearance in history. Unexpectedly small expenditures of men and material. Now the Eastern front is held by only a few divisions. It is a situation which we viewed previously as unachievable. Now the situation is as follows: The opponent in the West liesbehind his fortification. There is no possibility of coming to grips With him. The decisive question is: How long can we endure this situation?"

Passing to Page 3 of that document, line 3:

"Everything is determined by the fact that the moment is favourable now; in six months it might not be so any more."

The final passage on Page 4 of the translation, in the long paragraph about half-way down, beginning "England cannot live without her imports. We can feed . . . ":

"England cannot live without her imports. We can feed ourselves. The permanent sowing of mines on the English coasts will bring England to her knees. However, this can occur only if we have occupied Belgium and Holland. It is a difficult decision for me. None has ever achieved what I have achieved. My life is of no importance in all this. I have led the German people to a great height, even if the world does hate us now. I risk the loss of this achievement. I have to choose between victory or destruction. I choose victory. Greatest historical choice, to be compared with the decision of Frederick the Great before the first Silesian war. Prussia owes its rise to the heroism of one man. Even there the closest advisers were disposed to capitulation. Everything depended on Frederick the Great. Even the decisions of Bismarck in 1866 and 1870 were no less great. My decision is unchangeable. I shall attack France and England at the most favourable and earliest moment. Breach of the neutrality of Belgium and Holland is meaningless. No one will question that when we have won. We shall not bring about the breach of neutrality as idiotically as it was done in 1914. If we do not break the neutrality, then England and France will. Without attack the war cannot be ended victoriously. I consider it possible to end the war only by means of an attack. The question as to whether the attack will be successful, no one can answer. Everything depends upon the favourable instant."

Thereafter the winter of 1939 and 1940 passed quietly, the winter of so-called " phony war."

The General Staff and High Command Group all knew what the plan was - they had all been told. To attack ruthlessly at the first opportunity; to smash the French and English forces; to pay no heed to treaties with or neutrality of the Low Countries. "Breach of the neutrality of Holland and Belgium is meaningless. No one will question that when we have won."

That is what Hitler told the Oberbefehishaber. The generals and admirals agreed and went forward with their plan.

Now it is not true that all the steps in this march of conquest were conceived by Hitler, and that the military leaders embarked on them with reluctance and misgivings. To show this we need only hark back for a moment to what Major Elwyn Jones told the Tribunal about the plans for the invasion of Denmark and Norway.

The Tribunal will recall that Hitler's utterances in October and November, which I have just read, although they are full of threatening comments about France and England and the Low Countries, contain no suggestion of an attack on Scandinavia. Indeed, Hitler's memorandum of 9th October, from which I read, Document L-52, affirmatively indicates that Hitler saw no reason to disturb the situation in the North, because he said that, unless unforeseen factors appeared, the neutrality of the

Northern states could be assumed. Trade could be continued with those countries, even in a long war. But a week previously, on 3rd October, 1939, the defendant Raeder had caused a questionnaire to be circulated within the Naval War Staff, seeking comments on the advantages which might be gained from a naval standpoint, by securing bases in Norway and Denmark. That document is C-122, Exhibit GB-82. And another document introduced by Major Elwyn Jones, C-66, which is Exhibit GB-81, shows that Raeder was prompted to circulate this questionnaire by a letter from another admiral named Karls, who pointed out the importance of an occupation of the Norwegian coast by Germany. Admiral Karls, Rolf Karls, later attained the rank of Admiral of the Fleet and commanded Naval Group "North" and in that capacity is a member of the group as defined in the Indictment, just as Raeder is.

The Tribunal will also recall that the defendant Donitz, who at that time was Flag Officer Submarines, replied to this questionnaire from Raeder on 9th October, 1939. The document in question is C-5, Exhibit GB-83. Doernitz replied that from his standpoint Trondheim. and Narvik met the requirements of a submarine base, that Trondheirn was better, and that he proposed the establishment of a U-boat base there. The next day Raeder visited Hitler, and this visit and certain subsequent events are described in a document which has not previously been introduced.

Now, your Honour, owing to a confusion in numbering, the German document is C-71, but the translation appears in your book in Document L-323.and that will be Exhibit USA 541. The translation will be found in L-323, the middle of the page, entitled "Entry in the War Diary of the Commander-in-Chief of the Navy, Naval War Staff, on Weseruebung," that being the code name for the operation against Norway and Denmark:

"10th October, 1939. First reference of the Commander-in-Chief of the Navy (Naval War Staff) when visiting the Fuehrer, to the significance of Norway for sea and air warfare. The Fuehrer intends to give the matter consideration.

12th December 1939. Fuehrer receivied "Q" and "H" - those being presumably Quisling and Hagelin.

Subsequent instructions to the Supreme Command of the Armed Forces to make mental preparations. The Commander-in-Chief of the Navy is having an essay prepared which will be ready in January."

With reference to this essay Kapitaen zur See Kranke is working on "Weseruebung" at O.K.W. During the time which followed, H - Hagelin - maintained contact with the Chief of Staff of the Commander-in-Chief of the Navy. His aim was to develop the Party Q - Quisling - with a view to making it capable of making a coup and to give the Supreme Command of the Navy information on the political developments in Norway and military questions. In general he pressed the speeding up of preparations, but considered that it was first necessary to expand the organisation.

I think that is all I need read of that.

Another document, which is C-64, Exhibit GB-86 - already in the record - shows that on 12th December, the Naval War Staff discussed the Norwegian project with Hitler - I am not going to read from that document, your Honour - at a meeting which the defendants Keitel and Jodl also attended. In the meantime Raeder was in touch with the defendant Rosenberg on the possibilities of using Quisling; and Major Elwyn Jones very properly pointed out to the Tribunal the close link between the Service Chiefs and the Nazi politicians. As a result of all this, on Hitler's instructions, Keitel issued an O.K.W. directive on 27th January, 1940, stating that Hitler had commissioned him to undertake charge of preparations for the Norway operation, to which he then gave the code name "Weseruebung."

On 1st March, 1940, Hitler issued the directive setting forth the general plan for the invasion of Norway and Denmark. That is Document C-174, Exhibit GB-89, which Major Elwyn Jones put in the record. The directive was initialled by Admiral Kurt Fricke, who at that time was head of the Operations Division of the Naval War Staff and who at the end Of 1941 became Chief of the Naval War Staff and in that capacity is a member of the group as defined in the Indictment. So, as these documents make clear, the plan to invade Norway and Denmark was not conceived in Nazi Party circles or forced on the military leaders; on the contrary, it was conceived in the Naval part of the General Staff and High Command Group, and Hitler was persuaded to take the idea up. Treaties and neutrality meant just as little to the General Staff and High Command Group as to the Nazis.

As to the Low Countries, neither Hitler nor the military leaders were disturbed about treaty considerations. The Tribunal will remember that at a conference between Hitler and the principal military leaders in May, 1939, as shown in Document L-79, Exhibit USA-27, already in the record, when the intention to attack Poland was announced, Hitler in discussing the possibility of war with England said that the Dutch and Belgian air bases must be occupied by armed forces. "Declarations of neutrality will be ignored." And later in his speech to the Oberbefehlshaber, in November, 1939, Hitler said that they must first invade the Low Countries and "no one will question that when we have won."

Accordingly, one can well imagine that the winter of 1939 and 1940 and the early spring of 1940 was a period of very intensive planning in German military circles. The major attack in the West through the Low Countries had to be planned and the attack on Norway and Denmark had to be planned. The defendant Jodl's diary for the period 1st February to 26th May, 1940, Document 1809-PS, Exhibit GB-88, contains many entries reflecting the course of this planning. Some of the entries have been read into the record and others are now of interest.

The Tribunal will see from these entries which have already been read, that during February and early March there was considerable doubt in German military circles as to whether the attack on Norway and Denmark should precede or follow the attack on the Low Countries, and that at some points there even was doubt as to whether all these attacks were necessary from a military standpoint. But the Tribunal will not find a single entry which reflects any hesitancy from a moral angle, on the part of Jodl or any of the people he mentions, to over-run these countries.

I will make some references now to Document 1809-PS and some of the entries in it. I do not find a direct quotation in any one of them. The Court will note that on 1st February, 1940, General Jeschonnek, the Chief of the Air Staff and a member of the Group as defined in the Indictment, visited Jodl and made a suggestion that it might be wise to attack only Holland, on the ground that Holland alone would offer a tremendous improvement for Germany's aerial warfare.

On 6th February, Jodl conferred with Jeschonnek, Warlimont, and Colonel von Waldau, and what Jodl calls a "new idea" was proposed at this meeting: that the Germans should only carry out Action H (Holland) and the Weser Exercise (Norway and Denmark) and should guarantee Belgium's neutrality for the duration of the war.

I suppose the German Air Force may have felt that the occupation of Holland alone would give them sufficient scope for air bases for attacks on England, and that if Belgium's neutrality were preserved the German bases in Holland would be immune from attack by the French and British armies in France. If, to meet this situation, the French and British should attack through Holland and Belgium, the violation of neutrality would be on the other foot. But whether or not this new idea made sense from a military angle, it appears to be a most extraordinary notion from a diplomatic angle. It was a proposal to violate without any excuse the neutrality of three neighbouring small countries and simultaneously to guarantee the neutrality of a fourth. What value the Belgians might have attributed to a guarantee of neutrality offered under such circumstances it is difficult to imagine, and in fact, the "new idea" projected at this meeting seems a most extraordinary combination of cynicism and naivete.

In the meantime, as Jodl's diary shows, on 5th February, 1940, the "special staff" for the Norway invasion met for the first time and got its instructions from Keitel. On 21st February, Hitler put General von Falkenhorst in command of the Norway undertaking; and Jodl's diary records that "Falkenhorst accepts gladly."

On 26th February Hitler was still in doubt whether to go first to Norway or the Low Countries, but on 3rd March he decided to deal with Norway first and the Low Countries a short time thereafter. This decision proved final. Norway and Denmark were invaded on 9th April, and the success of the adventure was certain by 1st May. The invasion of the Low Countries took place ten days later.

So, France and the Low countries fell, Italy joined the war on the side of Germany, and the African campaign began. In October, 1940, Italy attacked Greece. The Italo-Greek stalemate and the uncertain attitude of Jugoslavia became embarrassing to Germany, particularly because the attack on the Soviet Union was being planned and Germany felt she could not risk an uncertain situation at her rear in the Balkans.

Accordingly, it was decided to end the Greek situation by coming to Italy's aid, and the Jugoslavian coup Xetat Of 26th March, 1941, brought about the final German decision to crush Jugoslavia also. The documents have already been introduced by Colonel Phillimore, and there is little that I need to add for my present purpose. The decisions were made; the Armed Forces drew up the necessary plans and executed the attacks. The onslaught was particularly unmerciful and ruthless against Jugoslavia for the special purpose of frightening Turkey and Greece. The final deployment instructions were issued by Brauchitsch and appear in a document R-95, Exhibit GB-127 which has not been read before. Two extracts from this are of interest. These extracts are very short:

"The political situation in the Balkans having changed by reason of the Jugoslav military revolt, Jugoslavia has to be considered an enemy even should it make declarations of loyalty at first.

"The Fuehrer and Supreme Commander has decided therefore to destroy Jugoslavia as quickly as possible."

And turning to paragraph No. 5, the "Time-table for the Operations":

"On 5th April, as soon as sufficient numbers of the Air Force are available and weather permitting, the Air Force should attack continuously by day and night the Jugoslav ground organisation and Belgrade."

The German attack on the Soviet Union I have little more to say about. The documents showing the aggressive nature of the attack have been put in by Mr. Alderman. I suppose it is quite possible that some members of the General Staff and High Command Group opposed "Barbarossa" as unnecessary and unwise from a military standpoint. The defendant Raeder so indicated in a memorandum he wrote on 10th January, 1944, Document C-66, Exhibit GB-81. C-66 is the translation, the only document I propose to read on this subject, from which a few extracts are of interest. The quotation starts at the very outset of the Document C-66:

"At this time the Fuehrer had made known his 'unalterable decision' to conduct the Eastern campaign in spite of all remonstrances. After that, further warnings, as no new situation had arisen, were found to be completely useless. As Chief of Naval War Staff I was never convinced of the 'compelling necessity' for Barbarossa."

And passing to the third paragraph:

"The Fuehrer very early had the idea of one day settling accounts with Russia; doubtless his general ideological attitude played an essential part in this. In 1937-38 he once stated that he intended to eliminate the Russians as a Baltic power; they would then have to be diverted in the direction of the Persian Gulf. The advance of the Russians against Finland and the Baltic States in 1939-40 probably further strengthened him in this idea."

And passing to the very end of the document, paragraph 7, page 4:

"As no other course is possible, I have submitted to compulsion. If thereby a difference of opinion arises between 1 S.K.L. and myself " that, if I may interpolate, is a division or tne Naval War Staff having. to do with operations - "it is perhaps because the arguments the Fuehrer used on such occasions (dinner speech in the middle of July to the Officers in Command) to justify a step he had planned, usually had a greater effect on people not belonging to the 'inner circle' than on those who often heard this type of reasoning. Many remarks and plans indicate that the Fuehrer calculated on the final ending of the Eastern campaign in the autumn of 1941, whereas the Supreme Command of the Army (General Staff) was very sceptical."

That, to be sure, indicates division of opinion as to the military chances of a rapid success, but the part last quoted indicates that other members of the group favoured "Barbarossa," and Raeder's memorandum actually says and substantiates what Blomberg's affidavit says, that some of the generals lost confidence in the power of Hitler's judgment, but that the generals failed as a group to take any definite stand against him although a few tried and suffered thereby. Certainly the High Command took no stand against Hitler on "Barbarossa" and the events of 1941 and 1942 do not suggest, that the High Command embarked on the Soviet War tentatively or with reservations, but rather with ruthless determination backed by careful planning. The plans themselves have all been read and cited to the Court previously.

That concludes the evidence on the criminal activities of the Group under Counts One and Two. The documents written by the military leaders are not the writings of men who were reluctant to plan and execute these manifold wars.

I want to make clear again the nature of the accusations against this Group under Counts One and Two. They are not accused on the ground that they are soldiers. They are not accused merely for doing the usual things a soldier is expected to do, such as making military plans and commanding troops. It is, I suppose, among the normal duties of a diplomat to engage in negotiations and conferences, to write notes and aide-memoires, to entertain at dinner parties and cultivate good will toward the government he represents. The defendant Ribbentrop is not indicted for doing these things. It is the usual function of a politician to draft regulations and decrees, to make speeches. The defendants Hess and Frick are not indicted for doing those things.

It is an innocent and respectable business to be a locksmith, but it is none the less a crime if the locksmith turns his talents to picking the locks of neighbours and looting their homes. And that is the nature of the charge under Counts One and Two against the defendants and the General Staff and High Command Group. The charge is that, in performing the functions of diplomats, politicians, soldiers, sailors, or whatever they happened to be, they conspired, and did plan, prepare, initiate and wage illegal wars and thereby committed crimes under Article 6 (a) of the Charter.

It is no defence for those who committed such crimes to plead that they practised a particular profession. It is perfectly legal for military men to prepare military plans to meet national contingencies, and such plans may legally be drawn, whether they are offensive or defensive in a military sense. It is perfectly legal for military leaders to carry out such plans and engage in war, if in doing so they do not plan and launch and wage wars which are illegal because they are aggressive and in contravention of the Charter. group, where drawing the line between legal and illegal behaviour might involve some difficulties. That is not an uncommon situation in the legal field. But I do not believe that there is any doubt or difficulty here, before this Tribunal, as to the criminality of the General Staff and High Command Group as a Group under Counts One and Two, or as to the guilt of the five defendants who are members of the group.

In the case of the defendants Goering, Keitel and Jodl the evidence is voluminous and their participation in aggressive plans and wars is more or less constant. The same is true of defendant Raeder, and his individual responsibility for the aggressive and savage attack on Norway and Denmark is especially clear. The evidence so far offered against Donitz is less voluminous for the reason that he was younger and not one of the top group until later in the war.

But numerous other members of the General Staff and High Command Group, including its other leaders, are shown to have participated knowingly and wilfully in these illegal plans and wars: Brauchitsch, the Commander-in-Chief of the Army, and his Chief of Staff Halder; Warlimont, the deputy of Jodl. In the nature of things these men knew all that was going on and participated fully, as the documents show. Reichenau and Sperrle helped to bully von Schuschnigg; Reichenau and von Schobert, together with Goering, were immediately sent for by Hitler when von Schuschnigg ordered the plebiscite.

At a later date we have seen Blaskowitz as an Oberbefehlshaber in the field, knowingly preparing for the attack on Poland; Field Marshal List educating the Bulgarians for their role during the attacks on Jugoslavia and Greece; von Falkenhorst "gladly accepting" the assignment to command the invasion of Norway and Denmark.

On the air side, Jeschonnek has been recorded proposing that Germany attack Norway, Denmark and Holland and simultaneously assuring Belgium that there is nothing to fear.

On the naval side, Admiral Karls, member of the Group, forsees at an early date that German policy is leading to a general European war, and at a later date the attack on Norway and Denmark is his brain-child; Krancke, later one of the group, is one of the chief planners of this attack; Schniewindt is in the inner circle for the attack on Poland; Fricke certifies the final orders for Weseruebung and a few months later proposes that Germany annex Belgium and Northern France and reduce the Netherlands and Scandinavia to vassalage.

Most of the nineteen officers I have mentioned were at that time members of the Group, as defined, and the few who were not subsequently became members. At the final conference for Barbarossa seventeen additional members were present, and at the two meetings with Hitler, at which the aggressive plans and the contempt for treaties were fully disclosed, the entire group was present.

The military defendants will perhaps argue that they are pure technicians. This amounts to saying that military men are a race apart from and different from the ordinary run of human beings - men above and beyond the moral and legal requirements that apply to others, incapable of exercising moral judgment on their own behalf.

What we are discussing here is the crime of planning and waging aggressive war. It stands to reason that that crime is committed most consciously and culpably by a nation's leaders - the leaders in all the major fields of activity which are necessary to and closely involved in the waging of war. It is committed by propagandists and publicists. It is committed by political leaders, by diplomats, by the chief ministers, by the principal industrial and financial leaders. It is no less committed by the military leaders.

In the nature of things, planning and executing aggressive war is accomplished by agreement and consultation among all these types of leaders. And if the leaders in any notably important field of activity stand aside or resist or fail to co- operate, then the programme will at the very least be seriously obstructed. That is why the principal leaders in all these fields of activity share responsibility for the crime, and the military leaders no less than the others. Leadership in the military field, as well as in other fields, calls for moral wisdom as well as technical astuteness.

I do not think that the responsible military leaders of any nation will be heard to say that their role is that of a mere janitor or custodian or pilot of the war machine which is under their command, and that they bear no responsibility whatsoever for the use to which that machine is put.

The prevalence of such a view would be particularly unfortunate to-day, when the military leaders control forces infinitely more powerful and destructive than ever before. Should the military leaders be declared exempt from the declaration in the Charter that planning and waging aggressive war is a crime, it would be a crippling, if not fatal, blow to the efficacy of that declaration.

Such is certainly not the view of the United States. The prosecution here representing the United States believes that the profession of arms is a distinguished profession. We believe that the practice of that profession by its leaders calls for the highest degree of integrity and moral wisdom, no less than for technical skill. We believe that in consulting and planning with the leaders in other fields of national activities the military leaders must act in accordance with International Law and the dictates of the public conscience. Otherwise the military resources of the nations will be used not in accordance with the laws of modern society but in accordance with the law of the jungle. The military leaders share responsibility with other leaders.

I use the word " share " advisedly. Obviously the military leaders are not the final and exclusive arbiters, and the German military leaders do not bear exclusive responsibility for the criminal holocaust which was committed. But the German military leaders conspired with others to undermine and destroy the conscience of the German nation. The German military leaders wanted to aggrandise Germany and, if necessary, to resort to war for that purpose.

> As the Chief Prosecutor for the United States said in his opening statement, The German military leaders are here before you because they, along with others, mastered Germany and drove it to war."

Your Lordship, that concludes the evidence under Counts One and Two, and if this would be a convenient stopping point -

THE PRESIDENT: You have another branch of the argument?

COLONEL TAYLOR: Counts Three and Four, your Honour, which will take considerable time.

THE PRESIDENT: Very well, we will adjourn now.

(The Tribunal adjourned until 1000 hours on 7 January, 1946)

About Coda Books

Most Coda books are edited and endorsed by Emmy Award winning film maker and military historian Bob Carruthers, producer of Discovery Channel's Line of Fire and Weapons of War and BBC's Both Sides of the Line. Long experience and strong editorial control gives the military history enthusiast the ability to buy with confidence.

The series advisor is David McWhinnie, producer of the acclaimed Battlefield series for Discovery Channel. David and Bob have co-produced books and films with a wide variety of the UK's leading historians including Professor John Erickson and Dr David Chandler.

Where possible the books draw on rare primary sources to give the military enthusiast new insights into a fascinating subject.

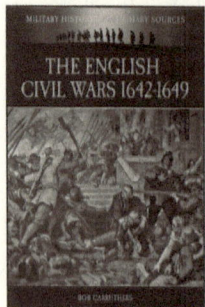
The English Civil Wars

The Zulu Wars

Into Battle with Napoleon 1812

Waterloo 1815

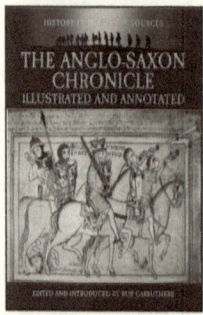
The Anglo-Saxon Chronicle

The Battle of the Bulge

The Normandy Campaign 1944

Hitler's Justification for WWII

Hitler's Mein Kampf - The Roots of Evil

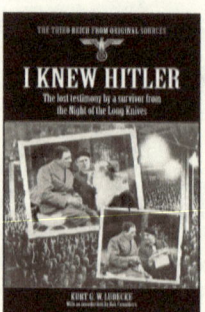
I Knew Hitler

Mein Kampf - The 1939 Illustrated Edition

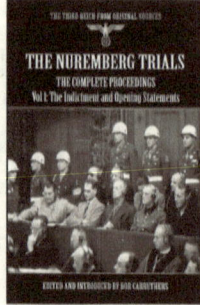
The Nuremberg Trials Volume 1

For more information, visit codahistory.com

Tiger I in Combat

Tiger I Crew Manual

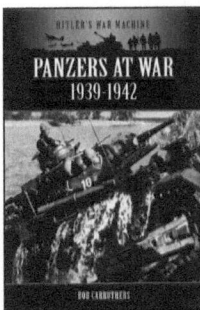
Panzers at War 1939-1942

Panzers at War 1943-1945

Wolf Pack - the U boats

Poland 1939

Luftwaffe Combat Reports

Eastern Front Night Combat

Eastern Front Encirclement

Panzer Combat Reports

The Panther V in Combat

The Red Army in Combat

Barbarossa - Hitler Turns East

The Russian Front

The Wehrmacht in Russia

Servants of Evil

www.ingramcontent.com/pod-product-compliance
Lightning Source LLC
Chambersburg PA
CBHW030523230426
43665CB00010B/736